hone    )7 487 7449

a¹        ¹⒱      ¬e⁻ts.ac.uk

# INTERNATIONAL TRADE REGULATION AND THE MITIGATION OF CLIMATE CHANGE

What can trade regulation contribute towards ameliorating the GHG emissions and reducing their concentrations in the atmosphere? This collection of essays analyses options for climate change mitigation through the lens of the trade lawyer. By examining international law, and in particular the relevant WTO agreements, the authors address the areas of potential conflict between international trade law and international law on climate mitigation and, where possible, suggest ways to strengthen mutual supportiveness between the two regimes. They do so taking into account the drivers of human-induced climate change in energy markets and of consumption.

THOMAS COTTIER is Professor of European and International Economic Law at the University of Bern and Director of the Institute of European and International Economic Law. He is also Managing Director of the World Trade Institute.

OLGA NARTOVA is a qualified lawyer in Russia, a research fellow at the Swiss National Centre for Competence in Research (NCCR) Trade Regulation of the University of Bern, and alternate leader of the project on energy in WTO law and policy.

SADEQ Z. BIGDELI is a graduate of the University of Tehran Faculty of Law and Political Science and a *summa cum laude* graduate of the MILE programme at the World Trade Institute in Bern, Switzerland.

# INTERNATIONAL TRADE REGULATION AND THE MITIGATION OF CLIMATE CHANGE

World Trade Forum

Edited by
THOMAS COTTIER
OLGA NARTOVA
and
SADEQ Z. BIGDELI

CAMBRIDGE
UNIVERSITY PRESS

CAMBRIDGE UNIVERSITY PRESS
Cambridge, New York, Melbourne, Madrid, Cape Town, Singapore,
São Paulo, Delhi, Dubai, Tokyo

Cambridge University Press
The Edinburgh Building, Cambridge CB2 8RU, UK

Published in the United States of America by Cambridge University Press, New York

www.cambridge.org
Information on this title: www.cambridge.org/9780521766197

First published 2009

Printed in the United Kingdom at the University Press, Cambridge

*A catalogue record for this publication is available from the British Library*

*Library of Congress Cataloguing in Publication data*
International trade regulation and the mitigation of climate change : World Trade
Forum / Edited by Thomas Cottier, Olga Nartova and Sadeq Z. Bigdeli.
p.   cm.
ISBN 978-0-521-76619-7
1. Foreign trade regulation – Environmental aspects – Congresses.   2. International trade –
Environmental aspects – Congresses.   I. Cottier, Thomas.   II. Nartova, Olga.   III. Bigdeli,
Sadeq Z.   IV. World Trade Forum (11th : 2007 : Berne, Switzerland)   V. Title.
K3943.A6I58   2009
343′.087–dc22
2009011369

ISBN 978-0-521-76619-7 Hardback

# CONTENTS

v

# CONTRIBUTORS

RUDOLF ADLUNG Senior Economist, Trade in Services Division, WTO Secretariat, Geneva

ARTHUR E. APPLETON Partner, Appleton Luff — International Lawyers, Geneva

DONAH BARACOL-PINHÃO Former Research Fellow, World Trade Institute, Bern

SADEQ Z. BIGDELI Former Research Fellow, World Trade Institute, Bern

FELIX BLOCH European Commission, Brussels

JENNIFER BURNETT United Nations Conference on Trade and Development (UNCTAD) Secretariat, Geneva

MIREILLE COSSY Counsellor, Trade in Services Division, WTO Secretariat, Geneva

THOMAS COTTIER Professor of European and International Economic Law, Managing Director, World Trade Institute, University of Bern

DANIEL C. CROSBY Partner, Budin & Partners, Geneva

PANAGIOTIS DELIMATSIS Assistant Professor of Law, Tilburg University, the Netherlands, Senior Research Fellow, World Trade Institute, Bern

ANTONIA L. ELIASON Associate, Allen & Overy, London

GARY N. HORLICK Partner, WilmerHale, Washington, DC

ROBERT HOWSE Alene and Allan F. Smith Professor of Law, University of Michigan Law School, Visiting Professor of Law, Fordham Law School and New York University School of Law (2007–2008), Principal Trade Expert, Renewable Energy and International Law (REIL)

GARBA I. MALUMFASHI Research Fellow, The Centre for Energy, Petroleum and Mineral Law & Policy, University of Dundee

GABRIELLE MARCEAU Counsellor, the Office of the WTO Director-General Pascal Lamy, Geneva

FABIAN MARTENS Attorney at law, Vischer, Zurich

SOFYA MATTEOTTI-BERKUTOVA Research Fellow, World Trade Institute, Bern

DESPINA MAVROMATI Legal Counsel at the Court of Arbitration for Sport, Lausanne, Switzerland

OLGA NARTOVA Research Fellow, World Trade Institute, Bern

CHRISTA PFISTER Attorney at law, Vischer, Zurich

STEFAN RECHSTEINER Attorney at law, Vischer, Zurich

DONALD H. REGAN William W. Bishop, Jr. Collegiate Professor of Law and Professor of Philosophy, University of Michigan

JOSÉ ROMERO Senior Scientific Advisor, Swiss Federal Office for the Environment, Bern

KARINE SIEGWART Head of Section, Swiss Federal Office for the Environment, Bern

THOMAS STOCKER Professor of Climate and Environmental Physics and Co-director, Physics Institute, University of Bern

GEERT VAN CALSTER Professor of Regulatory Law at K.U. Leuven Belgium, visiting lecturer at Oxford University, of Counsel (practising) with DLA Piper, London

JACOB D. WERKSMAN Program Director, World Resources Institute, Washington, DC

SIMONETTA ZARRILLI Legal Officer, the Division on International Trade and Commodities, United Nations Conference on Trade and Development (UNCTAD) Secretariat, Geneva

# FIGURES

# TABLES

# ABBREVIATIONS

| | |
|---|---|
| AB | Appellate Body |
| AEP | American Electric Power |
| AG | Advocate General |
| AMS | aggregate measure of support |
| AoA | Agreement on Agriculture |
| AOSIS | Alliance of Small Island States |
| APEC | Asia-Pacific Economic Cooperation |
| ASCM | Agreement on Subsidies and Countervailing Measures |
| BTA | Border Tax Adjustment |
| CAFE | Corporate Average Fuel Economy |
| CBD | Convention on Biological Diversity |
| CDM | Clean Development Mechanism |
| CEC | Commission for Environmental Cooperation |
| CERs | certified emission reductions |
| CIEL | Center for International Environmental Law |
| CITES | Convention on International Trade in Endangered Species |
| CLASP | Collaborative Labelling and Appliance Standards Programme |
| $CO_2$ | carbon dioxide |
| COP | Conference of the Parties |
| COP 13 | thirteenth Conference of the Parties |
| CPC | United Nations Provisional Central Product Classification |
| CTE | Committee on Trade and Environment |
| CTESS | Committee on Trade and Environment Special Session |
| CVD | Countervailing duty |
| DDA | Doha Development Agenda |
| DEFRA | Department for Environment, Food and Rural Affairs |
| DMD | Doha Ministerial Declaration |
| DNA | Designated National Authority |
| DSB | Dispute Settlement Body |
| DSU | Dispute Settlement Understanding |
| EAI | Environmental Area Initiative |
| EC | European Community |
| ECJ | European Court of Justice |

| | |
|---|---|
| ECN | Energy Research Centre of the Netherlands |
| EFTA | European Free Trade Association |
| EGS | environmental goods and services |
| EISA | Energy Independence and Security Act 2007 (US) |
| EPA | Environmental Project Approach |
| EPACT | Energy Policy Act 2005 (US) |
| EPFL | Ecole Polytechnique Fédérale de Lausanne |
| EPPs | environmentally preferable products |
| ERUs | emission reduction units |
| ESIS | Energy Standards Information System |
| ESTs | environmentally sound technology |
| ETS | Emissions Trading Scheme |
| EU | European Union |
| FAO | Food and Agriculture Organization (United Nations) |
| FDI | foreign direct investment |
| FSC | Forest Stewardship Council |
| GATS | General Agreement on Trade in Services |
| GATT | General Agreement on Tariffs and Trade |
| GEF | Global Environment Facility |
| GHG | greenhouse gas |
| GMOs | genetically modified organisms |
| GPA | Government Procurement Agreement |
| GSP | General System of Preferences |
| HFCs | hydrofluorocarbons |
| HS | Harmonized System |
| HWWI | Hamburgisches Weltwirtschafts Institut |
| IBEW | International Brotherhood of Electrical Workers |
| ICJ | International Court of Justice |
| IEA | International Energy Agency |
| IEC | International Electrotechnical Commission |
| IGOs | intergovernmental organisations |
| IIAs | international investment agreements |
| IISD | International Institute for Sustainable Development |
| ILC | International Law Commission |
| IMF | International Monetary Fund |
| IMO | International Maritime Organization |
| INC | Intergovernmental Negotiating Committee |
| INMETRO | National Institute of Meteorology, Standardization and Industrial Quality (Brazil) |
| IPCC | Intergovernmental Panel on Climate Change |
| IPRs | intellectual property rights |
| ISEAL | International Social and Environmental Accreditation and Labelling |

| | |
|---|---|
| ISO | International Organization for Standardization |
| ITO | International Trade Organization |
| KP | Kyoto Protocol |
| LDCs | least developed countries |
| LNG | liquefied natural gas |
| MDGs | Millenium Development Goals |
| MEAs | multilateral environmental agreements |
| MEP | Member of European Parliament |
| MFN | most-favoured-nation |
| NAFTA | North American Free Trade Agreement |
| NAMA | non-agricultural market access |
| NGOs | non-governmental organisations |
| NPR-PPMs | non-product related processes and production methods |
| NTBs | non-tariff barriers |
| ODA | Official Development Assistance |
| OECD | Organisation for Economic Co-operation and Development |
| OIE | World Organisation for Animal Health (formerly International Office of Epizootics) |
| PFCs | perfluorocarbons |
| PPMs | production and process methods |
| R&D | research and development |
| RE | renewable energy |
| RECs | renewable energy certificates |
| RES | renewable energy standards |
| RFS | renewable fuel standard |
| RPS | renewable portfolio standards |
| RRS | Round Table on Responsible Soy |
| RSB | Round Table on Sustainable Biofuels |
| RSPO | Round Table on Sustainable Palm Oil Production |
| RTFO | Renewable Transport Fuel Obligation Programme |
| S&D | support and development |
| SCM | Subsidies and Countervailing Measures Agreement |
| SGS | Société Générale de Surveillance |
| SPS | Sanitary and Phytosanitary Measures Agreement |
| STOs | specific trade obligations |
| TBT | Technical Barriers to Trade Agreement |
| TEDs | turtle excluder devices |
| TPA | third party access |
| TPES | total primary energy supply |
| TRECs | tradeable renewable energy certificates |
| TRIMS | Trade Related Investment Measures Agreement |
| TRIPS | Agreement on Trade-Related Aspects of Intellectual Property Rights |

| | |
|---|---|
| UK | United Kingdom |
| UN | United Nations |
| UNCED | United Nations Conference on Environment and Development |
| UNCLOS | United Nations Conference on the Law of the Sea |
| UNCTAD | United Nations Conference on Trade and Development |
| UNDP | United Nations Development Programme |
| UNEP | United Nations Environment Programme |
| UNFCCC | United Nations Framework Convention on Climate Change |
| UNGA | United Nations General Assembly |
| US | United States |
| WCO | World Customs Organization |
| WIPO | World Intellectual Property Organization |
| WSSM | World Standards Services Network |
| WTO | World Trade Organization |
| WWF | World Wildlife Fund |

The World Trade Forum series was established in 1997 to offer an opportunity for an international in-depth discussion of issues facing the world trading system. The topic chosen for the 11th World Trade Forum was: International Trade Regulation and the Mitigation of Climate Change. On 21 and 22 September 2007 more than seventy-five people representing international organisations and governments, as well as distinguished academic scholars, climate scientists and students of international economic law from many different countries met at the World Trade Institute of the University of Bern to discuss what role the multilateral trading system could play in promoting state participation in the fight against global warming. The forum was opened by a leading climatologist from the NCCR 'Climate', Martin Grosjean, who provided the forum with an overview of the science behind the climate change debate.

The theme of climate change is particularly timely because the Intergovernmental Panel on Climate Change (IPCC) 4th Assessment Report, the first volume of which was published in February 2007, re-affirms that human activities have indeed contributed to the warming of the globe. Earlier, in 2006, the Stern Review on the economics of climate change, supported by many economists, some of whom are Nobel Prize winners, stated that 'the benefits of strong and early action far outweigh the economic costs of not acting'. This year's World Trade Forum, after touching briefly upon the current state of scientific knowledge on climate change, outlined the background for the legal ways forward after the expiry of the Kyoto Regime in 2012. Scholars and experts participating in the various sessions of the Forum addressed the WTO Agreements relevant to the climate change debate and made suggestions which led to this collection of essays.

Such a high-level exchange of expertise would not have been possible without the guidance of Professor Dr Thomas Cottier, Managing Director of the World Trade Institute. The co-editors of this volume

Sadeq Z. Bigdeli and Olga Nartova are indebted to Thomas Cottier for selecting the theme of the conference and his significant role in helping shape the programme and encouraging high-level participation in the Forum. The editors are also indebted to the authors of the chapters in this collection not only for their valuable input to the content of the conference but also for making the effort to revise their drafts for publication. At the same time, the World Trade Forum could not have taken place without support of the discussants and participants who with their openness and active involvement in the debates contributed to the success of the event.

Organising the conference requires the work of a dedicated team and the efforts of all those involved were much appreciated. We wish to express our gratitude to Susan Kaplan and her assistants, Josephina Delahaye and Jane Müller, for preparing the manuscript. Many thanks also go to Sofya Matteotti-Berkutova, NCCR research fellow, for her work in preparing the conference web page, preparing online abstracts for the preliminary and final programmes and for undertaking many other tasks. Moreover, we would like to extend our sincere thanks to the administrative staff of the World Trade Institute, in particular Margrit Vetter for doing everything it takes to put on a successful conference. Special thanks are due to Christian Steiger who supervised the audio-visual equipment.

The World Trade Forum is a non-profit event, and we are very grateful for the support provided by the Ecoscientia Foundation. Also, this conference would not have been possible without funding from the Swiss National Science Foundation in support of the NCCR Trade Regulation and the invaluable counsel and guidance of Dr Susan Brown-Shafii, Scientific Coordinator of the NCCR project.

Our special thanks are due to Finola O'Sullivan of Cambridge University Press and her staff, in particular Brenda Burke and Richard Woodham, for their commitment to the book project and excellent support.

# PART I

Climate change mitigation: scientific, political and
international and trade law perspectives

# Earth in the greenhouse — a challenge for the twenty-first century

### THOMAS STOCKER

## Greenhouse gas concentrations in the long-term perspective

As part of the European Project for Ice Coring in Antarctica (EPICA), an ice core of 3,270 metres in length was drilled at Dome Concordia (75° 06′ S, 123° 21′ E, 3233 m.a.s.l., −54.5°C mean annual temperature, 2.5 cm $H_2O$ precipitation per year). This ice contains information on climate evolution over the last 800,000 years.[1] Important results of the analysis of the ice and the enclosed gas are now available and provide a unique context within which the present changes in the climate system should be interpreted.

The top layers of a polar ice sheet consist of firn (compacted snow), which is in contact with the atmosphere above. Air is exchanged with the atmosphere and can circulate freely in channels of the porous firn. Beyond a depth of about 80 metres, the high pressure of the overlying ice constricts the channels progressively until air bubbles are formed. Analysis of the air enclosed in these bubbles permits the reconstruction of past concentrations of the most important greenhouse gases: carbon dioxide ($CO_2$), methane ($CH_4$) and nitrous oxide ($N_2O$). Measurements demonstrate that the current concentration of $CO_2$ is higher by 27 per cent, and that of $CH_4$ by 130 per cent, than any concentration during the last 650,000 years before industrialisation. Many different and independent studies show that these increases are caused primarily by the burning of fossil fuels, the change of land use and the production of cement.[2]

---

[1] EPICA Community Members, 'Eight glacial cycles from an Antarctic ice core', *Nature* 429 (2004), 623–8.

[2] The major raw materials for cement ($3CaO \cdot SiO_2$ and $2CaO \cdot SiO_2$) are limestone ($CaCO_3$) and sand ($SiO_2$). The production process involves sintering at temperatures exceeding 1000°C during which the $CaCO_3$ dissociates into CaO and $CO_2$. The former builds a structure with sand, the latter is emitted to the environment. In 2004, $CO_2$ emissions

Figure 1 shows the $CO_2$ concentration over the last 650,000 years from measurements of the air entrapped in several different Antarctic ice cores.[3,4] The increase in the concentration of $CO_2$ during the past fifty years has passed beyond the range of natural fluctuations. These analyses also demonstrate the tight relationship between the $CO_2$ concentrations and temperature estimates: during ice ages, concentrations are low and in the range of about 200 parts per million (ppm), whereas during interglacials they are about 280 to 300 ppm. The present concentration is higher than 380 ppm and continues to increase.[5]

## The challenge of the twenty-first century

It is beyond doubt that the accelerated warming of the last fifty years has been caused primarily by the increase in the concentration of greenhouse gases and is hence man-made.[6] Numerous model simulations demonstrate that natural forcings, such as the change in solar radiation or volcanic events, as well as natural cycles, are of only secondary importance.[7] The evolution of the surface temperature over the last thirty years can only be explained in a quantitative way by the radiative forcing caused by an increase in greenhouse gases (figure 2). *Climate sensitivity*, i.e. the global mean warming due to a doubling of the atmospheric $CO_2$ concentration, and a fundamental measure of the effect of greenhouse gases, can now be better constrained owing to better paleoclimate reconstructions.[8] These two results reinforce and consolidate the basis on which calculations of future climate change rest.

associated with global cement production amounted to 3.8 per cent of the global $CO_2$ emissions of $7.9 \times 10^9$ tonnes of carbon per year (G. Marland, T. A. Boden and R. J. Andres, 'Global, regional, and national $CO_2$ emissions' in *Trends: A Compendium of Data on Global Change* (Oak Ridge, Tenn.: Carbon Dioxide Information Analysis Center, Oak Ridge National Laboratory, US Department of Energy, 2007). http://cdiac.esd.ornl. gov/trends/emis/tre_glob.htm.

[3] U. Siegenthaler, T. F. Stocker, E. Monnin, *et al.*, 'Stable carbon cycle-climate relationship during the Late Pleistocene', *Science* 310 (2005), 1313–17.

[4] R. Spahni, J. Chappellaz, T. F. Stocker, *et al.*, 'Atmospheric methane and nitrous oxide of the Late Pleistocene from Antarctic ice cores', *Science* 310 (2005), 1317–21.

[5] Current data on $CO_2$ from Mauna Loa (Hawaii) are available at www.cmdl.noaa.gov/ ccgg/trends

[6] S. Solomon, *et al.* (eds.), *Climate Change 2007: The Physical Science Basis* (Cambridge University Press, 2007).

[7] P. A. Stott, J. F. B. Mitchell, M. R. Allen, *et al.*, 'Observational constraints on past attributable warming and predictions of future global warming', *J. Climate* 19 (2006), 3055–69.

[8] G. C. Hegerl, T. J. Crowley, W. T. Hyde, *et al.*, 'Climate sensitivity constrained by temperature reconstructions over the past seven centuries', *Nature* 440 (2006), 1029–32.

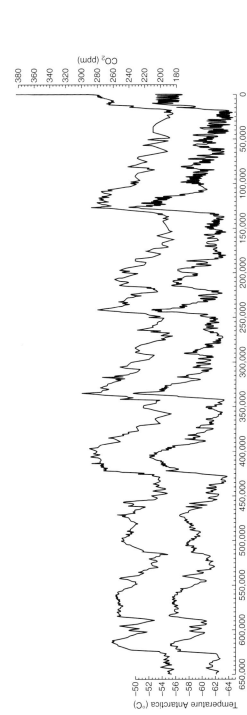

**Figure 1** Reconstruction of the atmospheric $CO_2$ concentration over the last 650,000 years measured in different Antarctic ice cores, combined with the increase in $CO_2$ of the last fifty years directly measured in the atmosphere (upper curve). Temperature in Antarctica is estimated based on measurements of the stable isotopes of water (lower curve). Data sources: U. Siegenthaler, T. F. Stocker, E. Monnin, D. Lüthi, J. Schwander, B. Stauffer, D. Raynaud, J.-M. Barnola, H. Fischer, V. Masson-Delmotte, and J. Jouzel, Stable carbon cycle–climate relationship during the Late Pleistocene, *Science*, *310*, 1313–17, 2005. J. R. Petit, J. Jouzel, D. Raynaud, N. I. Barkov, J.-M. Barnola, I. Basile, M. Bender, J. Chappellaz, M. Davis, G. Delaygue, M. Delmotte, V. M. Kotlyakov, M. Legrand, V. Y. Lipenkov, C. Lorius, L. Pépin, C. Ritz, E. Saltzman, and M. Stievenard, Climate and atmospheric history of the past 420,000 years from the Vostok ice core, Antarctica, *Nature*, *399*, 429–36, 1999. A. Indermühle, T. F. Stocker, F. Joos, H. Fischer, H. J. Smith, M. Wahlen, B. Deck, D. Mastroianni, J. Tschumi, T. Blunier, R. Meyer, and B. Stauffer, Holocene carbon-cycle dynamics based on $CO_2$ trapped in ice at Taylor Dome, Antarctica, *Nature*, *398*, 121–6, 1999. EPICA Community Members, Eight glacial cycles from an Antarctic ice core, *Nature*, *429*, 623–8, 2004.

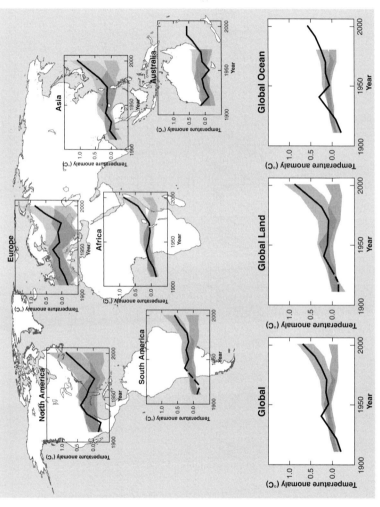

**Figure 2** Temperature change in the twentieth century on the six continents. Measurements (black curves) are compared with simulations using different climate models, which consider only changes of solar radiation and volcanic events (darker grey bands), or which also take into account the increase of greenhouse gas and aerosol concentrations as observed (lighter grey bands, following the observations in the last decades of the twentieth century).[9]

A question of fundamental importance for policy-makers is how large the probability is of staying below an agreed global warming target. This can only be addressed using climate models which permit a large number of simulations. Knutti *et al.*[10] have used the climate model of reduced complexity of the University of Bern[11] and assumed an estimated probability density function for climate sensitivity.[12] The results are summarised in figure 3. They show that the agreed climate target of the European Union, i.e. to limit global warming at 2°C, can be achieved, but that this requires rapid implementation and efficient reduction of $CO_2$ emissions. A capping of atmospheric concentrations at twice the pre-industrial concentrations, i.e. at around 560 ppm, would permit a global

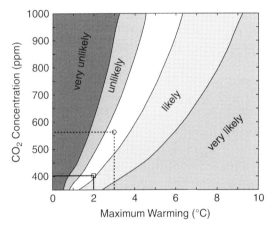

**Figure 3** Estimate of likelihood that for a given $CO_2$ concentration, a maximum warming will not be exceeded. 'Very unlikely' denotes < 10%, 'unlikely' < 33%, 'likely' > 66%, and 'very likely' > 90%.
Source: Knutti *et al.*[13]

[9]  IPCC, 'Summary for Policymakers' in S. Solomon, *et al.* (eds.), *Climate Change 2007: The Physical Science Basis* (Cambridge University Press, 2007), p. 18 *et seq.*
[10]  R. Knutti, F. Joos, S. A. Müller, *et al.*, 'Probabilistic climate change projections for $CO_2$ stabilization profiles', *Geophys. Res. Lett.* 32 (2005), L20707.
[11]  T. F. Stocker, D. G. Wright and L. A. Mysak, 'A zonally averaged, coupled ocean-atmosphere model for paleoclimate studies', *J. Climate* 5 (1992), 773–97.
[12]  R. Knutti, T. F. Stocker, F. Joos, *et al.*, 'Constraints on radiative forcing and future climate change from observations and climate model ensembles', *Nature* 416 (2002), 719–23.
[13]  R. Knutti, F. Joos, S. A. Müller, *et al.*, 'Probabilistic climate change projections for $CO_2$ stabilization profiles', *Geophys. Res. Lett.* 32 (2005), L20707.

warming target of about 3°C. It is evident from these calculations that the challenge increases rapidly with increasing $CO_2$ concentrations and more stringent temperature limits.

A global increase in temperature of 2°C is often assumed to be tolerable and has been declared as a climate target by the European Union. However, four points need to be considered.

First, while global temperature changes are an abstract metric, it is the regional changes that are relevant for the environment and society. Due to fundamental physical processes, the warming will be greater in areas of seasonal snow and ice cover. This is the snow/ice albedo feedback. In particular, at latitudes north of 60°N, the warming will be increased by at least a factor of two. Towards the end of the twenty-first century, large-scale melting of the Arctic sea ice cover[14] as well as accelerated loss of mass of the Greenland ice sheet are expected.[15] This feedback process is also responsible for a shortening of the winter season in Alpine areas. Even if the very ambitious climate target of 2°C can be achieved, tourism, water and hydro-power economies will be seriously affected in these areas.

Second, changes in the occurrence of extreme events have captured the attention of the public because these are costly and immediate burdens to society. Simple statistical considerations show that the frequency of the occurrence of extreme events is particularly sensitive to small changes in the mean values (figure 4). Therefore, changes in the mean climate manifest themselves in changing statistics of extreme events. A small increase in the mean summer temperature, as illustrated in figure 4, will lead to a strongly increased probability of heat waves. Calculations suggest that the historic heat wave of 2003 can already be attributed to global warming.[16] Estimates of the future probability of the occurrence of such heat waves show that a situation such as the heat wave of 2003 or stronger could occur two to three times per decade towards the end of the twenty-first century.[17] Paleoclimate reconstructions corroborate these

---

[14] G. M. Flato and Participating CMIP Modeling Groups, 'Sea-ice and its response to $CO_2$ forcing as simulated by global climate change studies', *Clim. Dyn.* 23 (2004), 220–41.

[15] P. Huybrechts, J. Gregory, I. Janssens, *et al.*, 'Modelling Antarctic and Greenland volume changes during the 20th and 21st centuries forced by GCM time slice integrations', *Glob. Planet. Change* 42 (2004), 83–105.

[16] P. A. Stott, D. A. Stone and M. R. Allen, 'Human contribution to the European heatwave of 2003', *Nature* 432 (2004), 610–13.

[17] C. Schär, P. L. Vidale, D. Lüthi, *et al.*, 'The role of increasing temperature variability in European summer heat waves', *Nature* 427 (2004), 332–6.

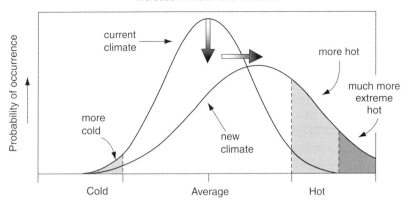

**Figure 4** Schematic probability distribution of summer temperature. A small increase of the mean (shift of the curve towards the right) causes a decrease of the frequency of cold summers. The occurrence of hot summers and extreme hot summers will increase by many factors of ten (light and dark shaded areas on the right, respectively).

analyses and demonstrate that the heat wave of 2003 was unique in the last 500 years![18]

Third, long-term changes must be considered, too. The greenhouse gases already emitted have a long lifetime. In particular, about 15 per cent of the emitted $CO_2$ will remain in the atmosphere for centuries. Due to its large thermal inertia, the ocean is far from being in equilibrium. The increase in sea levels will persist well into the twenty-second century and would do so even if emissions were reduced today. This is due to the slow uptake of heat into the ocean. This so-called *climate commitment* implies that we have not yet experienced all the consequences of past greenhouse gas emissions.

Fourth, the latest climate research has shown that several components in the climate system exhibit non-linear behaviour and tipping points. Among the best known is the northward extension of the Gulf Stream. Strong and rapid warming has the potential to destabilise this circulation, causing a strong reduction in it, or even a cessation.[19] Model simulations point to the possibility of an ice-free Arctic if fossil fuel emissions continue at a high

[18] J. Luterbacher, D. Dietrich, E. Xoplaki, *et al.*, 'European seasonal and annual temperature variability, trends, and extremes since 1500', *Science* 303 (2004), 1499–503.
[19] T. F. Stocker and A. Schmittner, 'Influence of $CO_2$ emission rates on the stability of the thermohaline circulation', *Nature* 388 (1997), 862–5.

rate.[20] The latest simulations suggest that there is a threshold in the range of a warming between 1.9 and 4.6°C beyond which Greenland could melt completely.[21] Vegetation cover, in particular the tropical rainforest, could also reach tipping point if warming continues.[22]

## Is there a magic fix?

Magic fixes for global warming are regularly proposed and make headlines in the media. But the large amounts of greenhouse gases which have been emitted during the past 250 years cannot be removed from the atmosphere within just a few years. Short-term measures such as piping greenhouse gas emissions into abandoned mines, or reforestation of some land areas, are futile efforts in comparison to the huge amounts of emissions. Only long-term strategies and global measures, such as the increase of fossil fuel efficiency and the gradual worldwide reduction in emissions will enable us to meet climate targets.

In addition to these indispensable mitigation measures which concern the origin of global warming, adaptation to the effects of past emissions and related climate change commitments will be necessary. Adaptation is highly region-specific. Not only *climate change mitigation* (as often claimed), but also *climate change adaptation* will be associated with high costs and the necessity for changes and investments in infrastructure. These costs are highly unlikely to scale linearly with the warming. Rather, greater warming and related changes will cause disproportionately large costs for adaptation. Whether we will be faced with a global warming of 2°C or 4°C is solely determined by the amount of greenhouse gases emitted from today onwards and hence is directly determined by our decisions at the local, regional and global levels.

## Bibliography

Cox, P. M., Betts, R. A., Collins, M., *et al.*, 'Amazonian forest dieback under climate-carbon cycle projections for the 21st century', *Theor. Appl. Clim.* 78 (2004), 137–56.

---

[20] M. M. Holland, C. M. Bitz and B. Tremblay, 'Future abrupt reductions in the summer Arctic sea ice', *Geophys. Res. Lett.* 33 (2006), L23503.

[21] J. M. Gregory and P. Huybrechts, 'Ice-sheet contributions to future sea-level change', *Phil. Trans. Roy. Soc. Lond. Ser. A* 364 (2006), 1709–31.

[22] P. M. Cox, R. A. Betts, M. Collins, *et al.*, 'Amazonian forest dieback under climate-carbon cycle projections for the 21st century', *Theor. Appl. Clim.* 78 (2004), 137–56.

EPICA Community Members, 'Eight glacial cycles from an Antarctic ice core', *Nature* 429 (2004), 623–8.

Flato, G. M. and Participating CMIP Modeling Groups, 'Sea-ice and its response to $CO_2$ forcing as simulated by global climate change studies', *Clim. Dyn.* 23 (2004), 220–41.

Gregory, J. M. and Huybrechts, P., 'Ice-sheet contributions to future sea-level change', *Phil. Trans. Roy. Soc. Lond. Ser. A* 364 (2006), 1709–31.

Hegerl, G. C., Crowley, T. J., Hyde, W. T., *et al.*, 'Climate sensitivity constrained by temperature reconstructions over the past seven centuries', *Nature* 440 (2006), 1029–32.

Holland, M. M., Bitz, C. M. and Tremblay, B., 'Future abrupt reductions in the summer Arctic sea ice', *Geophys. Res. Lett.* 33 (2006), L23503.

Huybrechts, P., Gregory, J., Janssens, I., *et al.*, 'Modelling Antarctic and Greenland volume changes during the 20th and 21st centuries forced by GCM time slice integrations', *Glob. Planet. Change* 42 (2004), 83–105.

IPCC, 'Summary for policymakers' in Solomon, S., *et al.* (eds.), *Climate Change 2007: The Physical Science Basis* (Cambridge University Press, 2007).

Knutti, R., Joos, F., Müller, S. A., *et al.*, 'Probabilistic climate change projections for $CO_2$ stabilization profiles', *Geophys. Res. Lett.* 32 (2005), L20707.

Knutti, R., Stocker, T. F., Joos, F., *et al.*, 'Constraints on radiative forcing and future climate change from observations and climate model ensembles', *Nature* 416 (2002), 719–23.

Luterbacher, J., Dietrich, D., Xoplaki, E., *et al.*, 'European seasonal and annual temperature variability, trends, and extremes since 1500', *Science* 303 (2004), 1499–503.

Marland, G., Boden, T. A. and Andres, R. J., 'Global, regional, and national $CO_2$ emissions' in *Trends: A Compendium of Data on Global Change* (Oak Ridge, Tenn.: Carbon Dioxide Information Analysis Center, Oak Ridge National Laboratory, US Department of Energy, 2007). http://cdiac.esd.ornl.gov/trends/emis/tre_glols.htm

Schär, C., Vidale, P. L., Lüthi, D., Frei, C., *et al.*, 'The role of increasing temperature variability in European summer heat waves', *Nature* 427 (2004), 332–6.

Siegenthaler, U., Stocker, T. F., Monnin, E., *et al.*, 'Stable carbon cycle-climate relationship during the Late Pleistocene', *Science* 310 (2005), 1313–17.

Solomon, S., *et al.* (eds.), *Climate Change 2007: The Physical Science Basis* (Cambridge University Press, 2007).

Spahni, R., Chappellaz, J., Stocker, T. F., *et al.*, 'Atmospheric methane and nitrous oxide of the Late Pleistocene from Antarctic ice cores', *Science* 310 (2005), 1317–21.

Stocker, T. F. and Schmittner, A., 'Influence of $CO_2$ emission rates on the stability of the thermohaline circulation', *Nature* 388 (1997), 862–5.

Stocker, T. F., Wright, D. G. and Mysak, L. A., 'A zonally averaged, coupled ocean-atmosphere model for paleoclimate studies', *J. Climate* 5 (1992), 773–97.

Stott, P. A., Mitchell, J. F. B., Allen, M. R., *et al.*, 'Observational constraints on past attributable warming and predictions of future global warming', *J. Climate* 19 (2006), 3055–69.

Stott, P. A., Stone, D. A. and Allen, M. R., 'Human contribution to the European heatwave of 2003', *Nature* 432 (2004), 610–13.

# 2

# A survey of Kyoto tools for greenhouse gas reductions: speculations on post-Kyoto scenarios

JOSÉ ROMERO AND KARINE SIEGWART

The United Nations regime for the protection of the global climate contains provisions related to trade. So far, there has been no conflict between climate protection and existing rules for international trade. But, in the future, conflicts may occur in a number of sectors when new investments in both mitigation and adaptation will be mobilised, and the development and transfer of environment friendly technologies to developing countries may pose problems related to intellectual property rights (IPRs). The Johannesburg Rio + 10 agreement provides the basic principle for mutual supportiveness of trade and multilateral environmental agreements (MEAs), in particular for climate protection.

## A. The threat of climate change

Given its potential impact on ecosystems and human activities,[1] climate change is recognised as one of the most important challenges for this century. Given also that greenhouse gas (GHG) emissions resulting from anthropogenic activities, such as the burning of fossil fuels, agriculture and deforestation, are among the causes of the recently observed changes in the climate system[2] substantial mitigation action and adaptation is urgently needed. The measures adopted are relevant to trade.

## B. Provisions of the UNFCCC and its Kyoto Protocol relevant to trade

The United Nations Framework Convention on Climate Change (UNFCCC) and its Kyoto Protocol (KP)[3] make numerous references to

---

[1] IPCC, Fourth Assessment Report, 2007, www.ipcc.ch   [2] *Ibid.*   [3] www.unfccc.int

trade. The decisions adopted for their implementation by their supreme organ, the Conference of the Parties (COP), consistently provide opportunities for both mutually supportive and conflicting situations with the current rules on international trade.

Provisions of the UNFCCC relevant to international trade are contained in Articles 2, 3 and 5. Article 2 provides that a time-frame sufficient to enable economic development to proceed in a sustainable manner should be allowed. This is in order for the UNFCCC to achieve its ultimate objective of stabilising GHG concentrations in the atmosphere at a level that would potentially prevent dangerous anthropogenic interference with the climate system.[4] Article 3, paragraph 5, provides that measures taken to combat climate change, including unilateral ones, should not constitute a means of arbitrary or unjustifiable discrimination or a disguised restriction on international trade. Finally, Article 5, paragraph 3, provides that Parties have to co-operate to promote a supportive and open international economic system that would lead to sustainable economic growth and development of all Parties, particularly developing country Parties, thus helping them to address the problems of climate change more effectively. The UNFCCC has introduced policies and measures that are trade relevant such as:

— those related to policies and measures pursuant to Article 4, paragraph 1;
— the provision of new and additional financial means through bilateral and multilateral channels according to Article 4, paragraph 3; and
— the transfer of technology (Article 4, paragraph 5, of the UNFCCC), in particular to developing countries.

The KP also has provisions relevant to trade in its Articles 2 and 3. Article 2, paragraph 2, provides that 'the Parties included in Annex I shall pursue limitation or reduction of emissions of greenhouse gases not controlled by the Montreal Protocol from aviation and marine bunker fuels, working through the International Civil Aviation Organization and the International Maritime Organization, respectively'. According to Article 2, paragraph 3 of the UNFCCC, Annex I Parties 'shall strive to implement policies and measures … in such a way as to minimize adverse effects … on international trade, and social, environmental and economic impacts on other Parties …' The KP has similar provisions in Article 3, paragraph 14.

---

[4]  Science establishes a direct link between global warming and the increase of atmospheric concentrations of GHG. The higher the concentrations the greater the warming and therefore the greater the potential to disrupt the climate system and the society.

Furthermore, specific provisions of the KP that have a highly trade-relevant content are:

— Article 2, paragraph 1 (a): sectoral policies and measures that may lead to conflicts with trade rules;
— the realisation of the reduction objectives contained in Article 3 has led to specific measures such as insurance (e.g. 'catbonds'), carbon-content accounting and transparency, labels, and public awareness in particular by consumers;
— innovative economic instruments, the so-called Kyoto mechanisms for carbon trading: joint implementation (Article 6 of the KP); Clean Development Mechanism (CDM) (Article 12 of the KP); and emissions trading (Article 17 of the KP).

So far, the implementation of the UNFCCC and its Kyoto Protocol has generated no conflicts with the established rules of international trade. Nevertheless, countries have considered it necessary to clarify the legal relationship between the instruments of the climate regime and trade, the fear of the climate policy-makers being that trade rules would supersede climate agreements. Following a proposal made by Switzerland, the Rio + 10 conference[5] that took place in 2002 in Johannesburg decided that MEAs and trade agreements should be mutually supportive,[6] as provided for in Article 3, paragraph 5, of the UNFCCC: 'Promote mutual supportiveness between the multilateral trading system and the multilateral environmental agreements, consistent with sustainable development goals, in support of the work programme agreed through WTO, while recognizing the importance of maintaining the integrity of both sets of instruments.'

In the interests of trade, the World Trade Organization (WTO) Ministerial Declaration in Doha in 2001[7] launched negotiations to enhance the mutual supportiveness of trade and the environment with a view to contributing to global sustainability as provided for in Article 3, paragraph 5, of the UNFCCC. In addition to the exchanges on national experiences, there have also been detailed exchanges and numerous submissions[8] on the concept of specific trade obligations (STOs) and

---

[5] www.iisd.ca/download/pdf/enb2251e.pdf
[6] World Summit on Sustainable Development, Johannesburg, 2002, Plan of Implementation.
[7] www.wto.org/english/thewto_e/whatis_e/tif_e/doha1_e.htm
[8] e.g. TN/TE/W/2 of 23 May 2002 (Argentina), TN/TE/W/4 of 6 June 2002 (Switzerland), TN/TE/W/72 of 7 May 2007 (Argentina, Australia).

the role they can play in enhancing the mutual supportiveness of trade and the environment. These have encompassed a wide range of STOs that are directed at complex environmental concerns. In particular, the negotiations to date have underlined that MEAs are an essential mechanism through which countries can address environmental objectives. It is also clear that trade measures will continue to be a feature of some MEAs. But it is also a fact that to date no specific difficulty has arisen in the relationship between MEAs and the WTO Agreements. Therefore, in principle, the international climate regime and international trade should neither interfere nor conflict with one another if the relationship between the trade and environment regime is clarified according to the principles of no hierarchy, mutual supportiveness, and deference. Such a clarification could take place within the Dispute Settlement Understanding of the WTO.[9] In view of the lack of practical experience within the WTO system it could be useful for WTO dispute settlement bodies to take advantage of the expertise available from MEAs in environmental issues.

## C.   Relationship between actions to tackle climate change and trade

Climate policies have to deal with the essential nature of our production and consumption patterns and are therefore recognised as a global development challenge. Mitigating the effects of climate change and adapting to its impacts will necessitate measures in all sectors.[10] It is envisaged that efficient and cost-effective means of mitigation and adaptation would make use of economic and market instruments.[11] This will require appropriate incentives which are likely to include agreements and regulations that will have an impact on international trade.

Since the entry into force of the UNFCCC in 1994 and its Kyoto Protocol in 2005, countries have been adopting appropriate policy and legal frameworks at the national[12] and international levels.[13] Enabling environments for investment and financial flows for the development of

---

[9]   e.g. TN/TE/W/68 of 30 June 2006 (European Communities).
[10]  Organisation for Economic Co-operation and Development (OECD), Climate Change: national policies and the Kyoto Protocol, OECD, 1999, Paris.
[11]  OECD, Environmental taxation in the OECD countries: issues and strategies, OECD, 2001, Paris.
[12]  http://unfccc.int/national_reports/annex_i_natcom_/items/1095.php
[13]  EU Greenhouse Gas Emissions Trading Directive (2003/87/EC).

effective mitigation and adaptation strategies have to be created in both developed and developing countries. Existing mechanisms, such as the CDM, will be strengthened and further developed and new ones will be created to provide incentives for investments and capital flows. For example, the CDM has not yet realised its full potential with respect to technology transfer. Projects that are effective in protecting the climate (e.g. the destruction of hydrofluorocarbons (HFC 23)) do not really address technology transfer and sustainable development.[14] An extension of the CDM with a more efficient mechanism for technology transfer in new sectors and countries is required.

### D.   The future of the international climate regime

What will the future climate regime after 2012 look like and what are the likely impacts of this regime on international trade? These questions should be considered in the light of current and foreseeable provisions resulting from the negotiations under the UNFCCC and its Kyoto Protocol.

The thirteenth Conference of the Parties (COP 13) in Bali in December 2007 will adopt decisions on these matters. Most probably the COP 13 will adopt a road map for negotiations to be concluded in 2009 for a comprehensive global climate regime with the participation of all countries. Depending on the objectives of the Bali road map, this agreement may well contribute to the 'greening' of investments and financial flows in the coming decades.[15]

Currently, the negotiations aim mainly at determining reduction commitments for Annex I Parties.[16] Based on scientific information[17] industrialised countries are requesting that developing countries participate in the global emission reduction efforts in view of their large share in global emissions which already amounts to more than 50 per cent. The extension of the international climate regime in the period after 2012 has been investigated by scholars and non-governmental organisations that have made proposals on these matters.[18] Their suggestions range from

---

[14]  Axel Michaelowa, 'CDM: current status and possibilities for reform', Paper No. 3 by the Hamburgisches Weltwirtschafts Institut (HWWI) Research Programme International Climate Policy, 2005.

[15]  For the outcomes of the Bali Conference see http://unfccc.int/meetings/cop_13/items/4049.php

[16]  www.unfccc.int

[17]  IPCC, Fourth Assessment Report, 2007, www.ipcc.ch     [18]  www.ccap.org

realistic and politically acceptable proposals to idealistic or unacceptable schemes. They concern not only the targets and the instruments, but also the extent of participation of developing countries in commitments to GHG reduction. Within the framework of the discussions under the UNFCCC and its Kyoto Protocol, Parties have already identified a number of elements of the future climate regime: mitigation, adaptation, technology and financing.

For mitigation, additional global investment and financial flows amounting to US$ 200–210 billion will be necessary in 2030 to return global GHG emissions to the current levels. These figures are from a recent study by the UNFCCC[19] and include the costs of technology research and development (R&D) related to climate change. Part of these investments and financial flows will need to be in developing countries where they are likely to be particularly cost effective.

For adaptation, the UNFCCC study estimates the overall additional investments and financial flows needed in 2030 to be US$ 30–50 billion. These estimates also include spending on technological R&D. A significant share of these resources will be needed in non-Annex I Parties (US$ 28–67 billion). Private sources of funding can be expected to cover a portion of the adaptation costs. Public resources will be needed in developing countries and to cover adaptation costs related to the impacts of climate change on the public infrastructure.

These amounts exceed the current funding available under the UNFCCC and its Kyoto Protocol, but are small in relation to the estimated global gross domestic product (0.3–0.5 per cent) and global investment (1.1–1.7 per cent) in 2030.

Potential areas of conflict between climate protection priorities and trade and new perspectives may be imagined that might conflict with international trade. In fact, new forms of intervention by the states are expected to foster technology transfer and new financial means for mitigation and adaptation. The potential conflicting areas are as follows:

— *The carbon market*: the carbon market will doubtless continue and expand after 2012. In fact, the European Union Emissions Trading Scheme (EU ETS) is almost independent of the Kyoto regime. Other

---

[19] UNFCCC, 'Report on the analysis of existing and potential investment and financial flows relevant to the development of an effective and appropriate international response to climate change', 2007, http://unfccc.int/files/cooperation_and_support/financial_mechanism/financial_mechanism_gef/application/pdf/dialogue_working_paper_8.pdf

regimes introducing the carbon certificates trade will be connected to the Kyoto regime and to the EU ETS. The carbon market may be challenged by some states or companies because it creates a sort of 'appropriation' of the atmosphere and the right to emit.

— *Technology development and transfer*: developing countries request preferential and non-commercial terms of access to technologies. They argue that these technologies are some sort of 'common goods' because they serve to combat a problem for which they are not mainly to blame. The promotion of technologies that are not yet commercially viable should be encouraged.

— *IPRs*: developing countries have requested that the period of rights over intellectual property is shortened. Some countries may not respect IPRs.

— *Compensation for the impacts of response measures and assistance for their economic diversification*: requested by oil exporting countries.

— *The CDM*: sectoral CDM, policy-based CDM. By establishing baselines and approved methodologies, the CDM establishes, de facto, a positive list of technologies and ('best' or 'better') practices that may be seen as discriminating against other practices.

— *Protectionism*: taxes based on the carbon content of the imported goods from countries that have not made GHG reduction commitments under the Kyoto Protocol.

— *Discrimination against users of fossil fuels*: de facto through policies aiming at reducing $CO_2$ emissions, but also of agriculture and forestry goods that do not satisfy certain environmental and/or climate standards.

— *Production and consumption patterns* may be addressed in the future as part of the international climate regime, as well as greening of the markets.

— *Financial issues*: the financial mechanism of the Convention, the Global Environment Facility (GEF), Official Development Assistance (ODA), specific national taxation policies and the mobilisation of new and additional resources may give rise to trade issues.

The way forward is through the participation of all the countries in combating and adapting to climate change. The Bali Plan of Action[20] adopted at the COP 13 in Bali in December 2007 corroborates this approach. Within the WTO Committee on Trade and Environment

---

[20]  For the outcomes of the COP 13, consult www.ccap.org

Special Session (CTESS) it has been decided at the ministerial level that efforts to safeguard the non-discriminatory multilateral trading system must go hand-in-hand with the commitment to sustainable development. The overall objective of the Climate Change Convention is to stabilise GHG concentrations at a safe level. The objectives of the WTO focus on the growth in economic welfare, employment, and production of and trade in goods and services. Sustainable development is also recognised by the WTO as a key objective. Turning to the principle of 'mutual supportiveness', the UNFCCC is coherent because it upholds an open and non-discriminatory international economic system and the special and differential treatment of developing countries. At the same time, the UNFCCC contributes to the overall goal of well-being by establishing rules, principles and institutions for the protection of the environment.

A final question: Principle 21 of the Stockholm Declaration (1972) as amended by the Rio Summit (1992) states that: 'States have, in accordance with the Charter of the United Nations and the principles of international law, the sovereign right to exploit their own resources pursuant to their own environmental and developmental policies, and the responsibility to ensure that activities within their jurisdiction or control do not cause damage to the environment of other States or of areas beyond the limits of national jurisdiction.' Does this responsibility impose restrictions on the trade of natural resources?

# 3

# International environmental law and the evolving concept of 'common concern of mankind'

THOMAS COTTIER AND SOFYA
MATTEOTTI-BERKUTOVA

## I.  Introduction

Legal and economic problems relating to climate-change mitigation transgress national boundaries and thus are at odds with the Westphalian system of territorially defined allocations of powers and responsibilities of government. This problem, of course, is not new and has significantly shaped the contours and concepts of international environmental law. States and the international community have shown considerable imagination and engaged in innovative legal engineering to cope with transnational issues. They have crafted emerging principles, rules, and monitoring mechanisms designed to strike a balance between two conflicting requirements: on the one hand, there is a pressing need to put an end to, or at least to slow down, the deterioration of the environment as well as forestalling new damage. On the other hand, there is a necessity for a realistic appraisal of the existing structures and the social and economic costs involved in this process both for developed states and even more so for developing countries. In addition, all of the above is undertaken within a framework of fragmented jurisdictions among states, which adds to the complexity of the task. For such reasons, progress at the legal level has been less conspicuous than one would have expected or desired. But progress has been made. The environment is no longer conceived of from a state-sovereignty-oriented perspective, as an asset that may belong to each state and in whose protection only the state concerned may be legally and practically interested.[1-2] Environmental law is increasingly abandoning the parameters

[1-2]  A. Cassese, *International Law*, 2nd edition (Oxford University Press, 2005), p. 487.

of territoriality, moving from transboundary pollution to shared or common concerns. The present chapter briefly explores this evolution. It focuses on the emerging concept of common concern in international environmental law with a view to preparing the ground for assessing its impact on the law of the World Trade Organization (WTO) and policy relating to the field of climate change.

Upon expounding the emerging contents of the principle, we argue that it will be mainly defined and shaped by specific provisions of treaty law. This includes the principles and rules of the multilateral trading system of the WTO. In many ways, environmental policies aiming at the reduction of greenhouse gases as well as policies of adaptation to changing climate conditions will affect, and be affected by, trade rules in the field of goods, services and intellectual property. Policies relating to climate change inevitably transgress national borders and need international co-ordination. The principle of common concern may give rise to unilateral measures and pressures which may be contained by international trade regulation. By contrast, trade regulation may impair the concretisation of common concern and reform of trade rules may be necessary. These issues and the dialectics between the two fields will be dealt with throughout this volume. This chapter prepares the ground with a view to helping to achieve coherence between the fundamental principle of common concern in climate change policies and the international trading system.

## II.   Traditional perceptions of jurisdiction in international law

### A.   *The legacy of territoriality*

The Westphalian state system of nation states, both unitarian and federalist, replaced an arcane and complex system consisting of overlapping jurisdictions of defunct feudal and medieval structures after the Thirty Years War. Since 1648, the jurisdiction of states to regulate, adjudicate and enforce has been essentially based upon the concept of territoriality. The story is well known. Boundaries became a predominant preoccupation in international law, both in terms of land and marine resources. Sovereignty was defined in territorial terms. The process of formal colonisation of the world's territorial resources by European powers, evolving from trade relations to the exercise of sovereign rights, was built upon these premises of modern international law. The same premises, and thus principles, also applied to the process of decolonisation, resulting in some 200 territorial sovereign states of all sizes: from huge expanses to tiny island states. Under the principle of sovereign equality and non-intervention, the law of the United Nations (UN) further consolidated the principle of territoriality. The prohibition on recourse to force, or the threat thereof, and the prohibition against interference with the domestic affairs of states under the UN Charter all build upon the territorially defined spheres of sovereignty and exclusive jurisdiction of states. The maritime revolution, beginning with the definition of the legal continental shelf in the 1950s and leading to the Exclusive Economic Zone in the 1970s, further enlarged the territorial concepts of overlapping jurisdictions. Codified in the 1958 Continental Shelf Convention and most prominently in the 1982 UN Convention on the Law of the Sea, the new zones reflected the emerging principle of permanent sovereignty of territorial states over natural resources. Not only land masses, but also most of the resource-rich parts of the seas have become compartmentalised in recent decades. Commensurate with sovereignty and jurisdiction, the responsibility for resource management and exploitation was exclusively vested in the territorial state. Sovereignty and responsibility expanded to include subterranean, surface and air space, essentially reaching as far as human exploitation of resources is technically feasible.

Eventually, communitarian traits emerged. The process of decolonisation brought about obligations to co-operate, and the structure of international law changed from mere co-existence to co-operation[3] under the UN Charter and the constitutions of specialised international organisations. Developing countries, claiming compensatory justice, enrolled in policies of special and differential treatment, in parallel to calls for import substitution and enhanced market access with the New International Economic Order movement in the 1970s. The technical feasibility of extracting resources beyond the territorial expanses in the high seas (manganese nodules) and possibly in outer space brought about strategies to counter appropriations on the basis of territoriality. The principle of common heritage of humankind of such resources was born. It pre-empted appropriation and reinforced the doctrine of *res nullius* and shared resources. In operational terms, the doctrine was

---

[3] See W. Friedmann, *The Changing Structure of International Law* (New York: Columbia University Press, 1964).

implemented for outer space with the Moon Treaty, and with the concept of the Area in the 1982 UN Convention on the Law of the Sea, securing participation and transfer of technology to developing countries in the potential extraction of mineral resources from the sea bed. Following the US policy review of the first Reagan administration, the interventionist regime of the Area was replaced by concepts closer to market-based extraction of such resources. It opened the path for ratification and entry into force of the Convention. The Area, however, has remained a dead letter due to geopolitical changes. There was no need to extract manganese from the sea bed due to abundant land-based resources in post-Apartheid South Africa and in Russia after the fall of the Berlin Wall. The implications, however, were felt elsewhere. Developing countries left the doctrine of common heritage of humankind and turned to emphasising the territorial concept of permanent sovereignty over natural resources. The Convention on Biodiversity, seeking to protect the global gene pool, operates under this principle. The same is true for wildlife, fisheries and other natural resources. International law has failed to evolve in terms of shared responsibilities beyond the doctrine of agreed co-operation. Recent claims to Antarctica, as much as continuing quarrels over the sovereignty and jurisdiction of remote islands with a view to establishing jurisdiction over maritime expanses of the continental shelf and the Exclusive Economic Zone are reminders that, in reality, international law and relations still largely operate within the Westphalian system.

Territoriality equally reflects the multilateral trading system and international economic law at large. Powers to regulate, adjudicate and enforce follow territorial patterns. Jurisdiction over persons and companies follows nationality and residence, both of which have a strong linkage to territorial attachment. The same holds true for trade regulation. Territorial concepts prevail. The WTO is open not only to territorial states, but also to customs territories operating a uniform regime of external trade in terms of tariff and non-tariff barriers. Trade regulations affecting imports and exports are legitimate because they affect the territory, industries and consumers located within its expanse. Trade restrictive measures, affecting others abroad, are justified provided a sufficient territorial nexus can be shown.[4] The same holds true in the

---

[4] See WTO Appellate Body Report on *US — Import Prohibition of Certain Shrimp and Shrimp Products*, WT/DS58/AB/R (12 October 1998).

field of anti-trust rules. Conduct, mergers taking place, and cartels operating abroad fall under the jurisdiction of domestic anti-trust authorities to the extent that they have an economic impact on domestic industries and consumers and can thus establish a sufficient nexus to the territory. It is for this reason that restrictions mainly motivated by causes abroad have remained highly controversial. This is true for production and process methods (PPMs) on grounds of environmental, labour and human rights concerns. The principle of territorial impact renders such measures difficult to justify under the traditional premises of international law. Albeit human rights are generally recognised and labour standards widely subscribed to by states, unilateral trade measures imposed in support of such rights abroad are anathema, often considered a matter of intervention in domestic affairs inconsistent with the principles of Article 2.4. of the UN Charter.

## B.   Limits and failures of territoriality

Technological advances increasingly challenge concepts of law based upon the territorial allocation of jurisdiction. In a number of areas, we observe a breakdown of territoriality as the principle is not able to regulate the matter effectively. This holds true in the field of communications. The most striking example is the World Wide Web which cannot be grasped and compartmentalised in terms of distinct national jurisdictions. Policing the web depends upon extensive co-operation and is likely to require centralised law enforcement agencies. The protection of domain names operates under the umbrella of international arbitration at the World Intellectual Property Organization (WIPO) which interestingly emerged on a de facto basis and is founded upon an international agreement. Other areas of communication reach the limits of territorial concepts: effective air traffic control cannot follow national borders and requires international regimes and co-operation. The operation and admission of ships by flag states often proves inadequate in terms of safety requirements and poses a serious risk to the marine environment. Territoriality also reaches its limits in the management of natural resources. The division and allocation of national jurisdiction over fish, gas and minerals by the continental shelf and the Exclusive Economic Zone not only creates complex problems of boundary delimitation, it also requires the management of overlapping resources by means of joint zones which are difficult to agree upon. Moreover, the distinction of exclusive zones and the high seas leaves resources located in the latter largely without adequate protection and management. They suffer the tragedy of the global commons: unsustainable exploitation and over-fishing. Importantly, this tragedy also extends to the exclusive zones of many coastal states, which seek fiscal revenues by extensive licensing and lack the means to police the waters with a proper navy. The situation is aggravated by the extensive subsidisation of large fishing fleets, depleting the fish stocks to the detriment of local fisheries. The dichotomy of territorial concepts and global commons and *res nullius* fails to provide an appropriate framework for protection and sustainable resource management.

Territoriality also accounts for the absence of key disciplines in international law, leaving certain matters almost exclusively to the nation states. This is particularly true for real estate and property regimes. While intellectual property protection has spearheaded international economic law since the nineteenth century, followed by trade regulation, real estate is clearly considered to be a matter of *rei sitae*. Disciplines and rules relating to real property in international law thus are minimal. Global law does not provide disciplines on property protection except for regional law.[5] Bilateral investment agreements and customary law merely address the rights of foreign right-holders and investors. They leave domestic relations and the position of domestic property owners and investors aside. The doctrine of *rei sitae* and non-intervention results in a lack of international disciplines, which translates into high costs. Real property regimes and land registration are retarded in many developing and even some industrialised countries. This is a major cause of delayed social and economic development as owners are often not defined and land cannot be used as collateral for investment. Also, it contributes to substantial inefficiencies in development assistance as resources dissipate and development is retarded due to the lack of proper legal institutions. The territoriality of law is thus one of the major causes of inequality and vast differences in social and economic development around the world.

## C.   Traditional remedies

The traditional response to the shortcomings of territoriality has been international co-operation and agreements. States are free to enter into

---

[5] European Convention on Human Rights, Third Protocol.

co-operation in any field of their activities and social life. Territorial boundaries may be overcome, or avoided, by schemes of co-operation. This can be observed in co-operation agreements relating to natural resources. The Antarctica Treaty is perhaps the most important and elaborate example.[6] In maritime law, states agree to establish joint zones of resource management and exploitation. In economic integration, territoriality and boundaries are reduced by means of abolishing trade barriers, while encouraging mutual recognition of regulations, and harmonisation of law by way of multilateral, regional or bilateral agreements. In development assistance, intervention in domestic affairs is based upon bilateral or multilateral treaty obligations and contractual arrangements defining conditionalities. Environmental issues are addressed in multilateral environmental agreements (MEAs), such as the Basel Convention, the Biodiversity Convention, the Framework Convention on Climate Change, the Montreal Protocol and the Kyoto Protocol. In this vein, states have taken recourse to the concept of common concern as a foundation for treaty-based regimes and co-operation. Both climate change and the conservation of biodiversity are considered to be matters of common concern in the relevant treaties. The point we wish to make is that traditional remedies all rely upon consent and mutual agreement. The shortcomings of territoriality are addressed by means of agreement between the parties concerned. It is unclear to what extent they can be addressed by means of unilateral action and intervention on the basis of rights and principles of international law within the framework of sovereign equality, non-intervention and self-determination of states. To what extent are states entitled to assume responsibilities for common and global goods beyond their territory and short of consent? It is at this point that we turn to the evolution of environmental law. We submit that it offers the basis and foundation for the emerging principle of common concern in international law. We recall the evolution of the core principles of environmental law and then turn to shape the contours and implications of the principle of common concern for climate change mitigation, adaptation and international trade regulation in this and other contributions to this volume.

---

[6] See S. Pannatier, *L'Antarctique et la Protection Internationale de l'Environnement*, (Zurich: Schulthess Polygraphischer Verlag, 1994), pp. 166–8; S. Pannatier, 'La protection du milieu naturel antarctique et le droit international de l'environnement', *European Journal of International Law* 7 (1996), 431–46.

## III.  The evolution of transboundary principles in international environmental law

### A.  From transboundary harm to common goods

The well-established general principle of international environmental law enjoins every state not to allow its territory to be used in such a way as to damage the environment of other states or of areas beyond the limits of national jurisdiction. The principle is based upon classical Roman law perceptions of good neighbourhood, equally shaping civil and common law. It is, however, no longer limited to this narrow dimension. In its generally accepted purport, the principle is not state sovereignty orientated. In other words, it is intended to protect the environment of other, and mainly neighbouring states. But the environment is seen not only as an asset belonging to states, but also as a common amenity, an asset which all should be interested in safeguarding, regardless of where the environment is or how it may be harmed.

This principle was first set out by the Arbitral Court in the *Trail Smelter* case.[7] It is substantially based on an even more general obligation, enunciated in 1949 by the International Court of Justice (ICJ) in the *Corfu Channel* case (every state is under the obligation 'not to allow knowingly its territory to be used for acts contrary to the rights of other states'). It was subsequently proclaimed, among other things, in Principle 21 of the 1972 Stockholm UN Declaration on the Human Environment. It was restated in two court decisions of 1979 and 1983, respectively, of the Rotterdam Tribunal in the case *Handelskwekerij G. — J. Bier B.V. Stichting Reinwater* v. *Mines de Potasse d'Alsace S.A.*[8] The ICJ affirmed the principle in the *Case Concerning the Gabcíkovo-Nagymaros Project*, where it stressed the importance it attached to 'respect for the environment', 'not only for states but also for the whole of mankind'.

The environment has come to be regarded as a common good and amenity. Yet, this has not had the consequences in the law which one would expect from the approach; no specific obligation to protect the environment has yet arisen in general international law with the characteristics of a community obligation, that is, an obligation towards all the other members of the international community, accompanied by a

---

[7] United Nations Reports of International Arbitral Awards UNIRAA 3 1905 (1938/1941).

[8] For the judgment of 8 January 1979 by the Rotterdam Court, see 11 *N.Y.I.L.* (1980), 326–33. For the judgment of 16 December 1983, see *N.Y.I.L.* 15 (1984), 471–84.

corresponding legal entitlement accruing to all the other members of the world community, to demand fulfilment of the obligation.[9]

## B.    From obligations erga omnes to common concerns

International lawyers have traditionally distinguished between legal obligations owed to another state, which can be enforced only by that state, and legal obligations owed to the whole international community of states, which can be enforced by or on behalf of that community. The latter are sometimes referred to as *erga omnes* obligations. This issue arose in an environmental context in the 1974 *Nuclear Tests* cases when New Zealand and Australia complained of the interference with the high seas freedoms of all states.[10] It may be right to take a cautious view of the *erga omnes* character of environmental obligations when the question to be determined is one of standing to bring proceedings before an international court; but if the International Law Commission (ILC) is correct, those obligations which concern the protection of the global environment will have an *erga omnes* character.

The idea that some legal obligations are owed to the international community as a whole however can be viewed from a broader perspective than procedural considerations. The characterisation of issues such as climate change as a common concern of mankind is important in this context because it places them on the international agenda and declares them to be a legitimate object of international regulation and supervision, thereby overriding the reserved domain of domestic jurisdiction or the possible contention that they relate to economic activities and resources which fall mainly within the executive territorial sovereignty of individual states.[11] The concept is more than a rhetorical gesture. What gives such obligations a substantive *erga omnes* character is not that all states have standing before the ICJ in the event of a breach, but that the international community can hold individual states accountable for compliance with their obligations through institutions such as the Conference of the Parties to the Climate Change Convention,[12] or other comparable bodies endowed, whether by treaty or General

---

[9]  Cassese, *International Law*, pp. 487–9.    [10]  *ICJ Rep.* (1974) 253 and 457.
[11]  P. W. Birnie and A. E. Boyle, *International Law and the Environment*, 2nd edition (Oxford University Press, 2002), p. 98.
[12]  1992 Convention on Climate Change, Article 7(2)(e), and Article 10.

Assembly resolution, with supervisory powers.[13] Another example arises in the case of a breach of the general principle prohibiting massive pollution of the atmosphere or of the seas, where any state, whether or not damaged, may invoke the 'aggravated responsibility' of the polluting state. In addition, the role of calling upon or requesting individual states, on behalf of the international community, to protect the environment is played in practice by the numerous international bodies established under the various conventions and treaties agreed upon in this area. Those international institutions act to safeguard community values and concerns. Their action is of crucial importance; they are indispensable in the present configuration of the world community.[14]

## C. From international to domestic concerns abroad

In certain contexts, the management of the state's own domestic environment is arguably a matter of common concern *independently* of any transboundary effects. Even before the Rio Conference,[15] multilateral treaties dealing with wildlife conservation, world heritage areas,[16] disposal of hazardous waste, and human rights had already touched on the international regulation of matters internal to the state concerned. By way of agreements, the international community addresses concerns which governments are supposed to deal with accordingly in domestic affairs. The Rio Declaration significantly extended the domestic reach of international environmental law by requiring states to enact effective environmental legislation[17] in order to facilitate access of individuals to information, the decision-making process, and judicial and administrative proceedings at the national level;[18] to apply the precautionary approach 'widely';[19] and to undertake environmental impact assessment 'as a national instrument'.[20] Moreover, to the extent that sustainable development can be regarded as a legal principle involving some degree of international supervision, it is argued that this aspect of domestic environmental protection may by implication also be a matter of 'common concern', although the Declaration itself does not say so.[21]

---

[13] Birnie and Boyle, *International Law and the Environment*, p. 99.
[14] Cassese, *International Law*, p. 488.
[15] United Nations Conference on Environment and Development: The Rio Declaration on Environment and Development, 13 June 1992, 31 *I.L.M.* 874.
[16] 1972 World Heritage Convention.
[17] Principle 11.   [18] Principle 10.   [19] Principle 15.   [20] Principle 17.
[21] Birnie and Boyle, *International Law and the Environment*, pp. 97–9.

## D. The impact of climate change

Contemporary climate change is a phenomenon of unprecedented scale and character.[22] This is why traditional legal concepts and mechanisms provided for by treaties and customary law do not have significant and sufficient impact. Numerous treaties have been concluded on specific matters; many of them, however, are framework agreements in that they merely provide a general agenda and directions for the further negotiations of agreements. That was the outcome of the recent United Nations Climate Change Conference, which took place in Bali, Indonesia, in December 2007. The conference culminated in the adoption of the Bali road map, which charts the course for a new negotiating process to be concluded by 2009, which will ultimately lead to a post-2012 international agreement on climate change. Ground-breaking decisions were taken, which form core elements of the road map. They include the launch of the Adaptation Fund as well as decisions on technology transfer and on reducing emissions resulting from deforestation. These decisions represent various tracks that are essential to achieving a secure future for the climate.[23]

States prefer to proceed with utmost prudence. They are prepared to be legally bound only by those rules the drafting of which they controlled or influenced, and which take into account their concerns, many of them shaped by conflicting interests of constituencies and thus without significant impact. In particular, governments are not willing to be bound by general rules emerging in the international community as a product of the majority of states. In short, states prefer to stick, as in other areas of law, to traditional consent[24] — despite pressing needs to bring about results. Accordingly, common concern so far is neither established as a proper self-executing, general principle of law, nor specified in contemporary international law. Nevertheless, it is not without shape and content, and has offered considerable guidance in drawing up international agreements in the field of climate change policies.

The features which appear important when seeking to define climate change as a global concern are its universal character and the need for common action by all states if measures for its protection are to work.[25]

---

[22] See Stocker in this volume.
[23] For the decisions adopted by the UN Climate Change Conference in Bali see http:// unfccc.int/meetings/cop_13/items/4049.php
[24] Cassese, *International Law*, p. 487.
[25] Birnie and Boyle, *International Law and the Environment*, pp. 97–9.

These elements can be found in a number of agreements already in force, notably the 1979 Geneva Convention on Long-Range Transboundary Air Pollution and the 1989 Montreal Protocol on Substances that Deplete the Ozone Layer, which do deal with atmospheric pollution. However, they do not specifically address the causes and effects of climate change as such.[26] Partly, these elements can be potentially found in customary international law, which may provide some general guidance on the legal implications of climate change. Existing customary law affirms the sovereign right of states to manage their own natural resources, although this right is by no means absolute. Customary law also prohibits a state from allowing activities on its territory to inflict serious damage to the environment of other states or on parts of the environment that do not belong to any state.[27] New rules may eventually emerge relating to common concerns. An unwritten international norm becomes part of customary law if it is consistently followed over a long period by a significant number of states which accept it as a legal obligation. For example, if a particular commitment to act is repeatedly expressed at important international conferences, and if all the participating states act in accordance with it, then the commitment may become an obligation under customary law. To what extent this is possible will be dealt with below in the context of the history of the principle of the common heritage of mankind.

Although the developments just referred to are tentative and of uncertain legal status and scope, they do point to the 'globalisation' of international environmental law, in the sense of meeting contemporary needs for global co-operation in dealing with global environmental problems.[28] For this reason, it is no longer possible to characterise international environmental law as simply a system governing transboundary relations among neighbouring states. It is in this context that the emerging concept of common concern becomes important.[29]

---

[26] *International Law and Climate Change*, reference on file with the author.

[27] *Ibid.*

[28] Kiss, 'Nouvelles tendances en droit international de l'environnement', *G.Y.I.L.* 32 (1989), 241; Handl, 'Environmental security and global change: the challenge to international law' *Yb.I.E.L.* 1 (1990), 3.

[29] Birnie and Boyle, *International Law and the Environment*, pp. 97–9.

## IV.  Legal implications of climate change as a common concern

### A.  Status of the atmosphere as common concern

The legal status of the global atmosphere was uncertain until UN Resolution 43/53 was adopted in 1988.[30] Even as late as 1985, the Vienna Convention on the Protection of the Ozone Layer could not specify the legal status of the atmosphere, apart from referring ambiguously to it as 'the layer of atmospheric ozone above the planetary boundary layer'.[31] In particular, no restriction on the external limits was contemplated. A couple of years before the adoption of the Resolution, the atmosphere was seen as a biogeophysical or global unity, and 'a natural resource of the Earth' rather than a typical example of *res communis*.[32]

Although as early as 1968 Prado had foreseen the characterisation of the atmosphere as a common heritage of humankind, the international community had to wait two decades to see another Maltese proposal suggesting that the atmosphere should be a common heritage of mankind.[33] The then Maltese Government proposed a General Assembly Resolution that climate change was part of the common heritage of mankind.[34] During the negotiations, the idea that the global climate is part of the common heritage of mankind failed. Instead, the common heritage of mankind was replaced with 'the common concern of mankind'.[35]

### B.  Emerging duties and obligations of states

Biermann argues that the status of the atmosphere as a common concern of mankind implies in particular three corollary duties: first, states are bound by certain environmental standards even without their consent, provided that these standards take account of different economic capabilities, in particular those of developing countries. Second, states are to

---

[30] The General Assembly Resolution 43/53 (6 December 1988) wherein it was recognised that 'climate change is a common concern of mankind, since climate is an essential condition which sustains life on earth' (paragraph 1).

[31] Article 1/1, 26 *I.L.M.* 1529.

[32] The WHO/UNEP meeting of experts held in 1978–1979 and designated by governments on the legal aspects of weather modification (Doc. WMO/UNEP/WG26/5).

[33] A. Pardo, 'Whose is the bed of the sea?', *Proc. American Soc. Int'l Law* 62 (1968), 225.

[34] UN Doc. A/43/241 (1988).

[35] K. Baslar, *The Concept of the Common Heritage of Mankind in International Law* (The Hague/Boston/London: Martinus Nijhoff Publishers, 1998), p. 306.

fulfil their legal obligations concerning the global environment both by domestic measures and by international assistance (duties of solidarity). Third, taking those duties into account, the international community may employ various means of enforcement to protect their common concern that have not yet been utilised in environmental issue areas.[36]

As we are already sharing the benefits of the atmosphere, which is a *sine qua non* of human survival, there is no need to emphasise that burdens should also be shared equitably among nations.[37] These obligations are to be assumed under the doctrine of 'common but differentiated responsibility' which evolved from the notion of the 'common heritage of mankind'. The latter concept gained stature in the UN Convention on the Law of the Sea,[38] as well as the international designation of certain areas (e.g. Antarctica and the deep seabed) and resources (e.g. whales) as 'common interests' of humankind.[39]

## C. Relationship to common heritage of mankind

Understanding the legal regime of the atmosphere as a matter of common heritage of humankind leads to different, albeit partly overlapping, implications from those of the doctrine of common concern. Partly in line with criteria on common concern, four elements are discussed. First, common heritage does not apply to environmental protection as strictly as it was devised to do for mineral resources: the airspace remains a matter of sovereign rights, but common heritage implies that they cannot be understood in terms of absolute rights which would deny the interests of the international community and future generations.[40]

In addition to this, there should be institutional machinery funded by the international community.[41] Common heritage goes along with an

---

[36] F. Biermann, 'Common concern of humankind: the emergence of a new concept of international environmental law', *Archiv des Volkerrechts* 34 (1996), 147.

[37] K. Ramakrishna, 'North-South issues, common heritage of mankind and global climate change', *Millennium Journal of International Studies* 19, No. 3 (1990), 441.

[38] United Nations Convention on the Law of the Sea, opened for signature 10 December 1982, 21 *I.L.M.* 1261. This concept dates to the 1950s and was also integrated into the Agreement Governing the Activities of States on the Moon and Other Celestial Bodies, 5 December 1979, 18 *I.L.M.* 1434.

[39] Biermann, 'Common concern of humankind', 147.

[40] Baslar, *Common Heritage of Mankind*, p. 306.

[41] The institutional provisions of the Montreal Protocol do not provide for the type of strong international mechanism envisaged in the case of the common heritage of mankind.

interventionist or mixed-economy regime as it was originally designed for the regime of the deep seabed at the UN Conference on the Law of the Sea (UNCLOS III). As Boyle suggests, treating the atmosphere as part of the common heritage of mankind would thus require far-reaching institutional changes and would, in effect, place atmospheric problems under collective management.[42] Biermann notes that an 'International Climate Authority' has been suggested by several political scientists.[43] According to them, the atmosphere needs a supranational authority as a custodian to protect the interests of humankind — 'an international body functioning on premises maximally scientific and minimally political, with its own standing to protect climate stability'.[44]

From the very beginning, the concept of common heritage of humankind has essentially incorporated ideas of redistributive justice, in particular to the benefit of the developing nations. The Prado doctrine sought to prevent the monopolisation of the future industry and the exploitation by the very few for the benefit of the very few. Such inherent redistributive qualities, as well as a necessity for international, even supranational regulation for effective implementation, are both absent in the traditional concept of *res communis* which denies territorial occupation, but allows for the unfettered exploitation of resources. These were conceived as being public, and freely exploitable without limits or any obligations whatsoever. In turn, common heritage seeks to bring about the reasonable exercise of rights, and the sharing of newly exploitable niches of the sea under general international law.

In this context, it is useful to learn some lessons from the international regulation of deep seabed mining under the concept of common heritage of humankind which illustrate the legal nature of this concept. This could reveal some similarities in the evolution and development of the concept of common concern. The 1970 Declaration of Principles Governing the Seabed and the Ocean Floor, and the Subsoil thereof, beyond the Limits of National Jurisdiction (1970 Declaration) assumed a key role in any attempt to define the general international law on deep seabed mining. Contrary to the views of developing countries at the time, any legal

---

[42] A. E. Boyle, 'International law and the protection of the global atmosphere: concepts categories and principles', in R. Churchill and D. Freestone (eds.), *International Law and Global Climate Change*, (Dordrecht: Graham and Trotman/Martinus Nijhoff, 1991), p. 10.
[43] Biermann, 'Common concern of humankind', 151.
[44] F. L. Kirgis, 'Standing challenge human endeavours that could change the climate', *A.J.I.L.* 84 (1990), 530.

position of the concept of common heritage could not be directly ascribed to its proclamation by means of a UN General Assembly (UNGA) resolution. Industrialised states (here the principal subjects of any obligations) have persistently resisted any such developments of customary law towards a majority rule under the UN Charter. Thus, the question of whether the concept of common heritage is a legal principle with binding force was a controversial one. The adoption of the 1970 Declaration without opposition and supported by a majority of industrialised states made the instrument eligible as one of the rare but possible candidates to carry, per se legally binding force. Prima facie, it seems possible to argue that the 1970 Declaration amounted to what de Visscher called *résolutions-accords*, establishing the concept of common heritage by agreement in the form of a UNGA resolution.[45] The situation was summarised by the late Mr Amerasinghe, President of UNCLOS III. He said:

> The Declaration cannot claim the binding force of a treaty internationally negotiated and accepted, but it is a definite step in that direction and ... it has — if I may adopt the words of Walt Whitman — that fervent element of moral authority that is more binding than treaties.[46]

This and further statements, however, do not allow any straightforward conclusions that the 1970 Declaration itself expressed or constituted the principle of common heritage as an explicitly accepted legal principle.

The critical question is, thus, whether a concept so firmly and unanimously accepted at the political level and pursued over a considerable number of years can remain without affecting the law. Can legal development and acceptance be blocked by insisting on a concept as mere policy even if unanimously pursued, in principle? Is it not a paradox to conclude, in an area of high legal significance, that moral or political authority is even more binding than the law? The danger of positivist perceptions, in such cases, is that due to the absence of any formal agreement, states remain seemingly free whereas, in fact, commitments have built up whose disruption may pose considerable threats to international stability and security. In other words: allegedly watertight distinctions between law and policy, usually cited in support of legal

---

[45] P. de Visscher, 'Observations sur les résolutions declaratives de droit adoptées au sein de l'Assemblée Générale de l'Organisation des Nations Unies' in E. Diez *et al.* (eds.), *Festschrift für Rudolf Bindschedler, Botschafter, Professor Dr. iur. zum 65. Geburtstag am 8. Juli 1980* (Bern: Stämpfli, 1980), p. 180.

[46] 5 UN GAOR (1933 mtg.) at 21, paragraph 245, UN Doc. A/PV. 1933 (1970).

security, are root causes of insecurity and instability of international relations — the very effects the idea of law tries to prevent. It is not a matter of giving up distinctions between law and policy, as a purely policy-orientated school of jurisprudence may do. Rather it is a matter of defining the thresholds of the law and legal obligations in a much more sophisticated, less formal, manner.

In this field so much is in transition and development, and so the conduct of states may provide the most reliable basis for the analysis of general rights and obligations. The equitable doctrine of settled expectations ('attitudes, expectations, perceptions and probable compliance'), proposed by Oscar Schachter, may prove to be the most helpful tool. Because it essentially relies on good faith (and therefore equity), and no longer rigidly on positivist categories of *lex lata* and *de lege ferenda*, it is particularly suitable to operate in infant fields still situated within the grey areas between law and non-law.[47]

The crucial test, thus, would ask which of the many norms at issue one could expect both industrialised states and least developed countries to comply with on the basis of attitudes and perceptions as expressed by conduct in the process of claims and counterclaims. Only congruent, or shared, expectations (which include an element of consent) can, in fairness, reach a settled status. The question thus is whether the concept of common heritage has achieved legal status under the approach of settled expectations. There is no single answer to that. Recognition of the general principle of common heritage in law, due to settled expectations, does not automatically entail an obligation to all the points set out in the 1970 Declaration or even the regime as negotiated at the UNCLOS III and expressed in Part XI and Annexes III and IV of the 1982 Convention on the Law of the Sea. The test of settled expectations has to be applied separately to all the various aspects. It may stand with respect to some, but be considered refuted in others, such as deep seabed mining upon the changes made due to the policy review imposed by the United States, at the time. The legal nature of common concern as a general principle can be assessed on similar foundations. It is essentially a matter of assigning levels of legitimate expectations and assessing the extent to which these expectations deserve protection under the principle of common concern. We submit that this stage has not yet been reached in terms of customary international law. But this may change in due course in relation to climate change.

---

[47] See O. Schachter, *International Law in Theory and Practice* (Dordrecht: Martinus Nijhoff, 1991).

## D.   Main content and message

While the legal nature of the principle of common concern, its scope, content and legal implications are unsettled, it is not devoid of content and direction, imposing some limitations on the exercise of sovereign rights by states within their own jurisdictions.

The language adopted itself was a matter of political compromise. Nonetheless, common concern indicates a legal status which is distinct from the concepts of permanent sovereignty, common property, shared resources, or common heritage of humankind which generally determine the international legal status of natural resources. As previously mentioned, in relation to climate change, UNGA Resolution 43/53 and the Climate Change Convention do not make the global atmosphere a common property beyond the sovereignty of individual states. But like the ozone layer, these instruments do treat it as a global unity insofar as injury in the form of global warming or climate change may affect the community of states as a whole. It is thus immaterial whether the global atmosphere comprises airspace under the sovereignty of a subjacent state or not: it is a 'common resource' of vital interest to humankind.[48] The recognition of the earth's climate as a common concern therefore implies not only the need for international co-operation to protect human interests, but also a 'certain higher status inasmuch as it emphasizes the potential dangers underlying the problem of global warming and ozone depletion [and suggests] that international governance regarding those "concerns" is not only necessary or desired but rather essential for the survival of humankind'.[49] By approaching the matter from a global perspective, the UN has acknowledged not only the artificiality of spatial boundaries in this context, but also the inappropriateness of treating the phenomena of global warming and climate change in the same way as transboundary air pollution, which is regional or bilateral in character.

If common concern is neither common property nor common heritage, and if it entails a reaffirmation of the existing sovereignty of states over their own resources, what legal content, if any, does this concept have? Its main impact appears to be that it gives the international community of states both a legitimate interest in resources of global significance and a common responsibility to assist in their sustainable

---

[48]   See recommendations of the International Meeting of Legal and Policy Experts, Ottawa, Canada, EPL 19 (1989), 78.

[49]   P. G. Harris, 'Common but differentiated responsibility: the Kyoto Protocol and United States policy', *NYU Environmental Law Journal* 7 (1999), 28.

development.[50] Moreover, insofar as states continue to enjoy sovereignty over their own natural resources and the freedom to determine how they will be used, this sovereignty is not unlimited or absolute, but must now be exercised within the confines of the global responsibilities set out principally in the Climate Change Convention as well as in the Rio Declaration and other relevant instruments.[51] Beyond this point, specific rights and obligations, in particular relating to responsibilities, remain to be properly defined in international law.

## V.   Open question of responsibilities under the concept of common concern

### A.   Liability

Under the general rules on 'ordinary' state responsibility, states incur international responsibility when they perform unlawful activities and thereby bring about damage to another state. However, the question arises whether the injuring state bears responsibility on account of fault (that is, if it failed to exercise due diligence) or, instead, regardless of any negligence, that is simply because of its risk-creating conduct. A further problem is whether states are responsible for activities that are not prohibited by international law, and nevertheless cause harm or damage to the territory of other states or outside them.

The spirit and the very thrust of modern law of the environment should encourage solutions capable of enhancing the safeguarding of the environment. It could therefore be maintained that, at least in the field of the environment, fault or negligence is not required for state responsibility to arise (that is, a state may be held accountable, hence liable to pay compensation, for serious damage to the environment even if it acted with due diligence). By the same token, it could be asserted that a state may also be held responsible for lawful activities, whenever they result in serious harm to the environment. The emergence of the rule in this sense can be seen from the *Trail Smelter* case, and the accidents of *Fukutyu Maru* and *Cosmos*, although in neither case did the relevant state admit its responsibility. Practice shows that in many instances states

---

[50]  UNEP, *Report of the Group of Legal Experts to Examine the Concept of Common Concern of Mankind in Relation to Global Environmental Issues* (1990).

[51]  Birnie and Boyle, *International Law and the Environment*, pp. 97–9.

are inclined to pay compensation for their own risky activities without, however, admitting any international responsibility.[52]

## B.    Compensation

Some experts argue that international law provides rules on liability and responsibility which require states or individuals that have caused environmental damage to restore the affected parts of the environment, pay compensation to those that suffered damage, or both. However, these rules are of limited value for problems such as greenhouse gas emissions, where the link between cause and effect can be difficult to prove.[53] The philosophy of *ex post* compensation rapidly reaches its limits, given that human factors causing contemporary changes have taken place over several generations. Moreover, they are most difficult to measure. The idea of compensation therefore translates into forward-looking strategies of creating incentives to reduce and eliminate emissions in the future. Past experience is taken into account in shaping future obligations.

## C.    Precaution

Potentially dangerous activities should be restricted or prohibited even before they can be proven to cause serious damage (the precautionary principle). Traditionally, activities were often not restricted or prohibited by legal rules until they had been proven to cause environmental damage. In other words, states were free to allow or were even obliged to allow, potentially hazardous activities, unless and until a causal link between an activity and a particular damage had been established. With a view to limiting the civil liability of governments in prohibiting potentially hazardous activities, environmental law developed the precautionary approach or principle. While the legal nature of this principle is still debated and controversial in general public international law, precaution has obviously been important and is most prominent in the field of climate change as the causes and effects of greenhouse gas emissions have only recently been established beyond reasonable doubt, and scientific certainty remains a matter of controversy. Scientists are still unsure about the exact timing and nature of the impacts of climate change, but if

---

[52] Cassese, *International Law*, pp. 497–9.
[53] *Key Legal Aspects of the Climate Change Convention*, reference on file with the author.

efforts to limit net greenhouse gas emissions are not initiated before scientific certainty is achieved, it may be too late to undo the damage. Therefore, the precautionary principle provides that activities threatening to cause serious or irreversible damage should be restricted or even prohibited even before scientific certainty about their impact is established. This principle has been discussed at many international climate conferences,[54] and it has also been included in some environmental policy statements and Conventions.[55] The Climate Treaty embodies a precautionary approach, since states agreed to take action despite the remaining scientific uncertainties about climate change.[56] This can be seen as an example of the evolution of the new principle in international environmental law and the concept of common concern of mankind may follow the same route in its development. It is fair to say that the principle has been accepted in treaty law, and a strong argument can be made that in the field of climate change mitigation it forms part of customary law. Even states that refused to sign the Kyoto Protocol operate domestic programmes recognising the importance of preventing further increases in greenhouse gas emissions and at the same time encouraging efforts to reduce pollution.

### D.   Obligations erga omnes and graduation

Global responsibility differs from existing transboundary environmental law in three respects. First, like human rights law, the global responsibilities in question may have an erga omnes character, owed to the international community as a whole, and not merely to other injured states inter se, as already discussed. Second, although held in common by

---

[54] e.g. the 'Brundtland Commission'; the Toronto Conference Statement; the European Community—European Free Trade Association (EC—EFTA) policy decision; Working Group I of the Intergovernmental Panel on Climate Change (IPCC), Working Group I of the International Negotiation Committee on Climate Change (INC), and the United Nations Conference on Environment and Development (UNCED) Preparatory Committee.

[55] e.g. the 1991 Bamako Convention on Hazardous Wastes adopted by the African States; the 1992 Paris Convention for the Protection of the Marine Environment of the North-East Atlantic; the 1992 Helsinki Convention on the Protection of the Marine Environment of the Baltic Sea Area; the preamble of the amended Montreal Protocol (1987/90); Resolution 44 (14) of the 1991 conference of the parties to the London Dumping Convention, and Principle 15 of the 1992 Rio Declaration.

[56] International Law and Climate Change, reference on file with the author.

all states, global environmental responsibilities are differentiated in various ways between developed and developing states, and contain strong elements of equitable balancing not found in the law relating to transboundary harm. Third, although the commitment to a precautionary approach mentioned above is now relevant to many aspects of environmental law, it is particularly evident in matters of global concern such as climate change.[57]

Since the climate is of such crucial 'common concern' to humankind, it follows that there is a responsibility on the part of countries to protect it. This begs the question of who is responsible for pollution affecting the climate. The answer is a function of each country's historical responsibility for the problem, its level of economic development, and its capability to act. This was suggested by Principle 23 of the 1972 Stockholm Declaration, which states that it is essential to consider 'the extent of the applicability of standards which are valid for the most advanced countries but which may be inappropriate and of unwarranted social cost for developing countries'.[58]

States thus have common but differentiated responsibilities for combating climate change. It is widely recognised that all states contribute to climate change and that all states may, to different degrees, suffer from it. Industrialised states have developed their economies over the past 150 years in part by treating the atmosphere as a free and unlimited resource, and they continue to generate the greatest quantity of greenhouse gases. Developing countries are now attempting to industrialise at a time when the atmosphere is no longer considered as free and unlimited. In addition, they still make a smaller contribution to climate change (although it will increase in the decades to come). The principle of common but differentiated responsibilities proposes that, while all states should act to prevent damage to the atmosphere, developed countries should take the lead. This principle is widely recognised.[59] Essentially, it is a matter of applying the 'polluter pays principle' to the field of climate change. It was incorporated into the 1987 Montreal Protocol and it underlies the dual

---

[57] Birnie and Boyle, *International Law and the Environment*, pp. 97–9.

[58] Declaration of the United Nations Conference on the Human Environment, 16 June 1972, Stockholm, *I.L.M.* 1416, 1420.

[59] The principle was strongly supported by all 'developing countries climate conferences' and was recognised by the UN General Assembly, the Second World Climate Conference, the Preparatory Committee of UNCED, the Toronto Conference Statement, the Hague Declaration, and the Noordwijk Declaration. It is also reflected in Principle 7 of the 1992 Rio Declaration.

standard of commitments for developed and developing countries established by the Climate Convention.[60] More to the point, while all countries must join in efforts to reduce emissions of greenhouse gases that contribute to climate change, the developed countries are required to take the lead by the Climate Convention.[61]

## VI. Minimal standards set out in the Climate Change Convention

Non-binding statements by international climate conferences influenced the drafting of the Climate Change Convention by the Intergovernmental Negotiating Committee for a Framework Convention on Climate Change (INC/FCCC).[62] The treaty-drafters referred to the statements to evaluate the concerns and proposals of various states and regions. In this way, a number of concepts and principles were reaffirmed and highlighted. The UN FCCC was adopted in May 1992 and opened for signature in June at the UN Conference on Environment and Development (UNCED) in Rio de Janeiro.[63] Conventions among states are a key source of international law. Also called treaties, they set out obligations that are binding on their party states. As a framework Convention, the Climate Treaty contains important principles and general obligations. Additional commitments may be agreed upon later in one or more protocols.[64]

As a framework Treaty, the Convention sets out principles and general commitments, leaving more specific obligations to future legal instruments. The key principles incorporated in the Treaty are the precautionary principle, the common but differentiated responsibility of states (which assigns industrialised states the lead role in combating climate change), and the importance of sustainable development (Article 3). The general commitments, which apply to both developed and developing countries, are to adopt national programmes for mitigating climate change; to develop adaptation strategies; to promote the sustainable

---

[60] *International Law and Climate Change*, reference on file with the author.

[61] P. G. Harris, 'Common but differentiated responsibility', 28–30.

[62] See P. Sands, 'The United Nations Framework Convention on Climate Change', 1 *R.E.C.I.E.L.* 270 (1992).

[63] Report of the Intergovernmental Negotiating Committee for a Framework Convention on Climate Change, May 1992, A/AC.237/18 (Part II) Add.1

[64] *International Law and Climate Change*, reference on file with the author.

management and conservation of greenhouse gas 'sinks' (such as forests); to take climate change into account when setting relevant social, economic, and environmental policies; to co-operate in technical, scientific, and educational matters; and to promote scientific research and the exchange of information (Article 4, paragraph 1).

The Convention also establishes more specific obligations for particular categories of states. It distinguishes between members of the Organisation for Economic Co-operation and Development OECD (listed in Annex II to the Convention), countries in transition to a market economy (Eastern European countries which, together with the OECD countries, are listed in Annex I), and developing countries. The Convention requires OECD countries to take the strongest measures, while the states in transition to a market economy are allowed a certain amount of flexibility. The Convention recognises that compliance by developing countries will depend on financial and technical assistance from developed countries; in addition, the needs of least developed countries and those that are particularly vulnerable to climate change for geographical reasons are given special consideration (Article 4, paragraphs 2–7).

The Convention is legally binding only on those states that have agreed to be bound by it. To meet its obligations under a Convention, a party may need to impose legal obligations on its nationals. For example, the Climate Change Convention obliges developed country parties to take measures aimed at limiting their greenhouse gas emissions. To fulfil this commitment, these states may need to adopt national legislation that will in turn encourage or require companies and individuals to limit their emissions.[65] More specifically, these minimal standards set out in the Convention and the Kyoto Protocol will be considered in other contributions to this volume. It confirms the experience that in matters of environmental protection states operate with caution and refrain from endorsing broad and encompassing principles short of technical implementation.

## VII.   Implications of, and on, international trade regulation

The concept of common concern is a treaty-based emanation. Its development is a dialectical process which may result in the recognition of the common concern as a general principle of international law beyond consent. It is still unclear to what extent the states are entitled to assume

---

[65] *Ibid.*

responsibilities for matters of common concern beyond their territory and short of consent but the evolution of environmental law offers the basis and foundation for the emerging principle of common concern in international law. This bears the risks of excessive unilateral intervention, and a sort of new imperialism — ecological imperialism, when the common concern becomes a justification for unilateral intervention and sanctions. Governments under domestic pressures may invoke the principle of common concern to justify measures having extra-territorial effect, close borders to products originating in other countries, impose additional burdens and barriers with a view to bringing about results beneficial to climate change mitigation, but that are also in tandem with domestic protectionist interests. For example, common concern may be invoked to support unilateral pressures to introduce safe nuclear technology, to apply $CO_2$ and other greenhouse gas emission controls and filters. It may be used to impose investment under the Clean Development Mechanism, to refrain from deforestation, to participate in emission trading schemes, to tax polluting activities, to refrain from supporting polluting technologies and to refrain from exporting environmentally unsound products. The motives of such action may be noble and deserving of support. At the same time, it creates tensions with established principles of international law in terms of self-determination and the prohibition of interference in the domestic affairs of other countries under the UN Charter. It is at this point that the relevance of the multilateral trading system of the WTO enters the stage. As will be seen throughout this volume, climate change measures relating both to mitigation and adaptation translate to a large extent into measures of trade policy. Multilateral rules therefore define the extent to which, in the name of common concern, unilateral measures may or may not be taken. Conversely, common concerns may require the multilateral system to adjust and to allow for specific action where today this may not be the case. Unilateral policies relating to product-related standards in the field of technical barriers to trade, including PPMs, labelling requirements, border tax adjustments, recourse to tariffs, the use of subsidies and recourse to countervailing duties, measures relating to government procurement and special and differential treatment under General System of Preferences (GSP) schemes will all need to be assessed and discussed in the light of WTO compatibility and, possibly, efforts at reform with a view to fleshing out the the emerging principle of common concern in the field of climate change policies. The same holds true in the field of services, in particular in relation to labour mobility (Mode 4) and rules facilitating the transfer of technology under the Trade-Related Aspects of Intellectual Property Rights Agreement (TRIPS). Indeed, the evolution of common concern towards a general principle of international law may lead to new rights and obligations of states to respect common concern. It may bring about new obligations to support the principle by means of affirmative action. It may trigger liability and state responsibility of the *erga omnes* type in case of failure to act, respect and support the common concern. In so doing, international environmental law and international trade law will need to find a new balance with a view to effectively supporting climate change mitigation and adaptation and the pursuit of welfare through an open trading system. Both are crucial to the well-being of future generations.

## Bibliography

Agreement Governing the Activities of States on the Moon and Other Celestial Bodies, 5 December 1979, 18 *I.L.M.* 1434.

Baslar, K. 1998. *The Concept of the Common Heritage of Mankind in International Law* (The Hague/Boston/London: Martinus Nijhoff Publishers).

Biermann, F., 'Common concern of humankind: the emergence of a new concept of international environmental law', *Archiv des Volkerrechts* 34 (1996), 426–81.

Birnie, P. W. and Boyle, A. E. 2002. *International Law and the Environment*, 2nd edition (Oxford University Press).

Boyle, A. E., 'International law and the protection of the global atmosphere: concepts categories and principles', in Churchill, R. and Freestone, D. (eds.) 1991. *International Law and Global Climate Change* (Dordrecht: Graham and Trotman/Martinus Nijhoff).

Cassese, A. 2005. *International Law*, 2nd edition (Oxford University Press).

Declaration of the United Nations Conference on the Human Environment, 16 June 1972, 11 *I.L.M.* 1416, 1420.

Friedmann, W. 1964. *The Changing Structure of International Law* (New York: Columbia University Press).

Handl, G., 'Environmental security and global change: the challenge to international law', *Yb.I.E.L* 1 (1990).

Harris, P. G., 'Common but differentiated responsibility: the Kyoto Protocol and United States policy', *NYU Environmental Law Journal*, 7 (1999), 27–48.

*International Law and Climate Change*, reference on file with the author.

Jennings, R., 'The role of the International Court of Justice in the development of International environmental protection law', 1/3 *R.E.C.I.E.L.* (1992), 240–4.

*Key Legal Aspects of the Climate Change Convention* at www.cs.ntu.edu.au/homepages/jmitroy/sid101/uncc/fs251.html

Kirgis, F. L., 'Standing challenge human endeavours that could change the climate', *A.J.I.L.* 84 (1990), 525–30.

Kiss, A., 'Nouvelles tendances en droit international de l'environnement', *G.Y.I.L.* 32 (1989), 241–63.

Pannatier, S. 1994. *L'Antarctique et la Protection Internationale de l'Environnement* (Zurich: Schulthess Polygraphischer Verlag), pp. 166–8.
  'La protection du milieu naturel antarctique et le droit international de l'environnement', *European Journal of International Law* (1996), 431–46.

Pardo, A., 'Whose is the bed of the sea?', *Proc. American Soc. Int'l Law* 62 (1968) 216–51.

Ramakrishna, K., 'North-South issues, common heritage of mankind and global climate change', *Millennium Journal of International Studies* 19, No. 3 (1990), 429–46.

*Recommendations of the International Meeting of Legal and Policy Experts, Ottawa, Canada*, 19 *E.P.L.* (1989), 78.

Report of the Intergovernmental Negotiating Committee for a Framework Convention on Climate Change, May 1992, A/AC.237/18 (Part II) Add.1.

Rest, A., 'Need for an international court for the environment? — Underdeveloped legal protection for the individual in transnational litigation', *E.P.L.* 24 (1994), 173–87.

Sands, P., 'The United Nations Framework Convention on Climate Change', 1 *R.E.C.I.E.L.* 270 (1992).

Schachter, O. 1991. *International Law in Theory and Practice* (Dordrecht: Martinus Nijhoff).

*The Convention on Climate Change: What Does it Say?* at www.cs.ntu.edu.au/homepages/jmitroy/sid101/uncc/fs250.html

United Nations Conference on Environment and Development: The Rio Declaration on Environment and Development, 13 June 1992, 31 *I.L.M.* 874.

United Nations Convention on the Law of the Sea, 10 December 1982, 21 *I.L.M.* 1261.

Vienna Convention on the Protection of the Ozone Layer, 1985, 26 *I.L.M.* 1529.

De Visscher, P., 'Observations sur les résolutions declaratives de droit adoptées au sein de l'assemblé générale de l'organisation des Nations Unis' in Diez, Emanuel *et al.* (eds.) 1980. *Festschrift für Rudolf Bindschedler, Botschafter, Professor Dr. iur. zum 65. Geburtstag am 8. Juli 1980* (Bern: Stämpfli), pp. 173–85.

4

# Domestic and international strategies to address climate change: an overview of the WTO legal issues

ROBERT HOWSE AND ANTONIA L. ELIASON

## I. Introduction

This paper seeks to provide an overview of the issues of World Trade Organization (WTO) law that are raised by domestic and international policy strategies to address climate change. The paper also provides a non-exhaustive survey of, and commentary on, the existing literature that concerns these issues.

Climate change, which has identifiable potentially catastrophic effects on the environment and human security in the broadest sense, cannot be halted, much less reversed, without the control and reduction of carbon dioxide ($CO_2$) emissions into the atmosphere. Current $CO_2$ levels in the atmosphere are higher than at any time in the last 450,000 years, and some analyses indicate that $CO_2$ levels are at their highest in twenty million years.[1-3] Associated with a rise in $CO_2$ levels is a rise in global temperatures, and current projections by the Intergovernmental Panel on Climate Change (IPCC) suggest that without measures to reduce emissions, over the course of this century global average temperatures will increase by 1.8–4.0 °C.[4] Rising temperatures are already causing Arctic ice to melt, glaciers to retreat and ocean levels to rise, threatening inhabitants of low-lying lands worldwide. Since these $CO_2$ emissions are, given current technologies, an inevitable byproduct of much of the energy consumed for transportation, industrial production, and domestic use, the

---

[1-3] *National Oceanic and Atmospheric Administration*, www.ncdc.noaa.gov/oa/climate/globalwarming.html#Q2
[4] *European Commission on Environment*, http://ec.europa.eu/environment/climat/home_en.htm

challenge of halting and ultimately reversing climate change is an enormously difficult one.

Several main international and domestic strategies have emerged and the paper will examine the WTO issues raised by each.

The first strategy, exemplified by the Kyoto process, is to seek quantitative reductions in or caps on the level of emissions through binding international commitments of each state. Trade measures have been proposed by some commentators and officials as a means of pressuring non-participating states, especially the United States (US), to ratify the Kyoto Protocol, or at least to shoulder the share of the burden for reducing emissions that would be allocated to them under the principles of the Kyoto Protocol. The Kyoto process also envisages emissions trading as a way of efficiently achieving reductions in emissions, and the resulting carbon market raises General Agreement on Trade in Services (GATS) issues, since what is traded is arguably a financial instrument.

A second and obviously complementary strategy to the Kyoto Protocol is to mandate the use of green or renewable energy, the consumption of which[5] does not create $CO_2$ emissions, and/or to reduce the cost of such energy relative to conventional energy sources. Such mandates can raise WTO issues where they affect goods and services traded between WTO Members, as can subsidies, including fiscal measures, to reduce the cost of renewable energy. Moreover, the reduction of tariff and non-tariff barriers (such as idiosyncratic technical standards) on renewable energy and the technologies and equipment needed to produce it may make a significant contribution to lowering the cost of renewables relative to conventional energy sources. Finally, mandates to use renewable energy can be traded in the form of tradeable renewable energy certificates (TRECs) and the development of a global market in such instruments will be affected by the financial services and other relevant rules in the GATS.

A third and also complementary strategy is that of energy efficiency. This can be achieved through product standards that specify a required performance level in terms of energy consumption. Subsidies may also be used to induce consumers and industrial users to switch to more energy-efficient goods, or adapt existing goods so as to make them more energy efficient. Again, where trade in goods and/or services is affected, WTO rules will be of relevance.

---

[5] Here it is important to note that such emissions may occur in the production of some kinds of green energy sources, such as biofuels.

## II.   Kyoto and the WTO

How to reduce greenhouse gas emissions has long been a focal point of the climate change debate. In particular, two questions arise in the context of measures designed to reduce emissions: how effective is the measure in reducing emissions and what are the implications for competitiveness and the economic costs of the measure? The concept of 'common but differentiated responsibilities' is enshrined in the United Nations Framework Convention on Climate Change (UNFCCC), recognising the historical contributions of states to the problem of climate change and the differing ability of states to respond to it.[6] In rejecting the Kyoto Protocol, which applies the principle of common but differentiated responsibilities and thus does not require developing countries to reduce their emissions, the US sent a clear message that considerations of economics and competitiveness would dominate its position on climate change legislation.

Such considerations relate to the effects on global trade of asymmetrical commitments to reduce emissions. In effect, if developed countries reduce their emissions while developing countries are exempted from making reductions, the cost disparity between goods produced in developed and developing nations could increase further, giving developing countries a competitive edge and harming the balance of trade for developed countries. Furthermore, companies in developed countries may choose to move production to countries where reducing emissions is not mandatory, thus undermining the reductions achieved in the developed country.

At the same time, the overwhelming reality is that because the US, the world's largest producer of $CO_2$, has refused to ratify the Kyoto Protocol, its effectiveness is limited. Successful tools for addressing global climate change require ways to balance environmental interests and economic growth; since global co-operation is necessary for climate change prevention mechanisms to be effective, mechanisms that require some countries to sacrifice disproportionately the possibilities of economic growth and development are unlikely to succeed. Joseph Stiglitz has argued that the refusal of the US to reduce its emissions constitutes a massive subsidy to its industries, since American firms are not paying the

---

[6] J. Robinson, J. Barton, C. Dodwell, M. Heydon and L. Milton, *Climate Change Law: Emissions Trading in the EU and the UK* (London: Cameron May, 2006), p. 28.

cost of damage to the environment.[7] He suggests that the signatories to the Kyoto Protocol immediately bring charges of unfair subsidisation to the WTO to address this.[8] In the long term, Stiglitz sees imposition of a global emissions tax to increase economic efficiency and avoid the distribution debate as a more viable solution than the Kyoto Protocol mechanisms, since such a tax would apply equally to developing and developed countries.[9]

## A.  Kyoto Protocol overview

The Kyoto Protocol to the UNFCCC was adopted on 11 December 1997 at the third Conference of Parties (COP 3), and entered into force on 16 February 2005. It strengthens the commitment of the UNFCCC to mitigate the effects of climate change by requiring mandatory limitations on emissions from Annex I parties (developed countries). To date, 175 countries have ratified the Kyoto Protocol, including Russia, China and India, although China and India do not have to reduce emissions under the terms of the Protocol.[10] Negotiations for the Kyoto Protocol began in 1995 with the Berlin Mandate, issued at COP 1, which launched a new round of talks in an attempt to strengthen the effectiveness of the UNFCCC. Upon its adoption, the Kyoto Protocol did not have comprehensive rules on implementation, requiring a further round of negotiations that culminated in the Marrakesh Accords, adopted at COP 7. The Kyoto Protocol covers six main greenhouse gases — $CO_2$, methane, nitrous oxide, hydrofluorocarbons (HFCs), perfluorocarbons (PFCs) and sulfur hexafluoride.[11]

Under the Kyoto Protocol, Annex I parties agreed to reduce $CO_2$ emissions to below 1990 levels, with individual targets set for each country. Implementation is to include domestic policy and regulatory measures as well as the use of the mechanisms available under the Protocol.[12] The Kyoto Protocol has two commitment periods — the first to end in 2007 and the second to run from 2008–2012. Those countries failing to meet their emission targets will be penalised by

---

[7]  J. E. Stiglitz, 'A new agenda for global warming', *Economist's Voice* 3 (2006).
[8]  *Ibid.*     [9]  *Ibid.*
[10]  UNFCCC website, http://unfccc.int/kyoto_protocol/items/2830.php
[11]  UNFCCC website, http://unfccc.int/kyoto_protocol/background/items/3145.php     [12]  *Ibid.*

having to make up the difference in the second commitment period with an additional 30 per cent penalty.[13]

The Kyoto Protocol established three main mechanisms to help Annex I countries cut the costs of meeting their emissions targets by using opportunities to reduce emissions in countries where it costs less — joint implementation, the Clean Development Mechanism (CDM) and emissions trading. Joint implementation allows Annex I countries to implement emission reduction projects (or projects that increase removal by sinks) in another Annex I country and count the emission reduction units (ERUs) the project produces against its own target. The CDM similarly allows Annex I countries to implement emission reduction projects in non-Annex I countries and use the resulting certified emission reductions (CERs) towards meeting their own targets. Finally, emissions trading allows an Annex I party to transfer some of its assigned emissions allowances to another Annex I party that has trouble meeting its emissions target. Notably lacking from the Kyoto Protocol is an effective enforcement mechanism. Although there is a monitoring mechanism, and the possibility that the failure to meet targets will be 'punished' as it were by an increase in the signatory's obligations, there is simply no multilateral means available to enforce the original obligation let alone the punishment for not meeting it.

This void leads to the possibility of governments taking unilateral measures to implement the Kyoto Protocol. To the extent that such unilateral measures have trade effects on other WTO Members, they would be regulated by WTO rules. Article 3.5 of the UNFCCC explicitly contemplates the possibility of unilateral trade action; direct or indirect effects on trade are acceptable under the UNFCCC provided that the measures in question do not constitute arbitrary or unjustifiable discrimination or a disguised restriction on international trade. Thus, Article 3.5 reads as follows: 'In their actions to achieve the objective of the Convention and to implement its provisions, the Parties shall be guided, *inter alia*, by the following: ... 5. The Parties should co-operate to promote a supportive and open international economic system that would lead to sustainable economic growth and development in all Parties, particularly developing country Parties, thus enabling them better to address the problems of climate change. Measures taken to combat climate change, including unilateral ones, should not constitute a

---

[13] *Ibid.*

means of arbitrary or unjustifiable discrimination or a disguised restriction on international trade.'

## B.    Carbon trading

The carbon market, as Graciela Chichilnisky states 'trades the right to emit carbon dioxide that originates from the burning of fossil fuels'.[14] Chichilnisky further emphasises that in order for a carbon market to exist and operate 'there has to be a firm agreement among the parties to reduce total emissions'.[15] It is arguably a short-term solution to the rising level of emissions, since in the long run, carbon trading does not provide incentives to reduce carbon emissions further — it provides incentives to stabilise pre-determined levels of carbon emissions, resulting in a situation where industry would probably protest against any form of subsequent reduction in emissions level that might affect them.

The UNFCCC and Kyoto Protocol establish the legal framework for international carbon trading.[16] This legal framework does not cover the aspects of carbon trading related to international trade, offering an opportunity for the WTO to become involved in addressing concerns pertaining to the carbon market. As yet, the WTO has not made a determination of whether carbon markets fall under its auspices. If they do, would a carbon market fall under the GATS as a financial service, under some other sectoral classification under the GATS (environmental or energy services?) or, viewed from a WTO law point of view, is the carbon market to be considered primarily in terms of how it affects the terms and conditions of production of the products for which carbon-based energy is an input? The answer may not be of an either/or character: as the Appellate Body held in *EC — Bananas*, the same regulatory scheme may affect trade in both goods and services and therefore both the disciplines of the covered agreements on trade in goods and those of the GATS may be applicable.

As defined in the carbon market envisioned under the Kyoto Protocol, carbon credits can be bought and sold through brokers, on exchanges and directly on a party-to-party basis. In some respects carbon credits resemble goods, while in others they are more akin to financial services.

---

[14] G. Chichilnisky, 'Energy security, economic development and climate change — carbon markets and the WTO' (2007), 3 (on file with authors).

[15] *Ibid.*, 25.

[16] Robinson, Barton, Dodwell, Heydon and Milton, *Climate Change Law*, p. 173.

Carbon credits have relatively transparent pricing, and in practice, carbon trading seems very much like a financial service — swaps, derivatives, futures contracts, options and the movement of large sums of money in exchange for pieces of paper with guarantees seem to fit a financial service rather than a good. That said, those same elements can be seen in commodities trading, and commodities are unquestionably goods.

Finding carbon markets to be financial services under the GATS would allow governments some latitude in taking prudential measures to protect the market. Article 2 of the Annex on Financial Services to the GATS states that 'a Member shall not be prevented from taking measures for prudential reasons, including for the protection of investors, depositors, policy holders or persons to whom a fiduciary duty is owed by a financial service supplier, or to ensure the integrity and stability of the financial system'. If the 'integrity and stability' of the carbon market is challenged, as may happen if flaws that result in the reselling of largely worthless carbon credits and sub-par emissions reductions are uncorrected, the broad language of the Annex on Financial Services will enable governments to support the market, thus undermining its value as a free market-based emission-reduction tool.

The carbon market is as yet largely unregulated, presenting opportunities for unscrupulous traders to dupe customers. As the first phase of the European Union's (EU's) Emissions Trading Scheme (ETS) demonstrated, even where a supranational body acts in a supervisory function, widespread manipulation of the system can exist.[17] While the carbon market is seeing explosive growth, particularly in the EU, such growth will not be boundless, particularly if the market is perceived as ineffective in reducing actual emissions. In order for the carbon market to achieve long-term, sustainable success, it must be regulated, and where the right to increase emissions is being traded across international borders, the potential for affecting trade is heightened.

The EU ETS is the best existing example of a functioning multinational carbon market. Established by the Emissions Trading Directive (Directive 2003/87/EC) and amended by the Linking Directive (Directive 2004/101/EC), the EU ETS is a cap-and-trade scheme which caps emission levels while allowing for the trading of carbon credits. Implemented

---

[17] Regulation 2216/2004 for a standardised and secured system of registries pursuant to Directive 2003/87/EC was amended in July 2007 by Regulation 916/2007 to address problems regarding the registration of emissions under the EU ETS.

in two phases, the first phase (2005–2007) highlighted some of the difficulties in applying market trading to climate change policy tools.

In January 2008, the Commission issued a proposal for the amendment of Directive 2003/87/EC, attempting to address some of the problems faced by the EU ETS in its first phase as well as expanding the coverage of the trading scheme to other sectors and gases.[18] Most significantly, the proposed amended Directive suggests the creation of harmonised rules for verification and accreditation to address the current difficulties caused by differing practices in the various Member States,[19] and changes the current multiple registry system (which permits each Member State to establish a registry to account for allowances) to a central Community one to ensure transparency and accountability.[20]

One of the recurring problems in the first phase was accounting for free carbon credits issued by governments to their industries. Article 9 of the Emissions Trading Directive establishes the structure of the national allocation plan, whereby Member States indicate the total quantity of allowances and distribution of allowances for the period in question. Within that national plan, Member States are free to allocate allowances as they choose, assuming the plan is based on 'objective and transparent criteria'. Article 10 provides for a method of allocation whereby for the first phase, Member States had to allocate at least 95 per cent of the allowances free of charge, and in the second phase, they have to allocate at least 90 per cent of the allowances free of charge. Industries in Member States received the credits and in turn were able to trade them on the carbon market for a profit, thus effectively earning them money in exchange for no emissions reductions at all. The United Kingdom (UK) Government's Department for Environment, Food and Rural Affairs (DEFRA), for instance, was found to have paid more than half of its £215 million allocated for a pilot greenhouse gas trading scheme to only four companies, which in turn spent significantly less than the amount they received on emissions cuts.[21] Additionally, a *Financial Times* investigation found examples of companies receiving carbon credits on the basis of efficiency gains from which they had already benefited,

---

[18] Proposal for a Directive of the European Parliament and of the Council amending Directive 2003/87/EC so as to improve and extend the greenhouse gas emission allowance trading system of the Community, COM(2008) 16 final, 23 January 2008.

[19] *Ibid.*, Article 10(a), Article 15.      [20] *Ibid.*, Article 19.

[21] F. Harvey and C. Bryant, 'DEFRA in storm over EU carbon scheme', *Financial Times*, 26 April 2007, available at www.ft.com/cms/s/0/48ad542a-f437–11db-88aa-000b5df10621, dwp_uuid=3c093daa-edc1-11db-8584-000b5df10621.html

companies and individuals significantly overpaying for EU carbon permits whose value had diminished since they did not result in emissions reductions, and widespread purchase by companies and individuals of 'worthless' credits that resulted in no emission cuts.[22] The proposed amended Directive would significantly revise the national allocation plan system, replacing the national allocation plan described in Article 9 with a method of reducing emissions allowances based on a linear factor that would take into account the national allocation plans for the period 2008–2012. Furthermore, the proposal replaces the method of allocation of Article 10 with an auctioning system to be implemented from 2013 onwards which would allocate at least 20 per cent of revenues generated to a specific list of activities related to reducing greenhouse gas emissions, facilitating climate change adaptation by developing countries and managing the emissions trading scheme.

Article 1.1(a)(1)(ii) of the Subsidies and Countervailing Measures Agreement (SCM) includes in its definition of a subsidy a financial contribution 'where government revenue otherwise due is foregone or not collected (e.g. fiscal incentives such as tax credits)'. Article 1.1(b) lays out the other criterion for a subsidy — that a benefit be conferred by the financial contribution in question. Thus, if under the EU ETS or any other carbon-trading system governments provide free carbon allowances that are then resold on the carbon market for a profit, this may be viewed as a subsidy. While Article 10 of the Directive requires the Governments of EU Member States to allocate most of the allowances free of charge, reselling those allowances would be likely to implicate the SCM.

The means that governments use to allocate carbon credits may raise concerns of unfair subsidies. Criterion 5 in Annex 3 to the Emissions Trading Directive provides a non-discrimination provision, prohibiting the undue favouring of certain undertakings or activities through discrimination between companies or sectors. This criterion raised the question within the EU of how state aid would be viewed by the Directive, resulting in a letter from the Directors General of the Environment and Competition Directorates General of the Commission to Member States in 2004, explaining four situations in the context of national allocation plans in which state aid issues may arise:

---

[22] F. Harvey and S. Fidler, 'Industry caught in carbon "smokescreen"', *Financial Times*, 25 April 2007, available at www.ft.com/cms/s/0/48e334ce-f355-11db-9845-000b5df10621, dwp_uuid=3c093daa-edc1-11db-8584-000b5df10621.html

1. where a Member State allocates more allowances than needed to cover projected emissions of an undertaking;
2. where a Member State over-estimates measures in sectors not covered by the ETS or intends to purchase additional credits under the Joint Implementation provision or Clean Development Mechanism;
3. where a Member State does not fully use its ability to auction or charge for allowances under the Directive; and
4. where a Member State provides for allowances to be banked between the first and second phase.[23]

Although the Commission could reject national allocation plans if it found an over-allocation of allowances by Member States to their installations, it has not yet taken a hard line approach on the issue.[24]

Another issue with the EU ETS and carbon trading schemes generally is the creation of industry specific barriers to entry. While Article 11 of the Directive says that Member States shall 'take into account the need to provide access to allowances for new entrants', the mechanism for allocation of allowances affords existing industries a competitive edge over new entrants, which are more likely to have to purchase their allowances. Furthermore, Article 28 sets out provisions to allow operators of installations to form a pool of installations engaged in the same activity. This system may lead to de facto cartelisation creating even greater barriers to entry into that industrial sector. These potential difficulties have been recognised by the Commission, which, in its proposed amended Directive, envisions the creation of a Community-wide new entrants' reserve of emissions allowances in order to reduce such barriers to entry.[25]

The EU ETS allows the free trade of allowances between people in the EU (Article 12(2) of the Directive). It also limits the possibility of concluding agreements with third countries to countries that are listed in Annex B of the Kyoto Protocol and that have ratified the Kyoto Protocol, meaning that without amendment, the EU ETS could not be linked with any US (among other) schemes.[26] To the extent that carbon trading services fall within a 'bound' sector in the European Community's (EC's) schedule, this could be seen as a violation of the national treatment obligation. Article XVII(1) of the GATS states that 'each Member shall accord to services and service suppliers of any other

---

[23] Robinson, Barton, Dodwell, Heydon and Milton, *Climate Change Law*, pp. 120–1.
[24] *Ibid.*, p. 121.    [25] Proposed amended Directive, COM(2008) 16 final, p. 9.
[26] Robinson, Barton, Dodwell, Heydon and Milton, *Climate Change Law*, p. 191.

Member, in respect of all measures affecting the supply of services, treatment no less favourable than that it accords to its own like services and service suppliers'. Since the EU and the US, for instance, are prevented from concluding agreements regarding emissions trading, the Directive could be viewed as discriminating against services and service suppliers of another Member while favouring national services and service suppliers. Additionally, this may be a violation of most-favoured-nation (MFN) obligations under Article II:1 of the GATS, since countries that have ratified the Kyoto Protocol could receive preferential treatment as compared to non-ratifiers.

In a recent article, Marisa Martin makes a detailed and in many respects persuasive argument that the exclusion of US service providers from participation in the EU carbon market is a violation of the EU's GATS commitments. Martin notes that in the US — Gambling case the Appellate Body interpreted a complete exclusion of a particular service or service provider of another WTO Member as a quantitative restriction within the meaning of Article XVI of the GATS; on this reasoning the EC would be in violation of the GATS, even if there were no discrimination within the meaning of the MFN and national treatment provisions of the GATS.[27] The question would become whether such a prima facie violation of Article XVI (and/or Article XVII) of the GATS could be justified under the general exceptions provisions in Article XIV of the GATS, and in particular the exception that allows measures necessary for the 'protection of human, animal or plant life or health'. Here, Martin notes: 'Whether the emissions brokers trade carbon allowances in the European Community or the United States does not alter the environmental effect — carbon emissions are reduced by the same amount in either location. The health impacts are exactly the same with or without the involvement of the US-based brokers. Therefore, the challenged measure does not at all contribute to a further reduction in greenhouse gases and in turn does not contribute to protecting human health.'[28]

This argument is persuasive as far as it goes; however, it abstracts from the possibility that the exclusion of non-Kyoto participants contributes to the health impacts in question by putting pressure on those non-participants to join the Kyoto process, thereby leading them to implement commitments to emissions reductions that have positive effects on

[27] M. Martin, 'Trade law implications of restricting participation in the European Union emissions trading scheme' Geo. Intl. Env. L.R. 19 (2007), 437.
[28] Ibid., 466.

health. This kind of conditionality can contribute to the achievement of an objective stated in a general exception in the case of the General Agreement on Tariffs and Trade (GATT), as the Appellate Body held in *Shrimp — Turtle*.[29]

## C.   Trade restrictions on imports from non-Kyoto participating countries

It is sometimes suggested that Kyoto Member States should restrict or ban imports of products from countries that refuse to participate in the Kyoto process, as a means of encouraging the target states to join the Kyoto Protocol. In the case of the Montreal Protocol on Substances that Deplete the Ozone Layer,[30] that treaty's effectiveness has often been credited to the success of the ban on trade with non-parties in chloro-fluorocarbons and related chlorinated hydrocarbons. The difference with the Kyoto Protocol is, however, fundamental: the Montreal Protocol was aimed at phasing out certain specific, defined chemical substances responsible for the depletion of the ozone layer while the Kyoto Protocol targets carbon emissions that are produced in a huge variety of industrial processes and in transportation, thus affecting a vast range of products and human activities. Thus, as Bhagwati and Mavroidis correctly note, the logical implication would be a virtual embargo on products from non-Kyoto countries.[31] Such a drastic measure would clearly be both politically and economically unfeasible (in the latter case because production chains are highly integrated between Kyoto- and non-Kyoto countries — especially the US and the EU — industrial activity in the EU would be seriously disrupted, and many jobs in the EU threatened, by such an embargo).

An alternative approach might be to ban only those imports that cause carbon emissions beyond a certain level over the lifecycle of the product. To enforce such a measure consistently, the importing state would have to require that the importer/exporter provide accurate information

---

[29] *US — Shrimp, United States — Import Prohibition of Certain Shrimp and Shrimp Products*, Appellate Body Report, WT/DS58/AB/R, adopted 12 October 1998, paragraphs 121, 141–2.

[30] The 1987 Montreal Protocol to the 1985 Vienna Convention for the Protection of the Ozone Layer, 26 *I.L.M.* 1550 (1987).

[31] J. Bhagwati and P. C. Mavroidis, 'Is action against US exports for failure to sign Kyoto Protocol WTO-legal?' *World Trade Review* 6 (2007), 300 (citing J. Bhagwati, *In Defense of Globalization*, p. 157).

concerning the life cycle carbon effects of the product; producing this information would be expensive and perhaps impossible given current production chains, something akin to the challenge of traceability with respect to genetically modified organisms (GMOs) but applied to *all* imports. In any case, since the approach of the Kyoto Protocol is not to limit emissions based on product life cycles but aggregate emissions for an entire country, the Kyoto Process itself would not generate any objective baseline for a product-specific limit on emissions.

The Appellate Body ruling in *Shrimp — Turtle* makes it clear that the exceptions in Article XX of the GATT may be used, in principle, to justify a measure that conditions market access for imports on the policies of the exporting country.[32] In the case of a product ban specifically intended to put pressure on non-participants to join Kyoto, as noted, a ban on all imports is unrealistic, politically and economically. The question would be therefore how to select some subset of products so as to satisfy the Appellate Body's criteria that, on the one hand, the measure contributes to the environmental goal in question and on the other hand, that it not be disproportionately wide in reach or scope. Furthermore, any selective inclusion of some products and exclusion of others could give rise to claims of 'arbitrary or unjustifiable discrimination' or 'disguised restriction on international trade', if the selection de facto or de jure disadvantages imports in relation to domestic products, or if it ignores differences in conditions in different WTO Members.

### D.   Carbon tax

A carbon tax can either be direct (directly taxing greenhouse gas emissions) or indirect (taxing emissions in inputs or final products).[33] For our purposes we will limit our discussion to an indirect carbon tax, which is the more widely used and easier to implement method of taxation. One conception of a carbon tax is that it would seek to tax products imported from non-Kyoto-compliant countries of origin so as to equalise the economic burden faced by domestic producers from the emissions reduction obligations imposed on them in consequence of the fulfilment of Kyoto commitments. Another conception of a carbon tax would be that of a tax on carbon emissions that applies to both domestic and imported products. We will consider each of these kinds of taxes in turn.

---

[32]   *US — Shrimp*, para. 121.
[33]   C. K. Harper, 'Climate change and tax policy' *B.C. Int'l & Comp. L. Rev.* 30 (2007), 411 at 429.

In the case of the first kind of tax, we must begin by characterising the measure under the relevant provisions of the GATT. Article II:1(b) of the GATT prohibits the imposition of other duties or charges on the importation of products in excess of bound MFN rates of custom duties. Article II:2(a) in turn clarifies:

> 2. Nothing in this Article shall prevent any contracting party from imposing at any time on the importation of any product:
>
>> (a) a charge equivalent to an internal tax imposed consistently with the provisions of paragraph 2 of Article III* in respect of the like domestic product or in respect of an article from which the imported product has been manufactured or produced in whole or in part;

It is reasonably clear that a tax that is intended to equalise the costs to producers of environmental compliance as between imported and domestic products, by imposing on imports a tax equivalent to the economic burden that domestic producers face from *command-and-control* regulation of emissions, would be characterised as an 'other charge' and prohibited under Article II of the GATT, as the charge is not 'equivalent to an internal tax imposed ... on the like domestic product'.

The issue then would be whether such a 'charge' could be justified under Article XX of the GATT, most notably as 'in relation to the conservation of exhaustible natural resources' (Article XX(g)). Based on the broad and evolutionary meaning of 'exhaustible natural resources' adopted by the Appellate Body in *Shrimp — Turtle*, which incorporates contemporary conceptions of biodiversity and sustainable development, it is unlikely to be controversial to state that the earth's atmosphere constitutes an 'exhaustible natural resource'. But is the measure 'in relation to' the conservation of the earth's atmosphere? On the one hand, it is certainly true that by internalising some of the negative environmental costs of imported products, the measure produces a market signal that is likely to contribute to lower levels of emissions (the standard behavioural effects of a Pigovian tax, with all of the qualifications).

It may also be argued that by reducing some of the competitive advantages that non-Kyoto-compliant countries gain from non-participation in the regime, the measure will, on balance, make it less worthwhile for those countries to resist joining. At the same time, it might be argued that the underlying purpose or intent, or at least one purpose, of the tax was to enhance the competitiveness of domestic products relative to imports.

Is such a purpose, which sounds protectionist, consistent with Article XX, even where the measure in question can objectively be seen as contributing to the conservation of exhaustible natural resources? It is arguable that the main control on such protectionism in Article XX is the chapeau, which imposes the conditions that to be justified under Article XX a measure must not constitute arbitrary or unjustifiable discrimination or a disguised restriction on international trade.

In the *Shrimp — Turtle* case, the Article 21.5 panel considered whether the US shrimp embargo was a 'disguised restriction'; the complainants had invoked the legislative history of the US measure, arguing that there were some legislators who viewed the embargo as a means of enhancing the competitiveness of the US shrimp industry. The panel, instead of examining the legislative history with respect to the intent of the measure, focused on its objective characteristics, asking whether the burden imposed on imported products or their producers was greater than in the case of domestic products or producers (paragraph 5.143). Thus, in the case of a carbon charge, the question with respect to a 'disguised restriction' would be whether the measure is applied in such a way so as to impose a disproportionate burden on imports. This poses the complex challenge of determining how to ensure that the rate of taxation imposed on an imported product is actually equivalent to the economic burden imposed on the like or competing domestic product through domestic command-and-control measures.

The second taxation concept is that of a tax on emissions that applies to both domestic and imported products. This kind of tax would seem to fall within the language of Article II:2(b) of the GATT, i.e. the Border Tax Adjustment concept; the essential question would then become its consistency with the national treatment obligation, Article III:2 of the GATT. This is consistent with the principle set out in the *Ad* Article III note that measures that apply to both imported and domestic products constitute internal measures for the purposes of the application of Article III, even if the measure is applied at the border in the case of the imported product.

Article III:2 addresses the issue of directly competitive or substitutable products and like products, requiring, in sentence two, that imported and domestic products be directly competitive or substitutable, that the products not be similarly taxed and that this treatment not afford protection to domestic producers.[34]

---

[34] C. Singh, 'Non-discrimination in tax matters in the GATT — national treatment', in J. Herdin-Winter and I. Hofbauer (eds.), *The Relevance of WTO Law for Tax Matters* (Vienna: Linde Verlag, 2006), p. 55.

Determining whether two products are 'like' or 'directly competitive or substitutable' has been held judicially to be a matter of a case-by-case examination of the facts, weighing all relevant evidence; the WTO Appellate Body has approved a technique of assessing both 'likeness' *and* whether products are 'directly competitive or substitutable' that consists of examining the factors enumerated in a GATT policy document, the *Border Tax Adjustment* report of the Working Party, namely physical characteristics, end uses, and consumer habits. In addition, customs classifications may be probative. While the issue of whether two products are 'directly competitive or substitutable' sounds like a matter of economic analysis, the Appellate Body (*Korea — Alcoholic Beverages*) has emphasised that this is a jurisprudential question based on the purpose of national treatment in protecting equal competitive opportunities, and may be based on common-sense considerations of reasonable consumer behaviour as well as empirical economic analysis of substitutability. A finding of likeness would normally entail a conclusion of greater affinity or similarity between the products in question than a finding of 'directly competitive or substitutable': this follows from the more stringent obligation imposed (identical rather than merely not 'dissimilar', as well as the fact that in the case of 'like products' — by contrast, with 'directly competitive or substitutable' products — the relevant treatment is not qualified by its limitation to cases where different tax treatment would afford 'protection' to domestic production).

Article I:1 of the GATT establishes the principle of MFN treatment. In imposing taxes on imports that come from countries without carbon emission reduction strategies, Member States face the possibility of claims of MFN violation. The question here is whether such an origin-neutral tax could be construed as de facto resulting in discrimination by origin. Again, as with national treatment, a central issue is the determination of likeness. Are two products that are identical in all respects except for the process (and consequent emissions) used to make them like for the purposes of the GATT?

This raises the question of whether a carbon tax/regulation is something that affects a product or a process. At the centre of the discussion on an indirect carbon tax is the distinction between products and production process methods (PPMs). An indirect carbon tax relates to the process or production method used — the tax relates to the emissions produced in the making of the product rather than those generated by the finished product itself. Pauwelyn suggests that a WTO permissible 'border adjustment'-framed carbon tax on imports would be likely to be found WTO compliant, and in the alternative, Article XX of the GATT could provide an environmental exception for carbon taxes.[35]

Whether a PPM-based tax is WTO compatible depends on whether it is possible to distinguish products based on the process used to make them. Pauwelyn cites the *US — Superfund* case as an example where products were found eligible for border tax adjustment without the need for determining likeness, and extrapolates that this would be applicable to products made with processes entailing different levels of emissions.[36] In *US — Superfund*, the government act in question 'imposed a new tax on certain imported substances produced or manufactured from taxable feedstock chemicals'.[37] With a carbon tax, the first issue is whether the carbon emissions can be viewed as incorporated in the product itself and second, if not, whether nevertheless the GATT/WTO rules on Border Tax Adjustment would permit such a tax.

A conventional engineering science perspective would consider the energy consumed in the production of a product (and the by-products of such energy, such as emissions) as 'work' to make the product and not as an input physically incorporated in the product itself. Assuming that this would be an appropriate perspective from which to view the issue as a matter of interpretation of WTO law, it would remain to be determined whether, in fact, border tax adjustment is available in respect of inputs in the production process that are physically incorporated or embodied in the product.

The Organisation for Economic Co-operation and Development (OECD) definition of border tax adjustment has been accepted by the GATT Working Party on Border Tax Adjustment, a key WTO instrument in the interpretation of the scope for border tax adjustment under the GATT: 'Any fiscal measures which put into effect, in whole or in part, the destination principle (i.e. which enable exported products to be relieved of some or all of the tax charged in the exporting country in respect of similar domestic products sold to consumers on the home market and which enable imported products sold to consumers to be charged with some or all of the tax charged in the importing country in respect of similar domestic products)'. This definition obviously does not

[35] J. Pauwelyn, 'US federal climate policy and competitiveness concerns: the limits and options of international trade law', Nicholas Institute for Environmental Policy Solutions, Duke University, NI WP 07–02, April 2007, p. 3.

[36] *Ibid.*, p. 28.

[37] *US — Superfund, United States — Taxes on Petroleum and Certain Imported Substances*, panel report, adopted 17 June 1987, L-6175, paragraph 2.1.

introduce any distinction as to whether, in the case where the adjustment is based on inputs, the products in question physically embody the input in question. Indeed, it appears that border tax adjustment is available in a much wider range of situations than a tax on inputs in production. The OECD definition as incorporated into the GATT Working Party states the issue as, fundamentally, one of non-discrimination: are similar taxes imposed on similar domestic and imported products? The issue thus becomes whether PPMs not incorporated physically in a product can be a basis for finding products 'unlike' for the purposes of Article III:2, first sentence. This is simply a reiteration of the whole PPMs debate, which is the subject of the contribution to this volume by Don Regan.

Pauwelyn nevertheless interprets Article II:2(a) as restricting the generality of the OECD/GATT Working Party definition of border tax adjustment. Article II:2(a) of the GATT reads:

> 2. Nothing in this Article shall prevent any contracting party from imposing at any time on the importation of any product:
>
> (a) a charge equivalent to an internal tax imposed consistently with the provisions of paragraph 2 of Article III* in respect of the like domestic product or in respect of an article from which the imported product has been manufactured or produced in whole or in part;

Pauwelyn understands the language 'manufactured or produced in whole or in part;' as intended to limit the permissibility of border tax adjustment to cases where the input is incorporated in the imported product itself. However, this neglects the context of Article II:2(a) of the GATT. This provision is found in Article II of the GATT, not Article III and by its terms does not add to the obligations of WTO Members with respect to the application of internal taxes to imported products as stated in Article III:2 of the GATT. Article II:2(a) of the GATT merely states that Article II of the GATT should not prevent the imposition of one kind of border adjustment tax, i.e. in respect of 'an article from which the imported product has been manufactured or produced in whole or in part'. Nothing in this language requires the inference that *other* forms of border adjustment taxes would be considered charges within the meaning of Article II of the GATT rather than internal taxes within the meaning of Article III:2 much less that *other* forms of border adjustment taxes would be per se violations of Article III:2.

It is noteworthy that with respect to border tax adjustments in the case of exported products, footnote 61 of the SCM provides that rebates on taxes on inputs in production for exported products should be regarded as border tax adjustments, not illegal export subsidies, wherever the inputs are 'consumed in the production process'. The definition of inputs consumed in the production process is as follows: 'inputs physically incorporated, energy fuels and oil used in the production process and catalysts which are consumed in the course of their use to obtain the exported product'.

This definition makes it clear that the relevant concept is whether inputs are used to create the final product, not whether they are physically embodied in it, at least with respect to energy, fuels and oil. It is true that there is no comparable language with respect to border tax adjustment in the case of *imported* products; but arguably there is no need for such language, since, again, the concept of border tax adjustment, as defined by the OECD and incorporated in the GATT Working Party allows for the normal application of Article III:2 of the GATT to such taxes. Further, based on the dynamic or evolutionary approach to treaty interpretation in environmental disputes that was adopted by the Appellate Body in *Shrimp — Turtle*, the language in footnote 61 may serve as part of the context for the interpretation of Article II:2(a) of the GATT: i.e. especially given the importance to the environment of taxing energy inputs; thus the language, 'from which the imported product has been manufactured or produced in whole or in part' should be read to include not only products incorporated physically into the imported final product but also that are *necessary* to its manufacture or production.

Thus, as Bhagwati and Mavroidis correctly identify it,[38] the real issue is whether under Article III:2 first sentence of the GATT, there is less favourable treatment of 'like' imported products.

Bhagwati and Mavroidis suggest that PPMs, under the jurisprudence of the Appellate Body in *EC — Asbestos*, may *only* be a basis for considering products 'unlike' for Article III of the GATT purposes where they result in different physical characteristics of the products, *even if* consumers distinguish between the different process and production methods. This interpretation of *EC — Asbestos* may be incomplete in two respects. It is true that, in *EC — Asbestos*, the Appellate Body, based on the facts, placed a considerable emphasis on one of the four factors, physical characteristics (and, in fairness to Bhagwati and Mavroidis,

---

[38] Bhagwati and Mavroidis, 'Is action against US exports for failure to sign Kyoto Protocol WTO-legal?', 299–310.

suggested that this factor will often weigh heavily towards a finding of *un*likeness where there are physical differences). Nevertheless, the Appellate Body in no way suggested that in other cases, with different factual dimensions, one or more of the *other* factors could be dispositive of a finding of unlikeness. On the contrary, the Appellate Body emphasised:

> These general criteria, or groupings of potentially shared characteristics, provide a framework for analyzing the 'likeness' of particular products on a case-by-case basis. These criteria are, it is well to bear in mind, simply tools to assist in the task of sorting and examining the relevant evidence. They are neither a treaty-mandated nor a closed list of criteria that will determine the legal characterization of products. More important, the adoption of a particular framework to aid in the examination of evidence does not dissolve the duty or the need to examine, in each case, *all* of the pertinent evidence. In addition, although each criterion addresses, in principle, a different aspect of the products involved, which should be examined separately, the different criteria are interrelated.
>
> For instance, the physical properties of a product shape and limit the end-uses to which the products can be devoted. Consumer perceptions may similarly influence — modify or even render obsolete — traditional uses of the products. Tariff classification clearly reflects the physical properties of a product.
>
> 103. The kind of evidence to be examined in assessing the 'likeness' of products will, necessarily, depend upon the particular products and the legal provision at issue. When all the relevant evidence has been examined, panels must determine whether that evidence, as a whole, indicates that the products in question are 'like' in terms of the legal provision at issue. We have noted that, under Article III:4 of the GATT 1994, the term 'like products' is concerned with competitive relationships between and among products. Accordingly, whether the *Border Tax Adjustments* framework is adopted or not, it is important under Article III:4 to take account of evidence which indicates whether, and to what extent, the products involved are — or could be — in a competitive relationship in the marketplace
>
> (paragraphs 102–3).

In evaluating a carbon tax imposed on imported and domestic products for consistency with Article III:2 of the GATT it would seem only sensible for the Appellate Body to consider the distinctive factual context in determining likeness: to exclude differences between the products that relate to potentially catastrophic global environmental harms would seem at odds with the Appellate Body's stricture, cited above, that all evidence probative of likeness in the particular context must be taken into account regardless of how it is sorted in terms of the different factors or criteria in the Border Tax Adjustment approach to likeness.[39]

Further, it is important to note that the analysis of 'likeness' by the Appellate Body in *EC — Asbestos* does not address PPMs; thus it may be somewhat misleading or at least subject to misreading for Bhagwati and Mavroidis to conclude that in *EC — Asbestos* the Appellate Body suggested that PPMs may only be considered as probative of unlikeness where they are somehow related to physical characteristics of the product. In *EC — Asbestos*, the Appellate Body concluded that asbestos products were unlike non-asbestos substitute products permitted in the EC, regardless of PPMs. In fact, the Appellate Body *rejected* an argument by Canada that France's legislation *wrongly* did *not* take into account PPMs, notably that Canada was using a PPM for asbestos that did not lead to the health consequences typically associated with products containing asbestos.

Bhagwati and Mavroidis themselves argue that, as a general matter, if consumer tastes and habits were to be the most relevant factor in ascertaining likeness, products with different impacts on the environment might well be treated differently by consumers, and therefore be seen as unlike: 'a reasonable consumer test (whereby "reasonable" means "informed") would lead to the conclusion that a consumer (in the eyes of the Appellate Body) who is aware of the environmental (and eventually health) hazard that global warming might represent, will treat the two goods … as unlike goods'.[40]

The difficulty under Article III:2 of the GATT may be much less one of whether, doctrinally, goods produced with significantly different levels of carbon emissions can be considered like products, than one of determining accurately whether a particular imported product is produced with significantly higher carbon emissions than a particular domestic product. This refers to the challenge, mentioned above, of ascertaining the carbon footprint of a particular imported product, which may have gone through production stages in several different facilities at different locations. Typically, domestic pollution taxes have been imposed with respect to a particular enterprise or polluting facility, not on finished

---

[39] R. Howse and E. Tuerk, 'The WTO impact on internal regulations: a case study of the Canada — EC Asbestos dispute', in G. de Burca and J. Scott (eds.), *The EU and the WTO: Legal and Constitutional Issues* (Oxford: Hart Publishing, 2001).

[40] Bhagwati and Mavroidis, 'Is action against US exports for failure to sign Kyoto Protocol WTO-legal?', 308.

products. Thus, there has generally not been the problem of attributing emissions to a finished product.

### E.    Applying cap-and-trade regulatory requirements to foreign producers

A different proposal is that of the International Brotherhood of Electrical Workers (IBEW) and American Electric Power (AEP): under the IBEW-AEP proposal, as we understand it, in order to gain access to the US markets, imports would either have to originate from a country that has an emissions control programme equivalent to the proposed US cap-and-trade programme or producers would have to acquire a carbon 'allowance' and imports would be accompanied by a certificate of this 'allowance'. Such an allowance might be acquired by purchasing carbon credits from an established emissions programme on the market or from a special international reserve.

How would such a measure be characterised within the framework of the GATT? In our view, it must be seen as part of a regulatory scheme that applies both to domestic and foreign products; the difference being in the manner of application, which in the latter case occurs through a method requiring that certification of regulatory compliance accompany products at the border. Like the other possible measures discussed above, the manner of application of the 'measure' to imports does require that the regulatory burden be expressed in the case of imports as a required allowance per unit of product. In light of the difficulties with converting emissions caps to a product-based equivalent, the proponents of the proposal have suggested it be limited to certain carbon-intensive products, such as primary goods or goods produced in bulk, where the emissions represented by the production of that good can be traced presumably to a single, discrete production facility.

The fundamental issue under the GATT would be whether as applied to imports the US programme is truly even-handed — i.e. 'equivalent' in the relevant senses to the burden imposed on like domestic products through emissions controls. This is a matter of applying the National Treatment standard in Article III:4 of the GATT.[41]

---

[41] We note that in the *US — Tobacco* (1994) case (*US — Tobacco, United States — Measures Affecting the Importation, Internal Sale and Use of Tobacco*, panel report, DS44/R, adopted 12 August 1994, paragraph 82), the adopted GATT panel ruling found that a measure that provided for an assessment or penalty where a certain domestic regulatory

Again, this will raise the issue of 'likeness' discussed above, and the related PPMs issue. Here, too, our view is that the approach of the Appellate Body in *EC — Asbestos* is sufficiently flexible and sensitive to the various kinds of differences between products mattering in different factual and regulatory contexts, that non-complying imported products could be distinguished as unlike on the basis of the failure to control or internalise environmental externalities in the production process. This assumes that it would be possible to establish that such differences matter to consumers; the stakes with respect to global warming, as we have already indicated, are high, and it may not be difficult to provide evidence for consumer awareness of the relationship of consumption habits to the problem and solution here.

In any case, again, as indicated by the Appellate Body in paragraph 100 of *EC — Asbestos* and correctly observed by Pauwelyn, even if the products in question were like, it would still be possible to draw regulatory distinctions between them provided there is 'no less favourable treatment' of the group of imported products relative to the 'group' of 'like' domestic products. Thus, assuming a finding of likeness, the question would be whether the actual design and operation of the scheme is truly even-handed *in its overall effects* on imports in relation to domestic products.[42]

Here, several design elements will be important. The first is the determination of what kind of foreign programme for control of emissions would qualify as being equivalent to the US programme for the purposes of the scheme. The proposal envisages that equivalence be established through negotiations with the other jurisdictions in question, which is a good way of avoiding a legal dispute. The second issue is the determination of what kind of per-unit 'allowance' would be required of an imported product where it originates from a jurisdiction that does not have an equivalent emissions control programme. Since US producers under the proposed domestic cap-and-trade scheme are permitted a certain free 'allowance' of emissions before being required to purchase credits or allowances, the proposal recognises that even-handedness

---

requirement was not met by an imported product was an 'internal law, regulation, or requirement' within the meaning of Article III:4 and not a fiscal measure within the meaning of Article III:2. Analogously here, we would see the proposed application of an 'allowance' requirement to imports not as a tax or charge, and even less an Article XI quantitative restriction, but as ancillary to the enforcement or administration of a US regulatory scheme that applies to both domestic and imported products.

[42] See also on this issue the Appellate Body report in *Dominican Republic — Cigarettes*.

would require that such a free 'allowance' be somehow extended to imports. In order to ensure no less favourable treatment of 'like' *products*, arguably it would be necessary to determine whether, on the one hand, a particular *product* had been produced in a facility where emissions did not exceed this cap (in which case the imports would not need to be accompanied by any purchased credits or allowances). On the other hand, if the cap was exceeded, the question is to what extent was the cap exceeded in that particular facility *in relation to the production of that particular product* and thus what amount of purchased credits or allowances would need to accompany a given unit of the product in question?

But, underlying all these issues, is the still more fundamental question of whether it is consistent with national treatment to apply the same cap in the case of foreign producers as is applied to domestic industries producing like products. A rational environmental policy in another jurisdiction, even one with the same global environmental goals, might employ different caps, depending on trade-offs with various economic considerations, technological concerns, and the mix of policy instruments (taxes versus command and control). It is arguable that consistency with national treatment in this instance requires the counterfactual exercise of imagining the kind of regulatory burden that foreign producers would have been subject to had they been under an environmental policy designed for *that jurisdiction*, that makes a contribution to the achievement of the global objectives equivalent to what is achieved by the US domestic policy.

The extent to which the application of the scheme to imports imposes an approach to and level of environmental regulation reflecting a trade-off between environmental and other interests that is more appropriate or burdensome for producers in some WTO exporting Members than others will also lead to concerns about compliance with the MFN obligation in the GATT. Thus, the IBEW-AEP proposal suggests that 'adjustments' be made to reflect economic development levels and other features of individual exporting countries.[43]

It should be noted that the IBEW-AEP proposal has been designed to allow justification of any prima facie violation of Articles III or I under Article XX(g) of the GATT, as a measure in relation to the conservation of exhaustible natural resources, and especially to reflect the Appellate

---

[43] IBEW-AEP International Proposal, attached to 'Testimony of American Electric Power submitted to Senate Subcommittee on Private Sector and Consumer Solutions to Global Warming and Wildlife Protection', 23 July 2007.

Body's interpretation of the chapeau of Article XX of the GATT in *Shrimp — Turtle*. As this measure seems designed to impose emissions control obligations on producers of imported products based on appropriate environmental policies given global objectives and the conditions in the country of production, and not to equalise the *economic* burden between domestic and foreign producers so as to preserve US industrial competitiveness, we are confident that it could be found to be 'in relation to' the conservation of exhaustible natural resources. The fact that some members of Congress and other interested parties may support the legislation because of a 'level playing field', and not because of environmental motivations is not relevant: the question, as indicated by the Appellate Body in *Shrimp — Turtle*, is whether there is a rational relationship between the measure, in its design and operation, and the objective of conservation of exhaustible natural resources. However, the selection of products to include or exclude from the scheme may raise issues of 'fit'; under the approach of the Appellate Body in *Shrimp — Turtle*, to be rationally connected to the conservation objective, the measure must not be disproportionately wide in scope or reach. It is unclear what standard the Appellate Body would use to apply this notion of disproportion, but in any case the proposal seems designed to target especially greenhouse gas (GHG)-intensive products, and does not seem to include or exclude classes of products so as to raise issues about the rational fit between the scheme proposed and the conservation objective.

The real issues under Article XX(g) of the GATT concerning the design of the scheme will be very similar to those under Articles I and III of the GATT. With respect to the requirement in the chapeau that the measure not be applied so as to result in arbitrary or unjustifiable discrimination between countries where the same conditions prevail, under the Appellate Body approach in *Shrimp — Turtle*, the question will be to what extent the scheme provides flexibility to achieve the environmental objectives in question through approaches that may differ from that of the US but may be more appropriate to the conditions in the exporting country. Here the emphasis in the proposal on attempting negotiations on regulatory rapprochement and equivalence before imposing requirements unilaterally is very well taken and suggests that its authors have been well advised on WTO law. Where a negotiated solution is not achieved, however, assessing whether there is adequate flexibility under the chapeau requirement will involve complex judgments of environmental policy and science and also about administrability and the reasonableness of compliance costs both to government and to the exporters, of various alternative ways of introducing flexibility.

A scheme that is designed to follow best regulatory practices as articulated in the work of international bodies such as the OECD and in the Kyoto process itself (to the extent that the process generates conceptions of appropriate policies and policy instruments to achieve climate change objectives), and that uses criteria that are transparent and based on internationally recognised standards and methodologies wherever possible would be likely to withstand WTO scrutiny under the chapeau of Article XX of the GATT: here it should be emphasised that the chapeau does not seek to eliminate all instances of discrimination but only those that are patently unreasonable, i.e. 'arbitrary' or 'unjustifiable'. Policy choices that are reasonable, transparent and objective, taking into account the situations of different countries and based on sound regulation and science, will not violate the conditions of the chapeau, even if it is inevitable that the result does not perfectly reconcile the overarching goal of attaining the environmental objective with a complete equalisation of effects or burdens on different WTO Members. Here, we note Gary Hufbauer's observation that '[t]he Appellate Body rulings in previous cases ... show considerable sympathy with environmental concerns and have increased the likelihood that trade restrictions in furtherance of GHG emissions controls would pass muster under WTO rules'.[44]

### F.   Countervailing carbon 'delinquents': the Stiglitz proposal

Noted Nobel laureate economist, Joseph Stiglitz, has suggested that the failure especially of the WTO Members not participating in the Kyoto Protocol to internalise the climate change costs caused by carbon emissions from the production of products is a 'subsidy' to the producers of such products, resulting in a distortion of international markets in the trade in goods. As a matter of WTO law, in order to be countervailable a subsidy must either be prohibited (the case with export subsidies) or 'actionable'. In order to be actionable, a subsidy must entail a financial contribution by government, must be specific to an industry or firm or a

---

[44]   G. Hufbauer, 'Climate change: competitiveness concerns and prospects for engaging developing countries', in Testimony before the Subcommittee on Energy and Air Quality, US House of Representatives, Committee on Energy and Finance, 5 March 2008.

group of industries or firms, and must confer a 'benefit' on the domestic producer of the subsidised products. Most WTO legal experts who have commented on Stiglitz's proposal have dismissed it as clearly not justified under the WTO rules in the SCM, since one or another of these criteria is obviously not met. According to Bhagwati and Mavroidis, 'a subsidy exists only if a government has made a financial contribution or has incurred a cost... The argument that the United States policy [of not participating in Kyoto] is a "hidden subsidy" is irrelevant and cannot justify an EU action under the SCM Agreement.'[45]

Nevertheless, it is not so easy to dismiss Stiglitz's view. Among the meanings of 'financial contribution' in the SCM is the government provision of goods or services other than general infrastructure. There are no pre-assigned property rights to the atmosphere; instead, states are generally thought to have prescriptive jurisdiction over this 'commons', subject to international obligations by treaty (e.g. the Kyoto Protocol) or custom. Thus, where a firm is allowed to emit carbon into the atmosphere up to a certain ceiling, this is not a consequence of some pre-existing property right in the atmosphere that is being exercised by the firm, but rather, of the assignment of such a right or entitlement by the state to the firm in question. Such a right or entitlement is a valuable asset, indeed (with the advent of carbon trading, discussed above) an asset that can be bought and sold in the marketplace. As already noted with respect to the assignment by the EC of 'free' allowances to enterprises under its carbon-trading scheme, the question arises as to whether the failure to charge a market price for the asset in question constitutes the provision of goods or services, and therefore a financial contribution within the meaning of Article I of the SCM.

In this context, it should be noted that Article 14(d) of the SCM provides:

> the provision of goods or services or purchase of goods by a government shall not be considered as conferring a benefit unless the provision is made for less than adequate remuneration, or the purchase is made for more than adequate remuneration. The adequacy of remuneration shall be determined in relation to prevailing market conditions for the good or service in question in the country of provision or purchase (including price, quality, availability, marketability, transportation and other conditions of purchase or sale).

---

[45] Bhagwati and Mavroidis, 'Is action against US exports for failure to sign Kyoto Protocol WTO-legal?', 302.

In the *US — Lumber* case, Canada challenged US countervailing duties in respect of softwood timber imports from Canada; the basis for imposing the countervailing duties was Canadian federal and provincial government practices concerning the provision of access to an exhaustible natural resource, raw timber.[46] The US argued that access to the resource was being priced in such a way that 'adequate remuneration' was not being paid to the government by the timber users; the US maintained that the appropriate benchmark for adequate remuneration was the price that access rights to the resource would fetch in an auction conducted on an arms-length-basis. The US insisted, contrary to the express terms of Article 14(d) of the SCM, that the benchmark should be auction prices in the US and not the Canadian market, on the grounds that there was no private market in Canada not influenced by government resource access practices. The Appellate Body held that, while the US could not simply import as a benchmark US prices, nevertheless in a case where there was no adequate private market in the exporting country, alternative methodologies could be considered, to determine whether there was 'adequate remuneration'.

In cases where there is a liquid emissions trading market in the country to whose exports countervailable duties are applied, the price of carbon on that market might be used to determine the 'benefit' within the meaning of Article 14(d) of the SCM that is conferred on firms by a given allowance or permission to emit carbon. In other cases, a market price might need to be constructed based on the observed price in functioning markets such as the EC, with due adjustment for differences in market and regulatory conditions affecting prices. However, there is no intrinsic reason why the provision of a right or entitlement to emit carbon up to a certain ceiling would not constitute a financial contribution within the meaning of the SCM; this constitutes access to an exhaustible natural resource (in this case the atmosphere) just as much as did access to timber in *US — Lumber*. And to the extent that the market price for carbon is not being charged by the government for this allowance or entitlement, there is, again, a 'benefit' conferred within the meaning of the SCM.

Whether in a given case the subsidy was specific would be a matter of interpretation; certainly in the case of some countries, if not most,

---

[46] *US — Lumber, United States — Final Countervailing Duty Determination With Respect to Certain Softwood Lumber From Canada*, Appellate Body report, WT/DS257/AB/R, adopted 19 January 2004.

energy-intensive industries would be likely to be highly disproportionate 'users' of such subsidies, thereby suggesting at least a prima facie case of de facto specificity.

## G. The EC carbon leakage proposal

As an alternative to countervailing duties to address the 'level playing field' issues raised by jurisdictions that fail to price the right to emit, thereby giving an advantage to their carbon-intensive industries, the European Commission has suggested that the EC might relax or reduce the emissions-reduction burden placed on its industries where failure to price emissions elsewhere could lead to production being shifted from the EC to the carbon renegade jurisdictions. According to the Commission document setting out proposals on climate policy for the EC, 'the Commission will identify by 30 June 2010 which energy-intensive sectors or sub-sectors are likely to be subject to carbon leakage. It will base its analysis on the assessment of the inability to pass through the cost of required allowances in product prices without significant loss of market share to installations outside the EU not taking comparable action to reduce emissions. Energy-intensive industries which are determined as being exposed to significant risk of carbon leakage could receive up to 100 per cent of allowances free of charge, or an effective carbon equalisation system could be introduced with a view to putting installations from the Community which are at a significant risk of carbon leakage and those from third countries on a comparable footing. Such a system could apply requirements to importers that would be no less favourable than those applicable to installations within the EU, for example by requiring the surrender of allowances. 'Any action … would … need to be in conformity with the international obligations of the Community including the WTO agreement.'[47]

The first method proposed, the provision of free allowances to EC industries where there is a threat of significant loss of market share due to the burden of emissions control, raises the subsidy issues discussed above, the financial contribution being the provision for goods or services for less than adequate compensation. Since the very rationale of the

---

[47] Commission of the European Communities, 'Proposal for a Directive of the European Parliament and of the Council amending Directive 2003/87/EC so as to improve and extend the greenhouse gas emission allowance trading system of the Community', Brussels, 23 January 2008, COM(208) 16 final, p. 8.

scheme would be the protection of EC market share against competition from producers in non-EU countries, this kind of measure would be likely to entail 'injury' of the kind that would allow for countervailability under the SCM, as well as the sorts of adverse effects that would allow a WTO complaint against the measure as an actionable subsidy. In addition, a finding of specificity would be likely as the very terms of this proposed scheme target it to a sub-set of industries whose competitive position in relation to non-EU producers is particularly affected by the burden imposed by emissions controls regulation.

The alternative proposal for 'carbon equalisation' through border measures on imports into the EU raises the kinds of issues discussed at length above concerning the US proposals with respect to 'border adjustment'.

## H.    The Clean Development Mechanism

The CDM is an alternative to direct emissions reductions under the Kyoto Protocol. Defined in Article 12 of the Protocol, the CDM allows Annex B (industrialised) countries to invest in projects designed to reduce emissions in developing countries in exchange for CERs, which can be used to meet the investor country's emissions targets. In order to obtain CERs from a CDM project, the industrialised country must first obtain approval from the developing country. Once approval has been obtained, additionality must be established — that is, the industrialised country (the applicant) must demonstrate that the proposed CDM project will reduce emissions more than if the project was not implemented. A baseline must also be set estimating future emissions in the absence of the CDM project. The project must then be validated by a third-party agency, after which the CDM Executive Board gives the final approval. The CDM Executive Board is also the body responsible for determining the methodologies to be used for CDM projects as well as the issuer of CERs. Recent registered CDM projects include biomass power plants in India, hydropower and wind power plants in China, and a methane recovery and electricity generation plant in the Philippines.[48]

Since CDM projects involve financing by Annex B countries to developing countries, affecting trade, various WTO provisions would potentially be applicable. In particular, CDM projects can be seen as falling under the GATS, since in exchange for funding projects in developing countries,

---

[48] UNFCCC website, http://cdm.unfccc.int/Projects/registered.html

Annex B countries receive CERs which are then transformed into energy production and consumption by Annex B consumers.[49] As this is likely to be seen as trade in services, the MFN provisions of GATS would then apply, and the national treatment and market access provisions, where a Member has bound the relevant sector(s) in its schedule. On the other hand, where trade in goods is affected (inputs in energy production) the WTO Agreements pertaining to trade in goods may apply.

Since CDM projects are heavily investment orientated, they could be viewed as investment measures under the Agreement on Trade-Related Investment Measures (TRIMS) if trade in goods is involved. Since the scope of the projects permitted by the CDM is broad, depending on the type of project, TRIMS issues could be raised. In the event that a CDM project is inconsistent with either national treatment (GATT Article III) or quantitative restrictions (GATT Article XI), it would be in violation of Article 2.1 of TRIMS.

The CDM poses an even more significant regulatory problem than the carbon market. While carbon markets are nascent financial instruments which are in the process of developing rules, in part, as in the EU, through trial and error, CDM projects are much more amorphous. One of the criticisms of carbon trading under a cap-and-trade scheme is that unlike its much touted forerunner, the US Acid Rain Programme, measuring the levels of carbon emissions is significantly more complicated than measuring levels of sulfur dioxide. CDM projects, which include growing forests in places such as Uganda,[50] pose a twofold problem — (1) many of these projects will not see environmental returns until some point in the relatively distant future; and (2) it is extremely difficult to estimate accurately the reduction in emissions that will result from the project. The EU ETS, which incorporates the use of CERs as carbon credits for regulated entities, has handled this uncertainty by excluding sinks (tree plantations designed to reduce $CO_2$ emissions) from CDM projects for which participants may receive carbon credits.[51]

---

[49] C. Carlarne, 'The Kyoto Protocol and the WTO: reconciling tensions between free trade and environmental objectives', *Colo. J. Int'l Envtl. L. & Pol'y* 17 (2006), 67.

[50] M. Green, 'In Uganda, money may grow on trees' *Financial Times*, 25 April 2007, available at www.ft.com/cms/s/0/48ad542a-f437-11db-88aa-000b5df10621,dwp_uuid=3c093daa-edc1-11db-8584-000b5df10621.html For some of the difficulties with the CDM and some proposed solutions, see R. B. Stewart and J. B. Wiener, *Reconstructing Climate Policy: Beyond Kyoto* (Washington, DC: American Enterprise Institute, 2003), pp. 118–19.

[51] Kyoto Protocol, MEMO/03/154 Brussels, 23 July 2003, available at http://europa.eu.int/rapid/pressReleasesAction.do?reference=MEMO/03/154&format=HTML&aged=0&language=en&guiLanguage=en

The EU has also taken steps to link the CDM and joint implementation to the EU ETS through Directive 2004/101/EC, the Linking Directive that amends Directive 2003/87/EC (the Emissions Trading Directive). Cost reduction and increased liquidity are two of the stated goals of the Directive (paragraph 3) — 'this will increase the diversity of low-cost compliance options within the Community scheme leading to a reduction of the overall costs of compliance with the Kyoto Protocol while improving the liquidity of the Community market in greenhouse gas emission allowances'. Without such a link, there would be no effective means to track the relationship between CDM projects and emissions trading, making accounting for emissions reductions more difficult.

Projected annual reductions in emissions through CDM projects currently amount to 278 million tons.[52] In 2003, global carbon emissions were 26 billion tons, indicating that CDM projects play a very small role in emissions reduction.[53] Michael Wara has argued that CDM projects have primarily succeeded in accomplishing the political goals of engaging countries such as China and India in the climate change discussion, but have had less success in actually reducing emissions.[54] Significantly, he notes that nearly two-thirds of emission reductions achieved through CDM projects have involved neither carbon emission reductions nor the energy sector, which is typically the largest emitter of carbon dioxide.[55] Wara points out that 'the CDM is both a market and a subsidy from industrialised to developing countries', but that as a subsidy, the CDM is inefficient, since it is not cost effective in reducing emissions.[56] The possibility of an actionable subsidy for CDM projects does exist under the SCM Agreement in the situation where a developing country encourages CDM projects in a specific sector while allowing emissions in that sector to increase, giving the developing country in question a financial edge over other developing countries.[57]

Two other WTO agreements may be relevant to CDM projects. Since CDM projects involve cross-border investments under the supervision of governmental authorities, the Agreement on Government Procurement may also be implicated. A non-Annex B country government is likely to

---

[52] M. Wara, 'Is the global carbon market working?', *Nature* 445 (2007), 595.
[53] *Ibid.*     [54] *Ibid.*     [55] *Ibid.*
[56] Wara, 'Is the global carbon market working?', 596.
[57] A. Petsonk, 'The Kyoto Protocol and the WTO: integrating greenhouse gas emissions allowance trading into the global marketplace', *Duke Envtl. L. & Pol'y F.* 10 (1999), 213.

employ some government procurement for the completion of a CDM project. Tendering procedures (SCM Article VII), supplier qualifications (SCM Article VIII), and selection procedures (SCM Article X) are among the provisions likely to be relevant to a CDM project. Finally, the Technical Barriers to Trade Agreement (TBT) may also apply where an Annex B country investing in a CDM project faces local technical regulations or conformity assessment procedures relating to products originating in the Annex B country.

## III.   Green or renewable energy[58]

### A.   *Policy measures to support renewable energy*

Where electricity itself is traded, policies that favour renewable sources of energy for electricity generation over non-renewable sources are unlikely to constitute discrimination under WTO rules, because the processes for generation are, in many respects, 'unlike' and WTO rules on non-tax policies only address discrimination between 'like' products. While it is sometimes suggested that process differences may not result in the determination that two 'products' are like as a matter of WTO doctrine, energy *is* a process, and the underlying physical nature of electrical energy is such that any distinction between 'process' and 'product' would be scientifically meaningless.

### i.   Non-tax measures

Some subsidies on renewables (e.g. on biofuels) may raise issues concerning the application and interpretation of the provisions of the WTO Agreement on Agriculture (AoA), which contains independent disciplines on domestic support measures for agriculture. The AoA explicitly exempts certain environmental and conservation subsidies from the requirement to reduce domestic support (Annex II, paragraph 12); if a measure falls within these provisions the AoA permits its retention at current levels. At the same time the AoA exempts such subsidies from suit as 'actionable' under the SCM,

---

[58] The following reproduces and/or summarises or expands earlier work by Robert Howse, in collaboration with Renewable Energy and International Law (REIL). See R. Howse, 'WTO disciplines and biofuels: opportunities and constraints in the creation of a global marketplace, International Food and Agricultural Trade Policy Council' (principal author, assisted by Charlotte Hebebrand, CEO, IFATPC and Petrus van Bork); and R. Howse and REIL, 'World trade law and renewable energy: the case of non-tariff measures', *J.E.E.P.L.* 6 (2006), 500.

but only during the 'implementation' period, i.e. before 1 January 2004. The question is *whether*, after 1 January 2004, when the *procedural* bar to complaints against these measures ended, the fact that such subsidies are explicitly *reserved* by WTO Members under the AoA affects the disposition of a WTO complaint under the substantive law of the SCM Agreement.

Determining whether subsidies to support renewable energy are legal under WTO rules is a complex undertaking; apart from domestic content-based subsidies, only export subsidies are prohibited outright under WTO rules. In the case of other 'domestic' subsidies, not only must it be shown that there is a financial contribution by the government and a competitive advantage ('benefit') conferred on the recipient, but the subsidy must also be 'specific' and cause certain defined 'adverse effects'. Many subsidies for renewable energy are unlikely to meet one or other of these criteria, and therefore, are unlikely to be actionable under WTO law.

WTO rules on technical standards require, *inter alia*, that states base their regulations on 'international standards'. Thus, international standard setting will have a very significant impact on the WTO-compatibility of measures concerning renewables. This includes any international standards that define a renewable energy source, and norms of reliability and safety among others, for renewable energy technologies and operations.

With demonopolisation and regulatory reform occurring in the electrical energy sector in many countries, and the functions of former integrated monopolies now being performed by discrete generation, distribution, grid management and retailing enterprises, the nature and structure of the electricity trade is changing; it is plausible to view these various discrete entities as providers of *services* of various kinds such that what are being traded across borders are these services, rather than electricity as a good. Where renewable energy obligations are being imposed on grid operators or retailers, for example, it may be appropriate to consider these obligations under the GATS rather than the GATT. Adding to the uncertainty, the Appellate Body has found overlap between the two treaties such that different aspects of the same measure could be disciplined in by both the GATT and the GATS.[59] Trade in renewable energy certificates would fall within the ambit of the WTO instruments on financial services. These certificates do not entail an

---

[59] *EC — Bananas, European Communities — Regime for the Importation, Sale and Distribution of Bananas*, Appellate Body report, WT/DS27/AB/R, adopted 9 September 1997, paragraph 221.

entitlement to *energy*, but rather an entitlement to be relieved of an obligation to purchase renewable energy that would otherwise fall on the bearer of the certificate, because the issuer of the certificate, in another jurisdiction, is prepared to bear that burden.

The nature of its financial services commitments may well affect a state's ability to confine a tradable certificate programme to being within its national borders. Since the unconditional MFN obligation in the GATS applies to financial services measures (unless within four months of the entry into force of the GATS a WTO Member lodged an MFN reservation with respect to the particular measure in question — GATS Second Financial Services Annex), questions could arise where a WTO Member's authorities recognise certificates issued by some other WTO Members' nationals but not those of other WTO Members, or where a Member seeks to operate an international certificate trading scheme based on reciprocal or mutual recognition.

## ii.   Tax measures

Differential taxation of fossil fuels as inputs in the production of energy is very likely to be consistent with Article III:2 of the GATT. The fuels in question are physically quite different from the technologies and materials involved in the production of renewable energy; consumers may well care about the environmental consequences that result from these physical differences (see *EC — Asbestos*), and even though it could be argued that the end uses (production of electrical energy) are the same, based upon the existing jurisprudence (*EC — Asbestos*), it is improbable that such a common end use would outweigh the other evidence pointing to unlikeness. A similar analysis would occur with respect to whether the products are 'directly competitive or substitutable'.

The legitimacy of favouring renewables through taxation instruments will not save a tax scheme that is discriminatory in other respects, for instance, as between different fossil fuels (e.g. oil versus coal). Similarly, the analysis of 'likeness' or 'directly competitive or substitutable' might have a different flavour were the WTO adjudicator to be faced with a scheme that favours domestic renewables inputs over imports. While issues of intent or motivation are not supposed to influence determinations of 'likeness' or 'directly competitive or substitutable', the adjudicator may well be influenced, at least subconsciously, by the overall purpose of national treatment, as stated in Article III:1 of the GATT, which is to avoid the 'protection' of domestic products.

### B.   Trade barriers to renewable energy

#### i.   Tariff barriers

Reduction of tariffs on renewable energy technologies and equipment, and on biofuels, would contribute to reducing the cost of renewable energy relative to conventional energy sources. The impasse in the Doha Round negotiations in general and especially the lack of progress in the Environmental Goods and Services (EGS) negotiations suggest that multilateral progress on the reduction or elimination of such tariff barriers is far from imminent. However, there is nothing to prevent individual WTO Members from establishing lower applied rates of tariff on the goods in question, provided that the applied rate is offered to all WTO Members (i.e. consistent with the MFN obligation).[60]

Technologies and equipment used for the production of renewable energy (such as components of wind turbines) typically do not have classifications that reflect their uses for these purposes under the Harmonized System (HS); similarly, with the exception of biodiesel, biofuels are classified with regard to their physical characteristics, and there is no HS sub-classification that applies to the substances in question when used as fuel. This raises the issue of how, without the cumbersome process of amending the HS itself at the World Customs Organization (WCO), WTO Members could reduce tariffs on the goods in question when used for renewable energy purposes. In fact, neither WCO nor WTO obligations would prevent a WTO Member from applying a *lower* rate of tariff than that bound for a six-digit or higher HS classification to some sub-set of goods within that classification, as long as it provided MFN treatment to 'like products'. The WTO Member could do this through introducing a further sub-classification in its domestic nomenclature. Although such action would be subject to the normal transparency obligations of Article X of the GATT, it would not require any permission from or negotiation with the WTO membership in general, or trading partners with export interests in particular. In this sense, it can correctly be described as a legally possible unilateral option.

This is illustrated by US practice with respect to ethanol. In 1980, the US introduced a 'secondary' import tariff of fifty cents per gallon on fuel ethanol; i.e. this tariff was added, in the case of imports of fuel ethanol

---

[60]   R. Howse and P. B. van Bork, 'Options for liberalising trade in environmental goods in the Doha Round'. ICTSD Trade and Environment Issue Paper No. 2., Geneva. Switzerland (2006).

alone, to the applied rate as classified in the HS headings for all ethanol (whether for fuel or non-fuel use). At the time, this was clearly a violation of US obligations under Article II of the GATT, since, with respect to some imports of ethanol at least, the US was applying a higher rate of tariff than the bound rate for the HS classification. But what if the US had done the reverse, namely singled out fuel ethanol for a lower applied rate than the bound rate for the HS classification in question? This would not have run afoul of the WTO rules: WTO Members are free to structure their actual applied tariffs on particular imports largely as they please, even based on considerations other than HS classification,[61] provided that the result is that the applied rate of tariff is never above the bound rate for the HS classification in question, and there is no discrimination between imports based on their national origin (the MFN obligation). Moreover, the US — in singling out fuel ethanol for separate treatment — would not be violating its obligation to use any HS classifications that exist at the six-digit level and above. This obligation does not exclude making further sub-classifications below those that exist in the HS system. Under Article II of the GATT, WTO Members cannot introduce, beyond the tariffs they have bound in their schedules, additional duties and charges on imported products.

Generally speaking, the tariff classifications applicable to biofuels have been based on conceptions of the substances in question as agricultural or chemical products, and are not specific to the use of the substances as fuels, biodiesel being an exception, as it now has its own HS classification. Thus, ethanol is classified on the basis of its chemical composition as undenatured (220710) and denatured (220720) alcohol in the HS, but these classifications refer to its chemical composition, and there is no separate classification or sub-classification specific to fuel ethanol that differentiates it from ethanol used for other purposes. WTO Members may have environmental and energy security reasons for wanting to reduce tariffs on these substances when used as fuels but not when they are destined for other uses in competition with domestic products. The fact that tariff classifications are not consistently aligned with the actual consumer market in question (the biofuel market) not only makes it difficult to ascertain the actual trade flows of biofuels, but also leads to a number of problems with respect to consistency, certainty and

---

[61] *Chile — Price Band, Chile — Price Band System and Safeguard Measures Relating to Certain Agricultural Products*, Appellate Body report, WT/DS207/AB/R, adopted 23 September 2002, paragraph 278.

non-discrimination in the application of existing WTO obligations. The European Union of Ethanol Producers claims for example that, because there is not a separate classification for fuel ethanol, Brazilian fuel ethanol has been entering Sweden not under the classification for denatured ethanol but under HS 3824.90.99 — a different classification that carries a much lower rate of duty. The argument here is apparently that the degree of denaturing is higher than what would be normal under HS 2207.20.

Importantly, HS classifications also determine whether or not a product is an agricultural product under WTO rules. Annex 1 of the WTO AoA states that the provisions of the Agreement apply to HS Chapters 1–24 (except for fish products) as well as to a specified list of products with other HS headings. We note that while in HS Chapter 22, ethanol is considered an agricultural good, biodiesel falls under Chapter 38 and is thus considered an industrial good. The AoA not only has separate rules that affect tariff rates (tariffication of certain kinds of quantitative restrictions), but also different rules with regard to subsidies and other domestic policies that affect trade, which will be addressed in section II of this chapter.

Further complicating the classification issue is the possibility (to the extent that the Doha Development Round may be revived) that some biofuels could be deemed as 'environmental goods' and subject to special negotiations to reduce trade barriers with respect to 'Environmental Goods and Services'. Paragraph 31(iii) of the Doha Ministerial Declaration calls for 'the reduction or, as appropriate, elimination of tariffs and non-tariff barriers to environmental goods and services'.

With respect to the requirement for MFN treatment of 'like products' in Article I of the GATT, the *Spain — Coffee* case suggests that end uses as perceived by consumers are a very important consideration in determining whether products are 'like' for the purposes of interpreting the MFN obligation;[62] subsequent jurisprudence on 'like products' in the WTO era has placed considerable emphasis on consumers' tastes and perceptions of products, i.e. not distorting the competitive relationship where products are competitive in the same consumer market. From this perspective, biofuels and physically similar products with non-fuel uses should be considered 'unlike' as they are not competing in the same consumer marketplace. If a WTO Member wished to reduce tariffs on

---

[62] *Spain — Coffee, Spain — Tariff Treatment of Unroasted Coffee*, panel report, L/5135 — 28S/102, adopted 11 June 1981, paragraph 4.6.

imports of biofuels largely or entirely for environmental reasons, the Member might logically wish to limit such reductions to imports of biofuels that have net positive environmental impacts based on the entire life cycle of the product. Would this kind of subclassification be consistent with the obligation of MFN for 'like products', or could it be successfully challenged by a WTO Member the failure of whose biofuels exports to meet the importing Member's environmental impact criteria is the only thing preventing it from qualifying for the tariff reduction?

In a finding that was adopted without being appealed, a WTO panel held that the word 'unconditionally' in the GATT Article I MFN obligation not to discriminate against imported 'like' products permitted distinctions that did not *discriminate* against imports *on the basis of national origin.*[63] Neutral environmental criteria, supported by international standards and multilateral environmental treaties, are not likely to be held to discriminate on the basis of national origin, either de jure (by distinguishing the national origin of the products on the face of the law) or de facto (where a criterion that is neutral on its face nevertheless appears in its design to favour imports from some countries more than others). Recent Appellate Body jurisprudence has, however, rejected that view, thereby implying that a wide range of considerations may inform the applied rate of a given WTO Member. What is crucial for the purposes of compliance with the GATT rules on tariffs is that an applied tariff never *exceeds* the MFN bound rate for the classification in question, regardless of whatever factors or considerations are used to calculate the tariff.

### ii.   Non-tariff barriers

To the extent that electrical energy is a good, the terms under which imported energy is afforded access to the national grid and distribution and transmission networks is governed by the TBT as well as various provisions of the GATT, including in some instances Article XVII, 'State Trading Enterprises'. These terms could be unfavourable to either foreign producers of *renewable energy* and/or producers of *renewable energy technology*.

**Subsidies**   Subsidies are a persuasive form of government intervention to support renewable energy. One issue that has already arisen in the

---

[63] *Canada — Autos, Canada — Certain Measures Affecting the Automotive Industry,* panel report, WT/DS139/R, WT/DS142/R, adopted 11 February 2000, paragraph 10.24.

context of the European internal competition law is whether minimum price requirements could be considered subsidies due to their effect of guaranteeing revenues in excess of what would exist without government intervention. In the *PreussenElektra* case, the European Court of Justice held that minimum price purchase requirements under German law could not be considered 'state aid' in European law because of the absence of any direct or indirect transfer of state resources.[64] In the WTO SCM, by contrast, a 'financial contribution' includes a situation where 'a government makes payments to a funding mechanism, or entrusts or directs a private body to carry out one or more of the type of functions illustrated in [SCM Article 1.1(a)(1)] (i) to (iii) ... which would normally be vested in the government and the practice, in no real sense, differs from practices normally followed by government'. Since Article 1.1(a)(1)(iii) of the SCM includes 'purchasing goods', the argument is that a situation where the government directs a private actor to purchase goods at a higher than market price is included within the meaning of 'financial contribution' even if the government does not incur any cost *itself*. In the *Canada — Aircraft* case (paragraph 160), the Appellate Body observed that 'financial contribution' could include those situations where a private body has been directed by the government to engage in one of the actions defined in Article 1.1(a)(1)(i)–(iii) of the SCM, even if the government does not bear the cost of such delegated action.

This being said, one should not jump to the conclusion that the German minimum price purchase requirements would fully meet the relevant definition of 'financial contribution', i.e. the definition that applies where the government entrusts or directs a private body. The relevant provision *also* requires that the function entrusted or delegated to the private body be one that is *normally* performed by the government. The German minimum price purchase requirements do not represent a delegation of a governmental function to any private body; rather they represent a *regulation* of the electricity market, and their directive character is in regulating market behaviour and transactions, not imposing a governmental function on a private body. Here, the observations of the panel in *Canada — Export Restraints* are relevant: '[I]t does not follow ..., that every government intervention that might in economic theory be deemed a subsidy with the potential to distort trade is a subsidy within the meaning of the SCM. Such an approach would mean that the

---

[64] Case C—379/98, *PreussenElektra AG* v. *Schleswag AG* [2001] E.C.R. I-2099.

"financial contribution" requirement would effectively be replaced by a requirement that the government action in question be commonly understood to be a subsidy that distorts trade' (paragraph 8.62). The requirement that a private body be performing a normally governmental function guards against the possibility that *all* 'command-and-control' regulation, which directs private bodies and which always has *some* distributive effect as between different private economic actors, could be deemed a subsidy.[65]

We have already alluded to some of the complexities of ascertaining whether the subsidy has conferred a 'benefit' on the recipient, i.e. a competitive advantage over and above general 'market' conditions. Some programmes for renewable energy may not confer a 'benefit' in this sense. Measures that merely defray the cost of businesses acquiring renewable energy systems or which compensate enterprises for providing renewable energy in remote locations, do not necessarily, for instance, confer a 'benefit' on the recipient enterprise. They simply reimburse or compensate the enterprise for taking some action that it would otherwise not take, and the enterprise has not acquired any competitive advantage over other enterprises, which neither take the subsidy nor have to perform these actions.

With respect to the requirement of *specificity*, subsidies that are provided to *users* of renewable energy may well not be specific if they are available generally to enterprises in the economy. This brings us to the consideration of 'adverse effects'. Often subsidies for renewable energy and renewable energy technologies reflect the absence of alternative sources of supply for renewable energy and/or the technologies. In such cases, there may be no competing producers from other WTO Members who can claim to be injured, or suffer other adverse effects, from the subsidies in question. Where subsidies are paid to users of renewable energy or renewable energy technology, and where those users can benefit from the subsidy regardless of whether they acquire

---

[65] In his fine contribution to this volume, Sadeq Bigdeli raises the possibility that such measures could be considered as 'price support' within the meaning of Article 1.1(a)(2) of the SCM. In our view, price regulation by government in the context of utilities and network industries more generally, ought not to be considered 'price support' under Article 1.1(a)(2). Because such utilities are often characterised by elements of monopoly provision and price regulation reflects a variety of public policy goals, including universal service, incentives for appropriate investment in infrastructure, it would be difficult and very intrusive into the operation of the democratic regulatory state for the WTO dispute settlement organs to assess whether, against some model of a perfect market, the tariffs in question constitute 'price support'.

the energy or the technology from domestic or foreign sources, again there may not be any 'adverse effects' on competing foreign producers.

Finally, we should mention the possibility that renewable energy subsidies could be challenged based on their 'adverse effects' not on imports of competing renewable but on foreign *non*-renewable energy products. Here we note that, generally speaking, the 'adverse effect' in question must be on a *like* product from another WTO Member. The meaning of likeness for the purposes of the SCM has been addressed only once so far in the jurisprudence, in the *Indonesia — Autos* case. In that case, the panel did not delineate very clearly the concept of 'like products', instead evoking a very broad notion that entails considering the kinds of factors that are at issue under Article III of the GATT as well as others perhaps, such as the way the industry had segmented itself. In *Indonesia — Autos*, the panel emphasised physical characteristics in its likeness analysis, but largely because, as it said, physical characteristics, *in the case of automobiles*, were closely linked to consumer-relevant criteria such as brand loyalty, brand image, reputation and resale value (paragraphs 14.173–14.174).[66]

Where the harm alleged is 'serious prejudice' within the meaning of Article 6 of the SCM, the requirement to identify a 'like product' exists explicitly with respect to serious prejudice due to price undercutting, but not with respect to the other kinds of effects identified in Article 6.3(c), notably significant price suppression, price depression or lost sales. In the *US — Cotton* case, in footnote 453, the Appellate Body held that it did not have to decide on the interpretative issue of whether a comparison with 'like' products should nevertheless be inferred in the case of significant price suppression, price depression or lost sales.

Related issues would arise if a WTO Member were to challenge subsidies on renewables, claiming adverse effects on producers of non-renewable *inputs* such as fossil fuels. The complex set of considerations that determines price and supply of fossil fuels in domestic and world markets (including futures and derivatives trading, political events, and in the case of petroleum, cartel-like behaviour), could make it very difficult to attribute the kinds of 'adverse effects' contemplated in Article 5 of the SCM to subsidies on renewables. With respect to 'serious prejudice', the Appellate Body has held in *US — Cotton* that 'it is necessary to ensure that the effects of other factors on prices are not

---

[66] *Indonesia — Autos, Indonesia — Certain Measures Affecting the Automobile Industry*, panel report, WT/DS54/R, WT/DS55/R, WT/DS59/R, WT/DS64/R, adopted 2 July 1998.

improperly attributed to the challenged subsidies [footnote omitted]' (paragraph 437). The Appellate Body further observed: 'we underline the responsibility of panels in gathering and analyzing relevant factual data and information in assessing claims under Article 6.3(c) in order to arrive at reasoned conclusions' (paragraph 458).

Subsidies for oil, coal gas and nuclear power are often cited as a very significant barrier to renewable energy. Perhaps inspired to some extent by initiatives on fisheries subsidies, one could envisage negotiations within the WTO with a view to Members agreeing to cap and reduce subsidies in the energy sector that are environmentally unfriendly. Such negotiations might also address the task of identifying a set of 'green box' renewable energy subsidies that Members agree to refrain from challenging, on account of consensus as to their positive environmental effects. A broader and much more speculative question is whether such negotiations could be linked to the fulfilment of commitments under international environmental regimes.

**Services** To the extent that the services provision is at issue and not just trade in goods, barriers to access to the grid, and transmission and distribution networks could be challenged where these affect the trading opportunities of service providers from other WTO Members. Assuming that the WTO Member being challenged has made commitments on the relevant energy services (few such commitments have been made to date), depending on the nature of the barrier either the national treatment or market access provisions of the GATS or both may be applicable. Given the lack of explicit commitments on energy services in the Uruguay Round, the changes in the structure of electricity systems and technological developments negotiations on energy services in the current Doha Round may present an opportunity to ensure that the commitments made reduce the barriers to renewable energy. The same goes for financial services negotiations in the current round, concerning the status and treatment of tradable renewable energy certificates in the future.

## IV.   Energy efficiency

A range of countries have implemented mandatory regulations and/or labelling schemes for energy efficiency in transportation vehicles and/or electrical appliances and equipment. Energy efficiency has a potentially significant contribution to make to the reduction of carbon emissions, but has received limited attention until recently.[67] Mandatory measures related to energy efficiency are 'laws, regulations and requirements' within the meaning of Article III:4 of the GATT and 'technical regulations' within the meaning of the TBT. In principle, there seems no reason why products would not be considered 'unlike' under Article III:4 of the GATT by virtue of the differences in performance with respect to energy efficiency. Such differences would normally depend on different design features of the products in question, and therefore there would be differences in physical characteristics. Consumers have both economic and environmental reasons to prefer energy-efficient over comparably performing non-energy efficient products. Thus, based on the approach to likeness in *EC — Asbestos*, the differential regulatory treatment of products based on energy efficiency would be widely permissible under WTO rules. At the same time, under the TBT, WTO Members are required to use international standards as a basis for their technical regulations where such standards exist (Article 2.4), and these regulations must be designed so as not to create unnecessary obstacles to trade, i.e. they must not be more trade restrictive than necessary to achieve the legitimate objective in question (Article 2.2). It is thus important that energy-efficiency regulations and labelling and certification programmes be designed using objective criteria and impartial conformity assessment procedures, to ensure that imported products are not unduly disfavoured or burdened.

There are few existing international standards for energy efficiency, although this is an area where the International Electrotechnical Commission (IEC) sees potential for future development (the IEC is the most important international standard-setting body for electrical equipment and electricity).[68] There are two main processes aimed at developing best practices, harmonising energy-efficiency standards, and providing technical assistance to developing countries in establishing and enforcing such standards: these are the CLASP process (Collaborative Labelling and Appliance Standards Programme), under US leadership, and the APEC Energy Standards Information System (ESIS). Assuming the guidelines, best practices, and other features developed by these organisations conform to the meaning of 'standards' in the TBT, it is questionable that they would be regarded as 'international

---

[67] See, generally, International Energy Agency, *Experience with Energy Efficiency Regulations for Electrical Equipment* (Paris: IEA, 2007).
[68] IEC-E-Tech News, May 2007, 'Energy efficiency household appliances'.

standards' within the meaning of the TBT, as these organisations are not open for membership by the standard setting bodies of all WTO Members (this is particularly clear with APEC, which is a regional grouping). This being said, it is likely that energy-efficiency regulations and labelling programmes that closely follow the guidelines, methodologies and best practices developed in these multi-jurisdictional expert bodies would be more easily defended as not being unnecessary obstacles to trade within the meaning of the TBT.

In the case of energy efficiency with respect to vehicles, a GATT panel ruling in the 1990s, the Corporate Average Fuel Economy (CAFE) panel, found a US tax applied to vehicles with fuel consumption of less than 22.5 miles per gallon (mpg) consistent with Article III:4. A different measure, a standard requiring that an automobile manufacturer achieve fuel efficiency of 27.5 mpg across its entire fleet was found to violate Article III:4 because the US applied it in a discriminatory way to the EU, counting only those vehicles imported into the US, which happened to have relatively low fuel efficiency, as opposed to the entire fleets of European manufacturers. (In the case of the US manufacturers, the entire fleet was counted, regardless of whether the vehicles were exported or sold domestically in the US.) The CAFE ruling is of limited precedential value, first since it is unadopted, and secondly since it appears to have been based on the 'aims and effects' approach to the national treatment obligation rejected by the Appellate Body in *Japan — Alcohol* and *EC — Asbestos*. Nevertheless, as we have suggested under the approach of the Appellate Body, it is very likely that products with different energy-efficiency characteristics would be considered 'unlike' (or for that matter, under the second sentence of Article III:2 of the GATT, directly competitive or substitutable), thus foreclosing the possibility of a violation of Article III of the GATT.

## V.  Conclusion

Properly interpreted, the existing law of the WTO should not pose obstacles to domestic or global policies designed to address climate change. Problems are most likely to arise where policies are intended in whole or in part to address competitiveness or 'level playing field' concerns about divergent domestic policies and regulatory burdens, as opposed to being intended to achieve climate change goals themselves, including by using trade pressure to induce countries not controlling emissions appropriately to adopt effective policies. In the case of renewable or green energy, governments have sometimes, along similar lines, designed incentives and other measures to promote renewables as industrial policy measures aimed at creating national industries and not simply at supporting the most efficient clean technologies. Some of the markets in question may not have got off the ground without protective, infant industry-type measures; on the other hand, today the development of more cost-effective green energy sources may be hampered by some of the traditional protective approaches in this area. Here, a sensitive application of non-discrimination norms is crucial to distinguishing between government intervention that supports 'green' consumption choices and innovation in green energy technologies, and those policies that close or restrict markets to competing, and perhaps more efficient producers from abroad. WTO subsidies disciplines may be implicated in some instances, especially in respect to biofuels. There are several respects, however, in which existing WTO law is not well adapted to realising the potential of trade liberalisation to reduce the costs of clean methods of production; these aspects, including the approach to customs classification inherited from the WCO, as it were, combined with a lack of international standards in some areas, are supposed to be addressed in part in the Environmental Goods and Services negotiations, but these negotiations are unfortunately stalled at a quite preliminary stage of discussion.

# PART II

Climate change mitigation and trade in goods

# 5

# How to think about PPMs (and climate change)

DONALD H. REGAN[1]

## I.  Introduction

The European Commission has apparently backed off from a proposal to tax imported goods produced by methods that generate excessive greenhouse gas emissions.[2] So the issue of whether such a tax would be legal under the WTO has become slightly less urgent than it recently appeared. But Pascal Lamy the Director-General of the WTO still thought the possibility of some countries imposing emission-based trade restrictions was worth mentioning prominently in his speech to the Trade Ministers Conference in conjunction with the Bali Conference on climate change after Kyoto.[3] And at that same conference, an official of the European Commission may have indicated that such restrictions are not off the table entirely.[4] Clearly, the impetus for such a tax to be levied by some nation or other is not going to go away until we have a universally accepted international regime for emissions control — which is to say, not any time soon.

Of course, as Lamy notes, there are all sorts of reasons to prefer a multilateral solution to the climate problem. Unilateral import restrictions based on emissions will be deeply resented by exporting countries. Unilateral restrictions are also likely to disrupt the economy of the importing country, if its supply chains and production have been globalised. Unilateral restrictions cannot in any event fully address the problem of high-emissions production when the products are sold in

---

[1]  William W. Bishop, Jr. Collegiate Professor of Law and Professor of Philosophy, University of Michigan. I thank Ted Parson for discussion of a draft, and my commentators Jacques Bourgeois and Daniel Crosby.

[2]  A. Bounds, 'EU turns away from carbon tax on imports', *Financial Times*, 26 November 2007.

[3]  From the WTO website, www.wto.org/english/news_e/sppl_e/sppl83_e.htm

[4]  ICTSD, 'Trade ministers discuss links between commerce and climate change in Bali', *Bridges Weekly Trade News Digest* 11, No. 43 (2007).

third-country markets (or in the home market of the high-emissions exporting country itself). Nor can they fully address the problem of investment capital flowing to high-emission countries. But it is one thing to say that we would prefer a universal or widespread international agreement. It is quite another to reach such an agreement. Until we do, unilateral action will have its proponents.

It might be suggested that no country will impose emissions-related import restrictions, for the same reasons that the EU never used more than a fraction of its authorisation for US$ 4 billion of trade sanctions against the US after it prevailed in the *FSC* (*United States — Tax Treatment for 'Foreign Sales Corporations'*) litigation.[5] This may be too sanguine; the cases are different in important respects. If we ask why the EU did not impose the authorised sanctions, a number of reasons come to mind. (1) Doing so would have greatly embarrassed general political and economic relations between the EU and the US. (2) There would have been great disruption to EU producers because of the interdependence of global production. (3) From a national welfare point of view, sanctions, which are just protective tariffs under a special permission, would hurt the EU economy overall more than they would help it, even aside from the disruption issues. Finally, (4) there was no group of EU producers certain to benefit from sanctions. In one way, of course, the possibility of sanctions was an invitation to any and every producer group that wanted a protective tariff to ask for one. But no group could be confident that effort spent lobbying would pay off, partly because no group had anything resembling a claim of right to protection.

If we now compare sanctions to an emissions-related import restriction, we see a number of differences. (1) The embarrassment to general political and economic relations with affected exporting countries may be much the same — no difference there. (2) With regard to disruptions to supply chains, however, there is a difference. There will of course be disruptions resulting from the import restriction, possibly substantial ones, but by hypothesis, the importing country had already decided to confront precisely such disruptions when it adopted its restrictions on domestic production (at least, if the import restriction takes the form of a tax). (3) There is also a difference with regard to the overall harm to the

---

[5] J. Bhagwati and P. Mavroidis, 'Is action against US exports for failure to sign Kyoto Protocol WTO-legal?', *World Trade Review* 6 (2007), 299–310, argue against the EU imposing such restrictions, and they introduce their discussion with the *FSC* sanctions analogy.

economy. The sanction/tariff creates no benefit except to domestic producers and the treasury; in the conventional understanding, these benefits are outweighed by the loss to consumers (or other users) of the product. In contrast, the emissions-based import restriction creates a distinct benefit in the form of reduced worldwide emissions. Whether or not the import restriction induces the exporter to change its production methods, it will (normally) reduce the demand for goods made with high-emission processes; it will thus reduce the intensity of use of such processes and the total damage done by them. The emissions-based import restriction might still be 'irrational' for the importing country in the sense that the extra cost to it of producing goods with the low-emissions process (or of buying only goods produced with the low-emissions process) is less than the benefit that accrues *to it* from the reduced use of the high-emissions process, since the benefit of that reduced use is spread over the whole world. But still, that sort of irrationality — which from another perspective is mere global good citizenship — is something the importing country had already com-mitted itself to when it decided to limit its *own* use of the high-emissions process in advance of comparable commitments by other countries. Finally, (4) in the case of the emissions-based import restriction, there is a particular producer group that can expect to benefit, and they have a very plausible claim of right to protection from imports produced using high-emission processes. This will affect both their motivation to lobby and the motivation of the political system to respond to their lobbying. There will also be another important lobby in favour of the restrictions, namely environmentalists, who play a role that has no analogue in the case of sanctions.

In connection with this last point, it is unfortunate (although not unusual) that when Lamy discusses emissions-based import restrictions in his Bali speech, he speaks as if the only possible justification for such restrictions is offsetting the competitive disadvantage to domestic pro-ducers caused by the domestic measures. If this were really the only thing to be said in favour of the restrictions (that they offset competitive disadvantage), they would be nothing more than protectionism — which is more or less the impression Lamy conveys. But as we have seen, there is something else to be said in favour of the restrictions: they can be expected to reduce the global emissions of greenhouse gases. This not only constitutes an additional, non-protectionist justification, it also changes the way we should view the 'offsetting competitive disadvantage' justification. As I shall explain in section III, when there is the appropriate sort of non-protectionist justification for the restriction, then offsetting the competitive disadvantage to domestic producers is desirable; indeed it is *necessary* if we are to achieve efficient location of production by the operation of comparative advantage.

If we suppose that it is at least possible that some country might want to impose emissions-based import restrictions, the next question is whether there is any legal problem with this under the WTO. Some might argue that the Appellate Body settled the legal issues in *US — Shrimp.*[6] But surely that is too quick. The Appellate Body has made it clear that, unless they change their mind, process-based trade restrictions are not flatly forbidden across the board. One such has been definitively upheld. But the decision in *Shrimp* attracted vehement criticism from many WTO Members and many scholars, and it continues to do so.[7] Although I think the Appellate Body was right both as a matter of treaty interpretation and as a matter of theory and policy, and I hope they will stick to their guns, I can also imagine them looking for ways to back away from *Shrimp* to some extent. There is no shortage of serious questions to be confronted. (1) Can we say, for example, that the capacity of the atmosphere to absorb $CO_2$ without serious damage to the climate is an 'exhaustible natural resource'? (2) If not, are the particular measures being challenged 'necessary' to the protection of human, animal, or plant life or health? (3) Are the precise discriminations between which products are admitted and which are not admitted 'justifiable' in the sense required by the chapeau of Article XX of the GATT (which *Shrimp I* makes clear is a requirement with teeth)? All of these questions presuppose that we have got to Article XX, where the burden of proof is on the respondent (importing) country. Given the practical difficulties of definition and administration that will attend any emissions-based import restriction,[8] the importing country would like to avoid that

---

[6] *United States — Import Prohibition of Certain Shrimp and Shrimp Products (Recourse to Article 21.5)*, WT/DS58/AB/RW (adopted 21 November 2001).

[7] As to the members' reaction, see C. Barfield, *Free Trade, Sovereignty, Democracy: The Future of the World Trade Organization* (Washington DC: AEI Press, 2001), pp. 48–50, p. 128. For an example of the scholarly criticism, see J. Bhagwati, *In Defense of Globalization* (Oxford University Press, 2004), pp. 153–8.

[8] Examples of the difficulties include: (1) defining the carbon emissions attributable to particular foreign products; (2) accounting for the fact that emissions permits have often been given away in the domestic system; (3) deciding how to treat products that have high carbon footprints because they come from countries that have chosen to meet their reduction commitments (under a Kyoto Protocol-style national emission-reduction target) in different ways from the importing country.

burden of proof, and it can do so if it can persuade the Appellate Body that its restriction is a permitted border tax adjustment under Article II.2(a), or that it falls under, and is consistent with, Article III as expanded by the interpretive Note *Ad* III. What are the prospects for that? Or, what if the challenge is under the Technical Barriers to Trade Agreement (TBT), where the issues are least restrictiveness and appropriateness to the local situation, and there is no textual analogue of Article XX at all? For that matter, does the TBT address unincorporated process-based restrictions?

It is clear, then, that there are many important legal issues concerning emissions-based import restrictions that are still unsettled. But there are a number of other excellent articles that discuss these legal issues in detail,[9] and for the most part I do not propose to go over the legal terrain again. Instead, I want to talk about how we should think about 'PPMs', including emissions-based import restrictions, in general. Because the legal issues are so uncertain, people's views about them are inevitably influenced by their underlying prejudices and pre-dispositions concerning PPMs. The Border Tax Adjustment provisions in particular seem to function as a Rorschach blot for revealing people's pre-dispositions. Unfortunately, these pre-dispositions are often based on confused thinking.

Many intelligent, thoughtful, well-informed people make claims about the economics and the political morality of PPMs that are muddled or just wrong. For example, I think many people are confused about the relationship between PPMs and comparative advantage. It is often said that PPMs interfere with the operation of comparative advantage. The truth is that sometimes PPMs are essential if comparative advantage, properly understood, is to have its proper influence. There is also confusion about when precisely one country's behaviour (or its producers' behaviour) creates an 'externality' vis-à-vis other countries. This confusion, coupled with another about whether PPMs are necessarily aimed at getting exporting countries to change their policies, makes PPMs appear 'coercive' even when they do not deserve to be regarded that way. My hope is that I can dispel some confusion, and that clearer thinking about the general nature of PPMs will lead to better legal decisions.

---

[9] e.g. R. Howse and A. Eliason, 'Domestic and international strategies to address climate change: an overview of the WTO legal issues', in this volume; J. Pauwelyn, *US Federal Climate Policy and Competitiveness Concerns: The Limits and Options of International Trade Law*', Working Paper NI WP 07–02, Nicholas Institute for Environmental Policy Solutions, Duke University (April 2007); P. Demaret and R. Stewardson, 'Border Tax Adjustments under GATT and EC law and general implications for environmental taxes', *Journal of World Trade* 28 (1994), 5–65.

## II.   What is a PPM?

The initials 'PPM' refer to 'process or production method'. On its face, the concept has nothing to do with trade restrictions of any kind. But 'PPM' is also now routinely used to refer to trade restrictions that are somehow based on the use or non-use by producers of particular processes or production methods. This broader usage is ambiguous in an important way. I suspect that for most people the paradigm PPM is a restriction that says, for example, 'we will not allow the import of widgets from any country that permits the use of certain processes or production methods for producing widgets'. This I shall refer to as a 'country-based' PPM. A different sort of PPM, however, is one that says 'we will not allow the import of widgets that were themselves produced using certain processes or production methods'. This I shall refer to as a 'product-based' PPM. The difference, of course, is that under the product-based PPM, widgets that are produced by approved techniques may be imported even if they come from a country that also permits the use of disapproved techniques.[10]

In what follows, 'PPMs' should be taken to refer only to *product-based* PPMs unless I specifically say otherwise. (I am also discussing only what are known as 'unincorporated PPMs' — restrictions based on processes or production methods that leave no distinctive trace in the physical constitution of the product when it arrives in the importing country. PPMs focusing on processes that do affect the physical constitution of the product are simply not controversial in the way unincorporated PPMs are.) The possible justifications for product-based and country-based PPMs differ in a number of ways, some of which I shall come back to later. But for now, let me suggest a 'moral' difference between the two sorts of PPM. To begin, forget about PPMs for a moment. I take it we think there is a significant difference between an importing country saying, (1) 'We do not want that product because of what it is in itself (an unsafe toy, a car without a catalytic converter, an item of Nazi memorabilia)', and the same country saying, (2) 'We do not want that (otherwise innocent) product because it comes from you (the particular

---

[10]  A third possibility is a 'producer-based' PPM, one that says 'we will not allow the import of widgets from any producer that uses certain processes or production methods for producing widgets (for any part of its production, not just the particular widgets we are importing)'. Although this is the category in which we would have to classify Corporate Average Fuel Economy (CAFE) standards, a bit awkwardly, I shall simplify the discussion in the text by ignoring this possibility.

exporting country).' Even if the exporting country is singled out by some general description of its behaviour (e.g. 'no widgets from countries that allow capital punishment'), the exclusion of innocent products because of the country they come from seems especially problematic. I do not mean to say it is never appropriate or allowable; just that it seems fundamentally more problematic than the exclusion of products that are objectionable in themselves. This antipathy towards country-based exclusion is one of the reasons for the intuitive appeal of the most-favoured-nation principle.[11]

Accepting the intuitive appeal of making some distinction between the two sorts of restriction I have mentioned, let us now reintroduce PPMs; and specifically, let us ask which of the two sorts of restriction the different kinds of PPM seem most akin to. The country-based PPM is obviously akin to (2), the restriction that says, 'We do not want that (otherwise innocent) product because it comes from you.' Indeed, it is straightforwardly an instance of (2), with the disfavoured countries singled out because they permit certain production techniques. The product-based PPM is not straightforwardly an instance of either (1) or (2), but to my mind, is much more like (1) than (2). It does not exclude any product because of its country of origin. Rather it excludes a product only because of the way *that product* was produced. With the example of climate change before us, it is clear that there can be good reasons to care about how a product was produced — reasons every bit as compelling as the reasons to want safe toys, or to exclude Nazi memorabilia, and so on. Of course, product-based PPMs can be abused for covert protectionist purposes; but so can product regulations that focus on the intrinsic physical properties of the products. If the question is about the general 'moral' status of a category of regulation, it seems clear to me that product-based PPMs are no more problematic in their general form than ordinary product regulations; and they are a world apart from country-based PPMs.[12] This discussion is intended only to make it

---

[11]  In fact, I think there are deep questions about the ideal contours and justification (in terms of economics, political economy, and political morality) of the most-favoured-nation principle that I have never seen properly addressed — but this is not the place for that discussion.

[12]  In some cases, of course, the country-based PPM (or a producer-based PPM, see n. 10 above) may be used by a country that would otherwise be content with a product-based PPM, because it is impossible to ascertain how a particular product was made except through a generalisation about products from that country (or that producer). So far as the law of the WTO is concerned, such country-based restrictions will still require a

initially plausible to distinguish between country-based and product-based PPMs. For readers who disdain this sort of argument, we shall see that there are economic differences and other political economy differences as well. So, to reiterate, when I talk about PPMs I shall be talking about *product-based* PPMs unless the context clearly indicates otherwise.

Now, a second point about the scope of 'PPMs'. For most people, the paradigm case of a PPM is a regulation, in the narrow sense in which a 'regulation' is distinguished from a tax. Think of the *Tuna/Dolphin* cases or the *Shrimp/Turtle* case, or a hypothetical law excluding products produced by workers paid a sub-standard wage. But in connection with climate change, we may well be thinking about *taxes* that distinguish between products on the ground of the techniques used to produce them. In the discussion that follows, I shall generally not distinguish between PPMs that involve regulation in the narrow sense and PPMs that involve taxation. I shall use the word 'regulation' to encompass both cases, again unless the context indicates otherwise. It is true that the WTO agreements have distinct provisions for the two cases; but the underlying conceptual issues are the same. And I think the legal results under the best reading of the various provisions are essentially the same for regulations (narrow sense) and taxes. There is one distinctive issue in connection with taxes: who gets the revenue? The Border Tax Adjustment provisions seem to presuppose that the best, or natural, answer to that question is 'the country of consumption', under the 'destination principle'. But it is clear that both the drafters of the border tax provisions and the authors of the Border Tax Adjustment Report were focusing on taxes imposed primarily for fiscal reasons, as opposed to the regulatory (Pigovian) taxes we are thinking about in connection with climate change. That is one of the reasons the border tax provisions seem so ill suited to addressing the problem of emission-based PPMs. In fact, if emission-based PPMs appear, the system that includes them is very likely to end up giving the bulk of the revenue to the producing country — which seems perfectly acceptable. In any event, this is one of the many problems of detail that I shall ignore in this paper, in order to concentrate on more fundamental issues.

---

special demonstration of justification. This 'evidentiary' use of country of origin or producer identity is one of the many wrinkles I shall ignore in the remainder of this essay. I shall assume that any country-based PPM under discussion is *not* justified by this sort of evidentiary argument.

### III.   PPMs and comparative advantage

I have heard both distinguished international economists and distinguished trade lawyers say that PPMs interfere with the operation of comparative advantage. This claim is at best misleading, and at worst false. The problem is that the notion of comparative advantage is ambiguous between what I shall call 'positive comparative advantage' and 'normative comparative advantage'. Consequently, the claim that PPMs interfere with the operation of comparative advantage is ambiguous also. I am prepared to concede for present purposes that PPMs always interfere with *positive* comparative advantage (although even this depends on how we define the alternative to the existence of the PPM). But the claim that PPMs interfere with positive comparative advantage, even if true, is no ground for objecting to PPMs. We would have a well-grounded objection to PPMs only if they interfered with *normative* comparative advantage. As to this, sometimes they do, but often they do not. Often a PPM is actually essential to the operation of normative comparative advantage, and hence to the achievement of efficiency.

So first, what is the difference between positive and normative comparative advantage? Let us start with the textbook example. England and Portugal both produce wine and cloth. In autarchy, the transformation rates of wine into cloth differ between the two countries. If we imagine that in each country we transfer the resources needed to produce a barrel of wine in that country from wine production to cloth production, we get more new cloth in England than in Portugal. If trade barriers are now removed, we will see English cloth traded for Portuguese wine and both countries will be better off. This is comparative advantage at work.

But notice that when we summarised the effect of removing trade barriers, we made two distinct claims: (1) English cloth will be traded for Portuguese wine, and (2) both countries will be better off. In the textbook example as we imagine it, and specifically with the implicit assumptions of no externalities and no regulation other than the initial trade barriers, these claims are both true; in this example they naturally go together. But in more complicated cases they can come apart.

Imagine two countries, Barataria and Pontevidro, both of which produce widgets and gadgets. In every physical, technological, and demographic respect, the economies are identical — the same climate, same resources, same technology, same sized populations with the same distribution of consumer preferences. The only technology for producing widgets generates greenhouse gases (in both countries, and to the same extent in both countries, since technology is identical). Gadget production generates no greenhouse gases. Now, despite the identicalness of the economies in all the respects mentioned, there is one difference: in the legal system. Barataria imposes a tax on the emission of greenhouse gases that correctly internalises the global-warming externality, while Pontevidro has no such tax. Now, in autarchy, the relative price of widgets will be higher in Barataria than in Pontevidro. So, if we remove trade barriers, we will see Baratarian gadgets traded for Pontevidran widgets. But does this make both countries better off? No. It cannot be that both countries are better off, because the world is worse off. There is neither gain nor loss from the fact that a certain number of widgets that used to be produced in Barataria are now produced in Pontevidro and a certain number of gadgets that used to be produced in Pontevidro are now produced in Barataria, since the technologies (including external effects) are identical in both places. But, because Baratarian consumers now have access to lower-priced Pontevidran widgets, there is more widget production overall than there was in autarchy, and hence more global warming. There was already too much widget production in autarchy, since Pontevidro was generating greenhouse gases by producing widgets for itself without taking account of the cost. But now it is even worse, because, as noted, one of the effects of opening up trade will be an increase in widget production overall.[13]

What are we to say about comparative advantage in this example, where removing barriers creates trade, but that trade makes the world worse off? In order to describe what has happened in terms of the operation of comparative advantage, we must distinguish between 'positive comparative advantage' and 'normative comparative advantage'. 'Positive comparative advantage' is just a matter of actual relative prices in the two countries in autarchy (or before the removal of some particular trade barrier we are considering removing). Positive comparative advantage is what explains trade flows when barriers are removed. In the Barataria/Pontevidro example, Pontevidro has a positive comparative advantage in widget production because of its non-taxation of greenhouse gases. In contrast, 'normative comparative advantage' reflects real

---

[13] The reader might wonder whether other benefits from trade could outweigh this disadvantage, but in this stylised example there are no genuine benefits from trade at all. If both countries properly internalised the cost of greenhouse gases (or for that matter, if neither did), then in autarchy the relative prices of widgets and gadgets would be the same in both countries, and opening up borders would have no effect. (I ignore possible externalities of scale.)

costs of production, including externalities, and it is this concept that tells us where production should be located for global efficiency. In the Barataria/Pontevidro example, even though Pontevidro has a positive comparative advantage in widget production as a result of ignoring greenhouse gases, it has no normative comparative advantage; there is no efficiency gain of any kind to be had from relocating production from what obtains in autarchy. To be sure, in our example there is also no *cost* from the mere relocation of production. The harm in our example when barriers are removed is not from the relocation of production, but from the overall increase in widget production. Still, in our example, where positive comparative advantage diverges from normative comparative advantage, allowing the trade flows called forth by positive comparative advantage is inefficient and reduces world welfare.

Our ultimate goal, remember, is to assess the claim that PPMs interfere with comparative advantage. Are we making any progress? In our Barataria/Pontevidro example as described so far, there is no PPM. The trade barriers in autarchy we assume take the form of across-the-board total embargoes on import or export; and once those barriers are removed, there are no barriers at all, therefore still no PPMs. But we can introduce a PPM. Let us imagine that, at the same time as the across-the-board embargoes are removed by both countries, Barataria imposes a tax on imports made by a production method that emits greenhouse gases, the tax being identical to Barataria's tax on domestic greenhouse gas emission. This is a PPM.[14] Furthermore, this PPM plainly interferes with *positive* comparative advantage. With the PPM in force, we will see the same difference between the relative prices of widgets and gadgets in Barataria and Pontevidro that we saw in autarchy, because the PPM still blocks the trade flows that would eliminate this difference; removing the PPM (while leaving the domestic tax in place) would induce trade flows.[15] But this PPM does not interfere with *normative* comparative advantage, because as we have seen, Pontevidro has no normative comparative advantage. The PPM merely puts Pontevidran and Baratarian

---

[14] It may occur to the reader that in this particular example, Barataria could get the same effect by eliminating its tax on emission of greenhouse gases entirely and imposing an origin-neutral internal tax on the sale of widgets. But this observation in no way undermines the appropriateness of using the case where the tax takes the form of a domestic process tax and a PPM for thinking about the effects of PPMs.

[15] If Barataria removed both the PPM and the internal tax, we would see no trade flows. Widget production would rise in Barataria and gadget production would fall, but after that adjustment, there would be no impetus to cross-border trade.

producers on the same footing. Removing the PPM would allow Pontevidran producers to exploit a positive difference between the legal systems of the countries, for which there is no normative justification. Removing the PPM would make the world worse off by inducing excessive widget production.

What is the upshot for the claim that PPMs interfere with comparative advantage? I am prepared to concede for present purposes that PPMs (assuming they bind at all) always interfere with positive comparative advantage.[16] But our hypothetical case is a counter-example to the claim that PPMs always interfere with normative comparative advantage. In our hypothetical case, the PPM does not interfere with normative comparative advantage; in fact, it increases efficiency, or reduces inefficiency, by preventing over-production of widgets beyond what occurs in autarchy. It is only the stylisation of the hypothetical case that has made possible some of the precise claims about the positive and normative consequences of various regulatory regimes; but it should be obvious that the general point I am making extends much beyond such stylised cases.

Notice that my claim is *not* that PPMs *never* interfere with normative comparative advantage. Sometimes they do — and this is true even though I always assume that the substance of any PPM is applied to domestic production as well as imports. Let us look at an example where a PPM does interfere with normative comparative advantage. We have only to change our current example in two ways. First, we assume that instead of generating greenhouse gases, widget production causes noise in the neighbourhood of the factory. Second, we assume that Pontevidrans and Baratarians have just one difference in their preferences: Baratarians are very sensitive to noise, and Pontevidrans are very insensitive. Hence Barataria, but not Pontevidro, imposes a noise abatement tax on widget production. As before, in autarchy there will be a difference in relative prices in the two countries, and removing trade barriers will induce trade flows. But in this case, the trade flows will actually make the world better off. There is a noise externality from widget production in Barataria, which the noise abatement tax internalises. There is no corresponding noise externality from widget production in Pontevidro. There is the

---

[16] This assumes that if we removed the PPM, we would leave all domestic regulation in place. If the alternative to the PPM is no PPM and the domestic tax or regulation is removed as well, then the change could move positive comparative advantage in either direction, or it could leave it unchanged. But discussion of positive effects in all cases is not my present concern.

same noise, but Pontevidrans do not mind it, so there is no externality. As a consequence, widgets really are relatively cheaper to produce in Pontevidro; the relocation of widget production to Pontevidro is a good thing, as is the increased global production of widgets that results once Baratarian consumers have access to Pontevidran widgets. In this case, if Barataria imposed a noise-based PPM that taxed on the basis of the noise level (the same as the domestic tax), it would interfere with Pontevidro's normative comparative advantage.

To summarise our conclusions thus far: The notion of 'comparative advantage' is ambiguous between positive and normative comparative advantage. Hence, the claim that PPMs interfere with comparative advantage is ambiguous between the claim that PPMs interfere with positive comparative advantage and the claim that PPMs interfere with normative comparative advantage. Even if PPMs always interfere with positive comparative advantage, that offers no ground for a general argument against PPMs, since interfering with positive comparative advantage is sometimes a good thing. In contrast, the claim that PPMs always interfere with normative comparative advantage would ground a general argument against PPMs, if it were true. But it is not.[17]

Lest the reader worry about my larger intentions, I am not recommending that the Appellate Body try to formulate all WTO law on the principle of normative comparative advantage. The task of the Appellate Body is to interpret a treaty; some parts of that treaty make sense as attempts to facilitate the operation of normative comparative advantage, and some do not. I am suggesting that when the Appellate Body is interpreting textual language that is in some respect unclear, but the basic object of which seems to be to encourage efficient regulation (as in Articles I, II, III, XI, and XX of the GATT, and the corresponding articles of the GATS, and the Agreement on the Application of Sanitary and

---

[17] It might be suggested that we can argue against PPMs in general on the grounds that *most* PPMs interfere with normative comparative advantage, and it is too much trouble, or too difficult, to distinguish between good PPMs and bad ones. So we ban them all. I am sceptical of both of the premises of this argument, but I shall not pursue the argument in this form. We should be extremely reluctant to condemn PPMs across the board if PPMs might be of significant help in addressing one of the greatest problems the world faces, namely global warming. If need be, I would separate out PPMs dealing with greenhouse gases and other climate related issues as a special category and, without regard to how we treat other PPMs, worry specifically about whether these climate related PPMs interfere with normative comparative advantage, and how we can tell, even if that requires investing more effort into making the required distinctions than would be worthwhile in connection with other PPMs. But I am not persuaded that is necessary.

Phytosanitary Measures (SPS) and TBT), then we would hope the Appellate Body would be influenced in its interpretation by correct views on how certain sorts of measure are connected in principle to efficiency. I should also say that I am not offering here a complete theory of normative comparative advantage. My reasons for not doing so are connected to the existence of the deep puzzles I mentioned earlier about the justification of the most-favoured-nation principle. I hope that the claims about normative comparative advantage that I have made in connection with particular examples can be accepted on their own, without a comprehensive theory.

Before going on, let me make some remarks about the 'level playing field' metaphor and about the use of the word 'distortion'. A standard argument against PPMs is that they interfere with comparative advantage, and I have explained why that is a misleading over-generalisation. A standard argument *in favour of* PPMs is that they are required to 'level the playing field' on which domestic and foreign producers compete. This is a precisely complementary and equally misleading over-generalisation. (Ironically, since many people see the fallacy in this argument *for* PPMs, that may encourage the overbroad rejection of PPMs.) Sometimes we should 'level the playing field', specifically when the disfavoured process creates the same externality when used in the foreign country that it creates when used at home (as in our greenhouse gas emission case). In this case, correcting for the externality in connection with domestic but not foreign production is both inefficient and 'unfair' to domestic producers. In contrast, if the disfavoured process does not create the same externality when used in the foreign country as it creates when used at home (as in the noise abatement case), then the playing field should not be levelled. Production ought to occur where it generates less social cost, and 'levelling the playing field' with a PPM will interfere with that. Nor is it 'unfair' to domestic producers that they should be charged for a social cost they impose, while their foreign competitors using the same process are not similarly charged because in context they do not impose a similar cost. In sum, we should 'level the playing field' precisely when a PPM does *not* interfere with the operation of normative comparative advantage but rather facilitates it; and we should *not* 'level the playing field' when a PPM *would* interfere with the operation of normative comparative advantage. Complementary overgeneralisations, as I said.

As to 'distortion', all that needs to be done is to point out that it is ambiguous in the same way as 'comparative advantage'. When it is claimed that a measure 'distorts' trade, it is natural to take this as a normative claim that the measure interferes with efficiency and is therefore bad; 'distort' in ordinary speech carries a negative normative connotation. But all too often people claim some measure distorts trade simply on the ground that it alters trade flows. This positive claim, even if true, does not entail any normative claim of inefficiency. Unfortunately, it strongly connotes such a claim; and I think people who speak carelessly about distortion often mislead not only their audience but themselves.

## IV.   PPMs, externalities, and 'coercion'

Let us now press forward again with the discussion of PPMs and comparative advantage. (Hereafter, by 'comparative advantage', I shall mean *normative* comparative advantage unless the context indicates otherwise.) The lesson we learn from comparing the greenhouse gas example with the noise abatement example is that, at least in this sort of case, whether a PPM interferes with the operation of comparative advantage or supports it depends on whether the targeted process creates an externality when it is used in the exporting country. This raises the question of what counts as an externality. I assume most of my readers would agree that greenhouse gas emission is an externality, whether the emitting country cares about the climate consequences (or even welcomes them) or not, but perhaps I am over-optimistic. In any event, it will be conducive to our general understanding if we consider briefly the question of the status of PPMs when there is disagreement, even reasonable disagreement, about the significance of the 'external' effects of the targeted process.

Take the case of tuna fishing using methods that kill dolphins. I assume the relevant species of dolphin is not endangered. Aside from the question of species preservation, some countries, such as the United States, regard it as morally offensive to kill such intelligent animals. They want the dolphins to live. Some countries (let us say Pontevidro again, to remain hypothetical) have no such feelings about dolphins. Suppose the United States enacts a law forbidding its domestic tuna fleet from using certain methods particularly dangerous to dolphins; and suppose it then adopts a PPM that excludes imports of tuna from other countries unless it has been fished by methods as dolphin friendly as those allowed US fishermen. Is this PPM defensible on my earlier analysis or not? Does the use of dolphin-unfriendly fishing techniques by the Pontevidran fleet impose an externality?

I have heard people argue that because of the disagreement about the importance of not killing dolphins, we cannot say on any objective grounds whether there is an externality here. (There is no disagreement, I assume, about what fishing methods kill dolphins at what rate. The disagreement is about whether that matters.) I have heard other people argue that there is definitely *not* an externality from dolphin-unfriendly fishing by the Pontevidran fleet, because *Pontevidro* does not value dolphins. Both of these claims are wrong. There is an externality here, in the sense that is relevant to thinking about efficiency. If the killing of dolphins by Pontevidran fishermen makes Americans unhappy, that is a genuine cost of such killing, and it is one the Pontevidran fishermen do not take into account. If this cost is not somehow internalised, Pontevidran fishermen will kill more dolphins than is efficient. That there is an externality here is simply not subject to doubt.

But notice I have said nothing as yet about how the cost to American sensibilities should be internalised. I think many people resist the claim that there is an externality in this case because they have in the back of their minds the 'polluter pays principle', or a broader analogous principle that says the 'active agent' causing an externality should pay, or be stopped, or at least be discouraged. But of course, the cost could equally be internalised if the United States offered to pay Pontevidran fishermen for not killing dolphins. And if we imagine for the moment that the US view about dolphins is thoroughly idiosyncratic, it may well seem that fairness requires that the cost should be internalised by the United States bribing Pontevidro to stop killing dolphins (or providing them with dolphin-safe technology, or whatever), rather than by Pontevidro being coerced by a PPM to stop killing them.

There is something in this claim that the United States should pay; but it should not seem completely right either. The specific measure the United States is proposing amounts to no more than a refusal to buy tuna that has been fished at the expense of dolphins' lives. Such a refusal to buy is not normally seen as 'coercion'. If I decide to switch from my old lawn-mowing service to a new one because the new one uses ethanol from sugar as a fuel for its mowers, I am not 'coercing' my old service to change their fuel, not even if I am such an important customer that they do in fact change their fuel to keep my business. A decision not to buy what one does not want is not 'coercion' of the seller; it is part of the normal operation of a market economy. And the United States imposing a PPM (*product-based*, remember) on Pontevidran tuna is just an instance of a consumer (now a 'collective' consumer) not buying what he (or it) does not want. For the reader who is troubled by this reference to a 'collective' consumer, I shall say more about that in a moment. But first, notice how limited, at least formally speaking, is the effect on Pontevidran fishermen of the US decision not to buy.

There is a great deal of Pontevidro's behaviour that the United States cannot hope to touch by a (product-based) PPM — for example, Pontevidro's catching some tuna by dolphin-unfriendly methods and exporting that tuna to third countries that do not care about dolphins. Even this behaviour imposes an externality on the United States. Again, that there is an externality should be uncontroversial. But even though there is an externality, we are not at all inclined to appeal to the notion that the active agent behind the externality should be made to stop, given our assumption that the US position is idiosyncratic. Rather, this is a case where we think the United States should get relief only if it is willing to pay Pontevidro to change its ways. But even if the United States should have to pay Pontevidro if it wants to change the way Pontevidro catches tuna for third-country markets (or its home market), it still seems that the United States should be free to refuse to buy *for itself* a product (dolphin-unfriendly tuna) that it does not want. This is not 'active agent pays', which is unacceptable as a general principle in the present circumstances. This, as I have said, is just the operation of the market.

Returning now to the 'collective consumer' issue, there are two differences that may seem significant between the US regulation on tuna and my decision about the lawn-mowing service. First, the United States definitely is coercing those consumers in the United States who do not care about dolphins and would like to buy cheaper tuna. But governments coerce their own citizens all the time; and they are justified in coercing them to prevent them from imposing externalities on their fellow citizens, as dolphin-indifferent consumers of tuna do on their fellow citizens who like dolphins (because purchases of dolphin-unfriendly tuna encourage dolphin mortality).[18] There may be some limits to this 'externality-preventing' justification; there may be some individual behaviour that a government is not justified in preventing solely on the ground that it makes others unhappy. But consuming dolphin-unfriendly tuna is not such behaviour. This is paradigmatically the sort of case where a government can regulate behaviour on pure

---

[18]  When dolphin-unfriendly tuna is purchased, then in the normal course of events, the retailer, wholesaler, distributor, and importer will resupply along the same supply chain, which means more dolphin-unfriendly tuna will be fished.

preference-maximising grounds. So this *internal* coercion is not a problem. And as to the Pontevidran fishermen, there is no coercion at all, merely the United States announcing what sort of tuna it wants to buy once all affected domestic interests are brought to bear on the consumption decision.[19]

Second, we might worry that the United States as a huge collective consumer has a degree of market power that an individual consumer almost never has, and that its ban on dolphin-unfriendly tuna may constitute exploitation of that market power. But we need to exercise the same kind of care in connection with the word 'exploitation' that I have already discussed in connection with 'comparative advantage' and 'distortion'. The United States is a huge presence in international trade. Consequently, a US PPM on tuna is likely to have a significant effect on foreign tuna fishermen, who may face a choice between changing their technology, which they may not have the capital to do, or losing market share. But we should not call this 'exploitation' of the US market power, which has a strong normative connotation of disapproval, unless it leads to inefficiency. Even if we think decency requires the United States to provide assistance to Pontevidran fishermen if they are in fact too poor to invest on their own in new fishing technology (the cost of which would presumably be mostly recouped in higher prices), still that is a matter of the particular circumstances of these fishermen. It is not a consequence of any general principles concerning the use of PPMs, principles which must govern relations between countries of all different relative sizes and

---

[19] The references in the text to preference maximisation and considering all affected domestic interests might seem to suggest that the US Government ought to consider the preferences of not only its own citizens, but also the Pontevidran fishermen. But as I have explained elsewhere, when the effects on Pontevidrans are market mediated, as they are here (that is, when the effects flow only from the terms on which someone is willing to engage in a market transaction with the Pontevidrans), efficiency does not require that they be considered by the United States. Donald Regan, 'What are trade agreements for? — two conflicting stories told by economists, with a lesson for lawyers', *Journal of International Economic Law* 9 (2006), 951–88. Remember the lawn-service example. Efficiency does not require that when I decide on what lawn service to use, I consider the interests of the lawn-service owners. Rather, I consult my own interests in deciding what I want to buy at what price; they consult their interests in deciding what to offer at what price; and (in the absence of monopolistic or monopsonistic behaviour) efficiency results. Notice that the external effects *within* the United States — the effect of Jones's purchase of dolphin-unfriendly tuna on Smith's sensibilities — are not market mediated. They flow from Jones's market behaviour, but as between Jones and Smith, they flow without any market relationship between them. That is why government intervention is required to achieve efficiency.

developmental levels. The claim that *in general* the user of a PPM should compensate affected exporters for their loss has no more moral or economic justification than Saudi Arabia's claim that it should be compensated if the other countries of the world succeed in reducing their demand for oil.

With regard to the question of whether the US PPM, in conjunction with the US market power, actually does lead to inefficiency, the answer is, 'No, not unless the United States is *purposefully* aiming at effects that it can achieve only because of its market power.' The full purport of that answer will hardly be immediately obvious; I have explained it and justified it at length elsewhere.[20] The crucial points for now are: (1) the mere fact that the US behaviour has certain *effects* because of the US market power that it would not have otherwise is *not* enough to cause inefficiency or to justify us in complaining of exploitation of market power; and (2) in the thumbnail sketch of the US motives for the PPM that I have given, there is nothing to suggest exploitation of market power or inefficiency (nor would there be even if the PPM were partly consciously motivated by a desire to 'level the playing field' for US fishermen, provided the concern for dolphins is genuine).

Perhaps a thought experiment will make it more intuitive that the PPM does not exploit the US market power. The reason we need a PPM (specifically, a PPM that goes beyond the provision of information to consumers) is that the class of people who consume tuna and the class of people who care about dolphins are not the same. Imagine for the moment that we hold the overall national profile of preferences over tuna prices and dolphin mortality constant, but we redistribute some of the preferences between individuals, so that the people who eat tuna and the people who care about dolphins are now the same. Now, assuming consumers have the means to distinguish dolphin-friendly tuna from dolphin-unfriendly tuna, we would see no purchases of dolphin-unfriendly tuna, even without any government regulation. But no one could claim that the purely private choices of all these consumers to reject dolphin-unfriendly tuna would count as the exploitation of market power or would create inefficiency. Returning now to the world of preferences as they are actually distributed, the function of the PPM in this world is simply to bring all relevant domestic preferences to bear on choices about tuna, just as happens in our imagined world of redistributed preferences without government intervention. So the PPM in the actual world is not exploitive either.

---

[20] *Ibid.*

Changing the topic somewhat, there is another reason PPMs are often thought of as 'coercive'. They are often assumed to be aimed at altering exporting countries' internal policies regarding production, a goal which is suspect. Now, it is true that PPMs *may* be aimed at altering other countries' internal policies. But this is not a necessary feature — certainly not of product-based PPMs, and in fact not even of country-based PPMs. With regard to product-based PPMs, the United States could quite sensibly maintain its ban on dolphin-hostile tuna even it were perfectly clear that Pontevidro would not change its national policy in response to the PPM, and in fact that no individual Pontevidran fisherman would change his behaviour. The United States might like to see such changes, but if it knows they are not going to happen, then bringing them about cannot be a part of its goal. Its goal, still fully adequate to explain the PPM, is just to minimise the demand for (and thus the production of) dolphin-hostile tuna, and perhaps also to avoid its own complicity in dolphin mortality.

The case might seem to be different with regard to country-based PPMs, since the importer may now exclude some shipments of dolphin-*friendly* tuna originating in the non-complying country. But even this might be justified (even if it is known that Pontevidro will not change its policy) as a means of reducing overall demand for dolphin-hostile tuna. Purchases by the United States of dolphin-friendly Pontevidran tuna might still increase the fishing of dolphin-hostile tuna if Pontevidran fishermen redirect to the US market dolphin-friendly tuna that they would have caught anyway and sold to dolphin-indifferent consumers, and if they then replace the redirected quantity with newly caught dolphin-hostile tuna. Once we start down this road, we will eventually realise that even the United States consuming its own fishermen's dolphin-friendly tuna may have the ultimate consequence that more tuna is taken by dolphin-hostile methods by fishermen of other countries. But it would be a mistake to treat the US failure to go all the way to the end of this line (which may also not be necessary, depending on the economic facts) as definitively revealing that a country-based PPM must be in bad faith (that is, must have a coercive or protectionist purpose). There are good reasons to be more suspicious of country-based PPMs than of product-based PPMs, but that is not to say that country-based PPMs are necessarily aimed at changing exporting countries' policies, nor that they are always illegal.

It seems possible that one of the reasons the Appellate Body's opinion in *US — Shrimp* was so unpopular is that the Appellate Body seemed willing to uphold some PPMs despite regarding all PPMs as intrinsically coercive. To my mind, it is not at all clear what the Appellate Body is actually saying about a whole tangle of issues concerning coerciveness, the purpose behind PPMs, and the relevance of the distinction between country-based and product-based PPMs (specifically, whether it was essential to the legality of the revised US PPM that it provided for shipment-by-shipment certification of shrimp from non-certified countries). I do not have space here for anything like a complete discussion. But in paragraph 161 and paragraph 165 the Appellate Body makes it very clear that it regards the unrevised PPM as coercive (it refers in paragraph 161 to the measure's 'intended and actual coercive effect', and it says in paragraph 165 that the measure is 'concerned with effectively influencing' other members' policies). And yet, the Appellate Body seems to object not to the coerciveness in itself, but to the particular goal of making other countries adopt turtle protection programmes identical to that of the United States, even where such measures were not necessary. And back in paragraph 121, the Appellate Body had said that 'conditioning access to a Member's domestic market on whether exporting Members comply with, or adopt, a policy or policies unilaterally prescribed by the importing Member may, to some degree, be a common aspect of measures falling within the scope of one or another of the exceptions (a) to (j) of Article XX'.

Now, 'conditioning access to a Member's domestic market on whether exporting Members comply with, or adopt, a policy' is not logically equivalent to trying to coerce them into adopting that policy; as we have noted, the importing Member might impose the condition on imports even though it knows no change in the exporting member's policy will result. But in conjunction with the later discussion that finds coercion in the US measure, it almost seems as if the Appellate Body is saying coercion is a common aspect of all measures falling within Article XX of the GATT.

The water is further muddied by the fact that it is not even true that conditioning access on the exporting member's policy is a common element of all measures that fall within Article XX (not even if we include cases where the conditioning does not amount to coercion). The measure by France in *Asbestos* that the Appellate Body upheld under Article XX (after also finding that it did not violate Article III) said nothing about Canada's policies.[21] It merely excluded asbestos and asbestos products, without regard to the country of origin or that country's policies.

---

[21]  *EC — Measures Affecting Asbestos and Asbestos-Containing Products*, WT/DS135/AB/R (adopted 5 April 2001).

The Appellate Body's seeming desire to defend coercion may reflect the tendency of exporting members to complain that any measure that excludes any of their products is 'coercive'. The Appellate Body is right, of course, that on this understanding of 'coercion' many coercive measures will pass Article XX. Indeed, on this understanding, many coercive measures should never even get to Article XX, because they will pass review under Article III. But this is not a reasonable understanding of 'coercion'. The Appellate Body should not indulge it or encourage it.

Given the general confusion about PPMs, the Appellate Body should not write opinions that reinforce the view that all PPMs are coercive, or that PPMs have any special affinity with coercion.

## V.    Three fragments of legal analysis

As noted above, I do not propose to go step by step through all possible lines of legal analysis of emission-based import restrictions; for the most part, that would merely repeat what others have said. I do want to make three quick points that I do not think duplicate what can be found elsewhere. All three points concern the question of whether PPMs violate the primary prohibitory provisions of the GATT, in particular Articles II and III. Of course, even if PPMs do violate the primary prohibitory provisions, they may be justified under Article XX of the GATT, like the import restriction in *Shrimp*. Some people think the Article XX issues are the only ones worth discussing, on the grounds that the Appellate Body will always find a PPM in violation of some primary prohibitory provision. But I shall say nothing here about Article XX; even if it ends up being the crucial provision, the basic framework for legal analysis under Article XX is reasonably clear.[22] Also, I am not persuaded that Article XX is the only provision in play. That PPMs are always prima facie illegal is certainly the conventional wisdom. But then, it was conventional wisdom before *Shrimp* that PPMs were not only prima facie illegal, but also unconditionally unjustifiable under Article XX. That conventional wisdom was overthrown in *Shrimp* when the Appellate Body simply applied

---

[22] What is clear is the *framework*. There will be excruciatingly difficult questions about the application to the facts of particular ideas: whether the restrictions on domestic and foreign production are comparable in the way that Article XX(g) implicitly requires, or whether some measure is 'unjustifiable discrimination', and in particular, how to apply in a very different context the basic idea of *Shrimp* that a measure must not require technology that is unnecessary in the exporter's circumstances. But to my mind there is little to be said about these issues until we have a concrete measure before us.

the treaty language. Since I think the treaty language also indicates that some PPMs are not even prima facie illegal, I have hopes that the Appellate Body may eventually confirm that as well. (Notice the Appellate Body has not yet considered a *product-based* PPM under Article II or III.) Since respondent members will obviously prefer to have their PPMs upheld at this very first stage, for burden of proof reasons if no others, the possibility is worth discussing. Along with Rob Howse, I have argued elsewhere that PPMs (*product-based* PPMs, remember) do not automatically violate Article III.[23] I shall not repeat what I have said already. These three new 'fragments' of legal analysis can be fitted into the general scheme Howse and I have developed.

### Fragment (1): a hypothetical case

Here I simply want to describe a hypothetical PPM that it seems to me we *must* conclude does not violate Article III; it cannot be justified under Article XX, because of the closed list of purposes, and yet it seems to me inconceivable that the drafters of the GATT would have wanted to forbid it. Here is the scenario: Home has an industry that produces widgets by a process that emits noxious odours affecting a substantial region around the factories. Home does not import widgets. As a result of political organisation by residents of the area around the widget plants, Home adopts a regulation forbidding the use of the odour-emitting process for widget production, and the producers switch to a more expensive, but less offensive process. At this point it becomes possible for foreign widget producers, who still use the cheaper, odour-emitting process, to export widgets to Home. As it happens, Foreign's widget factories are right on the Home/Foreign border; and it even happens that prevailing winds are such that the odour from the Foreign plants affects only residents of Home. So the residents of the border region combine with Home widget producers to secure a PPM, forbidding the sale in Home of widgets made with the odour-emitting process.

Now, I cannot believe that the drafters of the GATT would have wanted to forbid this PPM. It is both efficient and fair: the Foreign widget producers are generating an externality in Home; they have no *normative* comparative advantage over Home widget producers; the history of the

---

[23] R. Howse and D. Regan, 'The product/process distinction — an illusory basis for disciplining "unilateralism" in trade policy', *European Journal of International Law* 11 (2000), 249–89.

PPM makes it clear that Home's concern with the odour is not a mere excuse for protectionism; and all Home is doing is trying to avoid causing harm to itself by its own widget purchases. But is this PPM allowed by the GATT as it stands? If we take the legal issues out of order and ask whether this PPM can be justified under Article XX, it seems very doubtful that it can. There are no known health effects (on humans, animals, or plants) associated with the odours. The only way to bring this within Article XX would be to find that 'odour-free air' is an exhaustible natural resource. But if we add the plausible assumption that the odour dissipates entirely within twenty-four hours if the source is not continuously renewed, then to say this PPM was protecting an 'exhaustible natural resource' would be to give up completely on 'ordinary meaning in context'. It would make a mockery of the specific listing in Article XX. Much better to say that the PPM does not violate Article III (which is the relevant provision, because of the Note *Ad* III) in the first place. After all, this PPM has nothing to do with protectionism, which is what Article III is aimed at. In sum, we cannot plausibly claim that PPMs always violate Article III. This case is a counter-example.

## Fragment (2): the relevance of regulatory purpose

Here I may be cheating a bit. I have said a great deal elsewhere about the role of regulatory purpose under Article III of the GATT.[24] But I have not done so since the Appellate Body decided *Dominican Republic — Cigarettes*,[25] and in any event there are always new readers. Once we have decided that PPMs do not automatically violate Article III, it is inevitable that the issue will arise, in connection with PPMs, of the relevance of regulatory purpose. The conventional wisdom is that the Appellate Body has definitively rejected consideration of regulatory purpose. But the conventional wisdom is wrong, not just about the best reading of the treaty, but about what the Appellate Body has actually done. So, very briefly:

---

[24] D. Regan, 'Regulatory purpose and "like products" in Article III:4 of the GATT (with additional remarks on Article III:2)', *Journal of World Trade* 36 (2002), 443–78, and 'Further thoughts on the role of regulatory purpose under Article III of the General Agreement on Tariffs and Trade — a tribute to Bob Hudec', *Journal of World Trade* 37 (2003), 737–60.

[25] *Dominican Republic — Measures Affecting the Importation and Internal Sale of Cigarettes*, WT/DS302/AB/R (adopted 19 May 2005).

It is unfortunate that the two 'leading' cases about Article III are *Japan — Alcohol*[26] and *EC — Asbestos*.[27] Both cases tend to mislead readers about the Appellate Body's actual views and behaviour. (The focus on these cases is understandable, because of the timing of *Japan* and the anticipation that preceded *Asbestos*, but it is still unfortunate.) In *Japan — Alcohol*, the Appellate Body denied any interest in the subjective intentions of legislators, and people took this to mean that the Appellate Body was denying the relevance of regulatory purpose. But in *Chile — Alcohol*, which people somehow read without actually noticing what it says, the Appellate Body says explicitly, and more than once, that consideration of regulatory purpose is essential.[28] Indeed, it says *explicitly* that ascertaining regulatory purpose was the *precise point* of looking at the 'design, architecture, and structure' of the measure in *Japan*.[29] On the issue of regulatory purpose, *Chile* plainly overturns the conventional wisdom about *Japan*. It does not overturn *Japan*, since *Japan* never denied the relevance of purpose in the first place.

With regard to *Asbestos*, the Appellate Body seems to imply that regulatory purpose is not relevant to 'likeness' by its focus on the criteria in the Border Tax Adjustment Report, especially consumer preferences. But in finding asbestos and PCG fibres unlike, the Appellate Body is so bizarrely indifferent to the actual facts of consumers' revealed preferences that one wonders how seriously to take their analysis. In any event, they emphasise in the Delphic paragraph 100 that a finding of likeness is not the end of the matter, and they at least leave room for regulatory purpose to be relevant to the issue of 'less favourable treatment' for foreign goods. They say that there is less favourable treatment only if the 'group' of like imported products is treated less favourably than the 'group' of like domestic products. To my mind, the most plausible reading of this, although not the only one, is that there is less favourable treatment only if foreign products are disfavoured *because they are*

[26] *Japan — Taxes on Alcoholic Beverages*, WT/DS8 & DS10 & DS11/AB/R (adopted 1 November 1996).
[27] *EC — Measures Affecting Asbestos and Asbestos-Containing Products*, WT/DS135/AB/R (adopted 5 April 2001).
[28] *Chile — Taxes on Alcoholic Beverages*, WT/DS87 & DS110/AB/R (adopted 12 January 2000), paragraphs 62, 71.
[29] *Ibid.*, paragraph 71. The reader may remember that the *Chile* report talks about ascertaining 'objective' purpose; lest one think this means the Appellate Body will look at nothing but the face of the measure, elsewhere in the *Chile* opinion, the Appellate Body considers Chile's proffered non-protectionist explanations for its tax scheme, although it finds none of them persuasive.

*foreign*. And then in *DR — Cigarettes*, they come even closer to asserting explicitly the relevance of regulatory purpose: '[T]he existence of a detrimental effect on a given imported product resulting from a measure does not necessarily imply that this measure accords less favourable treatment to imports if the detrimental effect is explained by factors or circumstances unrelated to the foreign origin of the product, such as the market share of the importer in this case.'[30] This is not quite an explicit endorsement of consideration of purpose, but the only way to make sense of the reference to 'explanation' is in terms of regulatory purpose.[31] Certainly this statement gives the lie to any claim that consideration of purpose has been definitively excluded.

### Fragment (3): avoiding border tax issues

Although much ink has been spilled about how emissions-based taxes would fare under the border tax provisions of the GATT, in particular Article II.2(a), it seems to me we may be able to sidestep II:2(a) entirely. The Note *Ad* III has been most often discussed in connection with regulations and the relation between Articles III and XI, but it applies also to taxes and charges, and thus to the relation between Articles III and II; it is a 'border tax adjustment' principle in itself. Suppose we consider a measure that says in more precise terms something like: 'No widget may be sold, used, or consumed in this country unless taxes have been paid [to any government, here or abroad] [or other payments have been made to purchase emission permits] in connection with its production [and not remitted] that reflect the carbon emissions in its production history.' It is not entirely clear whether this is a regulation or a tax; perhaps it is a regulation in respect of widgets on which the relevant taxes have been previously paid, and a tax in respect of widgets on which they have not. But insofar as it is a tax, it seems to be a tax that 'applies to the product' (the relevant language of the Note *Ad* III), even though the amount payable depends on earlier taxes levied during the production process. So the tax should be reviewed under Article III. This avoids entirely the issues under Article II:2(a) concerning what counts as 'an article from which the imported product has been manufactured or produced in

---

[30] *DR — Cigarettes*, n. 25 above, paragraph 96.
[31] If we knew nothing of the jurisprudential context, we might take this quote from *Cigarettes* as saying that only origin-specific regulation is illegal under Article III. But we know that cannot be what it means.

whole or in part'. It might be suggested that this reading of the Note *Ad* III renders Article II.2(a) inutile. I have no space here for a full discussion, but here are two quick responses. First, we should be cautious with arguments from inutility, remembering that some redundancy is both inevitable and even desirable in most legislation. Second, Article II.2(a) retains a distinct function, even given the suggested reading of the Note *Ad* III, in authorising taxes in a *form* that would otherwise be unacceptable; in particular, a tax levied on imported gadgets at the border that compensates for an internal tax on some input physically incorporated into the imported gadgets, where there is no internal tax on gadgets themselves at all.

## VI.   Conclusion

Climate change is one of the most pressing, but also one of the most divisive, problems facing the world today. It is hardly surprising that it should threaten to create very divisive problems in the WTO. It is sometimes suggested that allowing unilateral emissions-based import restrictions might cause the collapse of the world trading system. And so it might. The converse possibility is not so often mentioned, but it also seems to me possible that, unless we achieve some multilateral solution to the climate change problem, trying to *forbid* unilateral emissions-based import restrictions might also cause the collapse of the world trading system. A country that is doing its part to reduce emissions will not be content to purchase high-emissions products from countries that are not doing their part, thus damaging both its producers and the climate. If its import restrictions are held to be WTO illegal, it may be unwilling either to change its regulations or simply to swallow the sanctions, as the EU was willing to do for a time in connection with *Hormones*. If the trading system is endangered either way — and I fear it may be — trying to figure out the 'right' legal solution to the PPM problem may be a waste of time in this context. We must have a multilateral climate agreement. But just in case it matters, I have tried to make it more likely that readers will think clearly about PPMs and get the right answers to the legal questions.

# 6

# Tilting at conventional WTO wisdom[1]

DANIEL C. CROSBY

## I.  Rebel without a cause?

Contemporary wisdom under the General Agreement on Tariffs and Trade (GATT) holds that physically identical products are 'like' for national treatment purposes, regardless of the climate change implications of their process and production methods (PPMs) including $CO_2$ emissions during production.[2] In his paper Professor Regan challenges the prevailing interpretation of World Trade Organization (WTO) law, and holds the truth to be self-evident that all products are *not* created equal, but are endowed by their creators with certain inalienable characteristics that can render them unlike otherwise identical products. He has further suggested that identical products are not like if treating them differently is justified by some non-protectionist purpose the regulator is pursuing. Professor Regan posits that conventional wisdom on PPMs has no basis in GATT/WTO treaty text and is not settled in jurisprudence. The goal of his paper is to change the mind-set of trade lawyers on this issue.

---

[1]  Comments on Donald Regan's paper on PPMs and climate change.

[2]  Although the text of Article III is ambiguous and the GATT product-process doctrine is not altogether coherent, this doctrine has been clarified with time and appears to be 'resting comfortably' in WTO jurisprudence. See R. E. Hudec, 'The Product-Process Doctrine in GATT/WTO Jurisprudence', in M. Bronckers and R. Quick (eds.), *New Directions in International Economic Law: Essays in Honour of John H. Jackson* (The Hague: Kluwer Law International, 2000), pp. 187–9 ('To be sure, the fact that six (or seven) panels have agreed with the product-process doctrine is a pretty strong indication of wide acceptability. In addition, a majority of the legal scholars who have written about the product-process doctrine recently, most of whom oppose the doctrine on (environmental) policy grounds, have assumed that it is settled in GATT/WTO law.'); and see S. Charnovitz, 'The law of environmental "PPMs" in the WTO: debunking the myth of illegality', *Yale Journal of International Law* 27 (2002), 91 (hereinafter Charnovitz) ('[T]he textual ambiguities in Article III have been resolved unfavorably to PPMs … WTO jurisprudence points to the likelihood that [a how-produced] standard would be deemed a national treatment violation.')

In terms of WTO law and practice, Professor Regan is calling for nothing less than revolution against the settled view that general GATT rules apply to 'products as products' and not to non-product-related PPMs. He raises the alarm that the (extra-systemic) dangers of disallowing PPMs are huge and has suggested that its is hard to think of an area in which trade rules, if enforced to prevent national regulation, could have greater worldwide cost.

This warning appears to exaggerate the WTO threat to PPMs, and to foment rebellion without an articulated cause, given that the WTO Appellate Body has established that Members may apply PPMs, even unilaterally, as long as they follow guidelines to satisfy the environmental exceptions to GATT rules.[3] Since existing rules can adequately accommodate climate change PPMs, is Professor Regan tilting at a non-issue?

## II.   Systemic considerations

### A.   Unilateral approach to externalities

Professor Regan has proposed that since externalities are in the eye of the beholder, the question of how or whether externalities should be internalised must be resolved in favour of the country purporting the existence of an externality (even based on idiosyncratic sensitivities). According to Professor Regan, it is 'simply not subject to doubt' that an externality arises '[i]f the killing of dolphins by [a member's] fishermen makes Americans unhappy', and leads fishermen to 'kill more dolphins than is efficient' (according to the standards dictated unilaterally by US law). This approach gives rise to a new and troublesome concept: 'Trade and ... happiness' — in this case in the eye of the American beholder. But what of the 'happiness' of fishermen in developing countries whose priorities (e.g. basic shelter, healthcare and education) may not match the priorities of wealthier friends of dolphins? The Regan revolution would 'legalise' such unilateralism and therefore

---

[3] Professor Regan's warning seems to perpetuate the 'pervasive myth ... that the WTO forbids PPMs'. See Charnovitz, above n. 2, at 63. Of course, Members must remain vigilant in monitoring the application of the exceptions to GATT rules and must be prepared to revisit and reassess conventional wisdom when demonstrably necessary to accommodate climate change imperatives. See e.g. application of Article XX in panel report, *European Communities — Measures Affecting the Approval and Marketing of Biotech Products*, WT/DS291/R, WT/DS292/R, WT/DS293/R, Corr.1 and Add.1, 2, 3, 4, 5, 6, 7, 8 and 9, adopted 21 November 2006.

allow members to decide when subjectively 'unlike' products will be subject to less favourable treatment. To say nothing of the economic and legal fallout, it seems impossible to reconcile this unilateral approach with our multilateral trading system.[4]

## B.   Coercive PPMs

Professor Regan expresses the view that a US unilateral PPM prohibiting the importation of dolphin-unfriendly tuna 'hardly sounds like coercion in the ordinary sense'. The legal dictionary definition of 'coercion' includes both 'direct' and 'legal, implied or constructive [coercion], as where one party is restrained by subjugation to other to do what his free will would refuse'.[5] Thailand's complaint in the *US — Shrimp* case exactly reflects this definition: Thai fishermen used turtle excluder devices (TEDs) 'largely due to the effectiveness of US *coercion* applied through the trade measure in dispute in this case' and that TEDs 'would not continue to be required in the absence of [US law] and the consequences of abandoning TEDs use for Thailand's exports to the United States'.[6] Such PPMs are certainly 'coercive in the ordinary sense,' and since they are not reconcilable with general multilateral trade rules, they should be dealt with under agreed *exceptions* to GATT rules.

---

[4] See concluding remarks of the *Shrimp* compliance panel: 'The best way for the parties to this dispute to contribute effectively to the protection of sea turtles in a manner consistent with WTO objectives, including sustainable development, would be to reach cooperative agreements on integrated conservation strategies.' Panel report, *United States — Import Prohibition of Certain Shrimp and Shrimp Products — Recourse to Article 21.5 of the DSU by Malaysia*, WT/DS58/RW, adopted 21 November 2001, upheld by Appellate Body report, WT/DS58/AB/RW, DSR 2001:XIII, 6529 (*US — Shrimp Compliance Proceedings*) at paragraph 7.1; and see 1996 Report of the Committee on Trade and Environment (WT/CTE/1, 12 November 1996), paragraph 169 ('WTO Member governments are committed not to introduce WTO-inconsistent or protectionist trade restrictions or countervailing measures in an attempt to offset any real or perceived adverse domestic economic or competitiveness effects of applying environmental policies; not only would this undermine the open, equitable and non-discriminatory nature of the multilateral trading system, it would also prove counterproductive to meeting environmental objectives and promoting sustainable development.')

[5] *Black's Law Dictionary*, 6th edition, (St Paul, Minn.: West Publishing Co., 1990), p. 258.

[6] Panel report, *United States — Import Prohibition of Certain Shrimp and Shrimp Products*, WT/DS58/R and Corr.1, adopted 6 November 1998 (emphasis added), modified by Appellate Body report, WT/DS58/AB/R, DSR 1998:VII, 2821, paragraph 3.101 (emphasis added).

## C.   Level playing field

From the developing country perspective, the international trade 'playing field' is not level, especially as concerns measures relating to trade and the environment. Developing countries acknowledge 'common but differential responsibilities' in the trade and environment debate since 'Northern countries [have] a greater responsibility for meeting the costs of adjustment because of their larger role in environmental degradation as well as their economic capacity to absorb more costs.'[7] Developing countries also harbour deep suspicions about 'green protectionism' of developed countries. This is a major reason for trade and environment deadlock at the WTO, which the Regan revolution would further entrench, to the detriment of the environment agenda.

### III.   Economic concerns: PPMs and comparative advantage

Professor Regan acknowledges that his revolution could lead to the distortion of 'normative' comparative advantage. He illustrates the problem through the case where Barataria imposes a noise abatement tax to internalise the 'cost' of noisy widget production to Baratarians, who are sensitive to such noise. No such tax applies in Pontevidro, whose citizens are not sensitive to the noise caused by widget production. Since Pontevidran citizens do not notice the noise, no externality exists in Pontevidro, and resulting migration of widget production to Pontevidro is, according to Professor Regan, a 'good thing' that reflects 'normative' comparative advantage.

We now introduce an idiosyncratic externality: Barataria considers that Pontevidran children should be protected from noisy widget production because Baratarians are 'unhappy' that Pontevidran children

---

[7] M. Shahin, 'Trade and environment: how real is the debate?' in G. P. Sampson and W. Bradnee Chambers (eds.), *Trade, Environment, and the Millennium*, 2nd edition (Tokyo: United Nations University Press, 2002), p. 41. The *Shrimp* compliance panel cited this principle as a basis for resolving the dispute. In its concluding remarks, the compliance panel, 'urge[d] Malaysia and the United States to cooperate fully in order to conclude as soon a possible an agreement which will permit the protection and conservation of sea turtles to the satisfaction of all interests involved and taking into account the principle that States have common but differentiated responsibilities to conserve and protect the environment'. *US — Shrimp Compliance Proceedings*, above n. 4, at paragraph 7.2 (footnote omitted; citing Principle 7 of the Rio Declaration on Environment and Development, the United Nations Conference on Environment and Development, June 1992 (Rio Declaration)).

must endure such noise. Perhaps Baratarian widget producers are also 'unhappy' with the relocation of production to Pontevidro and the resulting 'unfair' import competition. Barataria therefore applies a 'non-protectionist' PPM prohibiting the importation of widgets without the payment of a noise abatement tax.

Professor Regan acknowledges that the application of this PPM would distort Pontevidro's 'normative' comparative advantage, but considers the potential for such protectionist abuse to be exaggerated. The contrary view of many experienced trade practitioners is that compliance with treaty commitments must not be entrusted to optimism or naïveté regarding governments' capacity to withstand the protectionist overtures of their constituents.[8]

The application of GATT conventional wisdom would preserve Pontevidro's 'normative' comparative advantage. Barataria's measure — allegedly aimed at saving Pontevidrian children from unnoticed noise — violates Article III in the conventional sense in so far as noise emitted during production does not affect the likeness of widgets 'as products'.[9] Since Barataria could not justify its measure under Article XX *Exceptions*, the economic benefit that Pontevidro bargained for would be preserved.

## IV. Accommodation of PPMs under WTO law

Professor Regan urges that we resist the argument that '*most* PPMs interfere with normative comparative advantage, and it is too much trouble, or too difficult, to distinguish between good PPMs and bad ones. So we ban them all.' But conventional WTO wisdom does not take a 'ban them all' approach to PPMs — quite the contrary. The thrust of Professor Regan's argument in the PPM debate misses the mark because existing WTO rules and Appellate Body rulings explicitly support the application of PPMs considered 'good' under multilaterally agreed rules. Nevertheless, Professor Regan cautions that '[w]e should be extremely reluctant to condemn PPMs across the board if PPMs might be of significant help in addressing one of the greatest problems the world faces, namely global warming'.

---

[8] Similar concerns arise with regard to Professor Regan's faith in the system's ability to identify and discipline 'regulatory purpose' as a means of evaluating the WTO consistency of environmental measures.

[9] It should be noted that Barataria might try to apply a border tax on widgets from Pontevidro consistent with Article III of the GATT.

This statement also seems to perpetuate the 'pervasive myth … that the WTO forbids PPMs'.[10] PPMs are certainly *not* condemned across the board under existing WTO jurisprudence. *Au contraire*, the Appellate Body has specifically approved environmental PPMs — even unilateral and extraterritorial measures such as those in *US — Shrimp*.[11] However, the PPMs in that case were justified under Article XX *Exceptions*, rather than found legal under a revolutionary interpretation of Article III.

Given the accommodation of PPMs under WTO jurisprudence, the rejection of the Regan revolution does *not* equal condemnation of climate change PPMs. Although Professor Regan has not mentioned GATT environmental exceptions in his paper, these exceptions should take centre stage in the climate change PPM debate. Very simply put, Article XX states that 'nothing in [the GATT] shall be construed to prevent the adoption or enforcement' of climate change PPMs, as long as such measures comply with rules and principles as clarified through WTO case law. So, even though turtle-friendly and turtle-unfriendly shrimp are conventionally treated as 'like products' for the purposes of domestic tax and regulatory measures under Article III of the GATT, and even if a regulatory ban prohibits or restricts imports of atmosphere-unfriendly steel in violation of Article XI, no GATT rule 'shall be construed to prevent' a Member from applying environment-related PPMs consistent with the agreed exceptions to WTO rules. This wisdom was built into the original legal framework for international trade, and currently provides a basis for applying climate change PPMs under WTO rules.

## V.   Conventional conclusion

The conventional GATT/WTO view of non-product-related PPMs — that they are not permitted under Article III of the GATT but justifiable under Article XX — strikes an appropriate balance between Members' rights and obligations under the WTO and reflects the view that multi-lateral solutions to climate change challenges are superior to unilateral ones.[12] In the Appellate Body's most recent statement on the subject, it

---

[10]  See Charnovitz, above n. 2, 63.
[11]  See *US — Shrimp Compliance Proceedings*, above n. 4. In the end, the Appellate Body's broad approval of environmental PPMs may well justify developing countries' concerns as to lack of discipline in this area — far from the feared condemnation across the board.
[12]  See Rio Declaration, Principle 12, above n. 7 ('[U]nilateral actions to deal with environmental challenges outside the jurisdiction of the importing country should be avoided.

confirmed that unilateral environmental measures could be justified under Article XX as long as the Member at issue satisfies the continuing requirement to engage in 'ongoing serious, good faith efforts to reach a multilateral agreement'.[13]

Prevailing GATT wisdom on PPMs has helped to maintain the credibility of the WTO with its sundry stakeholders by balancing the complex and competing interests of developing and developed countries in the trade and the environment debate. Professor Regan's Revolution would legalise environmental unilateralism and undermine the minimal multilateral discipline that conventional wisdom has engendered at the WTO. If we unnecessarily abandon conventional wisdom on PPMs, a wise balance will be cast away along with the multilateral approach to trade and environment issues. Any PPM revolution should therefore be resisted unless and until conventional wisdom proves incapable of resolving the challenges that climate change will surely continue to visit upon the WTO system.

Environmental measures addressing transboundary or global environmental problems should, as far as possible, be based on an international consensus').

[13] See *US — Shrimp Compliance Proceedings*, Appellate Body report, above n. 4, at paragraph 153.

# 7

# Private climate change standards and labelling schemes under the WTO Agreement on Technical Barriers to Trade

ARTHUR E. APPLETON[1]

## I. Introduction

Private carbon and climate change labelling schemes allow consumers to make choices based on carbon emissions over the whole or a part of a product's life cycle.[2] Carbon labels raise consumer awareness and may increase pressure on producers and companies to reduce carbon emissions. Private climate change labelling schemes are proliferating rapidly. Labels reflecting 'air miles' and 'food miles' are now part of the marketing strategy of two UK supermarkets — Marks & Spencer and Tesco.[3] Other private standardisation and labelling organisations, including the Soil Association[4]

---

[1] Arthur E. Appleton, JD, PhD is a partner at Appleton Luff — International Lawyers (Geneva). I am grateful to Marcia Aribela de Lima Gomes Pereira for valuable research assistance. Any remaining errors are my own.

[2] A life-cycle analysis is an environmental analysis of each stage in a product's life to quantify the amount of pollution generated in a product's production, transport, use and disposal.

[3] In January 2007, Marks & Spencer announced it would label air-freighted products. S. Bowers, 'M&S promises radical change with £200 m environmental action plan', *The Guardian*, 15 January 2007, http://business.guardian.co.uk/story/0,,1990338,00.html. See also D. Adam, 'Emission impossible', *The Guardian*, 25 January 2007, www.guardian.co.uk/environment/2007/jan/25/supermarkets.ethicalliving

[4] The Soil Association favours local farm products and producers and is considering whether to refuse organic certification for farm products shipped by air. The Soil Association notes that one reason to buy locally is that it 'cuts down on air miles, the least environmentally-friendly form of transport'. See www.soilassociation.org/web/sa/saweb.nsf/GetInvolved/buy.html. See also, *'Should the Soil Association Tackle the Environmental Impact of Air Freight in its Organic Standards? A Basis for Discussion'*, *Air Freight Green Paper*, May 2007, at paragraph 6.1, p. 10 (*citing* the no air-freight policy of Bio Suisse), www.localfoodworks.org/web/sa/psweb.nsf/.77080a2b4f261f0380256 a6a00485fbe/0777428074797c4280257287005ce1ec/$FILE/air_freight_green_paper.pdf

and Bio Suisse,[5] are examining or have already decided (respectively) to deny organic certification for products transported by airfreight — a carbon-intensive form of transport. This paper first discusses the policy implications of private climate change labelling schemes, then scrutinises their legality under the WTO Agreement on Technical Barriers to Trade (TBT).[6]

## II. Policy perspective

### A. Climate change standards and climate labelling: the policy dimension

Private labelling schemes are not generally based on agreed international standards. As a result, they may risk confusing consumers. The potential for consumer confusion is compounded by the fact that private labels often focus on one narrow aspect of a product's life cycle (such as transport), which may present an incorrect view of that product's overall implications for climate change, and could undermine confidence in more sophisticated carbon and climate change labelling schemes.[7] Certain problems posed by private schemes are discussed below.

#### 1. Neutrality of standards and standardisation organisations

Private labelling schemes often lack neutrality and frequently serve local commercial and protectionist interests. Both the Soil Association proposal, if enacted, and the Bio Suisse labelling scheme serve to protect local farmers. A recent article in *The Times* suggests that English agricultural producers support the Soil Association and stand to benefit most

---

[5] Bio Suisse refuses to grant organic certification to products imported by air and favours local organic farm products or farm products from neighbouring countries. See. '*Bio Suisse Standards for the Production, Processing and Marketing of Produce from Organic Farming*', 1 January 2007, at 36, paragraph 5.10.1, www.biosuisse.ch/media/en/pdf2007/import/rl_2007_e.pdf. Bio Suisse rules applicable to imports are summarised at www.biosuisse.ch/en/biosuisseimportpolicy.php. Several Bio Suisse standards have a carbon component, for example Bio Suisse standards Article 2.5 (greenhouse heating), Article 5.10 (choice of greenhouse heating system), and Article 5.10.1 (air freight). See Mat and Klimat, '*bakgrund inför KRAVs klimatseminarium*', 26 April 2007, at 26, http://arkiv.krav.se/arkiv/klimat/Klimatbakgrund070410.pdf

[6] An in-depth study of GATT obligations is beyond the scope of this paper.

[7] On 26 July 2007 the Environmental Audit Committee of the UK House of Commons established a sub-committee to examine environmental labelling, including climate labelling. See www.parliament.uk/parliamentary_committees/environmental_audit_committee/eac_260707.cfm

from trade measures that keep cheaper African organic products out of the English market and thus favour Northern farming methods that may be more greenhouse gas intensive.[8] *The Times* article also suggests that the methodology used by some to calculate food miles fails to take into consideration the full array of greenhouse gases from European producers, for example carbon emissions coming from tractors, truck transport and hothouse heating systems. Likewise, a review of Bio Suisse standards reveals that Swiss producers stand to benefit most from these standards, followed by EU and Mediterranean producers if Swiss production is insufficient.[9] Developing countries in remote regions are the likely losers.

Private supermarket schemes may also produce discriminatory results and serve special interests. Marks & Spencer labels air-freighted food products and has stated its intent to reduce food miles by increasing food purchases from UK and Irish sources.[10] Tesco has ambitious plans to lower its carbon footprint by reducing its reliance on air transport to less than 1 per cent of its products.[11] Both schemes would favour UK producers.

## 2.  Accounting considerations

Carbon labelling schemes depend upon an assessment of carbon in some or all of a product's life cycle. This is a new form of accounting without a generally accepted methodology. A recent article in *The Guardian* points out that carbon accounting procedures are not straightforward, and notes Tesco's admission that it has no idea how 'to include indirect greenhouse emissions given off during [a product's] production and processing'.[12]

Many questions exist with respect to carbon accounting. In theory, precise carbon accounting would include all direct and indirect forms of energy from non-renewable sources used during a product's life cycle.

---

[8]  J. Clayton, 'Organic farmers face ruin as rich nations agonise over food miles', *The Times*, 2 August 2007, www.timesonline.co.uk/tol/life_and_style/food_and_drink/real_food/article2182994.ece. See www.soilassociation.org/web/sa/saweb.nsf/848d689047cb466780256a6b00298980/3263a3366e5940108025726f00402c29?OpenDocument

[9]  Bio Suisse criteria for the award of its Bud Label discriminate against agricultural imports, in particular those transported by air. Bio Suisse standards also favour the processing of imported agricultural products in Switzerland. See www.bio-suisse.ch/en/biosuisseimportpolicy.php

[10]  www.marksandspencer.com/gp/browse.html/ref=sc_fe_c_12_0_51360031_1/026-0253251-0330818?ie=UTF8&node=51444031&no=51360031&mnSBrand=core&me=A2BO0OYVBKIQJM#tackling

[11]  Tesco announced it will grant a preference to food imports from poor countries for the 1 per cent of products it will continue to import by air. Sir Terry Leahy, *Forum for the Future and Tesco*, 18 January 2007, www.tesco.com/climatechange/speech.asp

[12]  Adam, 'Emission impossible', *The Guardian*.

How far should one go? Should certain phases in a life cycle analysis receive greater weight for accounting purposes (production, transport, use or disposal)? How does one evaluate transport-related criteria which by their very nature discriminate against imports? How does one evaluate products produced using more polluting forms of energy? How does one evaluate foreign production processes that may be more suitable given a particular country's geographical, climatic and other conditions, including level of development? Should one count fuel used by a Northern farmer to go to work and to power farm equipment; or energy used to heat or perhaps even manufacture a Northern hothouse? What about energy used to manufacture fertilisers and pesticides for non-organic production, and fuel used to transport these products to the farm? What about refrigeration costs? Or landfill emissions from product waste? The list is almost endless. Without a uniform and coherent accounting system, consumers will face distorted figures and deceptive labelling practices. For example, by focussing on only one stage in a product's life cycle, private transport-related labelling schemes, such as air miles and food miles, give a one-sided view of a product's carbon footprint.

### 3. Developing country considerations

Climate change labelling schemes pose difficulties for industries in the South. Developing countries often lack carbon efficient technologies, making it more difficult to be certified for labels in the North. The time for and cost of obtaining a foreign certification to use a particular label can also discourage developing country exporters. When developed countries take transport considerations into account, the result is often de facto discrimination against developing country producers, particularly those trading in perishable items.[13]

Are private climate change labelling schemes that only reflect a single issue, such as food miles and air miles, a reliable indicator of carbon emissions? One recent industry study says no. 'World Flowers', a UK cut-flower packer, cites a study produced by Cranfield University comparing cut roses produced in Kenya and the Netherlands for the British market.

---

[13] The Soil Association is aware of the development implications of the proposal it is studying. A *Times* article quotes the chairman of the Soil Association's Standards Board as recognising that: 'When reducing our impact on the world's climate, we must carefully consider the social and economic benefits of air freight for international development and growth of the organic market as a whole.' Clayton, 'Organic farmers face ruin', *The Times*.

World Flowers submits, based on a life cycle analysis considering more than 500 inputs, that emissions released in conjunction with the sale of Kenyan flowers (including air freight emissions) are 5.8 times lower than those of Dutch hothouse flowers. World Flowers notes that the global warming potential over the next twenty years would be 6.4 times higher from roses grown in Dutch greenhouses than from roses grown on the equator in Kenya and flown to the United Kingdom.[14]

What are the likely effects of Northern labelling and certification schemes on the environment in the South? Probably negative unless one adopts the peculiar view that depriving people of development opportunities is healthy since it reduces environmental pressure. The opposite is often true. Poverty poses an important threat to the environment, including climate change.[15] Development may reduce certain forms of environmental pressure — for example deforestation resulting from charcoal production. Development also fosters an educational culture that provides people with knowledge to address domestic environmental problems.[16]

### 4. Efficacy, coherence and the legitimacy of labelling standards

Mileage calculations do not paint an accurate portrait of carbon emissions in a product's life cycle, serving instead to favour local industrial and agricultural producers. *If* the notion of 'food miles' and 'air miles' were carried to its logical conclusion by applying the same concept to *all* other trade sectors, we would wake up in a 'brave new world' where all industrial and agricultural goods, as well as trade in services involving travel, would be subject to 'mileage calculations'. This would reduce the

---

[14] Variables considered include packing, cooling, transport, energy consumption, and the manufacture, use and delivery of fertilisers, pesticides, vehicles, and building materials. *Comparative Study of Cut Roses for the British Market Produced in Kenya and the Netherlands,* 12 February 2007, www.world-flowers.co.uk/12news/Comparative%20Study%20of%20Cut%20Roses%20Final%20Report%20Precis%2012%20Febv4.pdf and www.world-flowers.co.uk/12news/news4.html

[15] See Frankel, 'Is trade good or bad for the environment? Sorting out the causality', *Review of Economics and Statistics* 87 (2005), noting trade may result in greenhouse gas reduction, available at http://ksghome.harvard.edu/~jfrankel/Is_Trade_Good_or_Bad_for_the_Environment.pdf

[16] The International Trade Centre (ITC) commissioned the Danish Institute for Strategic Studies to examine the economic effect on developing countries of EU schemes restricting imports by airfreight. See the study guidelines: *The Economic Impact of Restricting Airfreight Imports to the EU,* www.intracen.org/organics/documents/Economic%20Impact%20of%20Restricting%20Airfreight.pdf

gains from trade and cast doubt on the viability of the international trading system.

To the extent that labelling is employed, it should depict a product's entire carbon cycle and not just one phase that benefits a particular class of producers.[17] While single-issue carbon labelling and life-cycle carbon labelling may foster some degree of environmental awareness, neither will solve the climate change problem. More sophisticated economic tools are necessary if we are to reduce carbon emissions. In the short term, there is a need for an economic regime that uses taxes and other pricing policies to force polluters, and therefore consumers, to pay a higher price for carbon emissions, thus providing industry with an incentive to reduce or eliminate such emissions. In the long term, the threat of climate change will continue until our dependence on fossil fuels ceases.

## 5. Sovereignty concerns

The climate change debate also raises sovereignty concerns. For example, to what extent should one state be able to use trade measures to influence another state's carbon emissions? From the perspective of state sovereignty, some may take a restrictive view as trade policy remains an essentially state-centric system. However, from an environmental or consumer perspective the need for action appears broader. Environmental issues challenge fundamental notions of state sovereignty and jurisdiction, due in part to their cross-border implications.

WTO Members have retained great discretion over rules governing the production and transport of products within their territory. Standards and labelling regimes that affect foreign production and transport practices pose significant challenges to the sovereignty of WTO Members, to their economic development, and to the trading system. WTO Members are having difficulty reaching a consensus on how to manage the relationship between trade law and international environmental law, in particular with respect to the extent that trade measures can be used to encourage changes in foreign production practices. Progress in the Committee on Trade and Environment (CTE) and the CTE meeting in Special Session (CTESS) has been slow, and as will be seen below, many legal questions related to the TBT remain open.

---

[17] This conclusion suggests the need for government action to encourage the development of coherent labelling standards.

## III. Legal perspective: the TBT

The TBT is the most specific covered agreement applicable to climate standards and labelling. A WTO panel faced with a technical regulation or standard applicable to carbon emissions is likely to turn first to the TBT. The TBT differentiates between technical regulations (mandatory measures) and standards (voluntary measures) and sets forth rules applicable to both. Carbon labelling programmes may fall into either category depending upon whether or not a particular label is mandatory or voluntary. Although the distinction between mandatory and voluntary labelling requirements is important for ascertaining which provisions of the TBT apply, the rules applicable to both technical regulations and standards are similar.[18]

Pursuant to the provisions of the TBT, technical regulations and standards promulgated by 'central government bodies' and 'local governmental bodies', including both voluntary and mandatory labelling schemes, fall within the TBT.[19] Debate, however, exists as to whether technical regulations and standards applicable to non-product related processes and production methods (NPR-PPMs)[20] and *private* labelling schemes fall within the Agreement. Both questions are addressed below.

### A. The PPM issue

Pursuant to the WTO Agreement, Members are able to regulate manufacturing processes and production methods (PPMs such as carbon emissions from a factory) when production occurs within their jurisdiction. They are also able to regulate the labelling of PPMs for products produced and sold within their territory. Subject to certain conditions set forth in the TBT and GATT, Members may also regulate the transport, use and disposal of goods within their territory. Controversy arises when

---

[18] The most important TBT provisions applicable to mandatory schemes (technical regulations) are Articles 2 and 3, as well as Articles 5–9 on conformity assessment. For voluntary schemes (standards) the most important provisions are Article 4, Annex 3, and Articles 5–9. Most climate labelling schemes are voluntary, so the standards rules are of particular relevance.

[19] See Articles 2–4 of the TBT and the definitions in Annex 1.

[20] In the context of carbon labelling, the term non-product-related processes and production methods (NPR-PPMs) refers to carbon emissions associated with a product's production or transport that are indiscernible in the final product, e.g. how much carbon was produced generating the electricity used to manufacture the product, or to transport it by ship or plane to the country of sale.

a WTO Member applies its laws to influence NPR-PPMs outside its jurisdiction — matters associated with the production or transport of a product that are not detectable in the final product. For example, a WTO panel would allow a Member to label a car for sale within its territory based on its fuel efficiency and exhaust emissions. The controversial question is whether a Member may label an imported car based on carbon emissions produced during its manufacture or importation.

Do TBT provisions governing technical regulations and standards cover NPR-PPMs (unincorporated PPMs)?[21] This question is important from an environmental perspective since significant carbon is emitted in the production and transport of many products. If NPR-PPMs fall within the TBT, Members might condition importation and domestic sale on compliance with technical regulations governing NPR-PPMs (subject to TBT disciplines). Likewise, certain standards applicable to NPR-PPMs would fall within the Code of Good Practice (the Code). If the TBT does not apply, GATT provisions such as Articles I, III, XI and XX might apply.

The applicability of the TBT to NPR-PPMs is one of the principal uncertainties regarding the application of the TBT to carbon standards and labelling schemes. This uncertainty arises from ambiguity in the definitions of the terms 'technical regulation'[22] and 'standard'[23] in Annex 1 of the Agreement. Annex 1(1) and Annex 1(2) both use the phrase 'related processes and production methods' in the first sentence, but fail

---

[21] If a process or production method (PPM) causes a change detectable in the product itself, trade experts classify the PPM as 'product related' or 'incorporated'. If a PPM cannot be detected in the product itself, it is said to be 'non-product related' ('NPR-PPM') or 'unincorporated'.

[22] Annex 1(1) of the TBT defines a technical regulation as a:

> Document which lays down product characteristics or their related processes and production methods, including the applicable administrative provisions, with which compliance is mandatory. It may also include or deal exclusively with terminology, symbols, packaging, marking or labelling requirements as they apply to a product, process or production method.

[23] Annex 1(2) of the TBT defines a standard as a:

> Document approved by a recognized body, that provides, for common and repeated use, rules, guidelines or characteristics for products or related processes and production methods, with which compliance is not mandatory. It may also include or deal exclusively with terminology, symbols, packaging, marking or labelling requirements as they apply to a product, process or production method.

to use the term 'related' in the second sentence which refers to the 'labelling' of a product, process or production method.[24] The failure to use the term 'related' in the second sentence leaves room to argue that labelling requirements need not be 'product related'.

An *Explanatory Note* in Annex 1 provides little clarity. The note states that 'This Agreement deals only with technical regulations, standards and conformity assessment procedures *related* to products or processes and production methods.'[25] The *Explanatory Note* suggests that despite the language of the second sentence, only standards (including labelling standards) that are product related fall within the ambit of the Agreement. This interpretation depends on the meaning that one ascribes to the word 'related'. Does 'related' mean product related (detectable in the final product)? Or does 'related' have a broader meaning, such as merely associated with a product, process or production method? The scope of the TBT will depend on a panel's interpretation of the term 'related'.

The interpretation accepted by most WTO Members is that Annex 1 (1) and (2) signify that only 'product-related' PPMs are covered by the TBT, and therefore only product-related labelling requirements fall within the Agreement.[26] However, no WTO disputes have examined the application of the TBT to NPR-PPMs, nor have there been any WTO cases examining carbon standards or carbon labelling.[27]

---

[24] A. E. Appleton, *Environmental Labelling Programmes: International Trade Law Implications* (London: Kluwer Law International, 1997), pp. 92–3. Annex 1(1), which defines a 'technical regulation' refers to 'product characteristics or their related processes and production methods'. It also provides that a technical regulation may 'include or deal exclusively with … Labelling requirements as they apply to a product, process or production method.' The question arises whether the second phrase is qualified by the word 'related' in the first sentence. Annex 1(2), which defines a standard, refers to 'characteristics for products or related production methods'. The following sentence also states that a standard may 'include or deal exclusively with … labelling requirements as they apply to a product, process or production method'.

[25] Emphasis added.

[26] See Appleton, 'Environmental labelling schemes revisited: WTO law and developing country implications' in Sampson and Chambers (eds.), *Trade Environment and the Millennium*, 2nd edition (Tokyo/New York: United Nations University Press, 2002), p. 257. This point remains a source of contention among some WTO Members. Despite the controversy, for transparency reasons many Members notify life cycle eco-labelling schemes covering NPR-PPMs to the WTO.

[27] A voluntary environmental labelling scheme reflecting an NPR-PPM (whether tuna was 'dolphin safe') withstood a challenge based on Article I:1 of the GATT in the unadopted 1991 *Tuna — Dolphin* report. *United States — Restrictions on Imports of Tuna*, DS21/R, 39S/155, at paragraphs 5.41–5.44. See also Appleton, *Environmental Labelling*

The *US — Shrimp* case involved a unilateral import ban predicated on an NPR-PPM.[28] The import ban was examined under Articles XI and XX of the GATT, but none of the related *Shrimp* reports examined the PPM issue. The Appellate Body's decision in Malaysia's subsequent Article 21.5 of the DSU dispute ultimately allowed the United States to discriminate against Malaysian shrimp based on an NPR-PPM — the manner in which Malaysians harvest shrimp.[29] Being a case arising under GATT 1994, the Article 21.5 decision offers no direct guidance on the interpretation of Annex 1(1) and (2) of the TBT.

Why is the NPR-PPM question important? From the perspective of climate change there may be valid reasons for distinguishing a product based on NPR-PPMs, but from the trade perspective differentiating goods based on NPR-PPMs increases trade barriers and trade discrimination, particularly discrimination against developing countries. Many developing countries are adamant in opposing trade restrictions based on NPR-PPMs. In part this is because: (i) they may lack the technical capacity and capital to meet stringent environmental production standards; (ii) if standards for NPR-PPMs differ greatly among importing countries, economies of scale would diminish;[30] (iii) transport-related labelling has the potential to disadvantage exports of fresh produce from the South; and (iv) opening the door to the regulation of NPR-PPMs related to carbon emissions could open the door for trade discrimination based on other non-product-related criteria, including labour and human rights practices.

Environmentalists may criticise this view, but it is pragmatic and finds support in the *Shrimp* decisions. Implicit in the *Shrimp* decisions is the realisation that certain global problems require international

---

*Programmes*. The panel found that the voluntary US scheme at issue did not prevent tuna products from being sold freely with or without the 'dolphin-safe' label, nor did the scheme establish requirements that had to be met to obtain an advantage from the US Government. Any advantage that occurred was due to consumer choice (1991 Tuna report, at paragraph 5.42). It is unlikely this unadopted report, which arose under the GATT and pre-dates the TBT, would affect a panel's interpretation of the TBT.

[28] *US — Shrimp* dealt with a US requirement that shrimp be netted using turtle excluder devices. These devices allow sea turtles (many species of which are endangered) to escape from shrimp nets. *US — Import Prohibition of Certain Shrimp and Shrimp Products*, WT/DS58/R and WT/DS58/AB/R (1998).

[29] *US — Import Prohibition of Certain Shrimp and Shrimp Products*, Recourse to Article 21.5 of the DSU by Malaysia, WT/DS58/AB/RW (2001).

[30] If countries A and B apply different production-related emission standards for widgets, a widget producer in country C might need to build separate facilities to export to countries A and B.

co-operative solutions, and that co-operative efforts should be exhausted before recourse to unilateral measures. The reduction of greenhouse gas emissions from NPR-PPMs requires an international effort involving the entire community of nations — an effort more far reaching than that of the Kyoto Protocol. Without such an effort, Members who do not address greenhouse gas emissions may enjoy a competitive advantage. Only after an attempt has been made to negotiate a well-conceived co-operative solution should WTO Members be allowed to take unilateral measures in response to the environmental policies of Members that choose to remain outside the co-operative framework.

## B.   Mandatory carbon labelling schemes

Articles 2 and 3 of the TBT are applicable to most mandatory carbon labelling schemes (technical regulations) promulgated by central, local and non-governmental bodies. Articles 2 and 3 resemble Article 4 and Annex 3, so many of the comments offered on TBT provisions governing technical regulations can also be applied to TBT provisions applicable to voluntary labelling schemes that fall within the Code (standards).

Article 2.1 of the TBT sets forth non-discrimination requirements (MFN and national treatment obligations). No TBT case has interpreted Article 2.1, but it is probable that a panel would turn to WTO 'like product jurisprudence' for guidance. Would a panel applying Article 2.1 consider two very similar products manufactured using different manufacturing processes, or shipped using different means of transport, one carbon intensive and the other not, to be like products? The answer would almost certainly be yes if the panel applies the traditional four-part test reaffirmed in *Japan — Alcoholic Beverages*.[31] If so, regulations governing NPR-PPMs that result in de facto discrimination against or between foreign producers would violate Article 2.1.

Article 2.2 requires that technical regulations do not create 'unnecessary' obstacles to international trade. Certain legitimate objectives are identified, including protection of human, animal or plant life or health, or the environment. These provisions are sufficiently broad to encompass carbon labelling schemes. Article 2.2 also requires that trade measures in furtherance of a legitimate objective be 'necessary'. Trade measures must not be more trade restrictive than required to fulfil a legitimate objective, taking account of the risks that non-fulfilment

---

[31] *Japan — Taxes on Alcoholic Beverages*, WT/DS 8, 10 & 11/AB/R, at pp. 21–3 (1996).

would create. A technical regulation must be modified or withdrawn (be made less trade restrictive) in the event of changed circumstances.[32] The 'necessary' requirement is designed to minimise the burden of technical regulations and to prevent the abuse of technical regulations for protectionist purposes. The application of the 'necessary' test adds a degree of rigidity to the TBT since reasonable and less trade-restrictive alternatives are often available.[33] This requirement also suggests an important question: if a given carbon labelling scheme is largely ineffective in fulfilling a legitimate objective (reducing carbon emissions), is it really necessary? The answer may be no. The question of effectiveness is also raised by Article 2.4.

Article 2.4 requires the use of relevant international standards as a basis for technical regulations unless they would be 'ineffective or inappropriate' for the fulfilment of a legitimate objective. Article 2.4 encourages international harmonisation of standards,[34] and should encourage the harmonisation of product-related carbon standards. Questions remain as to what is an 'international standard'. Annex 1(2) defines a 'standard' as a 'document approved by a "recognised body"'. The TBT is silent with respect to what constitutes a 'recognised body'. This point is examined below in the discussion of standards.

Article 3 establishes rules for the preparation, adoption and application of the TBT by local government bodies and non-governmental bodies. Article 3.1 is poorly drafted and leaves open to dispute questions concerning the 'reasonable measures' Members must take to ensure compliance by these bodies with Article 2, in particular compliance by non-governmental bodies. Article 3.4 prohibits Members from taking measures that encourage local government bodies and non-governmental bodies to act inconsistently with Article 2. Article 3.5 holds Members 'fully responsible' for the observance of all provisions of Article 2 by local government bodies and non-governmental bodies and requires Members

---

[32] Article 2.2 of the TBT reads in part that 'technical regulations shall not be more trade-restrictive than necessary to fulfil a legitimate objective'. Article 2.3 provides that: 'Technical regulations shall not be maintained if the circumstances or objectives giving rise to their adoption no longer exist or if the changed circumstances or objectives can be addressed in a less trade-restrictive manner.'

[33] Whether a mandatory labelling requirement is trade restrictive depends on the type of label. Some labelling requirements are only designed to provide information and are not trade restrictive. Labelling requirements become trade restrictive when a product must meet certain norms to bear a label.

[34] Participation in international standardisation is difficult for developing countries that lack the financial and technical means to play an active role in this process.

to implement 'positive measures' to support the observance of Article 2 by these bodies. No WTO jurisprudence delimits the extent of a Member's responsibility under Article 3.5 for the acts of non-governmental bodies, including with respect to labelling schemes.

## C. Voluntary carbon labelling schemes

Most carbon labelling schemes are voluntary, with the result that Article 4 and Annex 3 of the TBT (the Code of Good Practice for the Preparation, Adoption and Application of Standards) may be applicable. In addition to the threshold question (treated above) as to whether the term 'standard' encompasses NPR-PPMs, other questions exist regarding the scope of the Code. First, there are questions arising from the definition of a 'standard' — a fundamental term for understanding the breadth of the Code. Second, there are questions with respect to the definition of a 'standardising body' as used in Annex 3:B of the Code. Third, there are questions about the meaning of 'non-governmental bodies' and whether private standardisation organisations fall within the definition.

### 1. Scope of the Code

(a) 'Standard' and 'standardising bodies'   The first two questions can be treated together: what is a 'standard' and what are 'standardising bodies'? Are firms with private certification and labelling schemes, such as the Soil Association, Bio-Suisse, Tesco and Marks & Spencer, developing 'standards' and acting as 'standardising bodies' within the meaning of the Code?

The definition of a 'standard' in Annex 1(2) uses the phrase 'document approved by a recognised body'. The term 'document' implies that a standard must be reduced to writing. The phrase 'recognised body' is obscure. The TBT does not state who can recognise such bodies, only giving guidance as to the definition of an 'international body or system', 'regional body or system' and various other 'bodies'. Annex 1(4) provides that an 'international body or system' is a 'Body or system whose membership is open to the relevant bodies of at least all Members.'[35] A 'regional body or system' is open to the relevant bodies of only some of the Members. 'Bodies' are defined by reference to the International

---

[35] Membership in several leading international standardisation bodies is not open to all WTO Members.

Organization for Standardization/International Electrotechnical Commission (ISO/IEC) Guide 2 as a 'Legal or administrative entity that has specific tasks and composition.'[36] These definitions are vague and provide insufficient guidance to determine what is a recognised body and who may recognise such bodies. Nor has the Appellate Body clarified the phrase. In its discussion of Annex 1(2) in *EC — Sardines*, the Appellate Body speaks only of a 'recognized body of the international standardization community',[37] but provides no further guidance.

The absence of a precise definition of a 'recognised body' means that members might call upon a panel to decide whether a particular entity is a recognised standardisation body. In looking at the issue of recognition, a panel would probably first examine whether an entity is recognised in the WTO Agreement as a standardisation organisation (e.g. ISO, IEC, OIE, certain organisations operating within the framework of the Intergovernmental Panel on Climate Change (IPPC), and the Codex Alimentarius Commission), or whether it falls clearly within the definitions of Annex 1(4)–(6) of the TBT. For standardisation organisations not explicitly mentioned in the WTO Agreement, a panel would also probably examine: (i) whether the entity is recognised by one or more WTO Members as a standardisation body, (ii) whether the private entity is involved in the standardisation activities of international standardisation organisations such as ISO and the IEC, (iii) whether any WTO Members apply standards promulgated by the entity, (iv) whether the body is open to the involvement of other WTO Members, (v) whether the body has accepted the Code of Good Practice, (vi) whether the aim of the standard furthers a legitimate TBT objective,[38] and perhaps (vii) whether the organisation is listed by the World Standards Services Network.[39]

Many non-governmental standardising bodies exist and more than seventy have notified WTO Members of their acceptance of the Code.[40]

---

[36] See the Explanatory Note to Annex 1, and Article 4.1 of ISO/IEC Guide 2: General Terms and their Definitions Concerning Standardization and Related Activities (1991).

[37] *European Communities — Trade Description of Sardines*, WT/DS231/AB/R (2002), at paragraph 227.

[38] The list in Article 2.2 of the TBT is not exhaustive.

[39] See www.fsc-deutschland.de/infocenter/docs/info/studien/iseal_01.pdf for the summary of a legal opinion produced by the International Social and Environmental Accreditation and Labelling Alliance (ISEAL) and the Center for International Environmental Law (CIEL) on whether Forest Stewardship Council Principles and Criteria are international standards under WTO rules. The legal opinion emphasises a listing by the World Standards Services Network, a less persuasive factor.

[40] WTO Document: G/TBT/CS/2/rev.13 (2 March 2007).

Are the Soil Association, Bio Suisse, Tesco and Marks & Spencer promulgating standards within the meaning of the Code? No WTO case has examined this question, but the answer is almost certainly 'no'. Although these companies put their criteria in writing, they do not appear to meet the requirements of a 'recognised body' suggested above.[41] Instead, their activities are private or commercial in nature — directed at the marketing of a product or service.

Turning to the second and related question, are these private entities 'standardising bodies' entitled to accept the Code within the meaning of Annex 3:B of the TBT? Again, the answer is probably 'no'. If an organisation or business is not promulgating 'standards' as defined in Annex 1(2) of the TBT, it is difficult to see how it can be classified as a 'standardising body'. If an organisation or business does not have 'recognised activities' in standardisation within the definition of ISO/IEC Guide 2 (as judged by the criteria set forth above), it is *also* difficult to see how it can be classified as a standardising body. In addition, the activities of these entities are not consistent with those of the international standardisation bodies described by the members in the Decision of the [TBT] Committee on Principles for the Development of International Standards, Guides and Recommendations with Relation to Articles 2, 5 and Annex 3 of the Agreement.[42] Their activities are not open to all members and their activities favour the interests of certain members over others.

Although for the reasons expressed above, it is unlikely that the Soil Association, Bio Suisse, Tesco and Marks & Spencer are standardising bodies, it cannot be said with certainty what a 'standardising body' is for purposes of the Code. The terms 'standardising bodies' and 'standardisation body' appear more than fifty-five times in the TBT, but are never precisely defined. Annex 3:B gives some indication as to the types of

---

[41] These companies have not notified their acceptance of the Code to the members, do not co-operate with the ISO, nor are they listed by the World Standards Services Network.

[42] See paragraphs 21–25 and Annex IV of the Second Triennial Review of the Operation and Implementation of the Agreement on Technical Barriers to Trade, WTO Document G/TBT/9. Annex IV, paragraph 8 provides in relevant part that: 'All relevant bodies of WTO Members should be provided with meaningful opportunities to contribute to the elaboration of an international standard so that the standard development process will not give privilege to, or favour the interests of, a particular supplier/s, country/ies or region/s.' Paragraph 9 provides in relevant part that: 'Impartiality should be accorded throughout all the standards development process with respect to, among other things: access to participation in work; submission of comments on drafts; consideration of views expressed and comments made; decision-making through consensus.'

'standardising bodies' to which the Code is open,[43] as does the Decision of the TBT Committee referred to above; ISO/IEC Guide 2 offers an inconclusive definition of 'standardisation body';[44] and the terms 'standard'[45] and 'body'[46] are each defined, albeit not well, in the TBT and ISO/IEC Guide, respectively. Even reading these definitions together, it is difficult to determine the precise meaning of the term 'standardising bodies'.

Turning to the third question, are private entities such as the Soil Association, Bio Suisse, Tesco and Marks & Spencer 'non-governmental bodies' pursuant to Annex 1(8)? Again the answer is probably 'no', but the answer here is less clear. Annex 3:B provides that the Code is open to non-governmental bodies. However the definition of a 'non-governmental body' in Annex 1(8) is vague: a 'Body other than a central government body or a local government body, including a non-governmental body which has legal power to enforce a technical regulation.' Does paragraph 8 cover all 'bodies' or only bodies that have the power to enforce a technical regulation? As already noted, pursuant to Annex 1 of the TBT the term 'body' is defined by ISO/IEC Guide 2[47] (paragraph 4.1) to mean any 'legal or administrative entity that has specific tasks and composition'. Does this definition refer to any corporation or partnership, or does the definition imply a grant of 'specific tasks and composition' (responsibility and membership) from a government body? If paragraph 8 is read as meaning any body in the broad sense (e.g. a corporation or partnership) then the second clause ('including a ...') has no meaning. Alternatively a comma could be read into the otherwise meaningless second clause (before 'which') resulting in a definition establishing that 'non-governmental bod[ies]' must have

---

[43] Annex 3:B opens the Code to 'standardising bodies' regardless of whether they are a central government body, a local government body, a non-governmental body or a governmental regional standardising body. These terms are defined, in part, in Annex 1(4)–(8).

[44] Article 4.3 of ISO/IEC Guide 2 defines a standardisation body as a 'Body that has recognized activities in standardisation.' Standardisation is defined in Article 1.1 as the 'Activity of establishing, with regard to actual or potential problems, provisions for common and repeated use, aimed at the achievement of the optimum degree of order in a given context.'

[45] See Annex 1(2) of the TBT.

[46] The term 'Body' is defined in paragraph 4.1 of ISO/IEC Guide 2 (discussed above).

[47] ISO/IEC Guide 2, General Terms and their Definitions Concerning Standardisation and Related Activities (1991). A 2004 version of Guide 2 exists but the TBT refers to the 1991 text.

legal power to enforce a technical regulation for the Code to apply. The latter interpretation is preferable since it gives the second clause legal meaning. It would, however, exclude many private labelling schemes from the scope of the Code on the grounds that they are not promulgated by 'bodies', or the entities lack the 'legal power to enforce a technical regulation'.[48] This latter phrase, the 'legal power to enforce a technical regulation', is also not defined. It is unclear whether the definition implies a government grant of power, or merely the ability to bring a complaint in court to enforce a mandatory technical regulation.

In conclusion, for the reasons discussed above, most 'private' climate change labelling schemes will fall outside the Code. This has advantages and disadvantages. On the one hand, if private schemes fall outside the Code, there is added space for harnessing the resourcefulness of private enterprise. On the other hand, labelling schemes that fall outside the Code are less transparent (not notified), less uniform (not based on international standards); and more likely to confuse consumers, be protectionist (in favour of local producers), and disadvantage developing countries. If the intent of the members is to widen the application of the Code, a goal that may be in the interest of developing countries, attention should be given to tightening the definitions of 'standard', 'standardising body' and 'standardisation body' and defining what constitutes 'reasonable measures' required by a member to assure that non-governmental bodies accept and comply with the Code.

**(b) Non-governmental bodies**   Pursuant to Article 4.1, only central government standardising bodies are bound by the provisions of the Code of Good Practice. Other standardising bodies have the option to accept and apply the Code. Members are obligated to take 'reasonable measures' to assure that regional, local and non-governmental standardising bodies accept and comply with the Code. Members are also responsible, pursuant to Article 4.1, for the 'compliance of standardizing bodies with the provisions of the Code of Good Practice … irrespective of whether or not a standardizing body has accepted the Code of Good Practice'. The seminal term is again 'standardizing bodies'. Pursuant to the Code, members have no responsibility under Article 4.1 if the body in question is not a 'standardizing body'. The activities of private sector

---

[48]   It would exclude the schemes of the Soil Association, Bio Suisse, Tesco and Marks & Spencer.

entities that are not 'standardising bodies' fall outside a member's direct responsibility.

## 2.  Private standards and the Code

WTO Members have discussed private standards and private labelling in both the TBT and Sanitary and Phytosanitary Measures Agreement (SPS) Committees. A joint UNCTAD/WTO Informal Information Session on Private Standards was held at the WTO on 25 June 2007.[49] There is recognition among some WTO Members and civil society that certain private environmental standards and labels, such as the Forest Stewardship Council (FSC) label (awarded based on NPR-PPMs),[50] are becoming globally accepted, but uncertainty as to whether WTO rules apply to these standards.[51] The FSC label provides an interesting example (even if only indirectly related to carbon labelling). It is widely recognised both at the international level and by consumers; its standards are referenced in specifications produced by several governments (including those of the United Kingdom and Denmark); it receives funding from the United Kingdom and Germany;[52] it is open to involvement by all members; and it is listed by the World Standards Services Network (WSSN) as an international standardising body.[53] However, FSC standards are based on NPR-PPMs.[54] For this reason, some WTO Members may be hesitant to permit the FSC to accede to the Code.

---

[49]  www.wto.org/english/tratop_e/sps_e/private_standards_june07_e/private_standards_june07_e.htm

[50]  The FSC develops standards for responsible forest management and accredits certification bodies. See www.fsc.org

[51]  *Business and Sustainable Development Global,* www.bsdglobal.com/issues/trade.asp, a site developed and maintained by the International Institute of Sustainable Development (IISD), notes that:

> the Forest Stewardship Council label for sustainably produced forest products is becoming a globally accepted standard, but is completely voluntary. Does WTO law apply to such standards?
> Some countries argue that it does, maintaining that the code of good practice demands that governments bring their national standard-setting bodies in line. Others argue that it does not, maintaining that WTO law applies only to governments. The discussions in the WTO will be interesting, and will carry heavy consequences for industries like forestry.

[52]  www.fsc.org/keepout/en/content_areas/29/71/files/Fact_Sheet_on_Procurement_2006_12_15.pdf

[53]  See www.wssn.net/WSSN/listings/links_international.html

[54]  See www.fsc-deutschland.de/infocenter/docs/info/studien/iseal_01.pdf. This summary of a legal opinion recognises the NPR-PPM question but sidesteps the issue. Note that

### 3. Obligations of standardising bodies bound by the Code

The Code establishes a number of obligations with respect to central government standardising bodies that are required to accept and comply with the Code, and for other standardising bodies that have accepted the Code. These obligations largely track those of Article 2. Standardising bodies are required to accord most-favoured-nation and national treatment to like products;[55] standards may not be prepared, adopted or applied with a view to, or the effect of creating unnecessary obstacles to international trade;[56] and standardisation bodies are required to base their standards on relevant international standards (or relevant portions of international standards) when they exist or when their completion is imminent.[57] Unlike Article 2.2, the Code does not explicitly set forth legitimate objectives for standardisation, however it does mention health and environmental problems in paragraph L. Also unlike Article 2.5, the Code does not establish a rebuttable presumption of validity for national and sub-national standards based on international standards, stating only that standardisation bodies that accept and comply with the Code 'shall be acknowledged by the Members as complying with the principles of this Agreement'.[58]

### 4. Conformity assessment procedures

Further ambiguity exists with respect to the treatment under the TBT of non-governmental bodies engaged in the development of climate standards and labels who manage their own conformity assessment procedures. The Code is silent with respect to conformity assessment. Articles 5–9 of the TBT deal with conformity assessment, with Article 8 containing the operative provision for non-governmental bodies. Article 8.1 provides that:

> Members shall take such reasonable measures as may be available to them to ensure that non-governmental bodies within their territories which operate conformity assessment procedures comply with the provisions of Articles 5 and 6, with the exception of the obligation to notify proposed

---

the FSC states that its policies and standards are transparent, independent ('no one interest dominates') and participatory ('FSC strives to involve all interested people and groups in the development of FSC policies and standards.') See www.fsc.org/en/about/policy_standards

[55] Paragraph D of the Code.    [56] *Ibid.*, paragraph E.
[57] *Ibid.*, paragraph F. Like Article 2.3, paragraph F contains an exception when use of the international standard would be ineffective or inappropriate.
[58] Article 4.2.

conformity assessment procedures. In addition, Members shall not take measures which have the effect of, directly or indirectly, requiring or encouraging such bodies to act in a manner inconsistent with the provisions of Articles 5 and 6.

Article 8.1 is vague, as are other provisions of the TBT applicable to member responsibility.[59] First, it provides no indication of what are 'reasonable measures'. Second, its scope with respect to standards is limited by definition to the activities of non-governmental bodies that have accepted the Code.[60] Third, while members must take reasonable measures to ensure that non-governmental bodies comply with Articles 5 and 6,[61] the obligations in Articles 5 and 6 only apply to central government bodies. Is the reference to Articles 5 and 6 in Article 8.1 meaningless, or did the members intend to expand the scope of member responsibility under Articles 5 and 6 to include the conformity assessment activities of 'non-governmental bodies'? Almost certainly the latter, but Article 8.1 is poorly drafted.

## IV. Conclusion

For developed countries, climate change is now of growing importance. Industry has realised this and views private standards and private labelling schemes as a response to consumer demand, and perhaps even as a means of creating demand. Do private labelling schemes fall within the TBT? Although the TBT is not clear on this subject, this paper concludes that private carbon labelling schemes generally fall outside the Agreement for several reasons: (i) they are not promulgated by recognised standardising bodies, (ii) they do not rely on 'standards' as defined in Annex 1(2), (iii) the non-governmental bodies in question may not satisfy the conditions of Annex 1(8), and (iv) the TBT probably does not apply to standards governing NPR-PPMs. Even if certain private carbon labelling schemes fall within the Agreement (and their acceptance of the Code has been notified to the members), the extent to which the Agreement's provisions on conformity assessment are applicable to non-governmental bodies is unclear, as are the reasonable measures that a

---

[59] See the comments on Article 3.5 (above).     [60] See Article 4.1 and 4.2 and Annex 3:B.
[61] Article 5 governs procedures for assessment of conformity by central government bodies. Article 6 governs recognition of conformity assessment by central government bodies.

member must take to ensure that non-governmental bodies comply with the provisions in the Code on conformity assessment.

For many developing countries, greenhouse gas reduction remains a luxury, and 'green protectionism' is a legitimate concern. Although the TBT may be adequate to protect against member-run green protectionism, it may be an ineffective tool to discipline private standardisation and labelling schemes with protectionist objectives. Private schemes are increasing in number. They have the potential to disadvantage exports from the South without bringing the environmental benefits that such schemes purport to deliver to the North. If the members intend to widen the application of the Code, a goal that may be in the interest of developing countries, members should give attention to clarifying the definitions of 'standard', 'standardising body' and 'standardisation body', and defining what constitutes 'reasonable measures' required by a member to assure that non-governmental bodies accept and comply with the Code.

While the TBT constitutes a major step forward from GATT practice, judging by the deficiencies cited above there is room for improvement. Unfortunately, rather than negotiating improvements, members are taking a wait-and-see approach. This means that members will have little choice but to refer important questions concerning private standards and private labelling schemes to WTO panels and eventually the Appellate Body. The resulting decisions may not be satisfactory.

Regardless of what panels and the Appellate Body decide, trade law in general, and labelling schemes in particular, will not bring an end to global warming. As only a small portion of climate change problems are trade related, there are limits to what one should expect from the international trade regime. If WTO Members are serious about addressing climate change, they need to look outside the trade regime towards more powerful tax and regulatory tools that promote cleaner sources of energy and limit greenhouse gas emissions throughout a product's life cycle.

# PART III

Trade in renewable energy sources

# 8

# Incentive schemes to promote renewables and the WTO law of subsidies

SADEQ Z. BIGDELI[1]

## Introduction

Presidents Ford and Carter's warnings in the 1970s on US dependence on foreign oil and Gore's warnings today on climate change have the same policy implication — move towards a low carbon economy. This is because carbon dioxide is the most important anthropogenic greenhouse gas (GHG) and its increasing concentration in the atmosphere since the pre-industrial period is primarily due to fossil fuel use.[2] In this respect, the international climate protection regime reflected in the UN Framework Convention on Climate Change and especially its Kyoto Protocol points in two directions — discourage fossil fuel subsidies and promote energy efficiency and renewable energy (RE) sources (Inferred from Kyoto Article 2.1.a (iv) and(v)).

From a pure theoretical economic viewpoint, subsidisation might not be the best way to promote renewables. Most economists would prefer to apply a proper taxation system which takes into account all environmental externalities related to fossil fuels. On a global level, an economically plausible cap and trade system may also be a way to achieve this. The lack of political consensus behind these 'market-based instruments', however, has led policy-makers to devise various domestic incentive schemes to promote renewables. Such schemes include subsidies among other regulatory schemes such as feed-in tariffs. Their primary

---

[1] The author has immensely benefited from extensive discussions with Mr Gary Horlick and Professor Rob Howse. I am also grateful to Mr Jesse Kreier and Mr Aaron Cosbey for their very useful comments. Views expressed here are solely those of the author.
[2] 'IPCC, 2007: summary for policymakers', in S. Solomon, D. Qin, M. Manning, *et al.*, (eds.), *Climate Change 2007: The Physical Science Basis. Contribution of Working Group I to the Fourth Assessment Report of the Intergovernmental Panel on Climate Change* (Cambridge University Press, 2007).

aim is to level the playing field between conventional and renewable energy sources, currently obstructed by the relatively high costs of RE technologies and also to some extent by subsidies on fossil fuels.

The magnitude of subsidies available for the RE sector is growing worldwide as a policy response to energy security concerns and climate change. The introduction of new incentive schemes to promote RE has become increasingly common especially in the US and EU region. The production of energy from RE sources is increasing rapidly which, along with the rise in demand for green energy, is leading to the emergence of new RE markets worldwide. This will result in the expansion of RE trade which could potentially lead to trade disputes. In this context, the question of the status of RE subsidies in WTO law is highly relevant — do the WTO rules on subsidies constrain climate protection policies pursued through policies for promoting RE, particularly subsidisation?

This paper is a synopsis of an extensive research project intended to address the above question. Section A seeks to identify a legally precise definition of the term subsidy in light of the WTO Agreement on Subsidies and Countervailing Measures (ASCM or the SCM) amid the diverging views put forward by economists and lawyers. Specific reference is made to the peculiarities of defining subsidies in RE markets. In accordance with the definition presented in section A, different types of subsidies existing in RE markets in general are identified in section B. In this section, instead of providing a run-down of the major subsidy schemes worldwide, incentive schemes are classified into four categories according to the intricacy involved in capturing them by Article 1 of the SCM. Recognising the specificities involved in biofuels and renewable electricity, sections C and D address different rules governing these RE sources. Section E then examines the 'specificity' requirement and section F deals with 'adverse effect' as pre-requisite steps for a country making a case in the WTO against subsidies. Section G, briefly analyses the realities of global trade in RE and considers the possibility of trade disputes arising in this sector in the near future. Finally section H offers suggestions as to the way forward.

## A.   Misconceptions about the definition of subsidy

There is no consensus upon the definition of the term subsidy even in the economic literature. According to a broad definition, a lax tax regime which does not fully take account of environmental externalities might be considered as a subsidy granted to the entity causing such an externality. These so-called implicit subsidies are not usually included in subsidy estimations due to difficulties in defining an optimal level for an environmental tax, which may vary in different jurisdictions.

Hence the Organisation for Economic Co-operation and Development (OECD) limits the definition of the term subsidy to 'any measure that keeps prices for consumers below market levels, or for producers above market levels or that reduces costs for consumers and producers'.[3] This definition is broader than what is normally perceived as a subsidy, in the narrow fiscal or financial sense of the word, since it includes any regulatory measures such as import duties and export restrictions, which have an effect on price or cost borne by producers or consumers. Many of these measures of a regulatory nature, as will be explained below, are excluded from the WTO definition of a subsidy due to a lack of a financial contribution or an element of income or price support by a government.[4]

### 1.   Article 1.1 lit (a) of the ASCM: financial contribution, or income or price support

For the first time in the history of the General Agreement on Tariffs and Trade (GATT), a definition of the term subsidy was included in the text of the ASCM as a result of the Uruguay Round negotiations in order to clarify the meaning of the term for purposes of WTO subsidies disciplines. Article 1 of the ASCM adopts a two-pronged definition of the term subsidy. In other words, there should be two conditions cumulatively applying to a situation in order for a subsidy to exist: the first condition is that there should be either a financial contribution by a government or any public body within the territory of a Member *or* any form of income or price support in the sense of Article XVI of the GATT.[5] The reference to 'income or price support' is extremely rare in WTO case law and I will briefly discuss that element later in the paper with respect to measures involving price regulations. In almost all

[3] OECD, *Improving the Environment through Reducing Subsides* (Paris: OECD, 1998), cited in UNEP, *Energy Subsidies, Lessons Learned in Assessing their Impact and Designing their Policy Reforms* (UNEP, 2004), at 23.
[4] Specifically with regard to export restrictions, a WTO panel in *US — Measures Treaties Export Restraints as Subsidies* ruled out the possibility of these measures being considered as subsidies. See report of the panel, WT/DS194/R, 29 June 2001 paragraph 9.1.
[5] For a discussion on what constitutes income or price support in the sense of GATT Article XVI see Section B.4.

subsidy cases so far, the finding of a 'financial contribution' by a government — along with finding a 'benefit conferred upon a recipient' as the second legal element of the definition of 'subsidy' — has been crucial in establishing the existence of a subsidy to which the ASCM disciplines would apply.

There are four broad categories of financial contribution stipulated in Article 1.1(a)(1) which include (i) a government practice involving a 'direct transfer of funds' whether actual (grants, loans, equity infusions, etc.) or potential (loan guarantees); (ii) government revenue that is otherwise due being foregone or not collected (e.g. fiscal incentives); (iii) a government provision of goods or services other than general infrastructure, or government purchase of goods; and finally (iv) government performing one or more of the type of functions illustrated in (i)–(iii) through a funding mechanism, or entrusted or directed private body if such functions would normally be vested in the government and the practice, in no real sense, differs from practices normally followed by governments.

These four categories of financial contribution mostly cover what economists generally consider a subsidy.[6] As mentioned earlier, however, most regulatory measures which are not of a financial or fiscal nature (such as border measures) are not captured by Article 1 of the ASCM although, from an economic standpoint, they may eventually confer the same benefit to their beneficiaries as the financial ones. With respect to item (i), 'direct transfer of funds' the mere existence of a government grant or loan arrangement suggests the existence of a financial contribution leading directly to the question of whether there is a benefit conferred upon a recipient. While there is no need to search for a market benchmark in the case of a government grant (a grant 'naturally' confers a benefit upon its recipient), one needs to compare the conditions of the terms of the government provision of equity capital, loans or loan guarantee to the 'usual investment practice' or what the market would provide in those circumstances in order for a benefit to be conferred (ASCM Article 14(a), (b) and (c)). Similarly with respect to item (iii) the

---

[6] With respect to the broadness of the definition of the term subsidy in WTO law, a comparison could be made with its counterpart in European law. The latter on the definition of 'state aid' includes a 'cost to government' condition which is lacking in Article 1 of the SCM. In this sense, it might be inferred that the EU law arguably contains a narrower definition of the term subsidy than the WTO. For more see C.-D. Ehlermann and M. Goyette, 'The interface between EU state aid control and the WTO disciplines on subsidies', (2006) 4 *European State Aid Law Quarterly*, 698.

mere existence of a government provision of goods or services or purchase of goods would entail a financial contribution. The government provision of goods or services or purchase of goods does not, however, constitute a subsidy (does not confer a benefit) 'unless the provision is made for less than adequate remuneration, or the purchase is made for more than adequate remuneration (see ASCM Article 14(d)).

Item (ii) on subsidies through fiscal measures perhaps deserves more attention to the first element (financial contribution) than to the second (benefit).[7] 'Tax credits' seem to be a perfect candidate for a financial contribution that confers benefit. There are a few items to be considered in the case of tax 'exemptions'. The first point with regard to the elusive concept of 'otherwise due' is that it 'depends on the rules of taxation that each member, by its own choice, establishes for itself' (*United States — Tax Treatment For 'Foreign Sales Corporations (US — FSC)*).[8] Hence it should be clear that WTO Members are free to define their rules of taxation as they wish. Their tax system may, however, involve a financial contribution if they apply differential fiscal treatment in 'legitimately comparable situations' through tax exemptions.[9] The Appellate Body (AB) in its original report on *US — FSC* pointed to the fact that the US itself acknowledged that the measure in question did represent a 'departure from the rules of taxation that would otherwise apply'. In other words, it was clear, even to the defendant, that the tax liability would be higher in the absence of the contested measure (paragraph 95). The AB went even further in its Article 21.5 of the DSU report stressing that it was not necessary for panels to try 'to isolate a "general" rule of taxation and "exceptions" to that "general" rule'. Instead, they should 'seek to compare the fiscal treatment of legitimately comparable income to determine whether the contested measure involves the foregoing of revenue which is "otherwise due", in relation to the income in question' (paragraph 91). It may be argued that the same rule could well apply to tax exemptions related to 'products' as well as 'income' — if a certain product is singled out from a set of products to be qualified for a tax

---

[7] For instance while the panel in *US — FCS* established the existence of a financial contribution through tax exemption for Foreign Sales Corporations (FSCs) the US, as the defendant, did not even argue on the question of benefit (paragraph 7.103).

[8] Appellate Body report *United States — Tax Treatment for 'Foreign Sales Corporations'* (WT/DS108/AB/R)/DSR 2000:III, 1619 (*US — FSC*) at paragraph 90.

[9] Appellate Body report *United States — Tax Treatment for 'Foreign Sales Corporations'*, WT/DS108/AB/RW, 14 January 2002, Recourse to Article 21.5 of the DSU by the EC (*US — FSC 21.5*) at paragraph 91.

exemption, there might be an element of financial contribution by government to the extent that taxed and exempt products are 'legitimately comparable'. I will turn to this point in section B.2.

The second point with regard to item (ii) — subsidies through preferential fiscal treatment — is that the ASCM, as interpreted by the AB, envisages a jurisdictional limit on how to define a benchmark for the level of environmental taxes below which a subsidy may be deemed to exist. The AB in *US — FSC* agreed with the panel that the term 'otherwise due' implies some kind of comparison between the revenues due under the contested measure and revenues that would be due in some other situation, and *the basis of comparison must be the tax rules applied by the member in question and not in other jurisdictions.*[10] Following this logic Stiglitz's (2006) opinion that '[N]ot paying the cost of damage to the environment is a subsidy [and hence open to challenges in the WTO], just as not paying the full costs of workers would be'[11] may not be legally precise. A Member who generally applies an environmentally lax tax regime may not be legally found to be subsidising polluting industries, as Stiglitz perceived, unless it has been demonstrated that it has provided a tax exemption to a certain entity while having done otherwise with respect to similarly situated entities.[12] This would imply that countervailing measures will not be endorsed by a WTO panel if they are used to remedy the competitiveness of imported products which have benefited from a lax tax regime in their production process.[13]

[10] *US — FSC* at paragraph 90.

[11] G. Stiglitz, *Economists' Voice*, July 2006, available at http://works.bepress.com/joseph_-stiglitz/, last visited 5 September 2007. Another example of Stiglitz's legal inaccuracy is where he states that 'Except in certain limited situations (like agriculture), the WTO does not allow subsidies.' This is technically wrong since the largest category of subsidies, called actionable subsidies, is allowed in the WTO *unless* their adverse effects on trade are demonstrated by a complainant. The AB has endorsed this point in Appellate Body report, *Canada — Measures Affecting the Export of Civilian Aircraft* Recourse by Brazil to Article 21.5 of the DSU (WT/DS70/AB/RW)/DSR 2000:IX, 4299, at 47.

[12] Howse and Eliason advocate an opposite view by examining the issue in the context of government provision of goods (item iii) in light of the AB rulings in *US Lumber*. See R. Howse and A. Eliason, 'Domestic and international strategies to address climate change: an overview of the WTO legal issues', in this volume.

[13] In the WTO, Border Tax Adjustment can arguably be used as a tool to address such concerns about competitiveness. For more see, J. Pauwelyn, 'US federal climate policy and competitiveness concerns: the limits and options of international trade law', Working Paper (Duke University, 2007).

## 2.    Is the determination of 'benefit' complex in the world of renewables?

The notion of benefit refers to the requirement that a subsidy must confer an advantage on a recipient, taking into account the conditions that such a recipient would otherwise have to face in a 'competitive market-place'.[14] What is crucial in the decisions of the AB in this respect is that in determining whether a benefit is conferred, the relevant analysis should not focus on whether the recipient is better off than its competitors in a market-place. Rather, the question is whether a recipient is better off than *it* would otherwise have been absent the financial contribution.

The above consideration of the notion of benefit has an important implication in the world of renewables. Howse *et al.* (2006) point out the complexity of identifying a 'benefit' in the renewables market where there is extensive government intervention.[15] Referring to the AB decisions on *Canada Lumber*[16] and *US Privatisation CVD*,[17] they conclude that a definition of a meaningful market benchmark for benefit is elusive in the biofuels market.[18] It could be inferred that Howse *et al.* perceive the determination of benefit as a major barrier to a finding of a subsidy in the RE (in this case biofuels) market.

I cannot fully concur with that conclusion. Of the above-mentioned cases, *US Lumber* deals with provision of goods by a government for less than adequate remuneration (ASCM Article 1.1. (a)(1)(iii)). In this case, as the AB stated, determining whether a benefit is conferred may be a complex matter if a market is extensively distorted by government interventions. In these circumstances despite the AB's permissive interpretation which basically allowed other jurisdictions to be looked at in a

---

[14] See the Appellate Body report, *Canada — Aircraft*, paragraph 157 where the Appellate Body stated that 'there can be no "benefit" to the recipient unless the "financial contribution" makes the recipient "better off" than it would otherwise have been, absent that contribution'.

[15] See R. Howse, P. van Bork and C. Hebebrand, 'WTO disciplines and biofuels: opportunities and constraints in the creation of a global marketplace', *International Food & Agricultural Trade Policy Council (IPC) Discussion Paper* (Washington DC: Renewable Energy and International Law (REIL), 2006).

[16] Appellate Body report *United States — Final Countervailing Duty Determination With Respect To Certain Softwood Lumber From Canada* (WT/DS257/AB/R)/DSR 2004:II.

[17] Appellate Body report *United States — Countervailing Measures Concerning Certain Products from the European Communities* (WT/DS212/AB/R)/DSR 2003:I, 5.

[18] With the existence of similar government intervention in other sectors of renewable energy, the same conclusion might be inferred in line with the arguments of Howse *et al.* (2006).

search for a benchmark, defining a meaningful benchmark, i.e. the market price of such goods or services, might still prove difficult. The second case is to consider whether the effect of a benefit from a previous financial contribution is continued beyond a privatisation process. There are of course complex situations, like these two cases, where an examination of benefit requires reference to the market price of goods or services. However, reiterating the opinion of the AB in *Canada Aircraft*, most types of financial contribution in the world of renewables, including grants, tax credits and tax exemptions, almost *by definition* confer a benefit upon their recipient. This is because grants, tax credits or tax exemptions normally make their beneficiary 'better off' than it would otherwise have been absent such government support. In the case of grants, for example, the issue of a market benchmark would be hardly likely to arise in the first place, as the market is very unlikely to provide grants. Tax credits and tax exemptions will also normally make their beneficiaries better off and therefore confer a benefit or an advantage upon their recipient.

One important exception would arguably arise in cases where a government imposes a regulatory burden on entities for environmental objectives and simultaneously provides them with financial or fiscal compensation to offset that burden. It might be argued that to the extent that the level of the financial compensation (like grants) or fiscal recompense (like tax exemptions) does not exceed the extra costs incurred by affected recipients, such a financial contribution does not confer a benefit.[19] This argument may have legitimate grounds particularly when the burden and the compensatory measure are found in one regulatory package. One remarkable but controversial example of such a case is the free allocation of allowances in a carbon cap and trade regime. For instance, the grandfathering provision of the EU Emissions Trading Scheme in its first phase provides for free allocation of at least 95 per cent of allowances among covered entities.[20] Most EU Member States distribute allowances based on the entities' historical emissions.[21]

---

[19] A similar argument is made by Sykes in A. Sykes 'The economics of WTO rules on subsidies and countervailing measures' (2003) *John M. Olin Law & Economics Working Paper No. 186*, University of Chicago, at 4.

[20] See Article 10 30/87/EC of the European Parliament and of the Council of 13 October 2003 establishing a scheme for trading of greenhouse gas emission allowances within the Community and amending Council Directive 96/61/EC.

[21] See J. de Sepibus, 'The European emission trading scheme put to the test of state aid rules' NCCR Working Paper 2007/34.

A free allocation of allowances which have financial value in the EU carbon market may well entail a financial contribution by EU governments to the recipients. It might be argued that, in the first phase, unless the level of allowances distributed for each entity does not go beyond their historical emissions or what they need to continue their business as usual, they do not confer a benefit. On the other hand, one might argue that the recipients could be potentially better off through selling on to the carbon market the allowances they have not utilised as a result of implementing efficiency measures. Following this line of argument, determining the existence of benefit should be examined on a case-by-case basis.

The above conclusion that there might be no benefit in cases of a regulatory package consisting of an environmental burden coupled with offsetting financial mechanisms might not find a strong basis in the ASCM. For instance Article 8.2(c), before its expiration, had envisaged extensive limitations for 'assistance to promote adaptation of existing facilities to new environmental requirements imposed by law and/or regulations which result in greater constraints and financial burden on firms'. Such assistance, for example, shall be limited to 20 per cent of the cost of adaptation. Hence where a government imposes a mandatory minimum quota of ethanol to be blended with gasoline while compensating for the extra costs which such a regulation would entail for fuel blenders, one might argue that a finding of no subsidy due to absence of benefit would not fit with the logic of the ASCM.

Finally with respect to other types of financial contribution, such as loans with rates more favourable than market rates and loan guarantees among others, Article 14 of the ASCM has provided clear guidance, as it refers to the market-place or 'usual investment practices', in describing how to establish the benchmark against which the existence of a benefit to a recipient in a renewables market would be determined.

### B. Identifying subsidies in the world of renewables: an ASCM-compatible analysis

#### 1. *Straightforward subsidies*

Various grants, tax credits, favourable loan programmes and loan guarantees are provided to the production, supply and consumption chains of RE sectors worldwide. The provision of grants (including capital grants and research & development (R&D) grants) in this sector is prevalent not only in developed countries such as the US, Canada, Australia, Japan and European countries, but also in China and India.[22]

In the US, the Energy Policy Act (EPACT) of 2005 provides for loan guarantees to carry out commercial demonstration projects for ethanol derived from sugarcane (section 1516). It also provides for US\$ four billion in grants for the period 2006–2015, to be spent on ethanol R&D. Furthermore, the recent Energy Independence and Security Act (EISA) of 2007 was aimed at increasing R&D grants for biofuels.[23] The majority of the US federal subsidies on biofuels, however, are in the form of volumetric excise tax credits. These tax credits are awarded 'without limit, and regardless of the price of gasoline, to every gallon of ethanol blended in the marketplace, domestic or imported' an average from US\$2,220–US\$2,650 million per year for the 2006–2010 period according to different estimations.[24] Koplow (2006) estimates the total amount of subsidies to the US biofuels sector at around US\$5.1–US\$ 6.8 billion for ethanol, and US\$0.4–US\$ 0.5 billion for biodiesel in 2006.[25] Production tax credits for renewable electricity have also been one of the most effective incentive schemes in the US providing 1.5 cent/kWh credit for wind, solar, geothermal and 'closed-looped' bioenergy facilities with other technologies receiving tax credits with a lesser value.[26] Although the largest subsidies in the US are authorised at the federal level, individual states also provide for tax credits and grants worth considerable amounts. In the EU, the Directive on energy taxation has enabled Member States to use tax incentives to stimulate demand for

[22] See the IEA's Global Renewable Energy Policies and Measures Data Base at www.iea.org/textbase/pamsdb/grresult.aspx?mode=gr, last visited 21 August 2007, bearing in mind that its data are not fully up-to-date. For the existing approach towards subsidising clean energy, see, N. Stern, *The Economics of Climate Change: The Stern Review. Report to the Cabinet Office, HM Treasury* (Cambridge University Press, 2006), p. 416. For subsidy schemes of various countries see K. Deketelaere, J. E. Milne, L. A. Kreiser, *et al.* (eds), *Critical Issues in Environmental Taxation Volume IV: International and Comparative Perspectives* (Oxford University Press, 2007).

[23] See the CRS Report for Congress on EISA 2007 at http://energy.senate.gov/public/_files/RL342941.pdf, last visited January 2008, at 6.

[24] See D. Koplow, 'Biofuels — at what cost? Government support for ethanol and biodiesel in the United States', prepared for the Global Subsidies Initiative (GSI) of the International Institute for Sustainable Development (IISD), Geneva, Switzerland, (2006) at 50.

[25] See Koplow (2006) at 56.

[26] These credits have been extended by the Energy Policy Act of 2005 until the end of 2008. See M. Mendonca, *Feed-in Tariffs, Accelerating the Deployment of Renewable Energy* (London: World Future Council, Earthscan, 2007).

biofuels. Nineteen Member States have used this opportunity.[27] Production subsidies, investment grants and R&D grants are also prevalent in the EU region.[28]

As mentioned before, grants and tax credits are the most straightforward subsidies as far as Article 1 of the ASCM is concerned, due to the 'benefit' being conferred on their recipient.

Many of these straightforward subsidies (mainly grants) target R&D activities deemed necessary for the development of new technologies in the field.[29] From the legal perspective it is important to note that all R&D subsidies are basically actionable according to the ASCM if proved to be specific. This is because the green light category, which included R&D subsidies and was created by virtue of Article 8.2, was provisionally applicable for five years. This provision was not extended by Members after its expiration according to Article 31.[30]

## 2.   Are tax exemptions on the basis of environmental policies subsidies?

Subsidisation through fiscal policies including tax credits, tax breaks or tax exemptions is one of the most prevalent forms of government support for renewables. The legal question here is whether there is any ground in the ASCM for excluding tax exemptions on the basis of environmental policies from tax exemptions as a government foregoing revenue, which is 'otherwise due' and hence an instance of financial contribution. In principle there is none. Indeed, as will be explained later, environmental exceptions are not defined in the ASCM structure as it stands today. In other words, taking into account the AB rulings in *US — FSC*, the mere fact that, say, a volumetric tax credit on biofuels or an exemption of a wind turbine from a sales tax has an environmental objective does not exclude it from being defined as a subsidy and therefore from the ASCM disciplines.

---

[27]   See Lorenzo and Nilsson, 'Transport biofuels in the European Union: the state of play', *Transport Policy* 14 (2007) 533–43, at 535.

[28]   *Ibid.*, see table 2 at 563.

[29]   The German Government has spent more than 3.5 billion Euros on R&D in RE since 1990. See P. Runchi, 'Renewable energy policy in Germany: an overview and assessment' (2005), available at www.globalchange.umd.edu/energytrends/germany/1/, last visited September 2007.

[30]   For R&D as green box subsidies under AoA see section C.

An important caveat here should be borne in mind in the case of taxation related to 'products' — as opposed to income tax — in situations where a tax is imposed on a certain polluting factor such as carbon. In this case, it could be argued that exempting a renewable resource from taxes imposed on the basis of carbon emissions does not entail a financial contribution — there is a 'potential' governmental revenue but it was not 'due' in the first place. The AB decision in US — FSC to respect the rules of taxation of each Member in determining what is 'otherwise due' and also its quest for 'comparable situations' supports this argument.[31] In this sense, a WTO panel in its analysis of a 'legitimately comparable' situation may arguably be justified in looking into the environmental objectives behind a tax policy.

It should be noted that a fully fledged carbon taxation system need not entail a tax exemption. In such a system, any emitter would pay a consistent rate of carbon tax according to the amount of $CO_2$ they emit. However, this question may arise where there are less inclusive 'versions' of carbon taxes. A good example of this case is the Swiss Climate Cent (CHF 0.015 per litre) to be levied on petrol and diesel fuels with a full exemption given to biofuels.[32] In this case, and for other so-called 'versions' of carbon taxes, one might find a 'comparable situation' in the sense of the US — FSC case between fossil fuels, on one hand and renewables which emit $CO_2$, albeit less, on the other. This is because, in the case of biofuels, carbon emissions, although generally lower than those from fossil fuels, are not zero even when full account is taken of emissions throughout their life cycle. Therefore, to the extent that biofuels emit $CO_2$ over their life cycle, a 'full' carbon tax exemption provided to them could contain a subsidy. In fact in this case, the way the Swiss Climate Cent Levy is designed runs counter to the environmental policy it pursues — the lower the life cycle emissions of the biofuels, the smaller

---

[31] See Appellate Body Report in US — FSC, WT/DS108/AB/R, adopted 20 March 2000, paragraph 90 and Appellate Body Report United States — Tax Treatment for 'Foreign Sales Corporations', WT/DS108/AB/RW, 14 January 2002, Recourse to Article 21.5 of the DSU by the EU, paragraph 92. Therefore each Member can restructure its taxation system in a way which does not contain a subsidy based on 'government revenue otherwise due' by imposing a lower rate of tax on environmentally friendly products instead of providing exemption as an exception to a general rule.

[32] Came into effect on 1 October 2005 until the end of 2007. See R. Steenblik and J. Simón, 'Biofuels: at what cost? Government support for ethanol and biodiesel in Switzerland', prepared for the Global Subsidies Initiative (GSI) of the International Institute for Sustainable Development (IISD), Geneva, Switzerland (2007).

the amount of the a subsidy created by the Climate Cent Levy exemption.[33] This has led to an ironic outcome where the Swiss Government is in effect providing greater subsidies to the more polluting biofuels producers.[34]

### 3.  Indirect subsidies (downstream or upstream subsidies)

There are circumstances in which a government bestows a financial contribution on an entity, but other entities enjoy a benefit as a result. Article 1 of the ASCM does not exclude situations in which the recipient of the financial contribution and of the benefit are not identical. To examine whether there is an 'indirect subsidy', it is sufficient to demonstrate that a benefit of a subsidy to an upstream entity is passed to a downstream entity or vice versa. The issue of 'pass-through analysis' has been the subject of many cases in the WTO where it is found that 'one company may be found to "benefit" from a "financial contribution" conferred on another company'.[35] The AB has noted, however, that such a passed-on benefit to an upstream or a downstream entity cannot be simply presumed to exist. It should be supported by factual evidence and examined on a case-by-case basis.[36]

In the case of RE industries, there are various indirect subsidies: upstream subsidies such as those on inputs to an RE producer. These subsidies include subsidies on feedstock as an input to biofuels or

---

[33]  For the sake of simplicity, one may think of the subsidy created by the Climate Cent Levy as a carbon tax exemption. In this case, the amount of subsidy is not the full amount of exemption (one cent per litre). But it is for the amount that biofuels are not taxed for the $CO_2$ they emit taking their life-cycle emissions into account.

[34]  The Climate Cent Levy, although serving as a good example, does not entail a significant amount of subsidy (68,400 CHF for biodiesel in 2006) generated from a tax exemption (145,000 CHF for biodiesel in 2006) whereas exemption from the Swiss Mineral Oil Tax granted to biodiesel and Straight Vegetable Oil (SVO) was approximately CHF 7.3 million in 2006. See Steenblik and Simón (2007).

[35]  The panel report on *United States — Imposition of Countervailing Duties on Certain Hot-Rolled Lead and Bismuth Carbon Steel Products Originating in the United Kingdom*, WT/DS138/R, 23 December 1999 at footnote 69. The report was upheld by the Appellate Body.

[36]  See Appellate Body report *United States — Final Countervailing Duty Determination with Respect to Certain Softwood Lumber From Canada* (WT/DS257/AB/R) / DSR 2004: II, 587, paragraphs 139–41. The Appellate Body in that case referred to previous cases such as Appellate Body report *Canada — Measures Affecting the Export of Civilian Aircraft* (WT/DS70/AB/R) / DSR 1999:III, 1377 and Appellate Body report *United States — Import Measures on Certain Products from the European Communities* (WT/DS165/AB/R) / DSR 2001:I, 373.

subsidies granted to producers of wind turbines, photovoltaic cells, etc. which are all eventually passed on to the producers of biofuels, wind energy, solar power, etc. Here it is important to distinguish between two situations: first, in the case where upstream and downstream producers are affiliated, for instance, they belong to the same company, passed-on benefit could arguably be presumed. This is mainly because the recipient and beneficiary are basically identical. Second, if the upstream and downstream companies are totally separate or operate at arm's length, the existence of benefit to the RE producer as a result of a subsidy to the upstream industry cannot be simply presumed. Rather it should be established by a complainant on a case-by-case basis through a consideration of the extent to which the subsidy has been passed through to the RE producer in the form of a lower price for the input.[37] This might not be an easy task since producers of inputs are likely to charge the producers of renewables a 'market price', which might itself be distorted because of the very existence of the subsidy depending on the conditions surrounding the market-place and the magnitude of the subsidy.

Downstream subsidies are RE consumption subsidies which could benefit industrial purchasers of renewables such as fuel blenders. Good examples are the EU Directive on energy taxation[38] which allows for exemptions for RE and also the US volumetric excise tax credits provided to the fuel blenders.[39] In this case, the fact that the EU Directive and the US tax credits do not exclude the purchase of imported biofuels from their scope, does not mean that a benefit is not conferred upon RE producers (domestic or foreign). This is because for a benefit to exist, it is not necessary for domestic beneficiaries to have a 'competitive advantage' over foreign producers. Rather it is sufficient that the beneficiaries are better off than they would otherwise have been in the absence of the subsidy. As Koplow (2006) mentions in the case of the US, although these subsidies are nominally provided to fuel blenders, they actually enable those blenders to pay a higher price for the biofuels they purchase than they could afford without the subsidy.[40] Thus these are subsidies indirectly granted to biofuel producers (both domestic and foreign).[41]

---

[37] See supra n. 36.
[38] See Article 16 of the Council Directive 2003/96/EC 'restructuring the Community framework for the taxation of energy products and electricity'.
[39] See supra n. 24.     [40] Koplow (2006) at 4.
[41] However these subsidies may not lead to a dispute because they do not normally cause any 'adverse effects'. See section F.

## 4.  Subsidisation through regulatory means: is this captured by the ASCM?

There are two main types of regulatory support for RE which are frequently used worldwide: minimum quota measures and minimum price mechanisms. In a minimum quota system, grid operators or fuel providers are required by law to allocate a minimum share for a specific source of RE. The terms mandatory blending target and RE standards (RES) or renewable portfolio standards (RPS) are used in the cases of renewable transport fuels and electricity, respectively.

The mandatory blending targets for biofuels are in use on both sides of the Atlantic. The 2003 EU biofuels Directive requires a blending target of 5.75 per cent calculated on the basis of energy content by the end of 2010.[42] This minimum target has been increased to 10 per cent in 2020 in the new proposal for a Directive recently presented by the Commission.[43]

In the US, the EPACT of 2005 envisaged that the first US mandatory target for biofuels of four billion gallons of ethanol and biodiesel in 2006 would be almost doubled in 2012.[44] Currently under the EISA of 2007, the new minimum target has been raised to nine billion gallons for 2008, rising to thirty-six billion gallons for 2022.[45] RES are mainly used in the US in around thirty states. However, the efforts to include RES in the EISA to be applied on the federal level were dropped as the result of the US President's threat of veto.[46]

These incentive schemes to promote renewables are not subsidies as far as the WTO law is concerned. This is because despite the clear existence of a benefit to the producers of renewables, there is a lack of financial contribution (or a price support) made by a government of any of the types stipulated by Article 1.1 of the ASCM.

Minimum price supports, however, such as those found in feed-in tariff systems, might arguably be considered as subsidies. Feed-in models which are predominant in the EU, but also in other countries such as

---

[42] See Article 3(1)(ii) of the Directive 2003/30/EC of the European Parliament and of the Council of 8 May 2003 on the promotion of the use of biofuels or other renewable fuels for transport.

[43] See the Proposal for a Directive of the European Parliament and of the Council on the promotion of the use of energy from renewable sources. Brussels, 23 January 2008 COM (2008) 19 final 2008/0016 (COD).

[44] See EPACT 2005 section 1501.    [45] Supra n. 23 at 5.

[46] See Statement of Administration Policy, H. R. 6 — Energy Independence and Security Act of 2007, December 2007.

some regions of India and Canada, are defined as a 'pricing law' guaranteeing RE operators a certain amount of profit by setting rates and also providing priority access to grids.[47] Article 1.1(a)(2) of the ASCM states that a subsidy is deemed to exist if 'there is any form of income or price support in the sense of Article XVI of GATT 1994' and a benefit is conferred to a recipient. On the latter, since feed-in laws 'ensure' profits which might not have existed in a normal market-place, they clearly confer a benefit on RE producers.

Knowing that benefit exists, the answer to the question whether these pricing laws contain a subsidy according to Article 1 depends on how one understands the term 'price support' particularly 'in the sense of GATT Article XVI'. Price support from an economic perspective is a government interfering in a market to increase the price of a product, for example by procurement means.[48] Article XVI makes price support mechanisms subject to the ones 'which operate directly or indirectly to increase imports of any product from, or to reduce imports of any product into its territory'. Hence it could be inferred from these two cumulative provisions that any regulation which benefits RE providers through minimum price support would be a subsidy within the ASCM to the extent that it increases exports or decreases imports. An early GATT panel alluded to the notion of price support as follows:

> a subsidy which provides an incentive to increased production will, in the absence of offsetting measures, e.g. a consumption subsidy, either increase exports or reduce imports.[49]

Nevertheless the same panel seemed to believe that there is only a subsidy if a government, by indirect or direct methods, maintains a price by purchases and resale 'at a loss'.[50] In other words, it applied a 'cost to government' condition to the definition of a subsidy.

Government 'purchases or resale at a loss' (as a subsidy) were later explicitly covered in Article 1.1(a)(1)(iii) of the ASCM with the explanatory Article 14(d). In these provisions, government provision of goods or services for less than adequate remuneration or government purchase of goods for more than adequate remuneration are labelled as subsidies.

---

[47] See Mendonca (2007).
[48] See A. V. Deardorff. *Terms of Trade: Glossary of International Economics* (Singapore: World Scientific Publishers, 2006).
[49] Panel report on subsidies and state trading: Report on Subsidies, L/1160, March 1960, paragraph 10.
[50] *Ibid.* at 11.

Howse (2005) invokes this paragraph to examine whether the minimum price purchase requirements similar to the one existing under German law, which gave rise to the *PreussenElektra* case,[51] contain a subsidy under the ASCM.[52] Referring to this provision and paragraph (iv), regarding government entrusting or directing a private body to make a financial contribution on its behalf, it concludes that there is no subsidy where a government mandates private bodies to purchase renewable electricity at a certain price. His argument is that minimum price supports do not represent a delegation of a government function to any private body as required by paragraph (iv). Rather, he argues, they represent a regulation of the electricity market.

Howse's (2005) argument may be legitimate in the context of Article 1.1(a)(1) with the caveat that the panel in *US — DRAMS* interpreted the term 'normally vested in the government' very broadly.[53] More importantly, that argument overlooks Article 1.1(a)(2), which envisages price support per se as a subsidy (if conferring a benefit). The question whether price regulations which confer benefit are captured by the term 'price support' remains to be developed in case law. It is submitted, however, that this could well be the case for the following reasons: first, it is covered by the ordinary meaning of the term 'price support' as required by Article 31.1 of the Vienna Convention on the Law of Treaties. Second, the GATT panel interpretation of price support to mean exclusively government sale or purchase 'at a loss' seems to be outdated in light of the panel[54] and AB ruling in *Canada Aircraft*. In that case, Canada's argument to restrict the term benefit to the occasions where there is a cost to government was rejected.[55] Third, confining Article 1.1(a)(2) to situations where a government maintains a price by purchases and resale

---

[51] European Court of Justice, 13 March 2001, Case C–379/98, *Aktiengesellschaft PreussenElektra* v. *Schleswag Aktiengesellschaft*.

[52] See R. Howse, 'Post-hearing submission to the International Trade Commission: world trade law and renewable energy: the case of non-tariff measures', 5 May 2005, REIL at 21–22.

[53] See the report of the panel in *United States — Countervailing Duty Investigation on Dynamic Random Access Memory Semiconductors (DRAMS) from Korea* (WT/DS296/R), 21 February 2005.

[54] Report of the AB in *Canada — Measures Affecting the Export of Civilian Aircraft* WT/DS70/AB/R, 2 August 1999 at 160.

[55] It is worth noting, however, that the panel deliberately left aside 'situations of alleged "income or price supports" within the meaning of Article 1.1(a)(2)' in its finding. See report of the panel in *Canada — Measures Affecting the Export of Civilian Aircraft* WT/DS70/R, 14 April 1999 at paragraph 9.120.

'at a loss' will render this provision inutile in light of Article 1.1(a)(1)(iii) which already captures such measures.

In the EU context, with the absence of a price support criterion and the existence of a 'cost to government' condition, it does not seem unusual that the European Court did not consider the German minimum price requirement 'state aid'. For the reasons mentioned above this might not be the case in the WTO.[56]

### C. Biofuel subsidies and the Agreement on Agriculture

#### 1. Inconsistency in biofuels' classification and implications for subsidy disciplines

Although WTO Members are not required by any WTO provision to classify products and commodities in a certain manner, most WTO Members are, at the same time, Members of the World Customs Organization (WCO). The WCO mandates its Members to apply its system of tariff classification known as the Harmonized System (HS) up to a six-digit level.[57] In the HS system, biodiesel, as one of the two important biofuels, is classified under chapter 38 and is clearly defined with specific reference, in the WCO Explanatory Notes, to its composition, production process and end-use as a fuel for diesel engines.[58] Ethanol as a biofuel, however, is not specifically referred to in the HS. This leaves ethanol to be classified merely according to its chemical composition making it subject to a more general categorisation as unnaturated (HS 220710) or denatured alcohol (HS 220720).[59]

---

[56] This view is supported in G. E. L. Hernandez de Madrid, *Regulations of Subsidies and State Aid in WTO and EC Law, Conflicts in International Trade Law* (The Hague: Kluwer Law International: 2007), pp. 120–3 and p. 449.

[57] Officially known as 'Harmonized Commodity Description and Coding System', available at www.wcoomd.org/home_wco_topics_hsoverviewboxes_hsconvention_hsnomencla turetable2007.htm, last visited January 2008.

[58] In the 35th Session of the WCO in March 2005, biodiesel was reclassified under 3824.90 described as 'a mixture of mono-alkyl esters of long chain fatty acids derived from vegetable oils or animal fats, which is a domestic renewable fuel for diesel engines and which meets the specifications of ASTM D 6751. It can also be used as a fuel additive'.

[59] According to UNCTAD both types of ethanol are used for production of biofuels, but it states that un-denatured ethanol is more suitable for use as a fuel. See S. Zarrilli, *The Emerging Biofuels Market: Regulatory, Trade and Development Implications* (Geneva: UNCTAD, 2006). According to the US Environmental Protection Agency 'ethanol produced for use as motor vehicle fuel is denatured specifically so that it can only be used as fuel'. See Regulation of Fuels and Fuel Additives: Renewable Fuel Standard

Annex 1 of the WTO Agreement on Agriculture (AoA) defines it scope to cover HS chapters 1–24 with the exception of fish and fish products. Hence, fuel ethanol classified under HS chapter 22, as opposed to biodiesel coming under chapter 38, is an agricultural product as far as the AoA provisions are concerned. Note that with the exception of production limiting programmes, *de minimis* support and development programmes designed on a support and development (S&D) basis, all domestic agricultural support which happens to distort trade in, or production of, agricultural products (amber box subsidies[60]) was subject to annual reductions over the six-year implementation period. Moreover, the current negotiations, if concluded successfully, will supposedly subject them to further cuts.

The fact that subsidy disciplines of the AoA apply to fuel ethanol 'as such', as opposed to biodiesel, might have significant implications: it could follow that any subsidy on ethanol production, on top of farm subsidies for producing feedstock for biofuels in general, should be included in the amber box. This is particularly so because the total aggregate measurement of support (total AMS) — a sum representing the level of amber box subsidies[61] — includes non-product-specific subsidies.[62] If the amber box includes the bulk of farm subsidies related to biofuel production and especially ethanol subsidies per se, the current commitment levels of both the EU (US$59.8 billion) and the US (US$19.1 billion) would already be exceeded as also suggested by the US Department of Agriculture.[63]

In order to avoid such a consequence, subsidising countries may seek two alternative solutions: the first is to argue that biofuel subsidies including those on ethanol are not agricultural support, but industrial subsidies by nature and hence they should be governed by the rules of the ASCM. For instance the US notifies its biofuels subsidies under Article 25 of the SCM under the heading 'energy and fuels' rather than agriculture. If the WTO adjudicating bodies endorse this in the course of a dispute, it will be for the complaining party to demonstrate that these subsidies have an 'adverse effect' on its like products.[64] The WTO, however, may

Program, Environmental Protection Agency, available at www.epa.gov/EPA-AIR/2006/September/Day-22/a7887a.htm, last visited January 2008.

[60] See Article 6.1 of the AoA. For more see J. McMahon, *The WTO Agreement on Agriculture* (Oxford University Press, 2006), p. 67.

[61] See Article 1(a) of the AoA.

[62] See Article 1(h) and paragraph (1) of Annex 3 of the AoA.

[63] US Department of Agriculture, '2007 Farm Bill Theme Paper: Energy and Agriculture', Washington, DC, August 2006, at 18.

[64] See section F. Do RE subsidies cause 'adverse effects'?

not accept this approach because these subsidies are indeed covered by the AoA by virtue of Annex 1, and in view of their direct distortive effects on agricultural products. In that case, the second solution is to invoke the so-called 'green box' exemptions for biofuel subsidies according to Annex 2 of the AoA.

## 2. Are green box opportunities 'real' for biofuel production subsidies?

The so-called 'green box', envisaged in Annex 2 of the AoA, contains agricultural support which is excluded from any disciplines of the AoA, especially from amber box caps. This includes farm subsidies which have 'no, or at most minimal, trade-distorting effects or effects on production'. In addition,[65] paragraph 1 of Annex 2 sets two general conditions for green box subsidies: the support should be through a publicly funded government programme not involving transfers from consumers. Second the support in question shall not have the effect of providing price support to producers. Other than these broad conditions which apply across the board to all green box measures, there are policy-specific criteria and conditions listed in paragraphs 2–12, applying to particular policies seeking green box exemptions under Annex 1. Three of these measures are probably of most relevance to ethanol subsidies: R&D subsidies (paragraph 2(a)), structural adjustment assistance provided through resource retirement programmes (paragraph 10) and payments under environmental programmes (paragraph 12).

In the previous section it was shown that there is an increasing amount of R&D subsidies, mainly in the form of grants, flowing to RE sectors worldwide. These subsidies, although potentially actionable under the ASCM, might be found to be exempt from amber box disciplines in the case of ethanol. This is because R&D subsidies, including general research, research in connection with environmental programmes, and research programmes relating to particular agricultural products, may qualify as green box measures as part of government service programmes (paragraph 2 chapeau and (a) of Annex 2). This is, however, subject to

---

[65] It is believed that green box subsidies, in addition to the specific conditions stipulated in Annex 2 must have 'no, or at most minimal, trade-distorting effects or effects on production'. The panel in US Upland — Cotton, however, did not decide on the issue of whether this statement only informs the general and policy specific criteria or it has to be regarded as a 'freestanding obligation'. See the panel report at paragraph 7.412.

the pre-condition that they do not involve direct payments to producers and processors.[66]

There might be other ways of claiming green box exemptions for biofuels including biodiesel. For instance, some commentators have seen a green box opportunity for biofuel feedstock producers in the sense of paragraph 10 of Annex 1.[67] Under this paragraph, supports provided to farmers to retire land from 'marketable agricultural products' for a minimum of three years with certain conditions are exempt from reduction commitments. The key issue here is what constitutes a 'marketable agricultural product'. First generation feedstock such as corn and soy bean, are surely captured by this term and thus farmers producing them as an input to biofuel will not be retiring land from production of a 'marketable agricultural product'. Moreover, it would have direct effects on food prices if farmers were to switch from growing food crops to producing energy crops as biofuels feedstock. Hence supports provided on this ground will not have 'no, or at most minimal, trade-distorting effects or effects on production' as required by the chapeau to Annex 2.

The issue might be more complex with respect to second generation feedstock.[68] Dana (2004) opines that green box measures could be used for producing feedstock for cellulosic ethanol, such as crop waste, corn husks, or grass which are not, in his opinion, 'marketed as agricultural commodities by other WTO Members'.[69] As most of these products are nevertheless agricultural products, the decisive question would only be a factual one — are they 'marketable' regardless of whether in a domestic or international market. It seems that in circumstances where farmers might even have to pay to dispose of crop waste, they could not be considered as marketable. Market developments for biofuels in the future

---

[66] Dana (2004) opines that R&D subsidies which involve direct payments to producers and processors are covered in paragraph 12 under government environmental programmes. See D. Dana, *Green Box Opportunities in the Farm Bill for Farm Income through the Conservation and Clean Energy Development Programs* (Chicago, IL: Northwestern University Law School, 2004), at 10.

[67] See Howse *et al.* (2006) and Dana (2004).

[68] The UN report on biofuels states that 'second-generation fuels are made from ligno-cellulosic biomass feedstock using advanced technical processes'. See 'Sustainable bioenergy, a framework for decision makers', (2006) UN-Energy. According to this report, as these technologies become commercially viable, the negative effects on land use and food security will be lessened, but will not disappear (at 33).

[69] Inputs to other forms of bioenergy, such as animal waste for heat production, could also be included in this category. See Dana (2004) at 10.

would imply that such farm support might gradually lose its 'green' status as these products become marketable. More relevant in the context of land retirement, as required by paragraph 10, would be the issue of farmers retiring land to produce non-food feedstock such as jatropha. Yet, jatropha as a non-food feedstock for biodiesel is already in the process of being commercialised in many developing countries such as the Philippines and India.[70]

Finally, payments under environmental programmes might be considered as green box support under paragraph 12. This is subject to conditions that such payments are part of a clearly defined government environmental or conservation programme and dependent upon the fulfilment of specific conditions under the government programmes, including conditions related to production methods. Most importantly, the payments shall be limited to the extra costs or loss of income involved in complying with the government programme.

Subsidies to ethanol consumers such as fuel blenders, which function as indirect subsidies to ethanol producers, potentially serves as an example of this type of green box measure.[71] This would be so, however, if governments merely compensated consumers (including fuel blenders) for the additional costs borne by them for purchasing or blending ethanol.

In any case, it should be noted that even if a subsidy scheme falls into the green box category, it will still remain actionable under the ASCM.[72] Controversies over the applicability of the ASCM to the AoA after the expiry of the Peace Clause[73] would appear less significant if one notes

---

[70] See UNCTAD, 'An assessment of the biofuels industry in Thailand', (2006), UNCTAD/DITC/TED/2006/7 and UNCTAD, 'An assessment of the biofuels industry in India' (2006), UNCTAD/DITC/TED/2006/6.

[71] In such cases, although one might question the 'environmental' benefits of biofuels, it could be argued that governments' sovereignty over how they devise their environmental regulations has to be recognised.

[72] This view is supported by R. H. Steinberg and T. E. Josling, 'When the peace ends: the vulnerability of EC and US agricultural subsidies to WTO legal challenge', *Journal of International Economic Law* 6 (2003), 369 and K. Halverson Cross, 'King cotton, developing countries and the "peace clause": the WTO's US cotton subsidies decision', *Journal of International Economic Law* 9 (2006), 149. For an opposite view see D. Chambovey, 'How the expiry of the peace clause (Article 13 of the WTO Agreement on Agriculture) might alter disciplines on agricultural subsidies in the WTO framework', *Journal of World Trade* 36 (2002), 305–10.

[73] The so-called 'Peace Clause' reflected in Article 13 of the AoA provided certain and limited exemptions for agriculture subsidies from being challenged in the WTO for the implementation period of six years.

that green box measures have 'no, or at most minimal, trade-distorting effects'. Thus, if a measure is really 'green' in this sense, there would naturally be no case under the general rules of the ASCM challenging green box measures, because the ASCM solely targets trade distortive subsidies.[74]

## D.    Electricity trade and relevant subsidy disciplines

Neither the GATT nor the GATS define what constitutes a good or a service. Hence it is necessary for WTO Members to reach a consensus as to the classification of an output of a specific production process. Such a consensus on the classification of electricity worldwide has yet to be documented. Going back to the history of the GATT 1947 at the time when this sector was entirely handled by state monopolies, negotiators did not seem to perceive electricity as a good.[75] Later on, the US, the EU and Canada, as opposed to Japan and Mexico, included electricity in their schedules of commitment to the GATT 1994. Overall, the international debate lately seems to be moving towards the recognition that generation of electricity, other than services incidental to power generation, is covered by the GATT, and transmission and distribution is covered by GATS provisions.[76]

Yet, as a matter of international law, there is no provision at the multilateral level requiring countries to classify electricity in either way. Although the HS notably classifies electrical energy as a commodity under chapter 27, it is under an optional heading allowing WCO members to decide otherwise.

The objective of this paper is not to argue for either case.[77] The implications of classifying electricity as a good or a service for its subsidy disciplines, however, should not be underestimated. This is because GATS subsidy disciplines, particularly those envisaged in its Article XV,

---

[74] Even Chambovey (2006:334) as the proponent of the non-applicability of the ASCM agrees that disputes are highly unlikely regarding 'genuine' green box measures.

[75] J. H. Jackson *World Trade and the Law of GATT (A Legal Analysis of the General Agreement on Tariffs and Trade* (New York: Bobbs-Merrill, 1969), p. 745.

[76] See G. Horlick *et al.* (2002) at 3. Also see UNCTAD Zarrilli 2003. Under the UN Central Product Classification, however, even generation of electricity if performed by a separate entity 'on a fee or contract basis' is also providing a 'manufacturing service' which could be covered by the GATS and does not constitute manufacturing a 'good'. See CPC Division 88, entitled 'Agricultural, Mining and Manufacturing Services' (Annex I).

[77] For arguments both ways see L. Albath, 'Trade and energy, investment in the gas and electricity sectors', *Oil Gas & Energy Law* (2004) at 88.

are much more lenient than the provisions of the ASCM.[78] In effect this means that Members perceiving electricity as a service may subsidise production, distribution, transmission and supply without facing a serious challenge under the GATS.[79] This may grant a full exemption for these countries to provide import substitution subsidies if they have not made a prohibitive national treatment commitment in their schedules of specific commitment. On the other hand, if electricity is recognised as a good, the rigorous disciplines of the ASCM would apply. For instance all import substitution subsidies per se would be banned.

When it comes to export subsidisation, the applicability of the ASCM would allow countries to resort to countervailing duty measures as an effective remedy to address the distortion that would be created as a result of an export subsidy. In these circumstances, countries classifying electrical energy as a service would arguably tie their own hands and not be able to invoke ASCM disciplines against exporting countries massively subsidising their electricity sector. From this angle, the lack of consensus among the WCO members reflected in the 'optional' classification of electricity, as stated in a WTO publication,[80] might lose its relevance over time. With the expansion of trade in electricity, especially development of a niche RE market, countries facing export competition might increasingly find themselves at a disadvantage vis-à-vis subsidising countries if they do not treat electricity as a good. This may cause a domino effect starting from major regions such as the EU and North American Free Trade Agreement (NAFTA) which have already clearly defined electricity as falling within the ambit of trade in goods.[81]

On the other hand, a Member whose policy is to provide domestic RE subsidies at the expense of RE imports being impeded or displaced in its market, as a way to promote its own RE industry, would probably prefer electricity to be treated as a service for the purposes of the WTO Agreement, so as to enjoy the leniency of the GATS subsidy provision.

On the whole, we will have to wait and see whether Members will officially put an end to this uncertainty, which could easily be done in the course of current negotiations on energy services; or whether they will

---

[78] Article XV of the GATS does not go beyond a request for consultations and exchange of information and leaves the issue to future negotiations.

[79] This is, however, subject to the MFN and, in scheduled sectors, national treatment obligations of the Members. For more on GATS subsidy disciplines, see R. Adlung, *Journal of International Economic Law* (2007), 235.

[80] See WTO Secretariat, *Guide to the GATS*, p. 261.

[81] See Article 602 paragraph 2 (h) of NAFTA and Annex EM to the ECT.

leave it to the WTO adjudicating bodies to do the job for them, similar to what the European Court of Justice (ECJ) did in the EU,[82] in the course of a dispute.

### E.  Are RE subsidies 'specific'?

In previous sections, different RE incentive schemes were identified as subsidies according to the definition provided in the ASCM and relevant case law. It should be noted that for a subsidy to be disciplined under the ASCM, it also has to be 'specific' as indicated by Article 1.2. Export contingent and import substitution subsidies which constitute the so-called 'prohibited' category are automatically deemed specific (Article 2.3). For the rest, the 'specificity' requirement implies that a subsidy must be granted to 'certain enterprises', defined as an enterprise or industry or group of enterprises or industries within the jurisdiction of the granting authority (Article 2.1). The rationale behind the specificity requirement is that a subsidy which is generally available throughout an economy should not be disciplined by the SCM. The provision does not make clear, however, what 'number' of enterprises or industries constitutes a 'group' which, if targeted with a subsidy programme, would make it specific.

Thus the concept of specificity faces serious uncertainties in the WTO and has yet to be developed in case law. So far, in almost all WTO cases, subsidies challenged under the ASCM were deemed specific.[83] It appears from the case law that a subsidy programme targeting only one industry, however large, would be deemed specific. In *US — Upland Cotton*, the panel based its finding of specificity on the fact that the subsidy programmes were 'not even generally available to the industry which can be categorized as the agricultural industry' (paragraph 7.1150). Notably the panel in *US Lumber IV* implicitly agreed that a subsidy targeting a large industry, (such as 'steel', 'autos', 'textiles', 'telecommunications', or the

---

[82]  The European Court of Justice in (ECJ) 1964 in *Costa/Enel* implicitly decided that electricity is to be treated as a good. Later on, in *Almelo* the ECJ explicitly regarded electricity as a good for the first time. See Albath (2004) at 89.

[83]  This has not been the case outside the WTO. For instance the US Department of Commerce in the case of *Final Negative Countervailing Duty Determination: Fresh Asparagus from Mexico*, 48 Fed. Reg. 21618 (13 May 1983) found that the irrigation facilities provided to the entire agricultural sector in the north-east of Mexico constitute a 'non-specific subsidy' programme.

like) could be deemed specific (paragraph 7.120).[84] Hence the denominator over which subsidised enterprises are measured for the purpose of finding 'specificity' seems to be the whole economy or at least the goods sector. In other words, a subsidy might target a large number of products within an industry or even a group of industries and still be deemed specific.[85]

More obvious cases are those in which a subsidy is 'explicitly' limited in terms of access to 'certain enterprises' in which case they are called de jure specific (Article 2.1(a)). On the other hand, in determining de facto specificity, for instance where a subsidy is not 'explicitly' limited to 'certain enterprises' whereas they are its predominant or disproportionate beneficiaries, account should also be taken of the diversification of an economy according to Article 2.1(c).[86]

In all these cases, it seems that the smaller the relative size of the beneficiary enterprises or industries, the higher the chances that they will be deemed specific. As mentioned above, it has not been made clear what exactly the relative size of such enterprises or industries should be to qualify them as 'certain enterprises' as defined above.[87] Therefore, determination of specificity remains a judgment call by a dispute settlement panel or investigating authorities to be assessed on a case-by-case basis.[88]

---

[84] See panel report in US — *Subsidies on Upland Cotton* (WT/DS267/R) and the panel report in *United States — Final Countervailing Duty Determination with Respect to Certain Softwood Lumber from Canada* (WT/DS257/R).

[85] In *US Lumber* the panel rejected Canada's argument that 'an "industry" should be interpreted as referring to "enterprises engaged in the manufacture of similar products"'. In that case the subsidy programme was deemed specific even though it covered 23 separate classes of industries, producing over 200 products (see the panel report at paragraph 4.52).

[86] For more on specificity under the WTO law, see Clark and Horlick (2004). For a comparison of specificity under WTO law and selectivity under EU law see Ehlermann and Goyette (2006) at 703.

[87] In the US system, Cameron and Berg have proposed a test under which a subsidy is de facto specific if the percentage of the total subsidy absorbed by the industry under a programme exceeds that industry's share of the country's gross national product. See Cameron and Berg, 'The countervailing duty law and the principle of general availability', *Journal of World Trade Law* 19 (1985), 497, 505.

[88] Confirmed by the panel, *US — Upland Cotton*, paragraph 7.1142. For more, see P. M. Alexander, 'The specificity test under US countervailing duty law', *Michigan Journal of International Law*, 807 (1989). He states that 'On the basis of its experience in administering the law, Commerce has found that the specificity test cannot be reduced to a precise mathematical formula. The determination of what constitutes a significant distortion of an economy requires line drawing on a case-by-case basis' (p. 12).

In general specificity, especially de facto specificity, might not be an easy test.[89] In the case of subsidies to RE producers, however, the determination of specificity could be straightforward in most cases. This is because, even if one takes the energy sector (and not the whole goods sector) as denominator, the relative size of the RE sector is significantly smaller than that of its non-renewable counterparts. At an aggregated global level, only 13.1 per cent of the world total primary energy supply (TPES) in 2004 came from renewable sources.[90] At the country level, which is relevant for the determination of specificity of a country's subsidy scheme, in almost all developed countries, with the exception of Austria, Iceland, New Zealand, Norway and Sweden, RE had a less than 20 per cent share in their TPES taking into account all combustible renewables and waste.[91]

Looking at transport biofuels specifically, their global share of the total road transport fuel consumption in energy terms was about 1 per cent in 2004.[92] At the country level in that year 'only in Brazil, Cuba and Sweden' did the share of biofuels in meeting total demand for transport fuel exceed 2 per cent.[93] Even Brazil's share, as the largest exporter of biofuels in the world, did not exceed 14 per cent.[94] Therefore, it could be inferred that all subsidies granted to the biofuels sectors in different countries are specific. Howse *et al.* (2006) argue that indirect upstream subsidies which are granted to biofuels feedstock as part of a general agricultural programme should be considered non-specific. This is because, in the case of corn, for instance, these support programmes benefit a variety of industries such as the processed food industry, the alcoholic beverages industry and the animal feed industry.[95] Nonetheless, following the same logic as the panel used in *US — Upland Cotton* and *US — Lumber*, that a specific subsidy may include numerous products and even cross many industries, might bring one to a different conclusion.

Similarly, in the case of electricity production, the quantity of renewables used in electricity production in 2004 did not exceed 17.9 per cent of which 16.1 per cent came from hydropower. The International Energy Agency's (IEA) Monthly Electricity Statistics of March 2007[96]

---

[89] For complexities of the specificity test, see J. D. Southwick, 'The lingering problem with the specificity test in United States countervailing duty law', *Minnesota Law Review*, May (1988). He suggests the replacement of the specificity test with a *de minimis* test.

[90] *Renewables in Global Energy Supply*, an IEA Fact Sheet, January 2007.

[91] *Ibid.*, inferred from table 1.    [92] IEA, *World Energy Outlook* (2006) at 387.

[93] *Ibid.*    [94] *Ibid.*, at 388 citing F. O. Licht (2006) and IEA Databases.

[95] See Howse *et al.* (2006).    [96] Available at www.iea.org

demonstrate that the size of non-hydro renewable electricity sectors of all IEA countries is very small. Hence, any subsidy programme in those countries targeting producers of non-hydro renewable electricity, not even singling out one particular technology, would most probably be deemed specific. In the case of hydro power, however, the specificity might be less straightforward in countries such as Canada, Iceland, New Zealand, Norway and Sweden, where the bulk of electricity production comes from this source. Yet, if one considers power generation as one large industry, any subsidy granted to this sector may be specific along the lines of *US — Upland Cotton* and *US — Lumber IV*.[97]

### F. Do RE subsidies cause 'adverse effects'?

The abundance of specific subsidies in the RE sector makes them subject to Parts III and V of the SCM which deal with actionable subsidies. This, of course, does not mean that these subsidies are necessarily banned in the WTO. It does, however, reflect the vulnerability of these RE subsidies in the sense that countries may unilaterally countervail them (Part V) or challenge them in a dispute if they can demonstrate that these subsidies have 'adverse effects' on their interests (ASCM Article 5).

The requirement to demonstrate adverse effects reflects the economic rationale behind the ASCM. That is, the only subsidies that would have to be disciplined at the WTO multilateral level are those that cause distortion in international trade. Export contingent and import substitution subsidies are per se prohibited due to their self-evident distortive effects on trade (Part II of the ASCM). For the rest, the distortionary effects of a subsidy have to be demonstrated in order for a country to countervail that subsidy or ask for its withdrawal through litigation. 'Adverse effects' of a subsidy, according to Article 5, could be manifested in an importing country's market in the form of an injury to its domestic industry (paragraph (a)) which could be offset by a countervailing duty measure. It could also happen if a subsidy causes 'serious prejudice' to the interest of another Member (paragraph (c)), which includes impediment or displacement of a product in the market of the subsidising country or in a third market (Article 6.3). In serious prejudice cases, a complainant could bring a so-called Track II claim against the subsidising Member which will then have to remove the adverse effects or withdraw the subsidy if a panel or the AB so decides (Article 7.8).

---

[97] See supra n. 84.

RE export subsidies (Article 3.1(a)) may be found, for instance, in the form of government provision of export credit guarantees or export credits at below market rates for RE with the conditions laid out in paragraphs (j) and (k) of Annex I of the ASCM.[98] Another type of prohibited subsidies, i.e. subsidies contingent upon the use of domestic over imported goods (import substitution subsidies), might also be found in the world of renewables. For instance in the case of biofuels, Loppacher and Kerr (2005) present an example from the US where a subsidy is given to refiners only if they use soy oil as a feedstock for biodiesel.[99] Considering the fact that the US produces 45 per cent of the soybeans grown in the world, they argue in favour of an import substitution subsidy prohibited under Article 3.1(b).[100] Although this is not a clear-cut instance of an import substitution subsidy, it might well be the case in light of *Canada Autos* where the AB envisaged a de facto concept for import substitution subsidies.[101]

As mentioned in section B: 4, minimum price requirements might also fit the definition of the term subsidy. Nonetheless, these schemes, such as electricity feed-in tariffs, are generally not likely to give rise to major disputes in the WTO due to a lack of adverse effects in cases where imports even handedly benefit from artificially high prices created by a minimum price requirement. This, of course, could only be the case where the scheme is applied on a non-discriminatory basis. Otherwise, they will involve restraints on RE trade, as Mendonca (2007) mentions,[102] if there are domestic production requirements.[103] In the latter case, a WTO panel might arguably find, in addition to a violation of the

---

[98] These measures will not be considered prohibited if they comply with the OECD Arrangement on Officially Supported Export Credits.

[99] L. J. Loppacher and W. A. Kerr, 'Can biofuels Become a global industry?: Government policies and trade constraints', prepared for *Energy Politics* (2005), www.dundee.ac.uk/cepmlp/journal/html/Vol15/Vol15_10.pdf, last visited October 2008.

[100] At the time of this study, we are not sure whether such a subsidy programme is maintained by the US Agriculture Department.

[101] In *Canada Autos* the AB decided that 'the Panel erred in finding that Article 3.1(b) does not extend to subsidies contingent "in fact" upon the use of domestic over imported goods.' See the report of the AB on *Canada — Certain Measures Affecting the Automotive Industry*, WT/DS139/AB/R, WT/DS142/AB/R, 31 May 2000.

[102] See M. Mendonca, *Feed-in Tariffs, Accelerating the Deployment of Renewable Energy* (London: Earthscan, 2007) at 13.

[103] This was the case in a Finnish scheme which was found inconsistent with the Treaty of Rome provisions on free trade by the ECJ. See judgment of the ECJ of 2 April 1998 in Case C-213/96, *Outkumpu Oy* [1998] ECR I–1777.

GATT national treatment obligation, an import substitution subsidy prohibited under Article 3.1(b) of the ASCM.

Challenging actionable subsidies may turn out to be more complicated than challenging prohibited ones due to the complexity of establishing a causal link between a subsidy and adverse effects especially in serious prejudice cases.

The finding of an adverse effect in the case of RE consumption subsidies or subsidies for blending biofuels with gasoline (as a means of supporting producers indirectly as discussed in section B:3) depends on the extent to which they are designed solely to benefit domestic industries. Biofuel consumption subsidies may not distort the flow of imports of biofuels insofar as they do not favour domestic over imported products. For example, in the case of volumetric excise tax credit for biofuels, the major ethanol subsidy in the US, it could be argued that there is no adverse effect of such subsidies on ethanol imported from Brazil or other places. This is because, currently, blenders will remain eligible for the tax credit whether they blend a gallon of domestic or of imported ethanol. It seems that in the present circumstances where tariffs are the major impediments to Brazilian imports of ethanol, establishing a causal link between tax credits and serious prejudice could be difficult.[104] The current regulatory environment in the US could simply change, however, if the law-makers started to think that taxpayers' money should only be used to encourage domestic production of ethanol. In general, providing subsidies exclusively to domestic producers, though permissible under Article III:8 of the GATT, might have adverse effects on imported like products and hence become actionable under the ASCM. For this very reason, resorting to tariffs will remain legally the safest way for the US to protect its biofuels industry.

This said, even non-discriminatory consumption subsidies may have an adverse effect outside the territory of the granting member. This is the subject of a recent complaint against US biodiesel tax credits made by the EU biodiesel industry.[105]

---

[104] It is true that currently high import tariffs on ethanol deprive the Brazilians from fully reaping the benefits of the blenders' subsidy or even simply realising their competitiveness in the US market. However, tariff measures, although they confer benefits to domestic biofuels industries, are not captured by the ASCM due to a lack of financial contribution. Rather, if they conform to the GATT 1994, they remain legitimate trade instruments of WTO members.

[105] Press Release, outcome of the 2007 European Biodiesel Board (EBB) General Assembly meeting, 'The EU biodiesel industry unanimously agrees to initiate legal action against US "B99" unfair biodiesel exports', 782/COM/07.

In the case of renewable electricity, consumption subsidies might arguably have adverse effects if they favour one 'technology' over another especially if they are based on the domestic technology endowments. This is because electricity supplies whether sourced from wind, solar or hydro, are basically like products. For example, consider a country subsidising consumers such as householders or office buildings to use solar panels as a result of which import of electricity to the subsidising region is decreased substantially. In such a hypothetical case, foreign RE producers (of hydro for instance) whose exports are replaced in the subsidising country may claim to be adversely affected by that subsidy.

### G.    Prospects for future WTO challenges against RE subsidies

Two elements might be considered in assessing the possibilities of WTO challenges against RE subsidies: one is the expansion of trade (but not necessarily production) in RE worldwide. The other is the manner in which RE subsidies are designed.

On the first element, it is reasonable to assume that the more the RE trade flow increases, the greater the chances of trade disputes.[106] There is little doubt that new RE market opportunities are emerging in RE and related technologies as a result of environmental, energy security and also agricultural policies:

— International trade in biofuels, being in its early stages, is small compared to total production of biomass energy and relative to global demand for biofuels.[107] Trade in biofuels feedstock, despite difficulties in making an accurate estimation due to its various uses, seems to be modest in the case of ethanol but considerable in the case of biodiesel.[108] Trade in ethanol is, however, growing rapidly and significantly and Brazil is taking a strong global lead in ethanol exports.[109] Different

---

[106] An economic study shows that 'if the level of subsidies for the development of biofuels industry in the two countries is different, trade disputes can arise'. See C. Viju, W. A. Kerr and J. Nolan, 'Subsidization of the biofuel industry: security vs. clean air?', paper prepared for presentation at the American Agricultural Economics Association Annual Meeting, Long Beach, California, 23–26 July, 2006.

[107] See IEA, *World Energy Outlook* (2006), at 416. Also see UNCTAD, *The Emerging Biofuels Market* (2006) at 35.

[108] See UNCTAD (2006). The EU is the major producer of biodiesel, whereas it imports a large bulk of feedstock such as palm oil from Asia as input.

[109] A 50 per cent market share of global ethanol exports belongs to Brazil. See UNCTAD (2006) at 36.

projections show a significant expansion in biofuels trade with increasing participation of developing countries, which will also increase the possibilities of challenges in the WTO.[110] This is where the IEA, while identifying the potential for a South-North trade flow in biofuels, considers subsidies as one of the major trade barriers to this scenario being played out.[111] It seems at first glance that in the present circumstances where major subsidisers, i.e. the EU and the US, are not major exporters, the potential for countervailing duty cases may be low. The current dispute over the US biodiesel subsidies,[112] however, suggests that developments may be much faster than expected. Furthermore, Article 5(c) serious prejudice cases[113] as well as claims regarding the violation of Article 6.1 of the AoA (amber box commitment levels) may be initiated particularly by developing country biofuel exporters. Currently the US is being challenged on its domestic support for, *inter alia*, corn and also on its biofuel tax subsidies. Canada's complaint is mainly regarding the US subsidies and other domestic subsidies for corn and other agricultural products. Among the disputed measures were the provisions of the 2002 Farm Bill that provide direct or indirect support to the US corn industry.[114] This could potentially include all the energy provisions of the 2002 Farm Bill containing subsidies that encourage production and the use of corn-based ethanol.[115] Brazil has further challenged, *inter alia*, the gasoline and diesel tax exemptions for biofuels,[116] which were later replaced by the volumetric ethanol excise tax credit in 2004.[117] A single panel was established to deal with both cases in December 2007 with a number of third parties.[118] In this case, it can be speculated that, according to the findings in sections C

---

[110] See *Petroleum Economist*, August 2007 at 14. The Brazilian Minister has predicted that with the arrival of second generation feedstock, around 100 developing countries would become energy exporters.

[111] See IEA, *World Energy Outlook* (2006) at 417.    [112] See supra n. 105.

[113] This is where the effect of a subsidy is to displace or impede the imports of RE into the market of a subsidising Member (Article 6.3(a)). The challenge for these cases remains to provide proof of a causal link between such displacement or impediment and domestic subsidies. However, the major trade barrier for biofuels in the future might be standards rather than domestic subsidies.

[114] Request for consultations by Canada, WT/DS357/1, January 2007.

[115] See R. Schnepf, 'Agriculture-based renewable energy production, Congressional Research Service', (2006) RL32712, www.fpc.state.gov/documents/organization/68294.pdf

[116] WT/DS365/1, request for consultations by Brazil, July 2007.

[117] See Koplow (2006) at 11.

[118] For a summary of the dispute, visit www.wto.org/english/tratop_e/dispu_e/cases_e/ds365_e.htm

and F, establishing a case against US subsidies to biofuels producers (feedstock and refineries) may be found less challenging than one against consumption subsidies (blenders' tax credits).

— In the case of electricity, for foreign competition to exist as a pre-requisite for a dispute to arise, there should be two main pre-conditions in a market: one is network liberalisation and allowing third party access (TPA). In the absence of competition, governments buying and selling electricity on a large scale may do so on a contractual basis according to their countries' needs. Nonetheless, their overall policy would be to reach overall self-sufficiency in terms of their net imports. The second pre-condition is the existence of sufficient interconnection capacities. Even with liberalisation of electricity markets, interconnection capacity between two countries would impose limitations on the volume of electricity trade to the disadvantage of exporting countries. These two factors, i.e. discretionary TPA and lack of investment in interconnection capacity, might serve as better protectionist tools for a country than subsidy disciplines such as countervailing duties (CVDs). With the expansion of liberalisation of electricity markets, however, and the emergence of a niche market for green electricity, the situation might change in the future. In the meanwhile, it is likely that subsidy cases in the WTO would remain limited to inputs to renewable electricity production such as emerging technologies in solar, wind, solar or thermal energy. These could well involve CVD and serious prejudice cases with increasing shares of renewables production and expansion of RE trade. Especially with a huge amount of R&D spending on these technologies worldwide, the fact that they no longer enjoy an exemption from the ASCM disciplines should be viewed with caution.

On the second element, one has to examine whether RE subsidies are designed in a trade distortive manner. Energy security policies may dictate to countries not to grant export energy subsidies the effect of which is likely to increase domestic prices of energy.[119] Import substitution subsidies, as might occasionally be found in some countries, are a recipe for a rather straightforward prohibited subsidy dispute. The chances of a dispute over other RE subsidies which remain actionable depend on whether they are designed in such a way as to bring their adverse effects to a minimum level. Non-discriminatory consumption

---

[119] See WTO *World Trade Report* (2006) at 57.

subsides may provide a good example of least trade distortive subsidy schemes from a legal point of view.

Overall, it is not very probable that the expanding number of RE subsidies, especially in the EU and US, will be designed in a non-trade distortive manner.[120] This is because energy security and agricultural policies seem to be a stronger motive behind RE promotion policies than the environmental one.

## H.   Suggestions on the way forward

The serious vulnerability of RE subsidy under the ASCM and the high chances of trade disputes imply that the WTO imposes considerable limitations on RE promotion policies, particularly on the way they are devised by its Members. But is this necessarily a bad thing for the environment?

It is essential to note first that in RE trade, as in trade in environmental goods and services, heated arguments over the conflict between trade liberalisation and the environment lose steam — liberalisation of trade in RE (assuming a net reduction in GHG emissions in their life cycle) and climate change mitigation indeed go hand in hand.[121] Assuming RE is produced in a sustainable manner, the more tariffs and trade distortive subsidies in the RE sector and related technology are removed, the better for the environment at least as far as $CO_2$ emissions are concerned.

Returning to the question raised in the introduction on the possibility of fragmentation between trade and the climate regime, the question is whether the fact that a WTO Member could successfully challenge RE subsidies means that trade and climate regimes are not coherent — one encouraging RE promotion policies and the other restraining them. It should be noted that from a purely legalistic viewpoint, there is no conflict between the two systems. The Kyoto Protocol merely encourages, and does not mandate, its members to promote RE let alone subsidise them.[122] On the other hand, the WTO regime, as explained

---

[120]  See L. J. Loppacher and W. A. Kerr, 'Can biofuels Become a global industry?: government policies and trade constraints' (2005), prepared for *Energy Politics*.

[121]  See Stern (2006) at 578.

[122]  The Kyoto Protocol does not use the specific term subsidy for RE. The Intergovernmental Panel on Climate Change (IPCC), however, suggests the use of production subsidies for RE. See IPCC, 'Summary for policymakers' in B. Metz, O. R. Davidson, P. R. Bosch *et al.* (eds.), *Climate Change 2007: Mitigation. Contribution of Working Group III to the Fourth Assessment. Report of the Intergovernmental Panel on Climate Change* (Cambridge University Press: 2007) at 19.

above, does not prohibit these subsidies insofar as they are not contingent upon export performance or import substitution. Actionability of all the remaining specific subsidies only insures against their potential adverse effects on their 'like' RE products. Hence one might further argue that the two regimes may well be found to be mutually supportive as far as international promotion of RE is concerned. This is because even if it is demonstrated in a case that a certain RE subsidy scheme causes an adverse effect, this would mean that such a subsidy is tipping the balance against a more efficient RE producer. In that case, putting an end to such distortive RE subsidies that hurt efficient RE producers would eventually lead to promotion of RE trade and hence benefit the environment. For this very reason, in our opinion, giving a blank exemption to RE subsidies by creating a green energy box in the ASCM[123] may run counter to the objective of promoting RE, particularly if it includes, directly or indirectly, any 'production' subsidies. In the same way that biofuels subsidies will not meet green box criteria if they have trade or production distorting effects, other RE subsidies may not benefit the environment on balance insofar as they keep more efficient producers out of markets. The idea of providing environmental exemptions for subsidies may appear more appealing in the case of conservation subsidies — a tax system that rewards energy efficiency might be defendable despite its potential trade distorting effects on less energy efficient 'like' products.

This said, however, RE subsidies have been defended by some economists on certain grounds.[124] They do not stand as major trade barriers to RE markets where high tariffs and restrictive standards are still prevalent. Moreover, subsidies might be considered as second best alternatives to proper taxation policies where politicians may not be able to afford to introduce sufficiently high carbon taxes to encourage the massive private investments needed in the RE sector. Yet, it may be argued that regulatory incentive schemes such as minimum price or quota measures, which are applied in a non-discriminatory way, take priority over production subsidies. Public support for R&D may also be justified to remedy the dearth of private investment in R&D.[125] There is, however, a legitimate

---

[123]  The idea is suggested by Howse (2005) at 29 endorsed by Stern (2006) at 578.

[124]  See for instance Stern (2006), IPCC (2007), n. 120 and T. Morgan, *Energy Subsidies: Their Magnitude, How they Affect Energy Investment and Greenhouse Gas Emissions, and Prospects for Reform* (Bonn: UNFCCC, 2007).

[125]  See for instance Stern (2006) and G. Prins and S. Rayner, 'Time to ditch Kyoto', *Nature* 449 (2007), 973–5.

concern in the cases where R&D subsidies are provided to the private sector in that they could simply open the door for disguised protectionism. As Sykes (2003) argues, it would be hard to ensure that money provided to firms for R&D does indeed result in more R&D rather than in an increase in production.[126]

Assuming that RE subsidies are legitimate on certain grounds, the question is to what extent the ASCM should be amended to accommodate those RE subsidies which could be justified on the above-mentioned grounds. The immediate answer to this question is the revival of Article 8.3, known as non-actionable subsidies. This green light category contained certain exemptions for R&D subsidies (Article 8.2(a)), regional development subsidies (Article 8.2(b)) and environmental subsidies (Article 8.2(c)). With the expiration of Article 8, by virtue of Article 31, currently all subsidies, except for non-specific ones, remain actionable.

It is certainly beyond the scope of this chapter to present a complete picture of the merits and shortcomings of reviving the category of non-actionable subsidies. I will therefore only emphasise two main points on the basis of the concerns raised above.

Any attempt to revive exemptions for R&D support should exclude from its scope direct payments to firms involved in production that should remain actionable due to the fungibility of money argument mentioned above. This carve-out has interestingly been taken into account in the area of agriculture (Annex 2, 2(2)), but this was not the case in the expired provision of Article 8.2(a). One may wonder further if other types of R&D subsidies (support for research activities conducted by higher education or research establishments) may ever cause an adverse effect in the first place and hence need blank exemption.

Article 8.2(c) on exemptions for certain environmental subsidy programmes merits more attention. In fact since the expiry of this provision in the year 2000, it is significant that the ASCM has been left without any GATT Article XX-like provision to cover environmental exceptions.[127] In reconsidering the green light solution, one should bear in mind that a subsidy will only need to be justified as non-actionable if it has

---

[126] See Sykes's (2003) argument about fungibility of money and n. 36 therein.

[127] A WTO report simply assumes the application of GATT XX exceptions to the SCM. See *World Trade Report 'Exploring the Links between Subsidies, Trade and the WTO'* (Geneva: World Trade Organization, 2006) at 201. Others like Gary Horlick and Andrew Green assume its non-application. The second view in my opinion is legally more sound. See Garry Horlick's comments on this chapter and A. Green, 'Trade rules and climate change subsidies', *World Trade Review*, 5 (2006), 411.

distortionary effects.[128] Otherwise, a specific subsidy which is not contingent on export or import substitution and does not cause adverse effects is not captured by the ASCM disciplines in the first place. Note that the types of exceptions envisaged in Article 8.2(c) for granting environmental subsidies are limited, *inter alia*, to covering 20 per cent of the cost of adapting to new environmental regulations which result in greater constraints and burdens on firms. In line with our discussions in section A:2 on the notion of benefit, these offsetting measures may not even constitute a subsidy due to a lack of benefit conferred let alone any adverse effect.[129] Accordingly, the revival of this provision may not have any substantial effects. It certainly fails to cover adequately all subsidies which presumably serve the environment but at the same time distort trade, for instance by displacing imports. On the other hand, even in cases where domestic RE subsidies result in a reduction of $CO_2$ on balance, this environmental objective may be better achieved through a non-discriminatory scheme which does not unnecessarily distort trade. As discussed above, RE subsidies can mostly be engineered in such a way as not to affect RE competitors adversely.[130] In fact, in most cases non-discriminatory subsidy schemes best fulfil environmental objectives, whereas protectionist schemes might essentially pursue other policies such as energy security.[131]

On this ground, any redefinition of an environmental exemption in the ASCM should be based on a necessity test similar to Article XX(b): it has to be shown that an environmental subsidy could not be designed in a less trade distortive manner to serve its objective effectively. In other words, all environmental subsidies have to be designed in the least trade distortive manner. This pre-requisite will strike a balance between

---

[128] That is why Article 9 of the ASCM stipulated a procedure aiming at minimising the adverse effects of non-actionable subsidies, if they were found to be serious and difficult to repair.

[129] This is in line with Sykes's (2003) argument at 4.

[130] This does not hold true in the case of minimum quota measures which, if coupled with substantially high tariffs, function as a protectionist tool which is not at all disciplined in the ASCM.

[131] In the US the primary goal of biofuels subsidies is to increase energy security (Loppacher and Kerr). Some might argue that energy security should also be considered as a legitimate ground for distortive subsidies. For a radically opposing view see S. Upton, 'Avoiding the wrong solutions to the wrong problems'. Policy Brief presented at the Conference on Climate Change and Security, 12 October 2007, Traders Hotel Singapore.

environmental benefits and trade costs of distortionary subsidies in favour of the 'planet' but against unnecessary trade protectionism.[132]

## Conclusions

Much of the support provided to the RE sectors takes the forms which fit the definition of subsidy according to Article 1 of the ASCM. These RE subsidies enumerated above (except for limited cases) are specific within the meaning of Article 2. If they are contingent upon export or import substitution or they cause adverse effects, RE subsidies are likely to result in trade disputes of different kinds and hence are vulnerable under the WTO system. However, a successful challenge of trade distortive RE subsidies may ironically benefit the environment on balance as it will level the playing field for the most efficient producers of RE and related technology. Yet, under a different scenario, the use of certain trade distortive subsidies for environmental purposes may be justified. In this context, the absence of an Article XX of the GATT provision in the ASCM should be given serious consideration. It is argued that the expired category of non-actionable subsidies falls short of fully achieving the goals since it is both over-inclusive (for instance in the case of R&D subsidies to producing firms) and under-inclusive (for instance in the case of subsidies targeting energy efficiency). It was also argued that any attempt to introduce particular environmental exceptions into the SCM Agreement should entail a necessity test similar to Article X(b) of the GATT to ensure that such exemptions will not be hijacked by domestic interest groups to the detriment of both trade and the environment.

Last, but certainly not least, it is worth mentioning that there is a huge potential for the ASCM to embrace climate protection objectives by effectively discouraging fossil fuel subsidies as a way to promote RE and protect the environment.[133]

---

[132] For more along this line of argument see Green (2006).
[133] See S. Bigdeli 'Will the "friends of climate" emerge in the WTO? Applying the "fisheries subsidies" model to energy subsidies', *Carbon and Climate Law Review*, issue 3 (2008), 78–89.

# 9

# The WTO and climate change 'incentives'

GARY N. HORLICK

The General Agreement on Tariffs and Trade (GATT) 1994 and the World Trade Organization (WTO) Agreement on Subsidies and Countervailing Measures (ASCM), as currently drafted, may not allow some of the policy choices discussed in the context of climate change, including in particular unilateral border taxes (especially as they are highly likely to be based on national values and existing availability of local resources); research and development for certain renewable energy sources; mandatory emissions permits; and so on. In addition, it should be noted that, to date, the ASCM has not proven effective in disciplining the numerous subsidies given in many countries to the production and consumption of fossil fuels. If climate change concerns had been more politically pressing when the ASCM was drafted, they would have been accommodated, together with the 'green light' (permitted) limited subsidies for research and development, environmental adaptation, and regional development programmes — but even those were allowed to lapse in 1999.[1]

As Sadeq Bigdeli's paper explains, the rules of the ASCM would constrain proposals to stimulate the use of renewable energy sources (although, as he notes, there are numerous subsidies for non-renewable energy which have not been challenged in WTO dispute resolution or

---

[1] A good first rule of GATT and WTO negotiations has been that Members will soon live to regret what they sought in the talks. For example, the European Community's (EC's) successful insistence on eliminating the compensation requirement for safeguards under Article XIX (for three years) in the Uruguay Round, or the insistence of the United States (US) in that Round on anti-dumping rules which Mexico promptly used against US farm exports. Viewed that way, the failure of the WTO Members to renew the 'green light' permission for certain environmental subsidies in Article 8 of the WTO Subsidies Agreement may not be surprising, even though that provision would not have provided the flexibility that policy-makers would need to implement many of the proposals for dealing with climate change and improved energy efficiency.

national countervailing duty (CVD) cases). Indeed, many proposals for energy subsidies, taxes and regulations are made with no knowledge of the ASCM rules, or indeed the WTO rules in general, or else rely on Article XX of the GATT 1994 (which does not apply to the ASCM) and/ or the rather dubious dictum of the WTO Appellate Body that an 'evolving interpretation' can rewrite text or prior decisions.

Under the ASCM rules, many if not most of the grants, loans and tax exemptions for both renewable energy and non-renewable energy involve financial contributions by the governments of the relevant territory and benefit to the recipients, and are de facto or de jure specific. Direct money and tax breaks would be treated as grants, while loans, loan guarantees, provisional goods and services, or purchases of goods would be compared against market benchmarks. Some of the more complex programmes proposed in the climate change context (such as tradable credits and certificates) could lead to interesting debates about the appropriate benchmark. The Appellate Body did not help by (mis)-reading Article 14(d) to allow benchmarks outside the territory of the relevant government.[2] A more interesting question is whether government-directed minimum prices for renewable energy are 'price supports' as listed in Article 1.1(a)(2) of the ASCM. Of course, not all cause material injury or serious prejudice or nullification and impairment (although some might ask why the assistance is given if it has no economic impact). And assistance by entities outside the territory (such as multilateral lending institutions or overseas development assistance) is not a subsidy at all.

Probably very few, if any, are prohibited export subsidies as governments do not usually subsidise the production of energy to be consumed in other countries.[3]

---

[2] Article 14(d) was written to preclude cross-border benchmarks — Mexico almost certainly would not have signed the Uruguay Round had it known that the Appellate Body would allow cross-border comparisons, specifically on energy prices.

[3] Countervailing duty cases were filed in the US in 1999 against imports of crude oil from Saudi Arabia, Venezuela, Mexico and Iraq, but they were quickly dismissed. Arguments could perhaps be made about some of the major projects (such as oil and gas pipelines or liquefied natural gas (LNG) import facilities) with substantial involvement of the exporting governments — consuming countries are unlikely to complain, and competing countries are probably more likely to do the same. There have of course been numerous arguments about alleged subsidies to downstream products — the so-called 'dual pricing' (lower energy or hydrocarbon prices for inputs sold domestically where the downstream product is exported and sold domestically), as raised by the European Union in the

More intriguing is the emerging trend of energy mandates, e.g. where the local government requires the use of a certain amount of ethanol in motor fuel, or a certain quantity of electricity from renewable sources.[4] Purely regulatory measures are not normally considered to be subsidies under the ASCM, for lack of a 'financial package'.[5] But what about discriminatory regulatory mandates, such as requiring the use of domestic renewable energy either de jure or de facto specific (much electricity, such as hydropower or wind power, in practice, could only be generated locally)? Or is that left to the mercies of Article III of the GATT 1994, and the 'evolving interpretation' in *Shrimp — Turtle*?

Looking to the future, the 'cleanest' way out of this mess would be an agreement negotiated among the WTO Members. There is precedent, as noted above — the 1994 WTO Subsidies Agreement included exceptions for 'permitted subsidies' for certain limited environmental purposes; certain limited research and development; and regional development programmes. Perhaps the political impetus behind the current energy concerns will provide the political will necessary to show that the WTO can, in fact, 'legislate' without a full scale 'round'.[6]

Some will argue that, as is often the case, it is highly unlikely that governments will negotiate well thought-out rules for climate change subsidies. The alternative is to rely on the existing texts through 'evolving' interpretations, with unforeseen consequences in other areas of the subsidies discipline. While a new negotiation to 'do it right' sounds terribly naïve (as shown by the bad rules forced into the Organisation for Economic Co-operation and Development (OECD) Shipbuilding and Steel Agreements, neither of which entered into force, fortunately),

---

current Doha negotiations. Numerous CVD cases were filed in the US against dual pricing, unsuccessfully. G. N. Horlick, 'Introduction Note — United States: Court of Appeals for the Federal Circuit Opinion in PPG Industries, Inc. v. United States', *I.L.M.* 30 (1991).

[4] G. Horlick, C. Schuchhardt and H. Mann, 'NAFTA provisions and the electricity sector', in NAFTA Environment Secretariat, *Environmental Challenges and Opportunities of the Evolving North American Market* (2002).

[5] *United States — Measures Treating Export Restraints as Subsidies*, WT/DS194R, 29 June 2001.

[6] Of course, the WTO has already legislated numerous times since 1995, not only on controversial issues such as access to medicines and 'conflict diamonds', including full scale negotiations on telecommunications, financial services, and zero-tariff electronic products, but there have also been numerous small and more detailed agreements negotiated within different WTO committees, such as the recommendation of the Committee on Anti-Dumping Practices concerning the time period to be considered in determining a 'negligible amount' of imports, G/ADP/11.

progress in the Doha negotiations on a Fisheries Agreement suggest it is possible. If a respectable agreement disciplining fisheries subsidies emerges in the Doha negotiations, it could be a model for a similar effort on climate change — one that protects a global commons while making adequate provision for the different circumstances in different countries. While there is the obvious difficulty of reaching such agreement in the absence of the trade-offs provided by a full WTO round, it is quite possible that climate change is sufficiently threatening to a wide range of countries, rich and poor, large and small, to generate the necessary political will.

## Conclusion

As Bigdeli points out, many of the policies recommended for responding to climate change may be found to be inconsistent with (though rarely prohibited by) the ASCM. The good progress in the Doha talks on a Fisheries Subsidies Agreement suggest that a similar effort on climate change may be worthwhile (even outside a WTO round.)

# 10

# Certifying biofuels: benefits for the environment, development and trade?

SIMONETTA ZARRILLI AND JENNIFER BURNETT [1]

## Introduction

According to the International Energy Agency (IEA) *World Energy Outlook* reference scenario, economic growth and increasing population will lead to an increase in global energy demand of 1.6 per cent per annum between 2006 and 2030.[2] While it is projected that fossil fuels will remain the dominant source of energy, increasing costs, security concerns and environmental consciousness have motivated countries to explore alternative energy sources.

Countries have begun to consider bioenergy[3] to be a viable alternative to fossil fuels. Biofuels, fuels derived from biomass,[4] are among the bioenergy alternatives which are being considered and are currently viewed, if carefully developed, as one of the means of slowing down the process of global warming and enhancing energy security, as well as

---

[1] The views expressed in this publication are those of the authors and do not necessarily reflect the views of the United Nations. This paper is an abridged version of the UNCTAD study *Making Certification Work for Sustainable Development: the Case of Biofuels* (UNCTAD/DITC/TED/2008/1). The authors wish to thank D. Andrew, G. Marceau, K. Mechlem, B. Oliveira, M. Otto and R. Steenblick for helpful comments on an earlier draft.

[2] IEA, *World Energy Outlook 2006* (2006).

[3] The term 'bioenergy' as used in this paper refers to electricity and any solid, liquid or gaseous fuel that is produced through the processing of biomass.

[4] Biomass is 'any derived organic matter available on a renewable basis, including dedicated energy crops and trees, agricultural food and feed crops, agricultural crop wastes and residues, wood wastes and residues, aquatic plants, animal wastes, municipal wastes, and other waste materials'. Found at www.energy.gov/energysources/bioenergy.htm

possibly providing countries with opportunities to diversify agricultural production and raise rural incomes.

Comparatively low production costs and better climate conditions in the developing world, coupled with limited land capacity in several developed countries to produce the amount of feedstock required to meet the internal demand, are driving an emerging market in biofuels and related feedstocks.

In parallel with the rapidly growing use of biofuels, concerns are being voiced about the sustainability of biofuels and feedstock production and interest in certification schemes to encourage sustainable production is intensifying.

Increased production and use of biofuels raises a number of crucial questions related, *inter alia*, to land diversion, food security, preservation of biodiversity and water use.

Certification is a form of communication along the supply chain that permits the buyer to be sure that the supplier complies with certain requirements. Certification allows product differentiation and provides information about certain characteristics of a product, in this case, its sustainability. Depending on how sensitive a market is to certain product attributes, certification, including voluntary certification, may have a significant market impact, affecting domestic and imported products. Sustainability principles, however, may be developed independently from certification, as guidelines for bioenergy planning for governments and risk minimisation for industry.

Interestingly, the European Commission has proposed that biofuels that fail to meet sustainability criteria should not count towards national biofuel targets and obligations and would not be eligible for tax reductions and other financial supports.[5] Likewise, other countries are linking biofuel certification with tax breaks and other incentives. These developments make sustainability an increasingly important attribute for biofuels and may also play a key role in international trade.

While ensuring sustainability[6] is a legitimate goal and certification may be an effective instrument to achieve it, certification initiatives also

---

[5] E. Thuijl and E. P. Deurwaarder, *European Biofuels Policies in Retrospect*, (Energy Research Center of the Netherlands (ECN), 2006), p. 8.

[6] There are several definitions of sustainability. It can be defined as 'the ability of natural resources to provide ecological, economic, and social benefits for present and future generations', www.uwsp.edu/natres/nres743/Glossary.htm; or can be seen as a 'top concept and strategy by which communities seek economic development approaches that benefit the local environment and quality of life', www.ci.austin.tx.us/zoning/glossary, or

raise a number of concerns related to their implications for small producers, especially in developing countries, their cost and effectiveness, their possible impacts on international trade, and their compatibility with multilaterally agreed trade rules.

The purpose of this paper is to provide an overview of existing or planned certification schemes, to assess their implications for developing countries, and to report on the possible ramifications of certification in the context of the World Trade Organization (WTO).

## Overview of certification schemes

The aim of this section is to provide a brief overview of the initiatives that have been developed or are being explored in relation to sustainable production of biofuels.

### *Logistical framework for certification*

The development of a certification scheme is an involved process. It requires an independent third party to assess quality based on a predetermined set of principles. Principles are usually established as general starting points that describe the objectives of certification. These objectives are then translated into measurable requirements in the form of criteria. Testing then uses indicators or verifiers which serve as quantitative or qualitative minimum requirements for certification.[7]

Ideally stakeholders are consulted and their input integrated into certification schemes that take into account various local conditions. Once the criteria and indicators have been established they must be tested to ensure that they are clear, appropriate and effective as well as

as an 'economic development with minimal environmental degradation, or equitable development that is environmentally sound', www.interfacesustainability.com/econ. html. Four different types of sustainability can be singled out: human, social, economic and environmental. *Human sustainability* means maintaining human capital. The health, education, skills, knowledge, leadership and access to services constitute human capital. *Social sustainability* means maintaining social capital. Social capital is investments and services that create the basic framework for society. *Economic sustainability* is maintenance of capital, or keeping capital intact. *Environmental sustainability* seeks to improve human welfare by protecting water, land, air, minerals and ecosystem services, www. wiley.co.uk/egec/pdf/GA811-W.PDF

[7] I. Lewandowski and A. Faaij, 'Steps towards the development of a certification system for sustainable bio-energy trade', *Biomass & Bioenergy* 30 (2005) 83–106; and *Testing Framework for Sustainable Biomass*, final report of the Cramer Commission (March 2007).

adequately understood and accepted by the users or stakeholders. These tests should be evaluated and used for modification and improvement of the scheme before the finalised criteria and indicators are implemented.

These are the ideal circumstances for the development of a certification scheme yet, as will be discussed later, this situation is not necessarily realised.

### Key actors in the development of certification schemes

The development of sustainable certification systems can be described from the point of view of the stakeholder groups involved.

#### National governments and regional groupings

Currently there are a number of countries and regional groupings active in the development of certification for biofuels and biomass.

*Belgium*: Belgium aims to have 6 per cent of its total electricity consumption coming from renewable energy sources by 2010. To support this goal the country has instituted a type of cap-and-trade system, comprising minimum quota obligations combined with a system of tradable certificates.[8]

Sustainable energy is a regional competence[9] in Belgium; certificate systems have been implemented in all three regions of the country (i.e. Brussels, Flanders and Wallonia) for renewable energy sources as well as combined heat and power.

Sustainability certification for imported biomass is a requirement only in Wallonia. There, the sustainability of the wood sourcing can be verified according to: forest certificates such as the Forest Stewardship Council; a traceable chain management system at the suppliers' end; or (in the absence of such certification) through all public documents originating from independent bodies making a review of forest management or control in the country under consideration.[10] However, all three Belgian regions require a traceable management system and a detailed

[8] K. Verhaegen, L. Meeus, and R. Belmans, *Towards an International Certificate System — The Stimulating Example of Belgium*, available at: www.esat.kuleuven.be/electa/publications/fulltexts/pub_1495.pdf

[9] Energy falls under the responsibility of both the federal and the regional authorities. The promotion of renewable energy sources is, however, a regional competence.

[10] J. Van Dam, M. Junginger, A. Faaij, I. Jürgens, G. Best, and U. Fritsche, 'Overview of recent developments in sustainable biomass certification', paper accepted for publication in a Special Issue on International Bio-energy Trade, *Biomass and Bioenergy* (2007).

energy balance for the supply chain. SGS (Société Génerale de Surveillance) International is the only company authorised by all Belgian authorities to grant green certificates.

*The Netherlands*: the Netherlands is a leader in establishing criteria for sustainable biomass and biofuel. In 2006 the Interdepartmental Programme Management Energy Transition established the project group, Sustainable Production of Biomass, also referred to as the Cramer Commission, with the aim to 'formulate a set of sustainability criteria for the production and conversion of biomass for energy, fuels and chemistry'. The final report of the project group was released in March 2007.

The project group promotes the 3P approach — people, planet, profit — and examines the sustainability of biomass based on greenhouse gas emissions; competition with food and local applications of biomass; biodiversity; environment; prosperity; and social well-being. For each theme, the project group formulated principles, criteria and indicators. In doing so, the group made use of existing standards when possible.

The Dutch project group has proposed that reporting occur at two levels: the company level and the macro level. At the macro level, reporting is the responsibility of the government and is likely to require intergovernmental co-operation. Macro-level reporting is primarily concerned with shifts in land use which may affect biodiversity, the greenhouse gas balance, and competition with food.

When drawing up the overall framework, the Cramer Commission made use of a broad consultation process; however, foreign producers were not involved.

*United Kingdom*: the Renewable Transport Fuel Obligation Programme (RTFO) is aimed at meeting the objectives established by the European Union (EU) Biofuels Directive. Since April 2008, the RTFO places an obligation on fuel suppliers to ensure that a certain percentage of their aggregate sales are made up of biofuels. The effect of this will be to require fuel companies to sell a minimum of 2.5 per cent renewable transport fuels in the UK in 2008–2009, increasing to 5 per cent in 2010–2011. The UK, acknowledging the risk that biomass could be produced from highly unsustainable sources, is developing an assurance scheme alongside the obligation to ensure that biofuels are produced from sustainable sources.

In June 2007, the government announced a package of measures on the sustainability of biofuels supplied under the RTFO which includes the aim to reward biofuels in accordance with the carbon savings that

Table 1 *Spotlight on Cramer Commission*

---

**PRINCIPLES**

**Theme 1: Greenhouse gas emissions**

The greenhouse gas balance of the production chain and application of the biomass must be positive.

Biomass production must not be at the expense of important carbon sinks in the vegetation and in the soil.

**Theme 2: Competition with food and local applications of biomass**

The production of biomass for energy must not endanger the food supply and local biomass applications (energy supply, medicines, building materials).

**Theme 3: Biodiversity**

Biomass production must not affect protected or vulnerable biodiversity and will, where possible, have to strengthen biodiversity.

**Theme 4: Environment**

In the production and processing of biomass, the soil and the soil quality are retained or improved.

In the production and processing of biomass, ground and surface water must not be depleted and the water quality must be maintained or improved.

In the production and processing of biomass, the air quality must be maintained or improved.

**Theme 5: Prosperity**

The production of biomass must contribute towards local prosperity.

**Theme 6: Social well-being**

The production of biomass must contribute towards the social well-being of the employees and the local population.

---

they offer from April 2010 onwards and to only reward biofuels if the feedstocks from which they are produced meet appropriate sustainability standards from April 2011 onwards. Furthermore, the government asserted that it intends to set indicative targets for the level of carbon and sustainability performance expected from all transport fuel suppliers claiming certificates for biofuels in the early years of the RTFO.

*Brazil*: Brazil is the world's largest ethanol exporter and the second producer. Brazil is in the process of developing a certification scheme aimed at ensuring that the biofuel sector follows environmental, social and labour standards according to national and international law. The National Institute of Meteorology, Standardization and Industrial Quality (INMETRO) is in charge of developing such a voluntary pro-gramme and has so far developed six preliminary principles and ten indicators.[11] In 2003, the Brazilian Government created the biodiesel programme which includes a social fuel seal. Under this programme, biodiesel producers may obtain tax benefits and credit if they purchase feedstock from family farmers, enter into legally binding agreements with them to ensure specific income levels and guarantee technical assistance and training to the farmers.[12] Furthermore, pending the completion of the certification programme, the Brazilian Government remains active in regulating the environmental impact of the sugar cane industry.[13]

*Canada*: Canada, which is a major producer and exporter of wood pellets and produces ethanol from grain, is currently relying on voluntary certification to promote sustainability in the biofuels industry. The EcoLogo[M] — Canada's national eco-labelling scheme — has criteria for renewable energy sources with specific criteria for biomass and biogas.

*Germany*: Germany is the world leader in biodiesel production. In January 2007 the Biofuel Quota Act came into force. The Act introduces a quota for the minimum addition of biofuels to petrol and diesel in Germany and empowers the government to establish sustainability criteria for biofuels that are eligible to participate in the quota system.

*European Commission*: at the European Council of March 2007, EU heads of state and government endorsed the European Commission's proposal for a mandatory target of a 20 per cent share of renewable energies in overall Community energy consumption by 2020, and a mandatory 10 per cent minimum target for the share of biofuels in transport petrol and diesel consumption by 2020. Ministers further agreed that the binding character of the biofuel target should be subject to production being sustainable, second generation biofuels becoming commercially available, and the Directive relating to the quality of petrol and diesel fuels being amended to allow for adequate levels of blending.[14] Hence, ministers invited the Commission to propose a

---

[11] Principles refer to compliance with environmental and labour laws; adequate work conditions; sustainable use of natural resources; biodiversity protection, recovery and conservation; water, soil and air protection; and socio-economic development of areas surrounding the production fields.

[12] J. Dam *et al.* (2007), see n. 10 above.

[13] J. Martines-Filho, H. Burnquist, and C. Vian, 'Bioenergy and the rise of sugarcane based ethanol in Brazil', in *Choices: A Publication of the American Agricultural Economics Association* (2006), JEL Classification: Q42,054,013 2(21), 91–6.

[14] Considering that the main purpose of binding targets is to provide certainty for investors, it was decided that the binding nature of the target should not be deferred until second generation biofuels became commercially available.

legislative framework for renewable energy that could include criteria and measures to ensure sustainable provision and use of biofuels.

On 23 January 2008, the European Commission introduced the draft Directive on the promotion of the use of energy from renewable sources,[15] which includes, among many other provisions, sustainability criteria for biofuels and other bioliquids.[16] The criteria are as follows: (a) the use of biofuels and other bioliquids shall lead to greenhouse gas emission savings of at least 35 per cent calculated through the life cycle of the product; (b) biofuels and other bioliquids shall not be made from raw material obtained from land with recognised high biodiversity value;[17] (c) biofuels and other bioliquids shall not be made from raw material obtained from land with high carbon stock;[18] (d) where biofuels and other bioliquids are made from raw material produced in the EU, they should also comply with the EU's environmental requirements for agriculture. Applying such criteria to imports from third countries is deemed administratively and technically unfeasible. Only biofuels that comply with sustainability criteria can count against national biofuels targets and renewable energy obligations, and be eligible for financial support.

The criteria proposed by the European Commission are environmental — 'environmental sustainability criteria' according to the definition of the Directive. The Commission opted to leave aside social criteria as well as criteria that relate to macro-level effects, probably because of considerations related to technical feasibility and WTO compliance. However, the draft Directive includes monitoring obligations for the Commission and reporting obligations for Member States on social and global issues, such as increases in commodity prices and land use changes associated with growing use of biomass.

Some tensions have already arisen regarding the intentions of the Commission to limit the scope of the criteria to environmental issues.

---

[15] Proposal for a Directive of the European Parliament and of the Council on the promotion of the use of energy from renewable sources, at http://ec.europa.eu/energy/climate_actions/doc/2008_res_directive_en.pdf

[16] 'Biofuels' means liquid or gaseous fuel for transport produced from biomass; 'bioliquids' means liquid fuel for energy purposes produced from biomass.

[17] The following are regarded as lands having high biodiversity value: (a) forest undisturbed by significant human activity; (b) areas designated for nature protection purposes; and (c) highly biodiverse grassland, that is to say grassland that is species rich, not fertilised and not degraded.

[18] The following are regarded as lands having high carbon stock: wetlands and continuously forested areas.

Some Member States, some members of the European Parliament (MEPs) and civil society would prefer to see the criteria cover a much broader range of issues, including deforestation, food price hikes and water shortages. As a consequence, in February 2008, the EU's energy ministers gave their go-ahead for an ad hoc working group to draw up core sustainability criteria for biofuels.

*The United States*: on 19 December 2007, President Bush signed the Energy Independence and Security Act (EISA).[19] The Act is designed to increase energy efficiency and the availability of renewable energy. Among many other provisions, the law sets a modified renewable fuel standard (RFS) which sets minimum annual levels of renewable fuel in US transportation fuel. The previous standard was 5.4 billion gallons (approximately 20.4 billion litres) for 2008, rising to 7.5 billion by 2012 (approximately 28.35 billion litres). The new standard starts at 9 billion gallons in 2008 (approximately 34 billion litres) and rises to 36 billion gallons in 2022 (approximately 137 billion litres).

The EISA includes several important definitions: new land use and greenhouse gas (GHG) reduction factors are introduced into the definition of 'renewable fuel' and only fuels that comply with the new definitions will count towards satisfying the RFS. These requirements may imply the need for a traceability and certification process such that purchasers of renewable fuels can be assured that the renewable fuel meets the carbon standard as well as the requirements related to land use, and the related possible need for third-party verification. In addition, an open question remains about how life cycle carbon will be calculated, i.e. what methodology will be used.

## Companies

While nations and international actors tend to have a broader view of certification, corporate initiatives tend to focus on their own sector when defining principles and criteria.

Companies have either taken steps to explore and establish certification schemes through international initiatives — such as the Round

---

[19] Energy Independence and Security Act. Public Law 110-140-Dec 19, 2007, at http://frwebgate. access.gpo.gov/cgi-bin/getdoc.cgi?dbname=110_cong_public_laws&docid=f:publ140.110.pdf. See also Congressional Research Service (CRS) Report for Congress. *Energy Independence and Security Act of 2007: A Summary of Major Provisions*, 21 December 2007, Order Code RL34294, at http://assets.opencrs.com/rpts/RL34294_20071221.pdf; and Beveridge and Diamond, *Renewable Fuel Standard Program Update*, 4 February 2008, at http://www.bdlaw.com/news-270.html

Tables on Sustainable Palm Oil Production and on Sustainable Biofuels — and collaborations with governments — for example the Cramer Commission; or they have established their own standards. The most advanced efforts by companies in the area of biomass certification have been made by companies in the electricity supply chain.

## Non-governmental organisations

Non-governmental organisations (NGOs) are active in certification at a number of levels, especially through the publication of position papers and research, and the participation in international networks and round tables. While NGOs agree on the need to have a set of sustainability principles, they have expressed different positions on the specific criteria that should be included in certification schemes. Additionally, they have not come to a consensus on the priority (e.g. between environmental and socio-economic criteria), strictness (e.g. use of genetically modified organisms and the GHG balance) and the level of detail given in criteria.[20]

In 2007, the World Wildlife Fund (WWF) International in collaboration with the Forest Stewardship Council (FSC), and the Dutch and UK Governments, published a paper entitled: 'Towards a harmonised sustainable biomass certification scheme'. The report promotes the 'Meta-Standard approach' and uses existing standards for agriculture and forestry.

## International initiatives

International efforts in the area of certification can be examined from the points of view of international networks and round tables.

*Round Table on Sustainable Palm Oil Production (RSPO)*: The RSPO Principles and Criteria for Sustainable Palm Oil Production were adopted in November 2005. They are currently being applied for an initial pilot implementation period of two years from the date of adoption. In June 2007, the RSPO finalised its certification scheme and plans to review the system after two years.[21]

*Ecole Polytechnique Fédérale de Lausanne (EPFL) — Round Table on Sustainable Biofuels (RSB)*:[22] the Round Table on Sustainable Biofuels is

---

[20] Dam, Junginger, Faaija, *et al.* (2006).
[21] www.rspo.org/Review_of_RSPO_Principles_and_Criteria_for_Sustainable_Palm_Oil_ Production.aspx
[22] Ecole Polytechnique Fédérale de Lausanne website: http://cgse.epfl.ch/page65660- en.html

an international initiative by the EPFL Energy Center. Its aim is to bring together farmers, companies, NGOs, experts, governments and inter-governmental agencies concerned with ensuring the sustainability of production and processing of biofuels. In October 2007, RSB released its 'Second version of global principles for sustainable biofuels produc-tion'. The principles refer to reduction of GHG emissions, human and labour rights, socio-economic development, food security, environmen-tal conservation, and soil, air and water protection.

*Round Table on Responsible Soy (RRS)*: the stated goal of the RRS is to promote economically viable, socially equitable and environmentally sustainable production, processing and trading of soy. In November of 2006, a final draft of the principles of the RRS was approved. The RRS has set out three main principles (economic, social and environmental responsibility) each with a number of sub-principles.[23]

## Issues of concern in the implementation of certification schemes

In order to understand fully the prospects for the future sustainability certification of biofuels, it is necessary to analyse some issues related to implementation.

### Issues with measurable indicators

Many of the criteria necessary for the certification of biofuels and related feedstocks are already employed in existing certification systems, mainly in the forestry and agricultural sectors, with the notable exception of criteria which refer to GHG emissions. However, it is important to recognise that for any biomass certification system to be effective it will have to employ precise and strong indicators. Unfortunately, although many criteria for environmentally and socially sustainable biofuels have been developed, not all of the indicators are well defined.

'Soft' indicators such as those that assert that farmers, workers etc. should not be 'unnecessarily exposed to hazardous substances or risk of injury', that call for the 'minimisation of wastes', that mandate that 'the activity should contribute to generation of jobs', that ensure 'equitable land ownership' or 'fair and equal remuneration' lack quantitative benchmarks applicable for assessment.[24]

---

[23] http://responsiblesoy.org/    [24] Lewandowski and Faaij (2005), 83–106.

The Cramer Commission has recognised that even when a considerable effort is made it is not always possible to use a 'quantitative indicator as a yard stick' in sustainability certification.

Perhaps most significantly, no functioning certification system currently employs measurable indicators for leakage effects, food and energy supply security, local benefits of biomass trade, alleviation of poverty, and greenhouse gas impacts. These are areas that many schemes that are under development are seeking to address.[25]

### Evaluating macro-level effects

Several certification initiatives have noted that the certification of individual products may fail to take into account important macro-level effects of biofuel production including: so-called 'leakage' effects, local food security and competition with other local applications, and effects on global commodity prices and the resulting effects on the purchasing power of different groups. How to test macro effects has not yet been worked out, but the Cramer Commission has suggested that the Dutch Government be responsible for accounting for such effects when assessing sustainability.

Leakage effects occur when the production of biomass displaces activities to other areas where they may cause undesirable land use changes. Because biomass production can induce land use changes outside the area of production, it can cause the carbon benefits gained in one area to be lost at another location. The problem is that leakage effects can reach global dimensions and therefore, they are particularly difficult to assess. Biofuel feedstocks are commodities that are traded on the global market and therefore leakage effects that occur across borders are probable. While effective national land use policies may deal with local leakages, they are incapable of protecting against displacement effects on the global scale.

Competition with food and other local applications of biomass is a real concern that certification schemes aim to address. Biofuel production can affect food security in different ways, namely via food prices, energy prices, farm incomes and rural incomes. These developments will produce winners and losers. At this time, there is no global consensus on how much biofuel production has contributed to the recent price spikes of agricultural and food products.

Calculating global leakages may thus be very difficult. Should macro effects be included in certification schemes, it would be necessary to

---

[25] *Ibid.*

Table 2 *Select examples of monitoring needed to evaluate macro-level effects of biomass production*[26]

| Effect | Data | Information to be reported |
|---|---|---|
| Food prices | Price information about food, with a distinction between autonomous trends (e.g. in the world market) and more local effects deviating from this trend. Price effects caused by biomass production must be considered in relation to (autonomous) exchange rate developments and the prices of raw materials. | Prices of food products for producers (farmers) and for consumers. The use of public statistics (national and those of the Food and Agriculture Organisation of the United Nations). |
| Deforestation and loss of nature reserves in relation to the supply of food, construction material, fertilisers, medicines, etc. | Monitoring of wooded acreage and nature reserves and effects on the availability of food, construction material, fertilisers, medicines, etc. | Satellite data for the monitoring of (shifts in) land use and vegetation. By national government and independent authority for higher scale levels and relevant regional organisations. |

develop assessment methods that are accurate and cost effective and that can reasonably be implemented for certification purposes. Still, the question remains of who will be responsible for tracking such macro effects (e.g. governments or certification bodies) and how accountability will be assured.

### Greenhouse gas impacts

Many certification schemes have prioritised the reduction of GHG emissions, since bioenergy is not necessarily carbon neutral. Any indicator that is developed should require the carbon benefit of the whole biofuels

[26] As proposed in the Final Report of the Cramer Commission, Table 3.4.1, p. 21.

chain to be demonstrated by comparing it to a baseline scenario. There remains some ambiguity and uncertainty as to how different biofuel GHG analyses are conducted, rendering it difficult to make any reliable comparisons between biofuels on the basis of their GHG performance.

## Implications for developing country producers

Certifying feedstocks and biofuels has implications especially for producers in developing countries.

### Cost of certification and conformity assessment

Certification will add significant costs to the production of biofuels. These expenses are associated with the additional costs of meeting the sustainability criteria for the production of biomass and the processing of biofuel, as well as the costs of proving compliance with established criteria. Furthermore, the costs will be highly dependent on the number, strictness and inclusiveness of the criteria established by the certification system. The need to prove adherence to a broad set of social standards will considerably raise the cost of certification. Additionally, the cost of certification borne by the producers is likely to vary with the scale of the production company. According to the Cramer Report, the additional costs of certification of smallholders are estimated at about 20 per cent of the production costs, but it may occasionally be more.[27] The danger is that the additional costs associated with certification may mean that small producers, particularly those in developing countries, will be unable to afford to comply with the requirements for certification. The result would be a loss of market share for small farmers and companies and a dominance of the market by large corporations. The Cramer Report has suggested that buyers might support access to the market for small producers by stipulating as a condition that a certain part of the biomass should originate from small producers. The same approach is followed by Brazil in its social programme for biodiesel. Additionally, the Dutch project group has proposed that sustainability requirements be simplified for small producers where necessary.

If certification requirements are established, they should be coupled with financing and technical assistance to improve the capacity of developing countries to master and apply certification schemes and prove

[27] p. 5.

compliance. This begs the question of who will supply such assistance and who will pay for such programmes. Will an established certification scheme make allowances for such support or flexibility to simplify the criteria based on the circumstances of the producer?

## The process of establishing certification schemes and participation of developing countries

The concerns repeatedly expressed by developing countries about certification refer to the fact that certification schemes do not always tailor solutions to local conditions; they may apply a one-size-fits-all approach, failing to take into account that one process or production method may be appropriate in one part of the world, but quite inappropriate in another. Some schemes may favour technologies that may be unavailable, unsuitable or prohibitively expensive for trading partners. Also, most certification and label schemes originate with significant input from domestic producers who may have vested interests in establishing particular requirements.

To ensure that certification contributes to sustainable production and does not become an obstacle to international trade, especially for developing countries, sustainability principles and criteria should be developed through a transparent and fair process where countries, both producing and consuming biofuels, are effectively represented. While rules developed at the country or local levels may encourage a level of discretion that complicates the standardisation process, if applied with appropriate prudence, criteria and indicators could be articulated and quantified in a way that facilitates engagement in sustainable production in all regions.

### *Implications of certification for the WTO*

Certification may enhance the market acceptability of biofuels, it may bring benefits in terms of tax breaks and other fiscal advantages, and only certified biofuels may count against blending targets: all this makes certification a more pressing issue and raises the profile of WTO provisions that may be relevant to certification of biofuels.

## WTO coverage of measures based on life cycle analysis

The Agreement on Technical Barriers to Trade (TBT) covers technical regulations and standards, including packaging, marking and labelling requirements, and procedures for assessment of conformity. The code of good practice for the preparation, adoption and application of standards (Annex 3 of the TBT) refers to the activities carried out by any standardisation body, including non-governmental bodies, which develop standards.

A 'grey' area in the field of labelling remains the TBT coverage of labelling programmes that refer to the way goods have been produced, even though the production methods are not reflected in the final characteristics of the product (non-product related processes and production methods — NPR-PPMs). The main concern about those measures is that, by establishing requirements for the way products should be manufactured, they limit the freedom of foreign producers to produce according to available technologies and following priorities and strategies set up by their governments. They would then represent an undue interference of one country in the sphere of discretion of another. Moreover, NPR-PPMs could quite easily be used for protectionist purposes, creating barriers to international trade which would negatively affect developing country producers in particular.

While numerous labelling programmes are based on the life cycle approach and therefore take PPMs into account, many WTO Members take the position that such programmes, by referring to PPMs that are not reflected in the final characteristics of the products, are not covered by the TBT.[28] If this were the case, they would then be scrutinised under the General Agreement on Tariffs and Trade (GATT), in particular under Articles I, III, XI and XX. This would, however, lead to the result that measures based on NPR-PPMs, in spite of their potential negative effects on international trade, would fall under a 'general' agreement — the GATT — while measures based on PPMs which are reflected in the final characteristics of the product would fall under a 'specific' and stricter agreement — the TBT even though the former requirements are potentially more trade restrictive than the latter. Hence, this interpretation that excludes NPR-PPMs from the coverage of the TBT does not seem very sound.

An additional question regarding the TBT coverage of labelling and certification initiatives concerns standards developed by private bodies which have not accepted the code of good practice (adherence to the code is voluntary), or which may not have the legal power to enforce the

---

[28] See *Report to the 5th Session of the WTO Ministerial Conference in Cancún — Paragraphs 32 and 33 of the Doha Ministerial Declaration*, WT/CTE/8, 11 July 2003, paragraphs 34–6.

standards they have set up (according to Annex 1, paragraph 8, a 'non-governmental body' is a body which has legal power to enforce a technical regulation. The 'legal power to enforce a technical regulation' is not defined by the code. It could possibly refer to the authority to grant or withdraw a label or to file complaints in the case of misuse of a label). Moreover, there is the case of 'hybrid' entities — such as the Round Table on Sustainable Biofuels — which are composed of representatives of public and private entities, international organisations and NGOs. It is unclear whether such entities could be regarded as international standardisation bodies[29] and the principles and criteria they develop as international standards, which would then be covered by a presumption of conformity with the TBT.

On the other hand, if these initiatives are regarded as private schemes which fall outside the scope of the TBT, they would escape from multilaterally agreed trade rules — such as non-discrimination, abstention from creating unnecessary obstacles to trade, proportionality and transparency. Nevertheless, they would have a significant impact on trade flows. There is still the possibility that private standards could be captured under the GATT as governmental measures if there is a strong link between the private action and the government in question, as in the case where a country decides to grant some incentives to certified biofuels and in doing so relies on the certification scheme developed by a private body.[30]

## Transparency

A vocal debate took place in the 1990s regarding the transparency of eco-labelling schemes. The concerns which prompted that debate within the WTO Committees on Trade and Environment and on Technical Barriers to Trade were that eco-labelling schemes — by being voluntary and often developed by private bodies — would fall under the transparency rules set by the code of good practice, which are

---

[29] According to Annex 1, international bodies or systems are those whose membership is open to the relevant bodies of at least all WTO Members. This definition is too succinct to be of real practical use.

[30] See paragraph 106–9 in *Japan — Trade in Semiconductors* (L/6309), report of the panel adopted on 4 May 1988, BISD 35S/116, where the panel found that it was not necessarily the legal status of the measure which was decisive in determining whether or not it fell under Article XI:1 of the GATT.

not very stringent. WTO Members reached an agreement to make efforts on a voluntary and non-binding basis to maximise the use of the code of good practice for eco-labelling programmes and to apply the notification obligations meant for mandatory measures to voluntary measures, including those developed by non-governmental bodies. A similar solution could apply to biofuel certification schemes, especially voluntary programmes developed by non-governmental bodies. The main benefit of such a solution is that producers and exporters would be informed in advance of the development of certification and labelling programmes and would have the opportunity to provide comments on proposals as well as time to adjust to the new requirements before their implementation.

## The 'like' products issue

*Defining 'like' products*: The criteria being developed to single out sustainably produced biofuels and feedstocks and distinguish them from biofuels and feedstocks which lack these characteristics raise a fundamental question over whether such a distinction between products which share the same physical characteristics and final uses is consistent with multilaterally agreed trade rules. The national treatment principle incorporated into Article III of the GATT implies non-discrimination between domestic and imported goods. This means that the importing country is not allowed to apply to foreign products measures more onerous than those applied to 'like' domestic products. Article 2:1 and Annex 3, paragraph D of the TBT restate the principle of non-discrimination set out in Article I:1 and Article III:4 of the GATT 1994. Within the context of biofuels, the question is therefore whether certified biofuels and non-certified biofuels may or may not be regarded as 'like' products.

The Working Party report on *Border Tax Adjustments*[31] identified three general criteria that would be relevant for analysing 'likeness': (i) the properties, nature and quality of the products; (ii) the end uses of the products in a given market; and (iii) the tastes and habits of the consumers, which vary from country to country. Later jurisprudence added tariff classification as a supplementary consideration (i.e. a fourth

---

[31] BISD 18S/97, adopted on 2 December 1970, paragraph 18.

criterion) in this respect.[32] The Appellate Body in the *Japan — Taxes on Alcoholic Beverages* case described the Working Party report on *Border Tax Adjustments* as setting out 'the basic approach for interpreting "like or similar products", generally, in the various provisions of the GATT 1947'.[33] In a subsequent case, the Appellate Body confirmed that the general criteria mentioned above provided a framework for analysing 'likeness', but reiterated that they were 'simply tools to assist in the task of sorting and examining the relevant evidence. They are neither a treaty-mandated nor a closed list of criteria that will determine the legal characterization of products. More important, the adoption of a parti-cular framework to aid in the examination of evidence does not dissolve the duty or the need to examine, in each case, all of the pertinent evidence.'[34] An overall determination of whether the products at issue could be characterised as 'like' thus requires that the evidence relating to each of the four criteria, along with any other relevant evidence, be examined and weighed.

In assessing whether products are 'like', the product/process distinc-tion has often been raised.[35] On the one hand, it has been argued that there is no real support in the text and jurisprudence of the GATT for the product/process distinction[36] and that this distinction is neither war-ranted nor useful in practice.[37] On the other hand, it has been suggested that there is a textual basis in Article III of the GATT and the Note *Ad* Article III for the product/process distinction and that the distinction

---

[32] *EEC — Measures on Animal Feed Proteins*, adopted on 14 March 1978, BISD 25S/49, paragraph 4.2; *Japan — Customs Duties, Taxes and Labelling Practices on Imported Wines and Alcoholic Beverages*, adopted on 10 November 1987, BISD 34S/83, paragraph 5.6; *United States — Measures affecting Alcoholic and Malt Beverages*, adopted on 19 June 1992, BISD 39S/206-299, paragraphs 5.24 and 5.71; *United States — Standards for Reformulated and Conventional Gasoline*, Report of the panel, WT/DS2/R, 29 January 1996, paragraphs 6.8 and 6.9.

[33] *Japan — Taxes on Alcoholic Beverages*, report of the Appellate Body, adopted on 1 November 1996, WT/DS8/AB/R, WT/DS10/AB/R, WT/DS11/AB/R, p. 20.

[34] *European Communities — Measures Affecting Asbestos and Asbestos-Containing Pro-ducts*, report of the Appellate Body, WT/DS135/AB/R, 12 March 2001, paragraph 102.

[35] However, it has been stressed that the 'trade policy elite has simply accepted the notion of a sharp divergence between measures on products and PPMs as if such a distinction had been written into the GATT all along, and not simply invented in the *Tuna — Dolphin* case': M. J. Trebilcock.and R. Howse, *The Regulation of International Trade* (London and New York: Routledge, 1999), p. 413.

[36] R. Howse and D. Regan, 'The product/process distinction — an illusionary basis for disciplining "unilateralism" in trade policy', *European Journal of International Law* 11 (2000), 264–8.

[37] A. Cosbey, 'The WTO and PPMs: time to drop a taboo', *Bridges* 5 (2001) No. 1–3, at 11–12.

should be retained to prevent protectionist abuses.[38] The product/process distinction is therefore an open issue. Jurisprudence related to Article XX (general exceptions) of the GATT, on the other hand, has evolved to interpret Article XX as covering measures that distinguish products on the basis of the production processes.[39]

In the *Asbestos* ruling,[40] the Appellate Body made a significant finding concerning evidence relating to the health risks associated with a product, stating: 'We are very much of the view that evidence relating to the health risks associated with a product may be pertinent in an examination of "likeness" under Article III:4 of the GATT 1994.'[41] Establishing links between the 'likeness' of two products and their respective impact on health has important implications, especially if we assume that other non-trade concerns, such as environmental protection or climate change mitigation, could also be used as elements to be taken into account when assessing 'likeness'. As far as biofuels are concerned, this approach might allow a distinction to be made based on the contribution of sustainable — as opposed to non-sustainable — biofuels and feedstocks to mitigating the environmental and health problems related to climate change. According to the Appellate Body's reasoning in the *Asbestos* case, however, the health risk associated with a product may be pertinent to the extent that because it reflects the physical properties of the product and affects the tastes and habits of consumers. It is also likely to influence the competitive relationships between products in the marketplace. More generally, the line of reasoning in *Asbestos* seems to suggest that non-trade concerns may be pertinent in an examination of 'likeness' under Article III:4 of the GATT when they have an impact on the 'competitiveness' or 'substitutability' of a product in relation to other products: 'a determination of "likeness" under Article III:4 is, fundamentally, a determination about the nature and extent of a competitive relationship

---

[38] J. H. Jackson, 'Comments on *Shrimp/Turtle* and the product/process distinction', *European Journal of International Law* 11 (2000), at 303–7.

[39] In the *US — Shrimp* case (*United States — Import Prohibition of Certain Shrimp and Shrimp Products*, Appellate Body report adopted on 12 October 1998, WT/DS58/AB/R), the Appellate Body stated that 'It appears to us, however, that conditioning access to a Member's domestic market on whether exporting Members comply with, or adopt, a policy or policies unilaterally prescribed by the importing Member may, to some degree, be a common aspect of measures falling within the scope of one or another of the exceptions (a) to (j) of Article XX.' (paragraph 121).

[40] *European Communities — Measures Affecting Asbestos and Asbestos-containing Products.*

[41] *Ibid.*, at paragraph 113.

between and among products'.[42] Non-trade aspects are relevant only in so far as they influence commercial factors.[43]

Hence, a particular emphasis should be put on how the domestic market treats the certified (presumably sustainable) biofuels and feedstocks compared to the uncertified ones, what is their competitive relationship in the market-place, and whether consumers perceive them as distinct products. Market studies on cross-price elasticity of demand and any other evidence indicating the extent to which the products involved are — or could be — in a competitive relationship in the market-place, would be part of the evidence relevant for determining 'likeness' under Article III:4 of the GATT.

The case of certification of biofuels and feedstocks presents, however, an additional complexity, since products may be distinguished not only on the basis of their possible impact on health or on the environment, but also with reference to labour and other social standards. At the first WTO ministerial conference in Singapore in December 1996, it was agreed that market access should not be linked with labour standards. While WTO jurisprudence has evolved to become more sensitive to non-trade concerns, especially in the health and environmental fields, it is highly questionable whether it would be equally open to accepting trade discrimination linked to labour and other social conditions, especially considering that Members have expressed themselves against it.

*Like products and domestic taxation*: the 'like products' issue may also be of relevance where domestic taxation is at issue, particularly because certain countries are planning to reserve tax breaks and incentives only to certified biofuels.[44]

---

[42] *Ibid.*, at paragraph 99.
[43] S. Zarrilli and I. Musselli, 'Non-trade concerns and the WTO jurisprudence in the *Asbestos* case: possible relevance for international trade in GMOs', *Journal of World Intellectual Property* 5 (2002).
[44] Under Brazil's social fuel seal, certification enables biodiesel producers to benefit from reduced rates of taxation on biodiesel. The rate of exemption is 100 per cent for biodiesel certified with the social fuel seal produced from castor oil or palm oil in the northern and north-eastern regions of the country, versus 67 per cent for biodiesel produced from any source in other regions that do not qualify for the social fuel seal. In March 2007, the Swiss Government amended its mineral fuel tax in a way that ties tax benefits for biofuels to a system based on various environmental and social criteria. Under the new rules, both domestic and imported biofuels that benefit from a reduced fuel excise tax require 'proof of a positive total ecological assessment that ensures also that the conditions of production are socially acceptable'. In addition, the government, 'taking into account of the amount of domestically available renewable fuels, shall establish the quantity of renewable fuels that can be exempted from the tax at the time of the importation'. The

According to Article III:2 of the GATT, regulations and taxation measures should not discriminate between 'like' products. If different biofuels — such as certified and uncertified biofuels — fall into the category of 'like' products, a country that applies different tax regimes to them may be considered to be violating its multilateral trade obligations unless it has legitimate reasons for imposing such a discriminatory system. We then go back to two issues: first of all, whether sustainability, or the lack of it, would be enough to make products 'unlike' and then lawfully subject to different tax treatments. The second issue is the following: if certified and uncertified biofuels were regarded as 'like' products, could the exceptions of Article XX(b) and (g) of the GATT be invoked to justify discriminatory tax treatments? These issues will be examined below.

### 'Less favourable treatment'

Assuming that certified and uncertified biofuels are found to be 'like' products, there is a second element that must be established before a measure can be held to be inconsistent with Article III:4 of the GATT: namely are 'like' imported products accorded less favourable treatment than 'like' domestic products? Only if a 'less favourable treatment' is detected can the measure be considered to be in violation of GATT Article III:4. 'The term "less favourable treatment" expresses the general principle, in Article III:1, that internal regulations "should not be applied ... so as to afford protection to domestic production" ... However, a Member may draw distinctions between products which have been found to be "like", without, for this reason alone, according to the group of "like" imported products "less favourable treatment" than that accorded to the group of "like" domestic products.'[45]

In the *EC — Biotech* case,[46] the panel reached an interesting conclusion in this regard. It stated that, in order to be a violation of Article III of the GATT, the 'less favourable treatment' of imported products should

---

European Commission has proposed that biofuels that fail to meet the sustainability criteria would not be eligible for tax reduction and other financial supports. The Cramer Report proposes that access to any subsidies for biofuels be contingent on satisfying its criteria and numerous sub-criteria. See: R. Doornbosch and R. Steenblik (2007), *'Biofuels: Is the Cure Worse than the Disease?'*, paper presented at the Round Table on Sustainable Development, Paris, 11–12 September, OECD, SG/SD/RT(2007)3, at 39–40.

[45] *EC — Asbestos*, paragraph 100.

[46] *European Communities — Measures Affecting the Approval and Marketing of Biotech Products (EC — Biotech)*, panel report, WT/DS291/R, WT/DS292/R, WT/DS293/R, 29 September 2006, paragraphs 7.2511–7.2516.

be explained by their foreign origin, rather than by other reasons, such as a perceived difference between products in terms of their safety or other characteristics. More specifically, the panel held that the fact that biotech products and non-biotech products were treated differently in the EU market was not the central issue; what was more relevant was that the different sets of rules which applied to them were not linked to their origin. Indeed, imported and domestic biotech products were treated equally, as were imported and domestic non-biotech products. Though different rules applied to these two categories of products, they were not justified by the origin of the products. It is noteworthy that the panel decided to analyse the 'no less favourable treatment' obligation before the 'like products' element. Having reached the conclusion that the complaining country — Argentina — had not been able to prove that its products had been treated 'less favourably' than domestic EC products, it did not need to address the issue of likeness between biotech and non-biotech products.

It is unclear whether the approach taken by the panel will be upheld by future WTO jurisprudence, especially by the Appellate Body. Should this be the case, it would represent a departure from the rather consolidated views that put 'likeness' at the core of the analysis under Article III of the GATT. The emphasis would shift from 'likeness' to 'less favourable treatment', hence partially depriving the issue of 'likeness' of its relevance.

Applying the panel's reasoning to biofuels could lead to the conclusion that different sets of rules could apply to certified and to non-certified biofuels and this would be consistent with WTO law, so long as the same set of rules applies to domestic and imported certified biofuels, and to domestic and imported non-certified biofuels. Nevertheless, this conclusion would hold only if the measures at stake were not aimed at de facto discriminating against foreign products under the pretext of distinguishing them on the basis of some differences unrelated to origin. The way biofuel certification schemes are developed and the opportunities which are given to foreign producers to be part of the process and to get their products certified without incurring into prohibitive and unjustified costs and delays would probably be highly relevant to assess whether a 'less favourable treatment' is in place. Jurisprudence in the *Shrimp* case may support this view.[47]

---

[47] See paragraph 166 in *United States — Import Prohibition of Certain Shrimp and Shrimp Products*, where the United States was found to be at fault for not consulting/negotiating with exporting countries and for imposing its own standards.

*The General Exceptions of Article XX of GATT 1994*: if a measure is found to violate Article III of the GATT, it requires justification under one of the sub-paragraphs of Article XX of the GATT and under its chapeau. Article XX of the GATT gives countries the legal means to balance their trade obligations with important non-trade objectives — such as health protection, the preservation of the environment or the protection of natural resources — which form part of their overall national policies.

To meet the requirements of Article XX(b) of the GATT — which refers to measures necessary to protect human, animal or plant life or health — the provision at stake (1) should fall within the range of policies designed to protect human, animal or plant life or health; (2) should be necessary to fulfil the policy objective; and (3) should fulfil the requirements of the chapeau of Article XX of the GATT.[48] In the *United States* — *Gasoline* case, the panel held that 'the policy to reduce air pollution resulting from the consumption of gasoline was a policy within the range of those concerning the protection of human, animal and plant life or health mentioned in Article XX(b)'.[49] Assuming that climate change can be considered an extreme form of air pollution, which can have negative repercussions on human, animal and plant life or health, measures aimed at mitigating climate change effects seem to be covered by paragraph (b).

GATT/WTO jurisprudence has interpreted 'necessary' as implying a 'least-trade-restrictive test': a measure cannot be considered 'necessary' if an alternative measure which is not inconsistent with GATT provisions or is less inconsistent with them is available and could reasonably be expected to be used. In the *Korea* — *Beef* case, the Appellate Body added some elements of clarification to interpret 'necessary' and held that '... determination of whether a measure, which is not "indispensable" may nevertheless be "necessary" within the contemplation of Article XX(d),[50] involves in every case a process of weighing and balancing a series of factors which prominently include the contribution made by the compliance measure to the enforcement of the law or regulation at issue, the importance of the common interests or values protected by that law or regulation, and the accompanying impact of the law or regulation on

---

[48] *United States* — *Standards for Reformulated and Conventional Gasoline*, paragraph 6.20.

[49] *Ibid.*, paragraph 6.21.

[50] The necessity requirement under paragraph (b) has been interpreted as corresponding to the one under paragraph (d), see *Thailand* — *Restrictions on Importation of and Internal Taxes on Cigarettes*, adopted on 7 November 1990, BISD 37S/200-228, paragraph 74.

imports or exports'.[51] One aspect of the weighing and balancing process is the extent to which an alternative measure 'contributes to the realisation of the end pursued'.[52] Moreover, '[t]he more vital or important those common interests or values are, the easier it would be to accept as "necessary" a measure designed as an enforcement instrument'.[53]

Recent jurisprudence has further developed the interpretation of the necessity test under Article XX of the GATT. In the *Brazil — Retreaded Tyres* case, the Appellate Body held that even measures which produced severe restrictions to international trade, such as import bans, could be regarded as necessary provided that they were apt to make a material contribution to the achievement of their objectives. Conversely, measures that made only marginal or insignificant contributions to the achievement of their objectives could not be regarded as necessary. However, the demonstration that a measure is apt to produce a material contribution to the achievement of its objectives 'could consist of quantitative projections in the future or qualitative reasoning based on a set of hypotheses that are tested and supported by sufficient evidence'. Interestingly, the Appellate Body added, 'Moreover, the results obtained from certain actions — for instance measures adopted in order to attenuate global warming and climate change — can only be evaluated with the benefit of time.'[54]

Applying these considerations to the certification of biofuels, we could draw some conclusions: first, it cannot be argued that climate change mitigation is not an important common interest; second, labelling and certification are 'soft' policy instruments, as opposed, for instance, to import restrictions and trade bans, hence for both these reasons biofuel certification may pass the 'necessary' test.

The additional criterion for a provision to meet one of the specific exceptions of Article XX of the GATT, including paragraphs (b) and (g), is that it fulfils the requirements of the chapeau of Article XX. In the *United States — Shrimp* case, the Appellate Body stated that there are three standards contained in the chapeau: (1) the measure must not constitute arbitrary discrimination between countries where the same conditions prevail; (2) the measure must not constitute unjustifiable

---

[51] *Korea — Measures Affecting Imports of Fresh, Chilled and Frozen Beef*, report of the Appellate Body, WT/DS161/AB/R, WT7DS169/AB/R, 11 December 2000, paragraph 164.

[52] *Ibid.*, paragraphs 166 and 163.    [53] *Ibid.*, paragraph 162.

[54] *Brazil — Measures Affecting Imports of Retreaded Tyres*, report of the Appellate Body, WT/DS332/AB/R, 3 December 2007, paragraphs 150 and 151.

discrimination between countries where the same conditions prevail; (3) the measure must not constitute a disguised restriction on international trade.[55] As far as biofuel certification is concerned, the issue seems to be whether distinguishing biofuels on the basis of their sustainability is a policy genuinely aimed at ensuring sustainability, or if it is a way to protect domestic producers who can more easily fulfil the principles and criteria set up in the certification schemes.

Let us now consider the exception of Article XX(g) of the GATT, which refers to measures relating to the conservation of exhaustible natural resources if such measures are made effective in conjunction with restrictions on domestic production or consumption.

According to panel practice, a country which wants its measure to be justified by paragraph (g) has to demonstrate that (1) the policy in respect of the measures for which the provision is invoked falls within the range of policies related to the conservation of exhaustible natural resources; (2) the measures for which the exception is invoked are related to the conservation of exhaustible natural resources; (3) the measures for which the exception is invoked are made effective in conjunction with restrictions on domestic production or consumption; and (4) the measures are applied in conformity with the requirements of the introductory clause of Article XX.[56]

In the *United States — Standards for Gasoline* case, the panel held that clean air was a resource, was natural and could be depleted; therefore, a policy to reduce the depletion of clean air was a policy to conserve a natural resource within the meaning of Article XX(g) of the GATT.[57] Measures aimed at climate change mitigation would then comply with this requirement.

The second criterion — 'relating to the conservation of exhaustible natural resources' — has been interpreted in a series of panel decisions as 'primarily aimed at' the conservation of exhaustible natural resources. In the *United States — Standards for Gasoline* case, the Appellate Body clarified that in order to qualify under this criterion, a measure should exhibit a 'substantial relationship' with the conservation of natural resources and should not be merely 'incidentally or inadvertently aimed at' this. In the *United States — Shrimp* case, however, the

---

[55] *United States — Import Prohibition of Certain Shrimp and Shrimp Products*, paragraph 150.
[56] *United States — Standards for Reformulated and Conventional Gasoline*, report of the panel, WT/DS2/R, 29 January 1996, paragraph 6.35.
[57] *Ibid.*, paragraph 6.37.

Appellate Body seems to have relaxed the 'primarily aimed at' test, by also allowing measures which are 'directly connected' with the conservation policy to pass the test of paragraph (g).[58] Again, biofuels certification may pass this test since certifying biofuels and encouraging producers to engage in sustainable production that reduces GHG emissions seem sufficiently connected to the conservation of clean air. This test is likely to be more easily passed if biofuel certification is one of the several policy instruments put in place by a country to deal with climate change and not the only one.

Moving to the condition that the contested measure shall be 'made effective in conjunction with restrictions on domestic production or consumption', paragraph (g) clearly requires a link between the measure at stake and restrictions on domestic production or consumption, though it does not require identical treatment for imported and domestic products. Hence we return to the situation analysed above where the relevant issue is whether the same set of rules applies to domestic and imported 'sustainable' biofuels, and to domestic and imported 'non-sustainable' biofuels.

Conformity with the chapeau of Article XX of the GATT has already been analysed.

In conclusion, if distinguishing between biofuels on the basis of their sustainability and applying different sets of rules to sustainable and to non-sustainable biofuels is regarded to be in violation of Article III of the GATT, these measures could, however, find justification under either paragraph (b) or paragraph (g) of Article XX of the GATT and under its chapeau. This assumes that the final goal of such measures is indeed preservation of the environment or health protection.

Things change radically, however, if the final goal of certification schemes is ensuring compliance with certain labour standards, enhancing food security or offering better income opportunities to feedstock producers. There is consensus on the fact that Article XX of the GATT contains a 'closed' list of general exceptions, therefore the above-mentioned considerations, in spite of their intrinsic value, do not fit into it and measures aimed at pursuing such goals, if otherwise

---

[58] 'This is, essentially, a requirement that a country adopt a regulatory program requiring the use of TED [turtle excluder devices] by commercial shrimp trawling vessels in areas where there is a likelihood of intercepting sea turtles. This requirement is, in our view, directly connected with the policy of conservation of sea turtles.' (paragraph 140). See P. C. Mavroidis, 'Trade and environment after the shrimps-turtles litigation', *Journal of World Trade* 34 (2000), 85.

inconsistent with WTO rules, cannot be justified under Article XX of the GATT.

## The way ahead

A wide range of stakeholders have embarked upon various initiatives with the aim of establishing sustainability certification systems for biofuels and feedstocks. The proliferation of individual standards may damage the efficiency and credibility of certification; hence it seems desirable to co-ordinate these efforts.

If an inclusive biomass certification system can be instituted, the next question is the appropriate strategy for implementing such a system.

A system of internationally agreed standards would be an option worth considering. A single set of standards would be easier to become familiar with than a multitude of different standards. Such a scheme would increase transparency in the market and provide clear indicators for producers. Most importantly, an international process would allow wide participation, including that of developing countries. The outcome of the process would then reflect the views and concerns of biofuel and feedstock producers in different regions and would also ensure that environmental and other concerns are balanced with market access expectations.

However, an international process is, by nature, long and complex. By contrast, the Round Table on Sustainable Biofuels, for example, has set a rather stringent time frame and hopes to be able to deliver a set of standards by the end of 2008.

A multilateral process conducted under the auspices of the United Nations (UN) would be ideal from a transparency, participation and fairness point of view. However, UN processes are particularly slow. On the other hand, while other international settings may have better chances of achieving results within a reasonable time, they might encounter a problem of legitimacy, since membership would not be universal.

The longer it would take to set internationally agreed criteria, the more difficult it would be to merge existing initiatives with an internationally agreed programme.

Some ideas for making progress include:

- The availability of scientific data, for example on the contribution of specific biofuels to the reduction of GHG emissions, could facilitate the decision-making process and ease the convergence toward a single set of principles and criteria.

- An appropriate balance should be found between including in the certification schemes criteria which are quantifiable and verifiable and leaving enough flexibility to adjust the schemes to the specific conditions in different producing regions.
- Regional meetings to discuss the criteria and approaches that best suit specific regions may be preferable to global meetings.
- Providing capacity building for assessment of compliance and conformity may represent a constructive approach, especially to foster the involvement of developing country producers.
- In addition to capacity building, compliance with sustainability principles could be linked to certain benefits — such as enhanced access to financing, linkages to other support services such as health and education and the establishment of local or regional networks — to encourage producers to engage in sustainable production and motivate them to make the extra investments required to meet the sustainability criteria.

## Conclusions

Present and predicted high oil prices and related energy security concerns and the increasing pressure to mitigate climate change effects, together with rural development aims, are expected to sustain an interest in biofuels. Hence, the production of and international trade in biofuels are expected to grow significantly in the years to come.

Consumers in many countries are expressing the wish to be informed about the sustainability impact of biofuels throughout their life cycle. Certifying biofuels may thus become a precondition for consumers' acceptance of these products.

Moreover, a number of countries and regional groupings are planning to require that only certified biofuels can count against the national or regional fuel blending targets, and are also linking biofuel certification with tax breaks and other incentives. These developments contribute to making certification an increasingly important issue, including in international trade.

Certifying biofuels on the basis of sustainability may play a role in ensuring that biofuels contribute to the fulfilment of energy, environmental and rural development goals, without having detrimental side-effects.

In developing certification schemes, some lessons from past experience may prove useful: inclusive processes that take into account differences between countries and regions lead to schemes which are generally more acceptable, reflect a fairer balance among different interests and concerns, and are more feasible to implement than schemes developed otherwise. An international process of standard development, possibly conducted under the aegis of the UN, would be ideal from the points of view of legitimacy and inclusiveness, while it would inevitably be slow and complex. The availability of clear scientific data, for instance on the actual contribution of biofuels to reducing GHG emissions, would facilitate the process and make it less controversial.

Linking certification with capacity building in the areas of compliance and assessment of conformity would promote the engagement of producers in sustainable production, especially in developing countries. Compliance could also be linked to incentives such as enhanced access to financing, linkages to other support services and the establishment of local and regional networks to increase productivity.

Differentiating products, including biofuels, on the basis of how they have been produced and of their impact throughout their life cycle remains, however, a complex issue both from the practical and legal points of view.

The criteria being included in the current certification initiatives are diverse and often far reaching. While some schemes put emphasis only on reduction of GHG emissions, others include issues such as environmental protection, social well-being and local prosperity. The applicable indicators are often not precisely formulated. Sometimes there is a lack of quantitative indicators. Social sustainability criteria are particularly difficult to quantify. As a result, certification has an inescapable aspect of subjectivity depending on the evaluation methods employed.

From a legal point of view, while the WTO system has evolved, mainly through jurisprudence, to become progressively more responsive to non-trade concerns and to product differentiation based on PPMs, the kinds of PPMs included in certification schemes for biofuels go far beyond those used so far and analysed in various WTO rulings.

This leads to the fundamental question of where it is appropriate to draw the line and what kind of product differentiation is legitimate and instrumental to reach sustainability goals. This is not a new issue in the international trade and development debate. What is new is that biofuels aim, among other goals, to tackle climate change, a phenomenon that can affect the development prospects of all countries and may deserve bolder behaviour and new attitudes, including more flexibility within the international trade system.

The magnitude of the climate change challenge, however, is not a guarantee against possible protectionist abuses by countries and companies. The role that farmer lobbies are playing in several developed countries in securing a high level of subsidies for feedstock producers confirms this point. While trade measures may help to support genuine efforts to tackle climate change, they may also be abused for protectionist purposes.

There is yet another dimension to consider. Would trade measures genuinely taken to address climate change challenges and developed in full conformity with multilaterally agreed trade rules be effective in achieving the expected results? Coming back to the specific theme of this paper, would the co-existence in the international markets of several ambitious and far-reaching biofuels certification schemes be instrumental in ensuring that climate change mitigation, energy security and rural development goals are achieved, while the potential negative side-effects of biofuel production and use are minimised?

While it would be very difficult to provide a conclusive answer to this question, it seems that certification schemes (i) developed through a participatory process; (ii) based on scientific evidence; (iii) accompanied by support measures to encourage engagement in sustainable production and to facilitate compliance especially by developing country producers; (iv) which do not entail unnecessary costs and delays in international trade; (v) which include criteria and indicators that can be evaluated quantitatively; (vi) which avoid reference to macro-level concerns that would be extraordinarily difficult to evaluate with reference to a single product and better dealt with at another level; may play a positive role in achieving sustainability goals without having a disproportionate disruptive impact on international trade.

If well planned, biofuels and feedstock production may offer a unique opportunity for developing countries to enter a new market which appears very profitable. Many of these countries enjoy the appropriate land and labour conditions for becoming efficient producers. Biofuels production may bring additional benefits to developing countries in terms of access to technology, to financing, and to market information. An appropriately designed certification scheme for biofuels should not be a hindrance to such developments and should ideally facilitate this process.

# PART IV

Climate change mitigation and trade in services

# 11

# GATS, financial services and trade in renewable energy certificates (RECs) — just another market-based solution to cope with the tragedy of the commons?

PANAGIOTIS DELIMATSIS AND
DESPINA MAVROMATI[1]

Freedom in a commons brings ruin to all.

G. Hardin[2]

## Introductory remarks

Trade in the energy sector is one of the areas that clearly demonstrates the importance of the service sector. As is the case with other trade areas, trade in energy is made feasible through a series of supporting services, ranging from distribution and transportation services to engineering and financial services. Energy constitutes the biggest business in the world economy, with a turnover of approximately US\$1.7–2 trillion per annum,[3] with energy demand mounting.[4] Energy has come to the forefront of the public debate in the last decade for two reasons: the first relates to the lack of a secure, continuous and, above all, unconditional energy supply in the *demandeurs*, mostly developed and transition

---

[1] We would like to thank Rolf Weber and Beatriz Gaitan as well as the WTF 2007 participants for their thoughtful comments. All errors are of the authors' alone.
[2] G. Hardin, 'The tragedy of the commons', *Science* 162 (1968).
[3] UNCTAD, *Energy Services in International Trade: Development Implications*, TD/B/COM.1/EM.16/2, 18 June 2001, 3.
[4] Energy demand will rise by over 50 per cent the next 20 years, with over 70 per cent of this increase stemming from developing countries. International Energy Agency, *World Energy Outlook 2006*, p. 65.

economies, which are still dependent on non-renewable carbon-based fossil fuels such as coal, oil or gas; 'pipeline diplomacy' has become the catchphrase for foreign policy that is inextricably intertwined with sufficient energy supply stemming from developing countries and, *a fortiori*, economic sustainability and national security. The second reason relates to the deleterious effects that production, distribution, and use of conventional energy may have on the climate, leading to environmental degradation.

Because of the recognition that these effects are of a transboundary nature threatening global commons,[5] several multilateral instruments have been used in the last two decades to tackle issues related to climate change mitigation.[6] The United Nations Framework Convention on Climate Change (UNFCCC) in 1992 and the ensuing adoption of the Kyoto Protocol in 1997[7] are the most prominent instruments to date that have attempted to address the issue of climate change and the negative impact of anthropogenic emissions of carbon dioxide and other gases on the atmosphere. Both these instruments reflect the need to address at a multilateral level the cross-border negative externalities caused by extensive emissions. The UNFCCC adopts a rather moderate approach by aiming to stabilise greenhouse gas (GHG) emissions at a level that prevents any anthropogenic interference with the climate system. Notably, the Kyoto Protocol sets up the framework for the first ever global, market-based scheme aimed at reducing emissions through trading of emission rights. In this respect, industrialised countries have agreed on binding and enforceable commitments.[8]

Until recently, energy-related services were supplied by state-owned vertically integrated monopolies either domestically or cross-border.[9]

---

[5] Note that WTO Members also endorsed the need for multilateral co-operation. Report (1996) of the Committee on Trade and Environment, WT/CTE/1, 12 November 1996, paragraph 171, section VII of the Report of the General Council to the 1996 Ministerial Conference, WT/MIN(96)/2, 26 November 1996.

[6] D. Freestone, 'The UN Framework Convention on Climate Change, the Kyoto Protocol, and the Kyoto Mechanisms' in D. Freestone and C. Streck (eds.), *Legal Aspects of Implementing the Kyoto Protocol Mechanisms: Making Kyoto Work* (Oxford University Press, 2005), p. 3.

[7] FCCC/CP/1997/L.7/Add.1. Decision 1/CP.3 Adoption of the Kyoto Protocol to the United Nations Framework Convention on Climate Change, Annex, reprinted in *International Legal Materials* 37 (1998), in force since 16 February 2005.

[8] These countries are listed in Annex I of the UNFCCC.

[9] See WTO, Council for Trade in Services, 'Energy Services', Background Note by the Secretariat, S/C/W/52, 9 September 1998, p. 1.

Hence, there was no scope for any trade whatsoever. However, as a result of intensive liberalisation attempts, core energy services (e.g. transport, transmission, and distribution) were unbundled and are now provided by private entities (sometimes former public monopolies which have been privatised) under conditions of competition in many countries. This trend has resulted in a great deal of confusion as to whether specific economic activities related to energy raise questions that should be dealt with under the General Agreement on Tariffs and Trade (GATT), the General Agreement on Trade in Services (GATS) or both.[10] It has also revealed possible imbalances that may appear due to this 'separating out' of previously fused activities.

Several market-based schemes that allow trading of units, rights, allowances or certificates have appeared in recent years. At the outset, a distinction should be made between schemes allowing the trading of emission rights or allowances such as the Kyoto Protocol or the European Union (EU) Emission Trading Directive[11] and schemes that set up the framework for the trade of renewable energy (or 'green') credits or certificates. The latter is in fact the other side of the coin when compared to emission trading. In the emission trading schemes, the tradable item is an entitlement to release a certain quantity of GHG emissions into the atmosphere. In a 'green' certificate market,[12] governments impose on the producers or distribution companies and retail suppliers the obligation that a minimum share of the electricity generated or supplied to the retail consumer (usually expressed as a percentage of the electricity portfolio of a producer or distributor) must come from renewable energy sources.[13] As will be demonstrated below, governments can use a 'green' certificate system to promote the use of renewables from low-cost sources and gradually reduce their dependence on non-renewable fossil fuels and

---

[10] Appellate Body report, *EC — Bananas III, European Communities — Regime for the Importation, Sale and Distribution of Bananas*, WT/DS27/AB/R, adopted 25 September 1997, DSR 1997:II, 591, paragraph 221; also Appellate Body report, *Canada — Autos, Canada — Certain Measures Affecting the Automotive Industry*, WT/DS142/AB/R, adopted 19 June 2000, DSR 2000:VI, 2985, paragraphs 159–66.

[11] Directive 2003/87/EC of the European Parliament and of the Council of 13 October 2003 establishing a scheme for trading of greenhouse gas emission allowances within the Community and amending Council Directive 96/61/EC [2003] OJ L 275/32, as amended by the Directive 2004/101/EC.

[12] Renewable Energy Certificates (RECs) are also known as green tags, renewable energy credits, tradable green certificates, or, in the US, as Renewable Portfolio Standards.

[13] S. Espey, 'Renewables portfolio standard: a means for trade with electricity from renewable energy sources?' *Energy Policy* 29 (2001), 560.

thus reduce their emissions. It will also be argued that linking this system with emission trading schemes would mitigate climate change.

Both emission trading and 'green' certificate schemes essentially aim at the mitigation of climate change by avoiding harmful emissions from fossil fuels. Another common feature of these two types of trading markets is that their potential is enormous, if developed properly. The GHG credit trading market, for instance, is expected to grow from US$10 billion by 2005 to over US$2 trillion per year by 2012, that is, by the end of the first commitment period set out in the Kyoto Protocol.[14] Regarding the green certificate market, in the US alone, the value of the market is expected to be over US$700 million in 2010.[15]

Since RECs are tradable on the financial markets, this paper attempts to identify whether the GATS and the Financial Services Annex are applicable to such transactions. Section I will provide a brief overview of the international regulation of trade in financial services under the GATS. The mechanics of trading in 'green' certificates and their relationship with emission trading under the Kyoto Protocol will be analysed in section II. An attempt will be made in section III to classify certificates as financial instruments that come under the definition of financial services in the Financial Services Annex to the GATS. Section IV concludes.

## I.   GATS and financial services

The GATS is the first multilateral, legally enforceable agreement dealing with trade and investment in services.[16] Whereas services and trade were considered as a paradoxical combination for decades or even centuries since the time of Adam Smith,[17] trade in services, despite the lack of exact data, is an important part of global trade representing more than 20 per cent of it. The economies of all developed countries are now regarded as 'services economies', while developing country economies are increasingly dependent on the performance of the domestic service sector. The GATS also provides a first inventory of regulations that dominate international trade in financial services. The financial sector is among the

---

[14]  Euromoney.com, 'Greenhouse gas trading warms up', January 2002.

[15]  E. Holt and L. Bird, *Emerging Markets for Renewable Energy Certificates: Opportunities and Challenges*, NREL Technical Report (2005), p. 2.

[16]  For an introduction to the GATS see, among others, P. Sauvé, 'Assessing the General Agreement on Trade in Services — half-full or half-empty?' *JWT* 29 (1995), 125.

[17]  P. Delimatsis, *International Trade in Services and Domestic Regulations — Necessity, Transparency and Regulatory Diversity* (Oxford University Press, 2007), p. 8.

infrastructural backbones of any modern economy.[18] A growing body of empirical studies demonstrates a strong positive link between the expansion of financial services and long-term economic growth.[19]

Financial services have economy-wide externalities. All branches of economic activity depend in essence on access to financial services. In that sense, financial services are far more important than their direct share in the economy implies.[20] Market-orientated economists insist on avoiding governmental interference except when it comes to 'market failure'.[21] Therefore, governments interfere with financial markets to reduce systemic risk and enhance the safety and soundness of the financial system.[22] Since the financial sector is often considered *sui generis* in that it encompasses certain services which have 'public goods' characteristics and, in turn, public goods provide a set of market failure possibilities, it seems, in principle, that government intervention is justifiable.[23] However, economic research has demonstrated that, in fact, the services sectors that are regulated the most, such as the financial sector, are the ones that possess growth-generating characteristics.[24]

Trade in financial services has experienced rapid growth in recent years.[25] Technological progress in communications, the spread of computer technology and electronic data processing, the internet-based supply of financial services and the unprecedented levels of multilateral

---

[18] WTO, *Economic Effects of Services Liberalisation: Overview of Empirical Studies*, S/C/W/26/Add.1, 29 May 1998.

[19] F. Eschenbach, J. F. Francois, and L. Schuknecht, 'Financial sector openness and economic growth' in: S. Claessens and M. Jansen (eds.), *The Internationalisation of Financial Services: Issues and Lessons for Developing Countries* (The Hague: Kluwer Law International, 2000), p. 103; A. Mattoo, R. Rathindran, and A. Subramanian, 'Measuring services trade liberalisation and its impact on economic growth: an illustration', *Journal of Economic Integration* 21 (2006).

[20] M. Kono *et al.*, '*Opening markets in financial services and the role of the GATS*' (Geneva: World Trade Organization, 1997), p. 7; D. K. Das, 'Trade in financial services and the role of the GATS: against the backdrop of the Asian financial crises', *JWT* 32 (1998), 83.

[21] L. J. White, 'Competition versus harmonization — an overview of international regulation of financial services' in C. E. Barfield (ed.), *International Financial Markets: Harmonization versus Competition* (Washington DC: AEI Press, 1996), p. 12.

[22] Also G. P. Gilligan, *Regulating the Financial Services Sector* (London: Kluwer Law International, 1999), p. 37.

[23] WTO, Council for Trade in Services, *Financial Services*, S/C/W/72, 2 December 1998, p. 9.

[24] Mattoo *et al.*, above n. 19.

[25] Also S. Claessens, 'Regulatory reform and trade liberalisation in financial services' in A. Mattoo and P. Sauvé (eds.), *Domestic Regulation and Service Trade Liberalisation* (Washington DC: World Bank, 2003), p. 132.

trade liberalisation through the GATT negotiating rounds have given a fillip to the expansion of such trade, particularly in a cross-border manner (mode 1 in the GATS parlance). All these factors have coalesced to increase the significance of the financial sector.

When the agenda for the Uruguay Round was negotiated in the mid-1980s, it was the US financial services industry that put pressure on its government for the creation of multilateral canons regulating trade in financial and other services.[26] Although negotiated intensively during the Uruguay Round, financial services negotiations were extended after the end of the Uruguay Round, mainly owing to strong pressure by the financial services industry in the US, which was seeking substantial improvements in the scheduled commitments under the threat of inscribing broad most-favoured-nation (MFN) exemptions in this sector.[27] After an interim agreement in 1995,[28] the negotiations were ultimately concluded in December 1997 through the adoption of the Fifth Protocol, thereby resulting in the full integration of financial services into the GATS.[29] The substantially improved schedules of commitments agreed upon in December 1997 were incorporated into the GATS by means of the Fifth Protocol, which entered into force in March 1999, four years after the establishment of the World Trade Organization (WTO) and only a few months before the beginning of the new round of services negotiations as foreseen in Article XIX of the GATS. For WTO Members that participated in the 1997 negotiations but accepted the Fifth Protocol after March 1999, commitments entered into force upon acceptance.[30] The Protocol initially remained open for

[26] Also J. Bhagwati, 'Splintering and disembodiment of services and developing nations', *The World Economy* 7 (1984), 140.

[27] Y. Wang, 'Most-favoured-nation treatment under the GATS — and its application in financial services', *JWT* 30 (1996), 113; and C. Arup, *The New World Trade Organization Agreements: Globalising Law through Services and Intellectual Property* (Cambridge University Press, 2000), p. 134; also M. G. Eckert, *Die Liberalisierung internationaler Finanzdienstleistungen durch das GATS — Unter besonderer Berücksichtigung internationaler Bankdienstleistungen* (Münster: LIT, 1997), p. 63.

[28] S. J. Key, *Financial Services in the Uruguay Round and the WTO* (Washington, DC: Group of Thirty, 1997), p. 4.

[29] WTO, *Fifth Protocol to the General Agreement on Trade in Services*, S/L/45, 3 December 1997. Also W. Dobson and P. Jacquet, *Financial Services Liberalisation in the WTO* (Washington, DC: Institute for International Economics, 1998), p. 80; P. Sorsa, *The GATS Agreement on Financial Services — A Modest Start to Multilateral Liberalisation*, IMF Working Paper, WP/97/55, May 1997.

[30] Note, however, that commitments may not have been implemented yet in the absence of formal ratification of the Protocol according to the domestic legal order. This is, for instance, the case for Brazil.

acceptance until 15 July 1999 and has been reopened for acceptance several times. By the conclusion of the negotiations, over one hundred WTO Members had made legally binding commitments in financial services, the second highest number after tourism.

In scheduling commitments in the financial sector, several Members, mostly Organisation for Economic Co-operation and Development (OECD) countries, used the Understanding on Commitments in Financial Services (the Understanding),[31] an optional, auxiliary text containing a 'formula' approach for scheduling commitments.[32] The Understanding provides an *à la carte* approach to scheduling which differs from the approach provided in Part III of the GATS. With its pre-determined set of commitments it has led to higher levels of liberalisation in the sector and was incorporated into the schedules of commitments of around thirty Members (counting the EC fifteen as one) on an MFN basis. The Understanding provides for the binding of the status quo; it adopts a negative list approach to scheduling commitments, and embodies a standstill commitment as well as broad liberalisation commitments relating to market access, national treatment, public procurement, and the offer of new financial services.[33] Nevertheless, even if a Member has undertaken commitments in the financial services sector based on the Understanding, it is still free to add any limitations on market access and/or national treatment.[34]

---

[31] I. Wilkinson, 'The Uruguay Round and financial services' in J. Bourgeois, F. Berrod and E. G. Fournier (eds.), *The Uruguay Round Results: A European Lawyer's Perspective* (Brussels: European Interuniversity Press, 1995), p. 415. For the negotiating history that preceded the adoption of the Understanding, see WTO, Committee on Specific Commitments, *Additional Commitments under Article XVIII of the GATS*, S/CSC/W/34, 16 July 2002, p. 18.

[32] S. J. Key, 'Financial Services' in: P. F. J. Macrory, A. E. Appleton and M. G. Plummer (eds.), *The World Trade Organization: Legal, Economic and Political Analysis*, Volume I (New York: Springer, 2005), p. 985. Note that, from a legal point of view, the Understanding is a unique WTO document, as it was included in the Final Act of the Uruguay Round but, in contrast to the Financial Services Annex, was *not* an integral part of the GATS.

[33] Paragraphs B.7 and D.3 of the Understanding. The purpose of this provision, which was strongly supported by the US financial services industry, is to allow innovative products introduced by financial institutions in their home countries — and approved by the competent home country authorities — also to be introduced by their offices in the host countries even if these services are not yet supplied in these jurisdictions. Key, above n. 28, p. 56, n. 27.

[34] Indeed, the introductory paragraph of the Understanding states that 'it does not prejudice the right of any Member to schedule its specific commitments in accordance with the approach under part III of the Agreement'.

Thus, depending on the method of scheduling commitments in the financial sector, WTO Members can be divided into two groups: The first group of countries undertook specific commitments under Part III of the GATS, whereas countries of the second group, developed for the most part, voluntarily assumed bolder liberalisation obligations as set out in the Understanding. Due to their more competitive financial service capacity and their ability to explore new markets through further liberalisation of that sector, several countries found the approach that the Understanding offered more appealing.[35] This is another illustration of the GATS variable geometry. The main concerns during the negotiations were whether the benefits resulting from a higher degree of commitments assumed by a limited number of Members should be extended to the entire WTO membership, including those Members that undertook their commitments under Part III of the GATS rather than under the Understanding. At the insistence of the overwhelming majority of Members, those that had not made commitments under the Understanding would nevertheless benefit from the greater financial services liberalisation that Members adopting the Understanding achieved.[36] This peculiar constellation, however, allowed for free-riding behaviour.

According to the Financial Services Annex, financial services include any service of a financial nature provided by a financial service supplier, including all insurance and insurance-related services (e.g. direct insurance, insurance intermediation) as well as all banking and other financial services (e.g. deposit-taking, lending, asset management and trading).[37] The list of financial services is extensive but non-exhaustive. The classification used in paragraph 5 is fairly broad and flexible. It is no coincidence that Members consider this list to be relevant to the current services negotiations and are encouraged to use this list rather than the W/120 one.[38]

---

[35] Of course, the pressure of the financial industry for tangible results also explains the breadth of the commitments undertaken. Also P. Sauvé and K. Steinfatt, 'Financial services and the WTO: what next?' in R. E. Litan, P. Masson and M. Pomerleano (eds.), *Open Doors: Foreign Participation in Financial Systems in Developing Countries* (Washington DC: Brookings Institution Press, 2001), pp. 352–3.

[36] WTO Members also benefited from extensive negotiations between Japan, the EU and the US that led to the scheduling of additional commitments regarding financial services. See also R. B. Woodrow, 'The 1997 World Trade Organization Accord on Financial Services: its impact and implications for the world insurance industry', *The Geneva Papers on Risk and Insurance* 25 (2000), 78.

[37] Financial Services Annex, paragraph 5(a).

[38] WTO, Council for Trade in Services (Special Session) and Committee on Trade in Financial Services, *Liberalisation of Financial Services*, Communication from Australia *et al.*, TN/S/W/43, S/FIN/W/43, 8 June 2005, p. 2.

In turn, financial service suppliers are defined as natural or juridical persons who supply financial services.[39] Importantly, those juridical or natural persons who are not yet providing financial services in the territory of the prospective host country or even in the territory of the Member where they reside are also considered as financial service suppliers, and thus benefit from the rights that flow from the GATS. Arguably, the GATS drafters intended to regard as financial service suppliers also those suppliers that are at the exploratory stage of a prospective commercial presence.[40]

The Financial Services Annex stipulates that only private entities can fall under the term 'financial service supplier'. In general, credit institutions, financial conglomerates, brokerage firms, insurance firms and non-bank financial intermediaries provide financial services, covering a wide range of different activities. Nevertheless, private entities that perform functions usually carried out by central banks or monetary authorities are considered as public authorities when exercising those functions, and thus fall outside the scope of the Financial Services Annex. It bears mention that, in this case, these private entities would essentially supply a service 'in the exercise of governmental authority', that is, neither on a commercial basis nor in competition with one or more service suppliers.[41]

## II.   RECs: definition, scope, context, mechanics

RECs are an important tool not only in the struggle to develop clean energy technologies to address climate change, but also in the attempt to diversify a country's energy supply and security.[42] Eligible RES can be, *inter alia*, wind power, biomass, biodiesel, solar power, wave power and small-scale hydropower.[43] Nevertheless, the sources that are eligible vary depending on the priorities regarding domestic energy policy and renewables, on consumer preferences, and/or the geographical idiosyncrasies of a given country. Currently, countries such as Sweden, Belgium, the Netherlands, Italy, the United Kingdom, and also the US and Australia,

---

[39] Financial Services Annex, paragraph 5(b).
[40] Also Dobson and Jacquet, above n. 29, p. 100.      [41] Article I:3(c) of the GATS.
[42] RECs should be distinguished from White Certificates, which are issued to comply with energy efficiency obligations imposed on suppliers. The issuance of a White Certificate confirms that the requested energy savings were made.
[43] Large-scale hydropower is considered as non-sustainable.

have implemented mandatory or voluntary schemes[44] that promote energy supply from renewable energy sources through the use of a system based on the issuance and trading of RECs. A number of utilities from several European countries have also developed and tested a harmonised voluntary pan-European scheme with tradable certificates, the so-called RECS (renewable electricity certificate system).

As implied earlier, a REC system is usually based on a government's decision to use a renewable energy quota obligation as the support mechanism for the use of renewable electricity. This quota obligation is administered by a system of tradable RECs. The possession of a specific number of RECs confirms that a supplier or distribution company has complied with the minimum share obligation. Once a year the RECs are redeemed and the competent authority verifies the compliance of the producers and distributors with their obligations. In the case of non-compliance, the producer or distributor responsible will be fined.

A renewable energy sources generator benefits from two different sources of income: the first stems from vending the physical electricity produced on the grid at the market price, while the second is associated with the number of 'green' certificates that it sells and corresponds to the renewable energy produced. The possession of a REC is evidence that entitles its holder to receive production support, which consists of the additional income generated through the sale of the green certificate. This second source of income can be seen as a reward for the environmental benefits that renewable energy technologies generate vis-à-vis conventional energy sources.[45] The objective is that, in the medium or long run, renewable energy will be able to compete with traditional sources without public support, for example, in the form of tax breaks, direct subsidies and payments. In this regard, it should be noted that one of the reasons that renewable energy has difficulties in competing with conventional energy sources at present is that the latter are subsidised directly or indirectly, and sometimes heavily. Furthermore, the current market prices of fossil fuels and nuclear power do not internalise the negative externalities generated.[46]

---

[44] For an analysis of these schemes, see R. Baron and Y. Serret, 'Renewable energy certificates: trading instruments for the promotion of renewable energy' in: OECD (ed.), *Implementing Domestic Tradeable Permits — Recent Developments and Future Challenges* (Paris: OECD, 2002), p. 111.

[45] P. E. Morthorst, 'The development of a green certificate market', *Energy Policy* 28 (2000), 1086.

[46] P. Menanteau, D. Finon and M.-L. Lamy, 'Prices versus quantities: choosing policies for promoting the development of renewable energy', *Energy Policy* 31 (2003), 800–1.

A REC is typically created when one megawatt hour (MWh) of electricity is produced from a qualified renewable energy source. In this respect, a REC is also an accounting tool which proves that the amount of energy from renewable energy sources was indeed produced. More specifically, RECs are intangible, tradable financial assets reflecting the commodity created by unbundling the environmental attributes of one MWh of electricity from a renewable energy source.[47] They take the form of electronic records administered through software that allows the issuance, tracking and registration of RECs, which are deposited and withdrawn in a central electronic registry of accounts of renewable energy sources generators. Since RECs can be unbundled from the underlying physical electricity and traded independently in their electronic form, they allow electricity suppliers, distribution companies or even consumers,[48] depending on the relevant legislation in force by the national system at issue, to purchase only the environmental attributes of electricity that was produced elsewhere.[49] They also allow financial service suppliers to act as intermediaries for the finalisation of such purchases.

The electricity generated will be sold as regular electricity. This means that the generation of renewable energy may be located on the other side of the national territory or even in another country, but the 'green' attributes can still be sold anywhere provided that the countries involved

---

[47] M. Gillenwater, *Redefining RECs (Part 1): Untangling Attributes and Offsets*, Discussion paper, Science Technology and Environmental Policy Program, Princeton University (2007), 1. Of course, RECs can also be sold bundled with the underlying physical electricity. Such a requirement may be in place in order to promote local promotion and generation of renewable energy sources. See E. A. Holt and R. H. Wiser, *The Treatment of Renewable Energy Certificates, Emissions Allowances, and Green Power Programs in State Renewables Portfolio Standards*, report prepared for Lawrence Berkeley National Laboratory (2007), 3.

[48] Even when consumers are called upon to consume a minimum amount of renewable-based electricity, it will more often than not be the distribution companies or retail suppliers that will be liable for the compliance (or lack thereof) of their consumers with the obligation to consume a given percentage of electricity from renewable energy sources. Evidence of this compliance will be provided by the submission of the corresponding number of RECs. See also Morthorst, above n. 45, at 1088.

[49] A REC will more often than not include the following information: a unique ID number; information about the producer; the date of issuance and the period of production that led to the issuance of this REC; unit and amount; the location and capacity of the plant; the RES used; its expiry date, if applicable; the support received for the production of renewable energy; and the environmental benefit, that is, how much pollution has been avoided thanks to the use of renewables in the production of electricity. This information allows double counting to be avoided and offers protection against erroneous guarantees of origin. All this information should be supplied and verified by the national issuing body, which is sometimes the national energy regulator itself.

mutually recognise their tradable certificate systems so that certificates issued abroad can be used to comply with the domestic minimum share obligation. Then, cross-border trade of certificates appears to be feasible. In the end, the renewable energy is produced somewhere on the globe and therefore the positive impact on the environment will occur.

RECs can be bought in order to comply with the imposed demand, that is, the minimum quota obligation relating to renewables that the government has stipulated, but they can also be bought, for instance, by environmental groups, to support the development of renewable energy sources. Individual companies can also buy RECs in an attempt to strengthen their environment-friendly profile. RECs can also be part of industry-driven, voluntary environment-friendly markets that aim to promote renewable energy sources. Finally, RECs can be imported in order for the importing country to meet its national renewable energy targets. For instance, pursuant to the EU Renewables Directive,[50] aside from the overall EU target of 21 per cent of electricity generation stemming from renewable energy sources by 2010, each EU Member State has committed to meeting individual national targets to this end. Importation of electricity from renewable energy sources produced in another Member State would be possible in order for the importing Member State to meet its national target. In this case a guarantee of origin would ensure the avoidance of double-counting of the energy produced. In this respect, the Directive calls for the establishment at the national level of the necessary mechanisms for the issue and mutual recognition of guarantees of origin regarding electricity generated in another Member State.[51]

The price at which these certificates are bought and sold represents the premium value that markets place on 'green' energy. Prices may depend on the location of the facility producing the certificates; the type of renewable energy sources and the power created; the supply and demand situation (for instance, inelastic demand together with unstable production of electricity due to weather conditions); the level of penalties for non-compliance; or even whether the certificate will be used by the

---

[50] Directive 2001/77/EC of the European Parliament and of the Council of 27 September 2001 on the promotion of electricity produced from renewable energy sources in the internal electricity market [2001] OJ L 283/33, as adapted by the Directive 2006/108/EC. According to the latter, after the accession of Bulgaria and Romania to the EU, the overall target for the EU27 is 21 per cent.

[51] *Ibid.*, Article 5.

purchaser to comply with a renewables minimum share obligation.[52] Research shows that prices of RECs can fluctuate significantly, especially when the minimum share (quota) is set too high.[53] This insecurity may deter potential investors from entering the market for renewables.[54] This, in turn, would lead to a small number of participants and an ensuing lack of liquidity, i.e. thin trading. Price volatility can be neutralised through the use of derivatives, e.g. futures with long-term contracts that would estimate the profitability of the projects at issue, or by allowing borrowing and banking. Allowing borrowing and banking, however, presupposes that the validity of the certificates will not expire at the end of the year, but will last for a longer period. This would allow the transfer of certificates to the coming years in case of excess supply or in the presence of speculations for higher prices in the future for such certificates (banking)[55] or the acquisition of more certificates than a producer, distribution company or consumer actually needs when the price is low so that they are able to cover renewables obligations in the future (borrowing).[56] For this, it is also necessary that the REC system has a significant lifespan.

Another way of avoiding unpredictable fluctuations is the adoption of minimum and maximum prices for certificates by the regulator.[57] While maximum prices (ceilings) would be necessary to avoid abuses in case of a shortage of RECs, minimum prices (floors) are equally — if not more — important at this initial stage of renewable energy source development for the short-term viability of the projects entailing renewables. It goes without saying that it is for the governments that establish a REC system to create sufficient demand, for instance, by imposing a minimum purchase obligation on the consumers.[58] Increasing environmental awareness of consumers is also expected to create additional demand

---

[52]  Indeed, compliance markets offer better options for REC trading than voluntary markets.

[53]  N. I. Meyer, 'European schemes for promoting renewables in liberalised markets', *Energy Policy* 31 (2003), 669.

[54]  C. Mitchell, D. Bauknecht and P. M. Connor, 'Effectiveness through risk reduction: a comparison of the renewable obligation in England and Wales and the feed-in system in Germany', *Energy Policy* 34 (2006), 297.

[55]  In the case of emissions trading, this possibility is called 'pooling'. Under this option, operators can pool their emission allowances (which, by the way, are usually distributed free of charge to the eligible operators) and name a trustee who will bear the responsibility to distribute sufficient amounts of allowances in case one of the participating operators fails to comply with its obligations. See, for instance, Article 28 of the EU Emission Trading Directive, above n. 11.

[56]  Morthorst, above n. 45, at 1093.     [57]  Menanteau *et al.*, above n. 46, at 810.

[58]  Governments also have the necessary tools to promote the diversity of RES.

for electricity generated from RES. In addition, the fact that the certificates issued can be traded either bilaterally or through the already-established financial markets may lead to cost-efficient production of renewable energy by the generators that use renewables technology. Finally, the size of a market is also decisive. Bigger markets can counterbalance the shortage of liquidity, narrow spreads and allow for a more cost-efficient development of renewable energy plants with optimal allocation of available resources for the highest possible production of energy.[59] Therefore, several countries, notably in Europe, are looking at the possibility of linking their REC system with similar systems in other countries. For such linkage to be successful, careful monitoring is needed to avoid double-counting and ensure the issuance of reliable guarantees of origin. In the medium or long run, regional markets or even an international market for RECs could emerge.

Setting the conditions for a well-functioning exchange of RECs can imply high administrative costs.[60] It would involve the creation of a mechanism that certifies that the producers generate energy from RES and issues certificates, and thereafter monitors and controls these processes; the establishment of a registry where certificates would be stored electronically and attributed a unique ID number; careful accounting and auditing to avoid, *inter alia*, double counting; and a surveillance mechanism that would lead to the imposition of penalties whenever the obligations of the renewable energy sources producers vis-à-vis minimum energy generation from renewable energy sources were not met. Other drawbacks of REC systems may include the lack of fair competition when different technologies (for instance, wind and solar energy) compete on the same market and benefit from the same support, or that such systems, due to their inherent complexity and the high transaction costs, may discourage small-scale producers of renewables.[61]

Of course, RECs are only one form of environmental commodity aimed at providing an incentive for the production of electricity from renewable energy sources. Among the other mechanisms to support supply of energy from renewables, the most common ones are: feed-in tariffs, tendering

---

[59] Morthorst, above n. 45, at 1089; also K. Verhaegen, L. Meeus and R. Belmans, *Towards an International Certificate System — The Stimulating Example of Belgium*, 6th Annual Global Conference on Environmental Taxation, Leuven, Belgium (2005), 3.

[60] European Commission, *The Support of Electricity from Renewable Energy Sources*, Communication from the Commission, COM(2005)627 final, 7 December 2005, 5.

[61] P. Agnolucci, 'The effect of financial constraints, technological progress and long-term contracts on tradable green certificates', *Energy Policy* 35 (2007), 3348.

systems and tax incentives. In a feed-in tariff scheme, electricity companies or distributors pay domestic generators of energy from renewable energy sources a specific price for the energy that they are obliged by law to purchase. This minimum price (or tariff) is determined by the government and guaranteed for several years. Hence, this instrument is in effect a subsidy granted to producers using renewable energy sources. When coupled with standardised costs for grid connections and short lead times, this scheme has the advantage of investment security and fairly unproblematic access to bank financing.[62] The tendering system consists of regular calls for tenders with respect to supply of energy from renewables whereby the provider quoting the lowest price gets the contract. This provider gets a fixed price/kilowatt hour (kWh) for the entire length of the contract period. The disadvantage of this system is that there is no certainty as to the continuation of this type of support. The risk that projects are not implemented because of low bids is also present.[63] Tendering systems seem to have been abandoned in Europe in favour of feed-in tariff-based systems or systems based on 'green' certificates. Tax incentives, on the other hand, are typically used as complementary policy tools to any policy that aims to promote renewables. There is a lot of learning by doing when it comes to the production of renewable energy and the best scheme to promote it. Governments experiment with several schemes or combinations thereof to find out what fits best with their domestic conditions.

Arguably, 'green' certificates systems, when designed properly, are compatible and can co-exist with or be integrated into other schemes aiming at climate change mitigation such as emissions trading.[64] The Kyoto Protocol, in its Article 17,[65] provides the framework for the first

---

[62] Meyer, above n. 53, at 667.

[63] European Commission, above n. 60, at 5; also Menanteau *et al.*, above n. 46, at 806.

[64] P. E. Morthorst, 'Interactions of a tradable green certificate market with a tradable permits market', *Energy Policy* 29 (2001), 345–53; M. Gillenwater, *Redefining RECs (Part 2): Untangling Certificates and Emission Rights*, Discussion paper, Science Technology and Environmental Policy Program, Princeton University (2007), 1; also Baron and Serret, above n. 44, p. 131.

[65] Article 17 of the Kyoto Protocol reads:

> The Conference of the Parties shall define the relevant principles, modalities, rules and guidelines, in particular for verification, reporting and accountability for emissions trading. The Parties included in Annex B may participate in emissions trading for the purposes of fulfilling their commitments under Article 3. Any such trading shall be supplemental to domestic actions for the purpose of meeting quantified emission limitation and reduction commitments under that Article.

global scheme of trading of emission rights for use in the fight against the global warming potential of GHG emissions.[66] For the countries that ratified the Kyoto Protocol, there is a set of legally binding emission limits and commitments to reduce GHG emissions. Instead of opting for command and control regulation and having recourse only to tax measures in order to achieve their commitments, several countries that ratified the Protocol adopted a market-based mechanism that would allow buying and selling of emissions allowances (Kyoto Units),[67] the so-called emission trading scheme (ETS). The Protocol allows the reduction of emissions abroad and hence parties can meet their commitments through the transfer or acquisition of Kyoto units worldwide.[68] Each Kyoto unit, that is, each entitlement to emit, represents one metric tonne of $CO_2$ equivalent.[69]

When compared to command and control instruments, emission trading appears to be a fairly cost-effective mechanism for reducing emissions. At the EU level, it was demonstrated that emission trading can reduce the cost of meeting the Kyoto commitments that the EU has undertaken by 35 per cent, representing a benefit of €1.3 billion per year until 2012. In the EU alone, the total size of the emissions trading market is estimated at €5–10 billion per year.[70] Hence, services related to emissions trading, such as brokerage, accounting or verification is a new but very promising and lucrative services sector (or sub-sector of financial services, as will be discussed in the next section). Again, for the time being, it appears that only large consulting firms and financial institutions from developed countries have the financial savvy to supply such services and frame deals among entities wishing to buy and sell emission rights, and thus business opportunities are not yet evenly distributed

[66] For a comprehensive analysis of the Article 17 mechanism, see R. de Witt Wijnen, 'Emissions trading under Article 17 of the Kyoto Protocol' in D. Freestone and C. Streck (eds.), *Legal Aspects of Implementing the Kyoto Protocol Mechanisms: Making Kyoto Work* (Oxford University Press, 2005), p. 403.

[67] R. de Witt Wijnen, p. 407; also M. Wemaere and C. Streck, 'Legal ownership and nature of Kyoto units and EU allowances' in Freestone and Streck (2005), p. 44.

[68] Trading is also allowed in the other two GHG reduction systems of the Kyoto Protocol, that is, the Joint Implementation (JI) and the Clean Development Mechanism (CDM).

[69] $CO_2$ equivalent is the universal unit of measurement used to indicate the global warming potential (GWP) of each of the six GHGs. It is used to evaluate the impacts of releasing (or avoiding the release of) different GHGs. The six gases and corresponding GWPs are: carbon dioxide (1); methane (21); nitrous oxide (310); halocarbons (HFC) (140 to 11,700); and sulphur hexafluoride (23,900).

[70] R. Dornau, 'The emissions trading scheme of the European Union' in Freestone and Streck (2005), p. 417.

between developed and developing countries. Nevertheless, developing countries are expected to achieve sustainable development notably through the CDM. The current lack of expertise when it comes to emissions trading markets hampers the achievement of this goal.[71]

A REC system should be considered as a complement to an ETS. The latter can lead to the reduction of GHG emissions, but not necessarily to the expansion of the use of energy generated by renewables. For such an expansion to occur, the establishment of a system with RECs is necessary. Such a system, when carefully designed and implemented, can stimulate the generation of energy from renewable energy sources. Viewed from this angle, then, an emissions trading scheme and a system with RECs (or any other support scheme relating to renewable energy sources) do not appear to be in conflict with one another.

## III.    Trade in RECs and the supply of financial services

As noted above, in a system with RECs, the electricity produced and its environmental attributes in the form of a 'green' certificate, that is, its 'greenness', are detached at the point of energy generation from renewable energy sources and traded individually. Thus, a distinct market for the environmental value of the certificates is created. Such a system is another regulatory instrument that assists a government in achieving its national targets for renewable energy. It can also be viewed as an accounting system that serves to certify energy production from renewables.[72]

In the exchange trading of RECs, there are several actors that can participate: producers, distribution companies and NGOs, or, more broadly, entities that have to meet the minimum share obligation and thus need to submit a given number of certificates at the end of a pre-specified period. This latter category can also involve consumers, depending on the regulatory regime at issue. This is a major difference between an REC system and the ETS as set out by the Kyoto Protocol. Under the latter, even if entities are authorised to participate in transfers and acquisitions of emission rights under Article 17 of the Kyoto Protocol, it is the parties to the Protocol, i.e. the sovereign states, that

---

[71] UNCTAD, above n. 3, at 18.

[72] The 'White and Green' Consortium, *A qualitative analysis of White, Green Certificates and EU CO$_2$ allowances — Phase II of the White and Green project* (Copernicus Institute, Utrecht University, 2004), 15.

are responsible for fulfilling their obligations under international law and ensuring that the participation of private entities in the trading of emission rights is in line with the parties' commitments and consistent with the applicable rules.[73]

For instance, the new Emission Trading Directive of the EU[74] provides that transfer of emission allowances can take place (i) between natural or legal persons within the EU; and (ii) between persons established in the EU and persons in countries listed in Annex B to the Kyoto Protocol and which have ratified the Protocol.[75] For this, a previous agreement is required between the Community and the country at issue regarding the mutual recognition of their respective emission trading schemes.[76] However, the Directive and the emission trading it introduces are the means for the Community to achieve its emission limitation and reduction commitments stemming from the Kyoto Protocol.

Brokers can also be allowed to participate in the trading of RECs and directly buy or sell RECs on behalf of their clients. As trading of RECs is most likely to occur electronically, the existence of a registry where all participating entities maintain an account is essential. Because of the high level of expertise needed when trading with transferable assets takes place, brokers and traders play a central role in the final shape of any deal, notably when the number of certificates and, *a fortiori*, the amounts of money at stake exceed a certain level. While brokers and financial institutions themselves do not have an obligation regarding emission reduction or minimum quota obligations relating to renewables, they are there to act as intermediaries to close deals between companies that do have obligations regarding energy from renewables. As the number of participants in trading grows, the monitoring and control of the trading taking place will become more difficult. On the other hand, a bigger market for RECs can ensure higher levels of liquidity, more reasonable and transparent prices with predictable fluctuations, and a low probability of market manipulation.[77] Simple rules for trading and the standardisation of contracts also make the market attractive for many

---

[73] De Witt Wijnen, above n. 66, p. 411.   [74] Directive 2003/87/EC, above n. 11.
[75] Thus, US companies are in principle excluded from participating in this scheme. Nevertheless, US parent companies can effectively participate in emission trading and supply-related services, such as brokerage and verification services, through their subsidiaries established in the EU market through the 'single passport' rule. For a discussion of these issues, see M. Wilder, 'Can companies or entities from a non-party to the Kyoto Protocol participate in the flexible mechanisms?' in Freestone and Streck (2005), p. 257.
[76] Directive 2003/87/EC, Articles 12, 25.   [77] Agnolucci, above n. 61, at 3348.

stakeholders and allow small- and medium-sized companies to participate as intermediaries in the trading of RECs. This, together with the
creation of common standards regarding the information that a REC
should include, could eventually lead to the mutual recognition of different REC systems or the harmonisation of rules on the issuance,
registration, verification, auditing and redemption of RECs with a view
to creating a global REC system.

Trading of RECs can take place on a bilateral, ad hoc basis (over the
counter). In this case, the amount of RECs traded can be significant. In
bilateral trading, the RECs are sometimes sold together with the electricity produced from renewable energy sources. The result of a bilateral
trade should be reported to the registry of RECs so that the transfer is
registered. This is not necessary when trading occurs through an electronic trading platform or an exchange in real time, e.g. in an electricity
trading exchange, as the registry would be connected with the platform
and would take account of the transaction directly. Such a platform leads
to more transparency and competition, much as securities exchange is
set and functions nowadays.[78] These two ways of trading RECs are in
competition and are expected to minimise trading costs.

Trading can involve direct purchases of certificates in primary markets,
but it can also entail trading with derivatives which have underlying RECs in
secondary markets. In the former case, there is a list of intermediary services
involved, such as brokerage or banking and insurance services. In the latter
case, buyers and sellers exchange derivative financial instruments for investment purposes. For instance, transactions can include financial derivatives
such as 'call options', according to which a company buys the right, but not
the obligation, to buy a specific quantity of certificates at a fixed price at a
specified future date; or they can involve futures contracts. Both trading
options can be attractive for financial service suppliers, as trading takes the
form of standard commodity trading where the supply of the related
financial services can also occur in a cross-border manner. For the producers, such options are also very attractive, since they allow for better risk
management. Excessive price volatility of RECs is thereby avoided.

As to the entities that will be authorised to be active in the trading with
RECs, it is for the government, when designing the trading scheme, to

---

[78] Transparent trading systems are considered to reduce price volatility. H. Allen,
J. Hawkins and S. Sato, 'Electronic trading and its implications for financial systems',
in Bank for International Settlements (ed.), *Electronic Finance: A New Perspective and
Challenges*, BIS Papers No. 7 (2001), p. 44.

establish clear eligibility criteria for the participating entities. For financial institutions and brokers, such criteria may include prior acquisition of a licence by the competent authority or prudential requirements such as minimum capital requirements or sufficient assets. They may also require the establishment of such entities in the territory of the country where the trading platform is set. It bears mention that, under the EU Directive on Financial Instruments (MiFID), Member States are required to allow in their regulated markets, e.g. their power exchange, the participation of 'remote members', that is, entities established in another Member State. The Directive requires that Member States make all the necessary arrangements to facilitate access to and use of their systems by such entities.[79] As the MiFID establishes several requirements relating to brokerage and intermediation services and pre- as well as post-trading, and RECs are tradable instruments of a financial nature, it is arguably applicable to the trading of RECs.

Trade in RECs, as depicted above, can raise several issues of relevance to the WTO[80] and more particularly the GATS and the regulation of trade in financial services. Energy or energy-related services is not a separate comprehensive category in the W/120, the services sectoral classification list. The same is true for the United Nations central product classification on which the W/120 is based. Instead, energy-related services, e.g. transport, distribution, construction, engineering, research and development and consultancy are dispersed across several existing sectoral classifications within the W/120. Only three sub-sectors in the W/120 are energy-specific: pipeline transportation of fuels (under 'transport services'), services incidental to energy distribution and services incidental to mining (under 'business services').[81] Overall, Members' commitments in energy-related services were limited at the closure of the Uruguay Round negotiations.[82] Nevertheless, because the final consumption of energy is the outcome of a series of associated activities,

---

[79] Directive 2004/39/EC of the European Parliament and of the Council of 21 April 2004 on markets in financial instruments amending Council Directives 85/611/EEC and 93/6/EEC and Directive 2000/12/EC of the European Parliament and of the Council and repealing Council Directive 93/22/EEC [2004] OJ L 145/1, Articles 31, 33, 42.

[80] Generally, Renewable Energy and International Law Project (REIL), *Post-Hearing Submission to the International Trade Commission: World Trade Law and Renewable Energy: The Case of Non-Tariff Measures*, 2005.

[81] WTO, above n. 9, p. 3.

[82] P. C. Evans, 'Strengthening WTO member commitments in energy services: problems and prospects' in A. Mattoo and P. Sauvé (eds.), *Domestic Regulation and Service Trade Liberalization* (Oxford University Press, 2003), p. 174.

market access may be a prerequisite in a considerable number of services sectors for energy service suppliers to provide their services adequately. This argument would call for the creation of a new entry in the services classification list that would allow Members to use energy-related services as a cluster and undertake commitments that would be consistent with one another to facilitate the supply of such services. As it stands, the current classification list allows for inconsistencies and the undertaking of commitments that are difficult to reconcile.

In the absence of an entry that lists energy-related services separately, trading of RECs can be regarded as falling under the provisions of the Financial Services Annex to the GATS. While the certificates are neither 'goods' nor 'services', trading of certificates will involve a series of financial services that financial institutions may supply until a deal for transfer of RECs is concluded, such as brokerage, trust, clearing and settlement. Consultancies and financial institutions can also offer services relating to derivative products trading, such as price-hedging instruments that would allow the seller to secure a future income[83] and the buyer to determine his costs. Such risk management services are usually supplied through forwards, swaps, or options in secondary markets. Certificates can also be offered by their owners as collateral against short-term lending.

Under entry number 7 of W/120, and in the Financial Services Annex in a more detailed manner, are several types of financial services that would allow for trading of RECs to be concluded.[84] In the services sectoral classification list, all financial services that would be involved in trades with RECs are listed under number 7.B f) (trading). The Financial Services Annex itemises the relevant financial services in a more comprehensive manner. In paragraph 5(a) of the Annex, as noted earlier, financial services are defined in a very broad manner to include 'any service of a financial nature'. An illustrative list of the activities falling under this definition follows. Nevertheless, it is worth noting that the list is so detailed and the financial services at issue so broadly described that it is hard to visualise an activity that is not already

---

[83] For the producer, price hedging allows hedging new investments and hedging the income from already existing plants. See also PricewaterhouseCoopers, *Organisation of RE Market and Trading of Green Certificates*, report for the Danish Energy Agency, Hellerup (1999), 73.

[84] Therefore, at first blush at least, it does not seem that services related to trading of RECs would come within the ambit of the category 'new financial services' as defined in the Understanding and described in section I of this paper.

included in the list, notably as far as 'banking and other financial services' are concerned.[85] The trading-related financial services are listed under paragraph 5(a)(x). For our purposes, RECs would most probably fall under (F). Indeed, the nature of this type of certificate as described earlier leads to the conclusion that they can be categorised as 'financial assets', or at least, fall under the 'catch-all' category of 'other negotiable instruments'. Paragraph 5(a)(xiii)–(xvi) also encompass services that will be supplied until a deal is finalised. These include asset management and trust services, settlement and clearing for financial assets, financial information and data processing services, as well as intermediation and other auxiliary services. On the other hand, issuance of certificates would most likely escape the purview of the GATS, as it is typically a task entrusted to public entities within the meaning of paragraphs 1(b)(iii) and 5(c) of the Financial Services Annex.

For the main obligations of the GATS such as MFN, market access, or national treatment to apply to the transactions relating to trading, Members should have undertaken commitments in the categories of financial services mentioned above (or, in the case of MFN, no MFN exemptions). The level of liberalisation for each Member is reflected in the number of services sectors that are listed in its schedule of commitments in conjunction with the number of restrictions that are embodied therein. Thus, the GATS has a variable scope of application, depending on the Member in question. Nevertheless, notably those Members that adopted the Understanding made comprehensive commitments in most categories of financial services that may relate to the trading of RECs, and several of them even allow the cross-border supply of such services. Therefore, respecting market access and national treatment will in most cases be required when financial service suppliers seek to supply such services, notably in the case that these suppliers are established in the WTO Member at issue.

In the case of cross-border trade of RECs, there are several issues that need to be clarified. For instance, the delimitation of competences between the supervising authorities of the two countries involved is a thorny issue that calls for regulatory co-operation. Another important issue is the taxability of transfers. Especially in over the counter trading, the amounts of money involved can be significant and therefore tax authorities in both countries may be tempted to charge the tax for the transaction in their jurisdiction. Arguably, the price that the seller will

[85] Financial Services Annex, paragraph 5(v)–(xvi).

get for the REC will be regarded as income and will be taxed accordingly. Because this could be considered as a disincentive to sell and thus could create problems to the proper functioning of a REC market, governments could set a lower tax for such transactions in the context of their strategy to promote renewables. However, if the taxation system does not treat such transactions differently, then the REC price will most likely reflect these charges.

Many of the measures regulating (or hampering) trading in RECs will be a subset of domestic financial services regulation. This means that such measures will often be non-discriminatory and fall under the broader category of prudential regulation measures that ensure the safety and soundness of the system.[86] This would mean that many financial service suppliers will be excluded from providing such services due to fairly high (and costly to comply with) requirements relating to available capital, assets and liquidity. An issue that arises from this conclusion is whether it would be worth envisaging special prudential standards, e.g. lower capital requirements, for those companies that deal exclusively with the supply of financial services in these new areas of trading in certificates or emission rights, as in this case the dangers for the financial system may not be so evident.

Furthermore, granting of licences may be warranted before any entity participates in trading with RECs. Such licences could be REC trading specific, but they can also involve any form of trading services. In such cases, the licensing requirements and procedures at issue would probably be non-discriminatory and would aim to ensure the quality of the service supplied and the protection of consumers. In this case, Article VI of the GATS would come into play, which entails certain transparency and due process requirements.[87]

## IV.   Conclusion

Trade, finance and investment are at the heart of sustainable development. The adopted market-based mechanisms such as trade in RECs or emission rights come as a recognition that private-sector-driven solutions can contribute to the reduction of harmful anthropogenic

---

[86] Paragraph 2(a) of the Financial Services Annex.
[87] For an analysis of these requirements, see P. Delimatsis, 'Due process and "good" regulation embedded in the GATS — disciplining regulatory behaviour in services through Article VI of the GATS', *JIEL* 10 (2007), 13–50.

emissions and the promotion of energy generation by RES. There are important issues to discuss in the near future. One of them is how it would be possible to link such mechanisms to achieve more environment-friendly and cost-effective results. Another important issue is how to create markets dealing with trade in renewables that cross national borders. There is a strong case for international trading in RECs and such initiatives have already been launched, albeit on a voluntary basis for the time being. As liberalisation efforts loom large in the energy sector worldwide and public awareness rises, the GATS may have a growingly important role to play with respect to energy services. In this context, Members may be interested to consider in the medium term whether a unified approach regarding energy-related services and trading of related financial instruments (such as RECs or emission rights) makes sense. A significant argument in favour of this approach would be that, as things now stand with the current classification system, Members may ultimately realise that they have already undertaken commitments in energy-related sectors, e.g. in financial services, that they had not intended to liberalise.

## Bibliography

Agnolucci, P., 'The effect of financial constraints, technological progress and long-term contracts on tradable green certificates', *Energy Policy* 35 (2007), 3347–59.

Allen, H., Hawkins, J. and Sato, S., 'Electronic trading and its implications for financial systems', in Bank for International Settlements (ed.), *Electronic Finance: A New Perspective and Challenges*, BIS Papers No. 7 (2001).

Arup, C., *The New World Trade Organization Agreements: Globalizing Law through Services and Intellectual Property* (Cambridge University Press, 2000).

Baron, R. and Serret, Y., 'Renewable energy certificates: trading instruments for the promotion of renewable energy' in OECD, *Implementing Domestic Tradeable Permits — Recent Developments and Future Challenges* (Paris: OECD, 2002).

Bhagwati, J., 'Splintering and disembodiment of services and developing nations', *The World Economy* 7 (1984), 133.

Bourgeois, J., Berrod, F. and Fournier, E. G. (eds.), *The Uruguay Round Results: A European Lawyer's Perspective* (Brussels: European Interuniversity Press, 1995).

Claessens, S., 'Regulatory reform and trade liberalization in financial services' in Mattoo and Sauvé (eds.), *Domestic Regulation and Service Trade Liberalization* (Oxford University Press, 2003)

Das, K. D., 'Trade in financial services and the role of the GATS: against the backdrop of the Asian financial crises', *JWT* 32 (1998), p. 83.

Delimatsis, P., *International Trade in Services and Domestic Regulations — Necessity, Transparency and Regulatory Diversity* (Oxford University Press, 2007).

'Due process and "good" regulation embedded in the GATS — disciplining regulatory behaviour in services through Article VI of the GATS', *JIEL* 10 (2007), 13–50.

Dobson, W. and Jacquet, P., *Financial Services Liberalization in the WTO* (Washington DC: Institute for International Economics Press, 1998).

Dornau, R., 'The emissions trading scheme of the European Union', in Freestone and Streck (eds.), *Legal Aspects of Implementing the Kyoto Protocol Mechanisms: Making Kyoto Work* (Oxford University Press, 2005).

Eckert, G. M., *Die Liberalisierung internationaler Finanzdienstleistungen durch das GATS — Unter besonderer Berücksichtigung internationaler Bankdienstleistungen* (Münster: LIT, 1997).

Eschenbach, F., Francois, F. J. and Schuknecht, L., 'Financial sector openness and economic growth' in Claessens and Jansen (eds.), *The Internationalisation of Financial Services: Issues and Lessons for Developing Countries* (The Hague: Kluwer Law International, 2000).

Espey, S., 'Renewables portfolio standard: a means for trade with electricity from renewable energy sources?', *Energy Policy* 29 (2001), 557–66.

European Commission, *The Support of Electricity from Renewable Energy Sources*, Communication from the Commission, COM(2005)627 final, 7 December 2005.

Evans, C. P., 'Strengthening WTO member commitments in energy services: problems and prospects' in Mattoo and Sauvé (eds.), *Domestic Regulation and Service Trade Liberalization* (Oxford University Press, 2003).

Freestone, D., 'The UN Framework Convention on Climate Change, the Kyoto Protocol, and the Kyoto Mechanisms' in Freestone and Streck (eds.), *Legal Aspects of Implementing the Kyoto Protocol Mechanisms: Making Kyoto Work* (Oxford University Press, 2005).

GATT, 'Services Sectoral Classification List', MTN.GNS/W/120, 10 July 1991.

Gillenwater, M., *Redefining RECs (Part 1): Untangling Attributes and Offsets*, Discussion Paper, Science Technology and Environmental Policy Program, Princeton University (2007) (available at: www.princeton.edu/~mgillenw/discussionpapers.htm).

*Redefining RECs (Part 2): Untangling Certificates and Emission Rights*, Discussion Paper, Science Technology and Environmental Policy Program, Princeton University (2007) (available at: www.princeton.edu/~mgillenw/discussion papers.htm).

Gilligan, P. G., *Regulating the Financial Services Sector* (London: Kluwer Law International, 1999).

Hardin, G., 'The Tragedy of the Commons', *Science* 162 (1968), 1243.

Holt, E. and Bird, L., *Emerging Markets for Renewable Energy Certificates: Opportunities and Challenges*, NREL Technical Report (2005).

Holt, E. and Wiser, H. R., *The Treatment of Renewable Energy Certificates, Emissions Allowances, and Green Power Programs in State Renewables Portfolio Standards*, report prepared for Lawrence Berkeley National Laboratory (2007).

International Energy Agency, *World Energy Outlook 2006* (Paris: OECD/IEA, 2006).

Key, J. S., *Financial Services in the Uruguay Round and the WTO*, G-30 Occasional Paper No. 54 (1997).

'Financial services' in: P. F. J. Macrory, F. J. Patrick, E. Appleton and M. G. Plummer (eds.), *The World Trade Organization: Legal, Economic and Political Analysis*, Volume I (New York: Springer, 2005).

Kono, M., Low, P., Luanga, M., Mattoo, A., Oshikawa, M. and Schuknecht, L., *Opening Markets in Financial Services and the Role of the GATS*, WTO Special Studies No. 1 (1997).

Mattoo, A., Rathindran, R. and Subramanian, A., 'Measuring Services Trade Liberalization and Its Impact on Economic Growth: An Illustration', *Journal of Economic Integration* 21 (2006).

Menanteau, P., Finon, D. and Lamy, M.-L., 'Prices versus quantities: choosing policies for promoting the development of renewable energy', *Energy Policy* 31 (2003), 799–812.

Meyer, I. N., 'European schemes for promoting renewables in liberalised markets', *Energy Policy* 31 (2003), 665–76.

Mitchell, C., Bauknecht, D. and Connor, P. M., 'Effectiveness through risk reduction: a comparison of the renewable obligation in England and Wales and the feed-in system in Germany', *Energy Policy* 34 (2006), 297–305.

Morthorst, P. E., 'The development of a green certificate market', *Energy Policy* 28 (2000), 1085–94.

'Interactions of a tradable green certificate market with a tradable permits market', *Energy Policy* 29 (2001), 345–53.

Oikonomou, V., *A Qualitative Analysis of White, Green Certificates and EU $CO_2$ Allowances — Phase II of the White and Green Project* (Copernicus Institute, Utrecht University, 2004), 15.

PriceWaterhouseCoopers, *Organisation of RE Market and Trading of Green Certificates*, report for the Danish Energy Agency, Hellerup (1999).

Renewable Energy and International Law Project (REIL), *Post-Hearing Submission to the International Trade Commission: World Trade Law and Renewable Energy: The Case of Non-Tariff Measures*, 5 May 2005.

Sauvé, P., 'Assessing the General Agreement on Trade in Services — half-full or half-empty?' *JWT* 29 (1995), 125–45.

Sauvé, P., and Steinfatt, K., 'Financial Services and the WTO: what next?' in E. R. Litan, P. Masson and M. Pomerleano (eds.), *Open Doors: Foreign Participation in Financial Systems in Developing Countries* (Washington DC: Brookings Institution Press, 2001).

Sorsa, P., *The GATS Agreement on Financial Services — A Modest Start to Multilateral Liberalisation*, IMF Working Paper, WP/97/55, May 1997.

UNCTAD, *Energy Services in International Trade: Development Implications*, TD/B/COM.1/EM.16/2, 18 June 2001.

Verhaegen, K., Meeus, L. and Belmans, R., *Towards an International Certificate System — The Stimulating Example of Belgium*, 6th Annual Global Conference on Environmental Taxation, Leuven, Belgium (2005).

Wang, Yi., 'Most-favoured-nation treatment under the GATS — and its application in financial services', *JWT* 30 (1996), 91.

Weiss, F., 'The General Agreement on Trade in Services 1994', *Common Market Law Review* 32 (1995), 1177.

Wemaere, M. and S., Charlotte, 'Legal ownership and nature of Kyoto units and EU allowances' in: Freestone and Streck (eds.), *Legal Aspects of Implementing the Kyoto Protocol Mechanisms: Making Kyoto Work* (Oxford University Press, 2005).

White, J. L., 'Competition versus harmonization — an overview of international regulation of financial services' in C. Barfield (ed.), *International Financial Markets: Harmonization versus Competition* (Washington DC: AEI Press, 1996).

Wilder, M., 'Can companies or entities from a non-party to the Kyoto Protocol participate in the flexible mechanisms?' in Freestone and Streck (eds.), *Legal Aspects of Implementing the Kyoto Protocol Mechanisms: Making Kyoto Work* (Oxford University Press, 2005).

Wilkinson, I., 'The Uruguay Round and Financial Services' in J. Bourgeois, F. Berrod and E.G. Fournier (eds.), *The Uruguay Round Results: A European Lawyer's Perspective* (Brussels: European Interuniversity Press, 1995).

de Witt Wijnen, R., 'Emissions trading under Article 17 of the Kyoto Protocol' in Freestone and Streck (eds.), *Legal Aspects of Implementing the Kyoto Protocol Mechanisms: Making Kyoto Work* (Oxford University Press, 2005).

Woodrow, R. B., 'The 1997 World Trade Organization accord on financial services: its impact and implications for the world insurance industry', *Geneva Papers on Risk and Insurance* 25 (2000), 78.

WTO, *Economic Effects of Services Liberalization: Overview of Empirical Studies*, S/C/W/26/Add.1, 29 May 1998.

Committee on Specific Commitments, *Additional Commitments under Article XVIII of the GATS*, S/CSC/W/34, 16 July 2002.

Council for Trade in Services, *Energy Services*, Background Note by the Secretariat, S/C/W/52, 9 September 1998.

Council for Trade in Services, *Financial Services*, Background Note by the Secretariat, S/C/W/72, 2 December 1998.

Council for Trade in Services (Special Session) and Committee on Trade in Financial Services, *Liberalization of Financial Services*, Communication from Australia, Bahrain, Canada, the European Communities, Japan, Norway, Oman, Panama, Singapore, Switzerland, the Separate Customs Territory of Taiwan, Penghu, Kinmen and Matsu, and the United States, TN/S/W/43, S/FIN/W/43, 8 June 2005.

Report (1996) of the Committee on Trade and Environment, WT/CTE/1, 12 November 1996.

# 12

# Assessment of GATS' impact on climate change mitigation

OLGA NARTOVA

## Setting the scene

According to the United Nations Framework Convention on Climate Change (UNFCCC), the principal reason for the earth's rising temperatures is a century and a half of industrialisation: the burning of ever-greater quantities of oil, gasoline and coal, the cutting down of forests, and the practice of certain farming methods.[1-2] The current dependency of the global economy on fossil fuels and the rapid increase in fuel consumption are influenced by international trade.

Trade and climate change policies are currently managed under separate legal regimes, although the international trade system offers various mechanisms for promoting environment-friendly development and contributing to climate change mitigation. In particular, liberalisation of trade in environmental goods and services (EGS) can help to achieve climate change objectives through reducing the cost of access to EGS, promoting environmentally preferable products and services, and creating incentives for technology transfer.

The Doha ministerial declaration provides a distinct mandate for negotiations on environmental goods and services and calls for 'the reduction or, as appropriate, elimination of tariff and non-tariff barriers to environmental goods and services'.[3] There are two important questions linking climate change and trade which come up in relation to the implementation of paragraph 31(iii):

---

[1-2] 'Outline for the IPCC Working Group I contribution to the Fourth Assessment Report', in S. Solomon *et al.* (eds.), *Climate Change 2007: The Physical Science Basis* (Cambridge University Press, 2007), accessible at www.ipcc.ch/activity/wg1outlines.pdf

[3] Paragraph 31(iii) of the Doha Development Agenda, available at www.wto.org/english/thewto_e/minist_e/min01_e/mindecl_e.htm

- What are environmental goods and services?
- What might be a pattern for liberalisation which would not only have an influence on climate change but would also suit both developed, export-oriented countries and developing WTO Members?

According to the Organisation for Economic Co-operation and Development (OECD), 'the environmental industry consists of activities which produce goods and services to measure, prevent, limit, minimise or correct environmental damage to water, air and soil, as well as problems related to waste, noise and eco-systems. These include cleaner technologies, products and services which reduce environmental risk and minimise pollution and resource use, although there is currently no agreed methodology which allows their contribution to be measured in a satisfactory way.'[4] More specifically, the environmental industry includes equipment (such as that used for water supply and delivery; treatment of wastewater; waste-handling; air pollution control; laboratory testing and prevention technology), services (such as engineering design; construction and management of utilities; collection and treatment of wastewater; waste collection and processing; management of hazardous waste; legal and consulting services; remediation services and strategic environmental management) and resources (such as water, recovered materials and renewable energy).[5]

Since environmental services is a fairly new sector, the main obstacle to analysing it is related to determining its extent. A number of studies have attempted to define and describe it; however, there is still no universally adopted technical or legal definition or classification of environmental services.

One of the reasons for this uncertainty is that there is no agreement on criteria for establishing the boundaries of the industry. Different groups of countries have their own individual understandings and approaches with regard to the definition and scope of environmental services.

First, traditionally there has been a so-called 'end-of-pipe' approach, which focuses on goods and services which are easily identifiable and used to clean up existing processes and production, for instance,

---

[4] OECD/Eurostat, *The Environmental Goods and Services Industry: Manual for Data Collection and Analysis* (Paris: OECD, 1999).

[5] J. Butkeviciene, 'GATS negotiations and issues for consideration in the area of environmental services from a development perspective', *UNEP-UNCTAD CBTF Workshop on Post-Doha Negotiating Issues on Trade and Environment in Paragraph 31*, Singapore, May 2002.

equipment for the treatment of wastewater or services for the disposal of solid waste.[6]

On the other hand, there is a growing interest in 'clean' technologies, production processes and products, which will reduce the need for clean-up and 'end-of-pipe' solutions. So the second approach to defining environmental goods and services is broader and includes environmentally preferable products (EPPs) and services. The United Nations Conference on Trade and Development (UNCTAD) defines EPPs as products which cause significantly less 'environmental harm' at some stage of their 'life cycle' (production, processing, consumption or disposal) than alternative products which serve the same purpose, or products the production and sale of which contribute significantly to the preservation of the environment.[7]

'Less environmental harm' is generally established according to the following criteria: (a) use of natural resources and energy; (b) amount and hazardousness of waste generated by the product during its life cycle; (c) impact on human and animal health; and (d) preservation of the environment. Thus, the environmental benefits may arise from the more environment-friendly production method either during the course of its use or during the disposal stage of the product. In this case, the primary purpose of the service is not to remedy an environmental problem. Although UNCTAD's definition of EPPs is widely recognised, WTO Members still lack a universally accepted definition for the purpose of negotiations.

Moreover, most environmental goods and services are not easily separable from their non-environmental connotations in practice, although all service sectors in the Services Sectoral Classification List (W/120)[8] are supposed to be mutually exclusive; hence, services in one sector cannot be covered by another. Thus, environment-friendly products and services in many, if not most, cases will have a non-environment-friendly counterpart. This leads to the discussion on like products and services.

---

[6] For more on this approach see M. Sugathan, 'Climate change benefits from liberalisation of environmental goods and services', in E. Rose and M. K. Gueye (eds.), *Linking Trade, Climate Change and Energy* (Geneva: ICTSD, 2006).

[7] For more information on the concept of EPPs see *Environmentally Preferable Products (EPPs) as a Trade Opportunity for Developing Countries*, report by UNCTAD Secretariat, UNCTAD/COM/70, Geneva, December 1995.

[8] Group of Negotiations on Services (MTN/GNS/W/120), July 1991.

Lack of a common definition of environmental services is one of the main challenges for negotiating the liberalisation of EGS as mandated in the Doha declaration. This paper attempts to deal with this and other challenges within the WTO negotiations relevant to climate-friendly environmental services. Section I will provide a brief overview of the international regulation of trade in environmental services under the General Agreement on Trade in Services (GATS) and examine the climate-related negotiation proposals of some WTO Members. Section II will attempt to assess whether current trade liberalisation efforts can be made more supportive of climate change mitigation. Section III will conclude by touching on an alternative pattern for negotiations.

## Classification

Defining the scope of environmental goods and services relevant to climate change objectives is a starting point for policy-makers and trade negotiators. The W/120 List, the current classification list used by the WTO Members in their schedules of specific commitments, is largely based on the United Nations Provisional Central Product Classification (CPC). The environmental services are included as the sixth sector category among the other twelve broad sectors. According to this list, environmental services include: sewage services (CPC 9401);[9] refuse disposal services (CPC 9402);[10] sanitation and similar services (CPC 9403); and other environmental services. The WTO Secretariat has pointed out that the latter include the remaining elements of the CPC environmental services category: cleaning of exhaust gases (CPC 9404),[11] noise abatement services (CPC 9405), nature and landscape protection services (9406), and other environmental protection services not included elsewhere (CPC 9409).

Many experts regard the current GATS classification as outdated and not suitable for a modern view of the industry and particularly for

---

[9] Sewage services are closely related to wastewater treatment services that aim essentially to speed up the natural processes which reduce contaminants to an acceptable level for discharge into the environment.

[10] Refuse disposal and sanitation services are virtually synonymous with solid waste management, which includes services to collect, transport, treat and dispose of waste from homes, municipalities, commercial establishments and manufacturing plants.

[11] Cleaning of exhaust gases closely resembles air quality control services designed to remove pollutants from a gaseous stream or to convert pollutants to a non-polluting or less polluting form prior to discharge into the atmosphere.

climate change mitigation for a number of reasons.[12] First, it covers only the above-mentioned 'end-of-pipe' environmental services and does not properly address services designed to prevent or reduce environmental harm or sustainable resource management services. Furthermore, it covers the services provided in the operation of certain facilities, plants and equipment, but not the design, engineering, R&D and consulting services necessary for building and upgrading them. And finally, it focuses on services supplied to the general community and overlooks those supplied directly to the industry.[13] Moreover, little international trade was taking place in the sector at the time the classification was developed: governments were providing most of the environmental services and private operators were not allowed or not willing to enter the market.

The OECD and the Statistical Office of the European Community (Eurostat) have developed a more comprehensive classification of environmental services.[14] The OECD classification is more connected to the climate change debate than that of the GATS and includes the following categories: pollution management,[15] cleaner technologies[16] and resource management.[17] It is noteworthy that the latter also includes services relevant to renewable energy. 'Cleaner technology and product' and

---

[12] For more, see Butkeviciene, *Workshop on Post-Doha Negotiating Issues and ICTSD, Background Note on State of Play in EGS Negotiations.*

[13] OECD, *Environmental Goods and Services — The Benefits of Further Global Trade Liberalisation* (Paris: OECD, 2001).

[14] OECD, *Manual for the Collection and Analysis of Data* (1999).

[15] The 'pollution management' group comprises activities that produce equipment, technology or services to treat or remove environmental effects. Generally, this includes end-of-pipe equipment, technology and related services that are clearly supplied for an environmental purpose only.

[16] The 'cleaner technology and product' group comprises any activity which continuously improves, reduces or eliminates the environmental impact of technologies, processes or products, but which are often supplied for purposes other than environmental ones and for which methods for assessment remain under discussion. This includes cleaner or resource efficient technology or products such as those that reduce energy consumption, recover valuable by-products, reduce emissions, or minimise waste disposal problems.

[17] The 'resource management' group comprises activities which prevent environmental damage to air, water and/or soil. This includes any activity that produces equipment, technology or specific materials, designs, constructs or installs, manages or provides other services for recycling new materials or products; for the generation of renewable energy (such as biomass, solar, wind, tidal or geothermal sources); for reducing climate change; for sustainable agriculture and fisheries (such as biotechnology applied to agriculture and fishery activities); for sustainable forest management; for natural disaster risk management; or related to eco-tourism.

'resource management' are considered to be key areas for climate change mitigation.

Many share the opinion that since the industry is going through changes in its structure (e.g. privatisation, consolidation) and in its goals (e.g. from compliance with environmental regulations to efficient use of resources), the W/120 classification requires an update. All the negotiating proposals on environmental services that have so far been put forward as part of the ongoing GATS negotiations address the issue of how the sector may be better classified.

In a submission as early as 1999,[18] the EU stated that the list did not, for instance, reflect changes in the environmental industry which was developing beyond traditional end-of-pipe/pollution control/remediation/clean-up towards integrated prevention and control of pollution, cleaner technology and resources and risk management. The EU has proposed an alternative classification in which the services are classified according to environmental medium, thus preserving the mutually exclusive character of the W/120 list. In addition, subsequent EU submissions in 2000[19] foresaw the creation of seven 'purely' environmental sub-sectors (as opposed to the three present ones), namely:

6A. water for human use and wastewater management
6B. solid/hazardous waste management
6C. protection of ambient air and climate
6D. remediation and cleanup of soil and water
6E. noise and vibration abatement
6F. protection of biodiversity and landscape
6G. other environmental and ancillary services.

The EC proposal also suggests a 'cluster' approach whereby other specific services — which facilitate the provision of environmental services, but which are also used for other purposes (dual-use services) — should remain classified elsewhere in the classification list but would also be subject to a special 'cluster' or 'checklist' that could be used as an aide-mémoire during the other sectoral negotiations. These are: business services with an environmental component; R&D with an environmental component; consulting, contracting and engineering with an

---

[18] WTO, *Communication from the European Communities and their Member States — Classification Issues in the Environmental Sector* S/CSC/W/25, 28 September 1999.
[19] WTO, *Communication from the European Communities and their Member States. GATS 2000: Environmental Services*, S/CSS/W/38, 22 December 2000, also S/CSS/W/3.

environmental component; construction with an environmental component; distribution with an environmental component; transport with an environmental component; others with an environmental component. The proposal encourages WTO Members to schedule liberalisation commitments without restriction for all sub-sectors as far as modes 1, 2 and 3 are concerned. However, some delegations have cautioned against Members making unintended commitments in a number of other sectors while liberalising under the 'cluster approach'.

The Australian proposal[20] supports the classification suggested by the EU and encourages WTO Members to use it for the negotiations on environmental services. It stresses the importance of liberalising mode 3 and calls for increased transparency of national regulations in the sector. The Canadian proposal[21] also upholds a cluster approach. It encourages liberalisation in all modes of delivery and in all sub-sectors contained in the present list of environmental services (core services) and in the other related services (non-core or dual-use services). The non-core services could be included in a checklist to be used as an aide-mémoire during the negotiations.

Colombia, while accepting the EU classification as a useful basis, has observed that imports of environmental services to developing countries can lead to increased foreign investment, technology transfer, wider coverage and improved environmental and sanitary conditions.[22] However, negotiations to liberalise the environmental sector must, if maintained, take into account each member's level of development. In order to facilitate trade in environmental services, the proposal urges developed countries to undertake liberalisation commitments on mode 4 so as to allow the movement of natural persons as suppliers of environmental services. Colombia has proposed the addition of three more services to the EU classification: (i) the implementation and auditing of environmental management systems; (ii) the evaluation and mitigation of environmental impact; and (iii) advice on the design and implementation of clean technologies.

The US proposal[23] also suggests setting up a core list of environmental services, which are those classified as such in the current classification,

[20] WTO, *Communication from Australia. Negotiating Proposal for Environmental Services*, S/CSS/W/112, 1 October 2001.
[21] WTO, *Communication from Canada. Initial Negotiating Proposal on Environmental Services*, S/CSS/W/51, 14 March 2001.
[22] WTO, *Communication from Colombia. Environmental Services*, S/CSS/W/121, 27 November 2001.
[23] WTO, *Communication from the United States. Environmental Services*, S/CSS/W/25, 18 December 2000.

and a list of environmentally related services, which are those necessary to the provision of environmental services, such as construction, engineering and consulting services. Both core and related services should be liberalised. Such liberalisation would be most beneficial in the context of modes 3 and 4. The proposal mentions that the liberalisation of the environmental services sector must not impair the ability of governments to impose performance and quality controls on environmental services and to ensure that service providers carry out their tasks in an environmentally sound way.

The Swiss proposal[24] suggests a classification of the core environmental services in six sub-sectors in a way very similar to that proposed by the EU: wastewater management; waste management; protection of ambient air and climate; remediation and clean-up of soil and water; noise and vibration abatement; protection of biodiversity and landscape; and other environmental and ancillary services. The list of related services would include: professional services relating to the environment; research and development relating to the environment; consultancy, sub-contracting and engineering relating to the environment; and construction relating to the environment. Switzerland seeks broader specific commitments with respect to market access and national treatment mainly under mode 3, but also under modes 1 and 2 (where technically feasible). Liberalisation of mode 4 would be particularly important for the related services.

It is noteworthy that some members have included a category called 'protection of ambient air and climate' as part of their proposal for updating the existing classification. In addition, other services that have positive implications for climate change, such as afforestation, can also be included.

A further problem associated with the classification of environmental services is their relationship with environmental goods.[25] The two issues have mainly been discussed separately while in the real world goods and services are often inseparable. Many suppliers of environmental services integrate their services with environmental goods, such as in the manufacturing, installation and maintenance of pollution control equipment.

---

[24] WTO, *Communication from Switzerland. GATS 2000: Environmental Services*, S/CSS/ W/76, 4 May 2001.

[25] For more on this discussion see C. Kirkpatrick, C. George and S. S. Scrieciu, 'Trade liberalisation in environmental services: why so little progress?', *Global Economy Journal* 6 (2006).

Accordingly, it is possible that the confusion between goods and services in the environment industry will complicate the application of the GATS and, if the situation cannot be addressed through the sector classification, it might be left for members to resolve on a case-by-case basis.

An appropriate classification is a pre-condition for scheduling meaningful commitments that would support climate change mitigation. However, taking into consideration the concerns of developing countries and given the wide range of positions, at this stage it is unlikely that the WTO Members will reach an agreement on the scope of environmental services.

### Liberalisation of trade in EGS and its impact on climate change mitigation

All the proposals described above are based on the assumption that further liberalisation of trade in the environmental services sector may lead to a 'win–win' situation where protection of the environment and economic growth are pursued in parallel.

Promoting the freer flow of environmental goods and services allows the removal of trade restrictions and distortions in this sector to have the potential to contribute to enhancing the quality of the environment, as well as expanding markets and offering new investment opportunities. Environmental goods and services contribute to cost-effective, resource-efficient and environmentally sound approaches to resource use, and to the minimisation of pollution and waste with subsequent gains in productivity and improvements in the performance of many industries and sectors.[26]

Improved market access for the environment industry increases the availability of services and goods while lowering their cost. The increased competition that will result from improved market access for foreign firms could lead to innovation and improved services. Less expensive and better quality services will serve to make environmental protection and climate change mitigation more efficient. Cheaper and more efficient environmental services and goods would also have benefits for the global environment in regard to developing countries, where domestic financial concerns may require careful balancing of environmental priorities with others. Eliminating market distortions that cause natural resources to be

---

[26] See the contribution by the United States on *Liberalisation of Trade in Environmental Services and the Environment* (WT/CTE/W/70).

undervalued leads to their more efficient use, and therefore directly supports climate change mitigation.[27]

From the perspective of climate change mitigation, the services to be considered for further liberalisation should be: services related to cleaner technology; types of fuel that emit less or no greenhouse gases; and services that assist in making more efficient use of energy or fuels. In other words, a new trade regime in environmental goods and services should facilitate the transfer of environmentally sound technology (ESTs).[28] There are three areas for which transfer and effective use of ESTs could be of particular importance for climate change mitigation: addressing air pollution; enhancing energy and material efficiency — this includes energy-saving devices and technologies and the use of renewable energy and materials, including biodegradable material; and complying with environmental requirements in export markets, particularly those relating to management of hazardous metals and chemicals and related traceability requirements.[29]

However, there are several challenges to be overcome in order to achieve the above-mentioned benefits and liberalisation of the trade in EGS. First, environment friendliness of a technology, good or service is a relative characteristic and thus cannot realistically be used as a starting point in negotiations. For instance, Qatar has proposed that energy-efficient natural gas-based technologies should be considered environment friendly. This argument is based on climate change objectives and

---

[27] Butkeviciene, *Workshop on Post-Doha Negotiating Issues* (2002).

[28] There are no commonly accepted definitions of environmentally sound technologies (ESTs), although they do share some generally recognised features — such as the fact that they are introduced in a highly regulated framework, they represent a response to urgent global environmental problems and they may benefit from public funding for research and development — and it is increasingly recognised that these features distinguish them from other technologies. It should be noted, however, that because of the evolving nature of environmental problems, what might be perceived as environmentally sound today may not necessarily be seen in the same way tomorrow. Moreover, a technology perceived as environmentally sound in one country may not be seen in the same way in another. However, in the interests of clarity, ESTs may be considered to refer to 'clean' technologies which have little impact on the environment in terms of pollution or which are high in energy efficiency compared to other technologies currently in use. (For more discussions on ESTs, see C. Almeida, 'Development and transfer of environmentally sound technologies in manufacturing: a survey', *UNCTAD Discussion Papers* No. 58 (1993); and OECD/Eurostat, *Environmental Goods and Services Industry Manual Classification* (Paris: OECD, 1999).)

[29] A. Vikhlyaev 'Environmental goods and services: defining negotiations or negotiating definitions?' in *UNCTAD Trade and Environment Review* 2003, UNCTAD/DITC/TED/2003/4.

is a response to the recognition of the role of natural gas in the Kyoto Protocol negotiations as part of the solution to stabilising greenhouse gases in the atmosphere.[30] However, natural gas is environment friendly only in comparison to fossil fuels, such as coal and oil, but not to wind power or hydrogen. Thus if the WTO Members liberalise their markets for natural gas-based technologies and wind power or hydrogen become economically feasible in the future they would not enjoy any trade advantages as tariffs on natural gas would be low or zero.

Furthermore, another aspect of the climate debate — energy efficiency — is also a relative and evolving concept. Technology changes with time and energy efficiency can be improved. Thus, trade-based discrimination according to energy efficiency may be difficult to manage.

Negotiations have also been plagued by concerns over services that could have both environmental and non-environmental uses. 'Dual classification' of services (for example, engineering services with an environmental component) poses a very interesting problem. Bearing in mind the *US — Gambling* case (DS285), Members should be careful in making commitments under broad sectoral headings as they may end up making unintended commitments. At the same time, trade in environmental services may be affected by lack of market access in the related sectors, such as legal, consulting and other services. Liberalisation would therefore have to include several sectors and negotiations on environmental services should be linked to other relevant negotiations, which complicates the process even more.

Compared to other sectors, such as tourism, financial services or telecommunications, liberalisation bound under the GATS in environmental services appears rather limited.[31] Although the potential benefits of trade liberalisation are recognised, there are several concerns on the implementation side.

## Climate change approach

Reaching an agreement between WTO Members on the above matters in the near future is challenging, given the variety of issues to be tackled, the

---

[30] WTO, *Submission by the State of Qatar — Negotiations on Environmental Goods: Efficient, Lower-carbon and Pollutant-emitting Fuels and Technologies*, TN/TE/W/19, 28 January 2003.

[31] See R. Adlung in this volume.

different positions and proposals, and the fact that the current Doha negotiations on environmental goods and services are making slow progress with no sign of any important step being made so far. Still, the GATS is a flexible instrument and allows the accommodation of Members' attempts at climate change mitigation.

The size of the environmental market is considerable and an alternative approach to negotiations would be to reduce the vast complexity of the matter and redefine the subject of the negotiations in terms of problem areas.[32] A negotiating package might include two or three such areas to provide WTO Members with a mandate that is politically balanced.[33]

An 'air pollution' cluster would directly relate to climate, and given that climate change is a global concern, WTO Members will have more incentives for reaching an agreement within such a narrowed-down negotiation framework than for agreeing on how to liberalise the whole EGS sector. For such negotiations to be successful the following must be achieved: balancing the interests of developed and developing countries; identification of a list of key technologies and services relevant to climate change; tackling barriers to trade in specific goods and services related to air pollution and climate; and avoiding 'pollution transfer'.[34] Under an environmental area initiative (EAI) approach, as proposed by T. Cottier and D. Baracol in this volume, negotiations would cover tariffs, making use of listings, non-tariff measures and services, and technical

---

[32] The suggestion has been made to consider the following problem areas: air pollution; access to and supply of clean water; treatment of wastewater and disposal of sewage (sanitation); solid waste management; promotion of renewable energies and fuel efficiency; promotion of extensively produced agricultural goods. For more on the Environmental Area Initiative see T. Cottier and D. Baracol in this volume.

[33] A. Vikhlyaev, 'Defining negotiations or negotiating definitions?' (2003).

[34] The pollution transfer issue might fit into the WTO agenda, similarly to exports of domestically prohibited goods. The issue covers products which are exported even though their sale and use are banned or severely restricted domestically on the grounds that they are hazardous to the environment. This is of particular concern to many developing and least developed countries, which often lack the capacity or resources to deal with such products. Avoiding 'pollution transfer' is particularly relevant for the negotiations on the liberalisation of environmental goods and services related to air pollution and the climate. The question is whether developing countries will be able to absorb climate friendly technologies at the quick pace needed, considering that OECD countries are or will be shifting energy-inefficient technologies (from used vehicles to industrial facilities) to developing countries, due to the lack of environmental legislation or climate-specific commitments. For a more detailed discussion on EGS negotiations, see P. Iturregui and M. Dutschke, HWWA Discussion Paper 335 (2005).

co-operation, as well as linkages to other regulatory areas, including IPRs to the extent to which they are relevant for the chosen field.[35]

To strengthen the potential contribution of international trade law to climate change mitigation, WTO Members should take a comprehensive negotiating approach applicable to both goods and services, from the design and production of equipment to providing the services related to its installation and application. The main reason for linking goods and services is that opening up the air pollution control services sector while maintaining high tariffs and non-tariff barriers on goods such as air pollution control equipment may obstruct market access.

The lack of linkage in negotiations on environmental goods and services as well as the drawback of the 'list' approach in taking account of their integrated nature have been noted. Where appropriate, parallel liberalisation of environmental goods and services has been suggested by the EU.[36] Canada,[37] Cuba[38] and India,[39] in their submissions, have highlighted the close linkage between environmental goods and services. They have pointed out that environmental services are often supplied through goods and the separation of environmental goods and services in an environmental activity is difficult owing to their integrated nature. Canada and the EU[40] have indicated that their lists of environmental goods have been informed by the type of products used in environmental services. The project approach to environmental goods negotiations suggested by India also points out the need to ensure synergy between environmental goods and services that are frequently provided on an integrated basis commercially.

As a first step to combining and interfacing the environmental goods and environmental service areas, it would be important for trade negotiators to monitor developments on both fronts.[41] It was suggested that a checklist may be created for environmental goods that are integral to the provision of environmental services in those sectors where the number and extent of requests are significant. Ultimately, goods, services and technology would form an integrated cluster addressing a particular environmental problem — climate change.

[35] T. Cottier and D. Baracol-Pinhão in this volume.
[36] See also informal note by WTO Secretariat TN/TE/W/63.
[37] TN/TE/W/50.    [38] TN/TE/W/55.    [39] TN/TE/W/51.    [40] TN/TE/W/47.
[41] A. Vikhlyaev, 'Defining negotiations or negotiating definitions?'

## Conclusion

Within the WTO, the process of negotiations for environmental goods and services is showing little progress and it is important to reduce the vast complexity of the matter and redefine the subject of the negotiations in terms of problem areas, one of which could be air pollution and the climate. If climate concerns are not adequately addressed, trade provisions could have an adverse impact on world emissions. For this purpose, it is important to balance the interests of countries and promote a list of key technologies expressed in terms of goods and services, taking into account the need for a new classification of environmental services.

## Bibliography

Almeida, C., *Development and Transfer of Environmentally Sound Technologies in Manufacturing: A Survey*, UNCTAD Discussion Papers No. 58 (1993).

Butkeviciene, J., 'GATS negotiations and issues for consideration in the area of environmental services from a development perspective', *UNEP-UNCTAD CBTF Workshop on Post-Doha Negotiating Issues on Trade and Environment in Paragraph 31*, Singapore, May 2002.

Iturregui, P. and Dutschke, M., '*Liberalisation of Environmental Goods & Services and Climate Change*', HWWA Discussion Paper 335 (2005).

Kirkpatrick, C., George, C. and Scrieciu, S. S., 'Trade liberalisation in environmental services: why so little progress?', *Global Economy Journal* 6 (2006).

OECD, *Environmental Goods and Services — The Benefits of Further Global Trade Liberalisation* (Paris: OECD, 2001).

OECD/Eurostat, *The Environmental Goods and Services Industry: Manual for Data Collection and Analysis* (Paris: OECD, 1999).

'Outline for the IPCC Working Group I Contribution to the Fourth Assessment Report' in S. Solomon *et al.* (eds.), *Climate Change 2007: The Physical Science Basis* (Cambridge University Press, 2007), accessible at www.ipcc.ch/activity/wg1outlines.pdf

Sugathan, M., 'Climate change benefits from liberalisation of environmental goods and services' in E. Rose, and M. K. Gueye (eds.), *Linking Trade, Climate Change and Energy* (Geneva: ICTSD, 2006).

UNCTAD, *Environmental Preferable Products (EPPs) as a Trade Opportunity for Developing Countries*, Report by UNCTAD Secretariat, UNCTAD/COM/70, Geneva, December 1995.

Vikhlyaev, A., '*Environmental goods and services: Defining negotiations or negotiating definitions?*' In *UNCTAD Trade and Environment Review 2003*, UNCTAD/DITC/TED/2003/4

WTO, *An Alternative Approach for Negotiations under Paragraph 31(III) — Submission by India*, TN/TE/W/51.

*Canada's Initial List of Environmental Goods — Submission by Canada*, TN/TE/W/50.

*Communication from Australia. Negotiating Proposal for Environmental Services*, S/CSS/W/112, 1 October 2001.

*Communication from Canada. Initial Negotiating Proposal on Environmental Services*, S/CSS/W/51, 14 March 2001.

*Communication from Colombia. Environmental Services*, S/CSS/W/121, 27 November 2001.

*Communication from the European Communities and their Member States — Classification Issues in the Environmental Sector*, S/CSC/W/25, 28 September 1999.

*Communication from the European Communities and their Member States. GATS 2000: Environmental Services*, S/CSS/W/38, 22 December 2000, also S/CSS/W/3.

*Communication from the Republic of Cuba — Environmental Goods*, TN/TE/W/55.

*Communication from Switzerland. GATS 2000: Environmental Services*, S/CSS/W/76, 4 May 2001.

*Communication from the United States. Environmental Services*, S/CSS/W/25, 18 December 2000.

*Contribution by the United States on Liberalisation of Trade in Environmental Services and the Environment*, WT/CTE/W/70

*Group of Negotiations on Services*, MTN/GNS/W/120, July 1991.

*Market Access for Environmental Goods — Communication from the European Communities*, TN/TE/W/47.

*Submission by the State of Qatar — Negotiations on Environmental Goods: Efficient, Lower-carbon and Pollutant-emitting Fuels and Technologies*, TN/TE/W/19, 28 January 2003.

*Synthesis of Submissions on Environmental Goods — Informal Note by the Secretariat*, TN/TE/W/63, 17 November 2005.

# 13

# GATS' commitments on environmental services: 'hover through the fog and filthy air'?[1]

RUDOLF ADLUNG[2]

## Introduction

Environmental services to date have drawn relatively few commitments under the General Agreement on Trade in Services (GATS) and seem to play only a modest role in the ongoing negotiations. Even if current offers materialised, the sector would still be trailing well behind other services such as banking, insurance and telecommunications with which, at first glance, it has some features in common. These include, not least, the dual nature of the activities concerned which, as in the case of sewage or refuse disposal services, may be destined either for private consumers or industrial users (including public facilities). Other commonalities are strong government involvement as producers and/or regulators, the co-existence of efficiency goals with distributional objectives and constraints (e.g. the perceived need to ensure universal access across all population groups), and the existence of various scheduling and classification problems due, *inter alia*, to the diverse nature of the activities covered.

However, whereas environmental services played second fiddle during the Uruguay Round and since, the results of the extended negotiations on telecommunications and financial services, both terminated in 1997, have been generally referred to as the most significant achievements under the GATS to date.[3] This is particularly evident in the case of telecommunications,

---

[1] Shakespeare, *Macbeth*, Scene I ('Fair is foul, and foul is fair: Hover through the fog and filthy air.')

[2] All views expressed are those of the author and cannot be attributed to the WTO Secretariat or WTO Members.

[3] L. B. Sherman, '"Wildly enthusiastic" about the first multilateral agreement on trade in telecommunications services', *Federal Communications Law Journal* 51 (1999), 61–110; P. Sauvé and K. Steinfatt, 'Financial services and the WTO: what next?', in R. Litan, *et al.* (eds.), *Open Doors: Foreign Participation in Financial Systems in Developing Countries* (Washington DC: Brookings, 2001), pp. 351–86.

where participants not only managed to agree on a novel set of competition disciplines, enshrined in a so-called reference paper, but were also ready to accept certain guidelines and/or understandings on difficult scheduling issues and/or problems of legal interpretation.[4] Also, telecommunications is the only sector where a significant number of World Trade Organization (WTO) Members committed on future liberalisation moves. About 60 per cent of the schedules submitted by some seventy Members in 1997 and implemented under the Fourth Protocol contain so-called phase-in commitments that must be met by specified dates.[5] With the exception of recently acceded countries, it is impossible to find similar cases in any other producer-related sector, whether environmental services, banking, transport or construction.

## Patterns of current commitments and Doha Round offers

Figure 5 provides an overview of the scheduling priorities of WTO Members in a number of core service sectors in which they currently maintain commitments on market access and national treatment and/or have made offers in the Doha Round. By June 2007, seventy-one schedules with initial offers and thirty schedules containing revised offers had been submitted (covering ninety-five and fifty-four WTO Members, respectively). These offers essentially consist of inclusions of new sectors in current schedules and/or the removal or reduction of existing limitations under one or more of the four modes of supply (cross-border trade, consumption abroad, commercial presence, and presence of natural persons). Of course, the figure provides only a tentative indication of governments' policy focus; the commercial substance of the underlying commitments may vary widely, depending, for example, on the number of sub-sectors covered and the levels of liberalisation implied under individual modes. The role of tourism as a focal sector for commitments may be ignored in the current context. Given the absence of long-entrenched domestic operators and a strong self-interest in many countries in attracting international hotel chains, this sector was an obvious candidate for commitments even for otherwise hesitant Members.

---

[4] These included, for example, the treatment of access problems resulting from frequency-related technical constraints and scheduling approaches to cover, or exclude, alternative transmission channels (radio, satellite, cable, etc.) that might be used to provide a particular service. See also M. C. E. J. Bronckers and P. Larouche, 'Telecommunications services and the World Trade Organization', *Journal of World Trade* 31 (1997), 5–48.

[5] R. Adlung, 'The contribution of services liberalization to poverty reduction: what role for the GATS?', *Journal of World Investment & Trade* 8 (2007), 565.

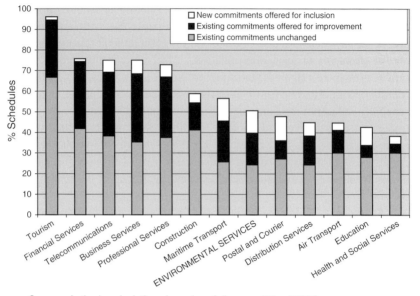

*Source*: Author's calculations based on Adlung and Roy (2005).

**Figure 5** Patterns of commitments in selected service sectors: existing schedules and Doha Round offers, September 2005
Note: 'Business Services' exclude Professional Services. Coverage of Air Transport is confined to three auxiliary services (repair and maintenance, selling and marketing, computer reservation systems). Health and Social Services consist mostly of hospital services and welfare services provided by social institutions.

Reflecting the breadth of the schedules submitted in recent WTO accession cases, the number of commitments has continued to increase across virtually all sectors. As of June 2007, sixty-seven WTO Members (including twenty-five EC Member States) maintained commitments on environmental services. In contrast to some other sectors, these are relatively evenly distributed across the sub-categories contained in the classification list generally used for scheduling purposes (MTN.GNS/W/120), even extending to segments that are somewhat hidden within a residual sub-category of unspecified 'other environmental services'.[6] For example, using the latter sub-category, fifty-two Members have inscribed commitments on 'cleaning services of exhaust gases'. In general, the commitments made under the most economically relevant mode of

---

[6] For more details, see Olga Nartova's contribution in this volume and WTO, *Guide to the GATS* (The Hague: Kluwer Law International, 2001), pp. 296–8.

supply, commercial presence, are subject to relatively few limitations on market access and national treatment. Nevertheless, as indicated before, the general level of commitments in this sector is anything but breathtaking.

What factors could explain the reticence of many WTO Members — despite the high political profile of environmental issues? Definitional and classification problems spring to mind. Olga Nartova's paper in this volume provides a very useful analysis of such problems that would need to be addressed in order to create a framework for commitments that is more closely in line with economic realities in the sector.

### Economic drive in some sectors …

While scheduling and classification problems can cause frictions and delays, experience suggests that these can be overcome if a sufficient number of Members is prepared to engage. It is more than coincidence that this was the case in telecommunications and, to a lesser degree, financial services, where the economic stakes were high:

- First, domestic commercial users — from traditional manufacturing industries to internet-based retailers and financial brokers — exerted pressure on governments to liberalise. This was particularly evident in telecommunications where the combination of rapid technical progress and profound regulatory reforms had added to the locational attractiveness of early liberalisers such as the United States or the United Kingdom. An increasing number of other governments had little option but to follow suit in order to protect their countries' status as international business centres.

- Second, internal reform pressures, building up since the mid-1980s, coincided with the emergence of an external negotiating forum in the form of the GATS. Export industries in economically advanced countries were able to mobilise 'their' governments to seek access commitments from what was considered to be a critical mass of other WTO Members. And the demandeurs had at their disposal a particular leverage: at the time of the extended services negotiations, they had not yet accepted a fully most-favoured-nation (MFN)-based outcome in the two sectors concerned and, thus, retained the possibility of retaliatory action.

Domestic economic (self-)interest might have been the prevailing force, however. For once at least, many governments were able to overcome traditional mercantilist instincts. This is evidenced not least by six WTO

Members, which had not participated in the telecommunications negotiations, but nevertheless volunteered commitments at a later stage. The most recent examples were Egypt and Honduras in 2002 and 2005, respectively. They apparently expected that policy bindings, and the ensuing protection from slippages or reversals, would reduce notional investment risks and thus encourage commercial engagement, whether from domestic or foreign entrants, in the sectors concerned.

### Why not in environmental services?

Although the Doha Round would offer an opportunity for environmental services and other 'laggards' to catch up, in terms of commitments, there has been limited progress to date (figure 5). Several factors may have prevented the sector from moving centre stage:

- Environmental services consist of a highly diverse set of economically and technically distinct activities, from refuse disposal to sewage and noise abatement services. Owing to the lack of commonalities and economic weight, relevant operators may find it more difficult to articulate and pursue their commercial interests in a focused manner than their counterparts in telecommunications or financial services. And this is true not only from the vantage point of suppliers, but also of (potential) clients.
- Government involvement is still rampant in a number of segments. Typically, water and sewage services or refuse collection are (still) considered a core government responsibility in many jurisdictions. If there has been privatisation, it has frequently consisted of public administrations no longer involving their own facilities, but using private suppliers on a contractual basis. However, even such relations tend to defy coverage under relevant GATS provisions. Article XIII:1 provides that 'the procurement by governmental agencies of services purchased for governmental purposes and not with a view to commercial resale' is not subject to most-favoured-nation treatment (Article II), nor the provisions governing market access (Article XVI) and national treatment (Article XVII). Although Article XIII:2 contains a negotiating mandate on government procurement of services under the GATS, there has been virtually no progress in more than ten years.[7]

---

[7] Of course, environmental services are also covered, across virtually all sub-sectors, by the schedules submitted under the Plurilateral Agreement on Government Procurement.

- Of course, refuse disposal services, sewage services, cleaning services of exhaust gases, among others are also, and possibly to an increasing extent, consumed by private commercial users. However, some potentially important industries, such as electricity generation, are highly concentrated, well-connected politically and amply cushioned from competitive pressures in many countries. Given this particular status, it may prove easier for them to accommodate and pass on high costs, including for exhaust cleaning, than companies subject to tight market constraints.

- A further element of uncertainty relates to the existence (or absence) of appropriate environmental standards. In contrast to financial, telecommunications or transport services, there is no genuine demand for environmental services. Relevant markets are essentially created through government regulation. Who would purchase, for example, sewage or air-cleaning services out of sheer altruism? Thus, while virtually all Members, twenty-one in total, which joined the WTO between January 1995 and June 2007 scheduled one or more environmental services with relatively few restrictions, the economic significance of these commitments is almost impossible to ascertain in the absence of concomitant information about pertinent standards and enforcement mechanisms.

## Scope for new initiatives?

There is a potentially relevant instrument under the GATS, whose use for environmental services has not been explored to date: Additional Commitments pursuant to Article XVIII. Again, telecommunications may provide some guidance. Given the legacy of monopoly arrangements in many countries, participants in the extended negotiations agreed on a set of transparency requirements, competition disciplines and institutional obligations concerning, *inter alia*, the creation of an independent regulator in the sector. Many Members inscribed the relevant reference paper — in a few cases with country-specific variations — in the fourth column ('Additional Commitments') of their schedule. The basic purpose was to ensure that the new access obligations are not undermined by non-transparent rules and regulations, anti-competitive

However, relevant concessions are exchanged only between the signatories to this Agreement (forty-odd WTO Members if EU Member States are counted individually). Moreover, the scope is limited to a range of listed entities and made subject to minimum threshold values.

practices, and the like. In environmental services, while the underlying rationale would be similar, such Additional Commitments could (or should) consist of undertakings to develop, implement and enforce pertinent standards. Like any other commitments, these could be phased in gradually in order then to be rendered enforceable via WTO dispute settlement.

The GATS is certainly flexible enough to accommodate such sector-specific intentions. Where there is a (political) will, there is a way under the Agreement. Otherwise, commitments on environmental services may continue to hover in an economic fog …

### Bibliography

Adlung, R., 'The contribution of services liberalization to poverty reduction: what role for the GATS?', *Journal of World Investment & Trade* 8 (2007), 549–71.

Adlung, R. and Roy, M., 'Turning hills into mountains? Current commitments under the General Agreement on Trade in Services and Prospects for Change', *Journal of World Trade* 39 (2005), 1161–94.

Bronckers, M. C. E. J. and Larouche, P., 'Telecommunications services and the World Trade Organization', *Journal of World Trade* 31 (1997), 5–48.

Sauvé, P. and Steinfatt, K., 'Financial services and the WTO: what next?', in R. Litan, *et al.* (eds.), *Open Doors: Foreign Participation in Financial Systems in Developing Countries* (Washington DC: Brookings, 2001), pp. 351–86.

Sherman, L. B., '"Wildly enthusiastic" about the first multilateral agreement on trade in telecommunications services', *Federal Communications Law Journal* 51 (1999), 61–110.

WTO, *Guide to the GATS* (The Hague: Kluwer Law International, 2001).

# PART V

Climate change and technology transfer, investment
and government procurement: legal issues

# 14

# International transfer of technologies: recent developments in the climate change context

FELIX BLOCH[1]

## Introduction

International legal aspects of technology transfer have been subject to international negotiations, and to scholarly debate among international lawyers for decades. In the 1970s and 1980s, technology transfer was an important matter in the discussions on a so-called 'new international economic order' and provisions on the transfer of deep seabed mining technology were a major stumbling block for the entry into force of the United Nations Convention on the Law of the Sea (UNCLOS). In the context of protecting the global environment, technology transfer has returned to the agenda of political decision-makers as an important item. As in those previous discussions, the transfer of environmentally sound technology raises important issues of law and policy, but the answers may not be the same as those given previously. Compared to the discussions on a 'new international economic order', the setting of the 'contemporary international economic order' is more than ever characterised by an increasing number of bilateral free trade agreements and bilateral investment treaties and by the overarching importance of the World Trade Organization (WTO).[2] Another important difference from those earlier discussions is that today a dozen important international agreements for the protection of the environment have been negotiated and have entered into force, all of them containing provisions obliging

---

[1] The views expressed are those of the author. This paper is partly based on the author's PhD thesis *Technologietransfer zum internationalen Umweltschutz* (Bern: Peter Lang, 2007).

[2] See for an accurate 'requiem' for the 'NIEO' debate, T. Wälde, 'A requiem for the "new international economic order"', in G. Hafner, G. Loibl, A. Rest, *et al.* (eds.), *Liber Amicorum Professor Seidl-Hohenveldern* (The Hague: Kluwer Law International, 1998), p. 771.

developed countries to transfer technologies to developing countries in order to assist them in protecting the environment. While a closer scrutiny reveals that all these agreements have common features, but also significant differences in terms of the normative value of the individual technology transfer provisions,[3] this contribution addresses only the legal rules contained in the climate change agreements. Apart from fitting into the necessarily limited space, this seems to be most appropriate in terms of the overall theme of this World Trade Forum.

The paper first provides a brief overview on recent political developments relating to the transfer of technology to developing countries in the climate change context. It then looks at the normative framework set by the Climate Change Convention and its Kyoto Protocol and addresses the relationship between the technology transfer obligations laid down in that framework and the WTO law.

## A.   Renewed commitment for climate-friendly technology transfer

At the annual summit of the Group of Eight leading industrialised nations (G8) in the Baltic resort of Heiligendamm in June 2007, climate change was put high on the agenda by the Presidency. The Heads of State and Government of the leading industrial nations concluded:[4]

> Technology is a key to mastering climate change as well as enhancing energy security. We have urgently to develop, deploy and foster the use of sustainable, less carbon intensive, clean energy and climate-friendly technologies in all areas of energy production and use. We have to develop and create supportive market conditions for accelerating commercialisation of new less carbon intensive, clean-energy and climate-friendly technologies. Furthermore, to ensure sustainable investment decisions worldwide, we need an expanded approach to collaboratively accelerate the widespread adoption of clean-energy and climate-friendly technologies in emerging and developing economies.

Hence, the G8 industrialised countries committed themselves, at the political level, to 'stimulate global development, commercialisation, deployment and access to technologies' and to 'promote major emerging

---

[3] Normative differences can be understood in relation to the importance that developed countries attach to the protection of the environmental good in question, F. Bloch, *Technologietransfer zum internationalen Umweltschutz* (Bern: Peter Lang, 2007) 280.

[4] See the summit declaration 'Growth and responsibility in the world economy', at paragraph 54.

and developing economies' participation in international technology partnerships and collaborations'.

In line with this political commitment, recent scientific studies have repeatedly highlighted the need for such climate-friendly technology transfer and have certainly helped to create the necessary political momentum for such a declaration.

The most notable contribution in this respect was made by the Intergovernmental Panel on Climate Change's Working Group III to the fourth Assessment Report on 'Mitigation of Climate Change',[5] which stressed 'high agreement' and had 'much evidence' leading to the following conclusion: 'The range of stabilization levels assessed can be achieved by deployment of a portfolio of technologies that are currently available and those that are expected to be commercialised in coming decades. This assumes that appropriate and effective incentives are in place for development, acquisition, deployment and diffusion of technologies and for addressing related barriers.' It went on to state that '[I]nvestments in and world-wide deployment of low-GHG emission technologies as well as technology improvements through public and private Research, Development & Demonstration (RD&D) would be required for achieving stabilization targets as well as cost reduction. The lower the stabilization levels […], the greater the need for more efficient RD&D efforts and investment in new technologies during the next few decades. Appropriate incentives could address these barriers and help realize the goals across a wide portfolio of technologies. This requires that barriers to development, acquisition, deployment and diffusion of technologies are effectively addressed.'

In a similar way, but from a more economic perspective, the Stern Review[6] stated that '[T]he development and deployment of a wide range of low-carbon technologies is essential in achieving the deep cuts in emissions that are needed.' It emphasised that '[G]reater international co-operation to accelerate technological innovation and diffusion will reduce the costs of mitigation' and stated that '[T]he private sector is the major driver of innovation and the diffusion of technologies around the world. But governments can help to promote international collaboration

---

[5] See Summary for Policymakers, formally approved at the 9th Session of Working Group III of the IPCC, 30 April–4 May 2007.

[6] See the Executive Summary (long), www.hm-treasury.gov.uk. For more detailed conclusions see N. Stern, *The Economics of Climate Change* (Cambridge University Press, 2007), in particular chapters 16, 23 and 24.

to overcome barriers in this area, including through formal arrangements and through arrangements that promote public-private co-
operation such as the Asia Pacific Partnership. Technology co-operation
enables the sharing of risks, rewards and progress of technology development and enables co-ordination of priorities.' However, it also warned
that 'A global portfolio that emerges from individual national R&D
priorities and deployment support may not be sufficiently diverse, and
is likely to place too little weight on some technologies that are particularly important for developing countries, such as biomass.' Finally, he
concluded that 'International R&D co-operation can take many forms.
Coherent, urgent and broadly based action requires international understanding and co-operation. These may be embodied in formal multilateral agreements that allow countries to pool the risks and rewards for
major investments in R&D, including demonstration projects and dedicated international programmes to accelerate key technologies. But formal agreements are only one part of the story — informal arrangements
for greater coordination and enhanced linkages between national programmes can also play a very prominent role.'

It is for scientists and not for lawyers to evaluate these prospective
changes of the earth's climate and the possible technological responses to
the related problems. However, if the diffusion of environmentally sound
technologies is indeed, as stated by the Heads of State and Government of
the G8, an essential policy goal, it seems important to identify and
evaluate the existing legal rules relevant for achieving that goal.

### B.   Technology transfer 'disciplines' under the climate change treaties

The normative framework of international climate protection is constituted by the United Nations Framework Convention on Climate Change
(UNFCCC) of 9 May 1992 (see point 1. below) and the Kyoto Protocol to
that Convention of 11 December 1997 (see point 2. below). With 192
instruments of ratification deposited, the Framework Convention has
gained almost universal acceptance.

### 1.   Setting up a framework for combating climate change: the UNFCCC

When the forty-fourth General Assembly called for the negotiation of the
Convention in 1989, it was clear from the outset that technology transfer

would have to be a cornerstone of any climate change treaty. The Assembly also decided that 'the concept of assured access for developing countries to environmentally sound technologies and assured transfer of those technologies to developing countries on favourable terms and the relation of that concept to intellectual property rights should be explored in the context of the elaboration of a framework convention on climate, with a view to developing effective responses to the needs of developing countries in this area'.[7] This resolution echoed the strong bargaining power of developing countries, which essentially took the position that developed countries had until then consumed most of the energy and emitted most of the greenhouse gases and that it was therefore up to them to save energy and to curb such emissions. Moreover, the industrialised countries would have to pay for any parallel action in developing countries. Otherwise, developing countries made it clear that they did not intend to ratify any agreement that would come close to supporting 'eco-imperialist' attitudes. Clearly, the fear of industrialised countries relating to the protection of intellectual property rights was also present from the beginning.

Developing countries were also encouraged to take this position because of the success they had had in the negotiations on the Montreal Protocol on Substances that Deplete the Ozone Layer of 1987. This Protocol was substantially strengthened in 1990, including an unprecedented provision obliging each developed country party to 'take every practicable step to ensure that the best available, environmentally safe substitutes and related technologies are expeditiously transferred' to developing countries 'under fair and most favourable conditions'.[8]

The principal goal for developing countries in the negotiations leading to the UNFCCC was thus twofold. Not only did they seek to avoid any environmental protection obligations without compensatory financial and technological support from developing countries, but also they insisted on similar financial and technology transfer commitments by the developed countries.[9]

---

[7] Resolution 44/207 of 22 December 1989.

[8] See Article 10A of the Protocol as adjusted and amended by the Second Meeting of the Parties (London, 27–29 June 1990). For an account of those negotiations see R. Benedick, *Ozone Diplomacy* (Harvard University Press, 1998). See also H. Ott, 'The new Montreal Protocol: a small step for the protection of the ozone layer, a big step for international law and relations' (1991) 24 *Verfassung und Recht in Übersee*, 188–208.

[9] See D. Bodansky, 'The United Nations Framework Convention on Climate Change: a commentary' (1993) 18 *The Yale Journal of International Law*, 451–558 at 479.

The first idea is now enshrined as a principle in Article 4(7) of the Convention. It reads:

> The extent to which developing country Parties will effectively implement their commitments under the Convention will depend on the effective implementation by developed country Parties of their commitments under the Convention related to financial resources and transfer of technology and will take fully into account that economic and social development and poverty eradication are the first and overriding priorities of the developing country Parties.

This provision, which introduces another concept of conditionality, is noteworthy for at least two reasons. While it may at first sight seem odd that an environmental agreement contains a provision that comments on the low political priority of the actual goal of that agreement[10] by some parties, this can be explained by the fear of developing countries that action to curb climate change could inhibit their developmental policies regarding 'economic and social development and poverty eradication'. Second, this provision ensures that when developing countries are asked to contribute to efforts to reduce greenhouse gas emissions, they can always argue a lack of 'effective implementation' by the developed country parties of their transfer of technology and/or financial resources obligations.

This provision reflects a remarkable aspect of the principle of common, but differentiated responsibilities and may yet prove to be of particular relevance when certain developing countries are asked 'to shoulder some of the shared obligations', as US President George W. Bush once put it.[11] And it may therefore be no coincidence that the 'New International Climate Change Framework' announced by President Bush in May 2007 closely links efforts to be made by developing countries to the commitment of 'advancing global transfer and adoption of clean energy technologies'.

The second goal that was boldly pursued by developing countries during the negotiations, binding commitments by the developed countries to transfer technology and financial resources, is echoed in several

---

[10] This objective of the Agreement is set out in its Article 2 ('The ultimate objective of this Convention and any related legal instruments that the Conference of the Parties may adopt is to achieve, in accordance with the relevant provisions of the Convention, stabilization of greenhouse gas concentrations in the atmosphere at a level that would prevent dangerous anthropogenic interference with the climate system.').

[11] Speech announcing 'Clear skies & global climate change initiatives' at the National Oceanic and Atmospheric Administration in February of 2002. See www.whitehouse.gov

provisions of the UNFCCC, but the technology transfer obligation is most clearly set out in Article 4(5). It reads:

> The developed country Parties … shall take all practicable steps to promote, facilitate and finance, as appropriate, the transfer of, or access to, environmentally sound technologies and know-how to other Parties, particularly developing country Parties, to enable them to implement the provisions of the Convention. In this process, the developed country Parties shall support the development and enhancement of endogenous capacities and technologies of developing country Parties.

It is clear that the wording of this provision was inspired by Article 10A of the Montreal Protocol; nonetheless, a closer look reveals some significant differences. While Article 10A contains an obligation to 'take every practicable step *to ensure*' (emphasis added) that technologies are 'expeditiously' transferred, the UNFCCC contains the obligation to 'take all practicable steps *to promote, facilitate and finance, as appropriate*, the transfer of, or access to, environmentally sound technologies' (emphasis added). This wording, which was undoubtedly drafted with great care, implies a considerable degree of flexibility as to the precise obligations of developed countries. An obligation to 'promote or facilitate' is clearly less onerous than an obligation to 'ensure' the transfer of technology, and the option to allow 'access to technologies', rather than ensuring 'expeditious transfer', may imply a more passive attitude towards transferring technologies.

Apart from the 'primary' technology transfer obligation contained in Article 4(5) of the UNFCCC, an obligation to finance the transfer can be found in the second sentence of Article 4(3) in conjunction with Article 11, whereby a 'mechanism for the provision of financial resources on a grant or concessional basis, including for the transfer of technology', is established.[12]

The parties to the UNFCCC initially decided to designate the already existing Global Environment Facility (GEF) as the 'operating entity' of the financial mechanism. The GEF has a unique institutional set-up,

---

[12] 'The developed country Parties … shall also provide such financial resources, including for the transfer of technology, needed by the developing country Parties to meet the agreed full incremental costs of implementing measures that are covered by paragraph 1 of this Article and that are agreed between a developing country Party and the international entity or entities referred to in Article 11, in accordance with that Article. The implementation of these commitments shall take into account the need for adequacy and predictability in the flow of funds and the importance of appropriate burden sharing among the developed country Parties.'

operating through the United Nations Development Programme (UNDP), the United Nations Environment Programme (UNEP) and the World Bank as 'implementing agencies' without a legal personality of its own.[13] Climate change is one of the 'focal areas' of support, and programme activities are closely supervised by the parties to the UNFCCC.

From a legal perspective, one may wonder how to characterise the relationship between the two obligations, the one contained in Article 4(5), and the one of the financial mechanism to finance transfer. It seems evident that these obligations are closely interrelated. Financing the transfer of technology is one available 'appropriate' measure under Article 4(5) of the UNFCCC and financing under Article 4(3) must comprise the transfer of technology. Clearly, the provision of Article 4(5) cannot be reduced to contributions to the financial mechanism; otherwise, Article 4(5) would have no real meaning of its own. However, the extent to which a party could convincingly argue that it has fulfilled its technology transfer obligation under Article 4(5) by contributing to the financial mechanism as the only 'appropriate' measure is unclear. In any case, one important conclusion that seems possible is that parties have an option under the UNFCCC to 'pay' for technology transfer. This is important for all those industrialised states that rejected any obligation detrimental to the protection of intellectual property rights connected to climate-friendly technologies. The parties to the UNFCCC have experienced considerable difficulties in drawing operational conclusions from these provisions[14] and while it is easy to list the obligations, it is more difficult to translate them into concrete action. What would constitute a 'practicable step' to promote the transfer of environmentally sound technologies? What would be a 'practicable step' to facilitate 'access to' technologies? It appears that parties enjoy some margin of appreciation in applying these obligations and the deliberate vagueness of the

---

[13] For a recent overview on the GEF, see L. Boisson de Chazournes, *The Global Environment Facility as a Pioneering Institution, Lessons Learnt and Looking Ahead*, GEF Working Paper 19, (Washington DC, 2003) and the annual reports contained in the *Yearbook of International Environmental Law* (Oxford University Press). On the role of the GEF in financing global environmental protection, see also R. Dolzer, 'Konzeption, Finanzierung und Durchführung des globalen Umweltschutzes', in V. Götz, P. Selmer and R. Wolfrum (eds.), *Liber amicorum Günther Jaenicke* (Berlin: Springer, 1998), pp. 37–61.

[14] On the discussions on technology transfer within the various bodies established by the Convention, see F. Bloch, *Technologietransfer zum internationalen Umweltschutz* (Bern: Peter Lang, 2007) 203, 220.

provision would not appear to give a government in any developing country a right to claim the transfer of a specific technology.

Leaving these legal headaches aside, it is apparent that a wide array of activities has been undertaken by developed countries to improve technological co-operation with developing countries in the field of climate change. Likewise, the GEF has developed a number of operational programmes which helped to finance measures intended to reduce greenhouse gas emissions. As an example, between 1991 and 2004 the GEF spent US$1.74 billion on climate change mitigation and adaptation and has generated some US$9.29 billion of co-financing. This may be insufficient, and it should certainly not be used as an excuse for industrialised countries to claim that they have provided enough funds already, but nevertheless, the UNFCCC has encouraged many concrete projects for technology transfer, and it cannot be said that technology transfer is not happening under the UNFCCC.

Still, developing countries have not hesitated to accuse developed country parties to the UNFCCC of a failure to comply with these commitments, and in reality these accusations arose because not enough is happening to meet the enormous challenge facing the developing world today, rather than as a legal challenge of non-compliance. Indeed in order to establish clear non-compliance with any of the above-mentioned technology transfer obligations, the framework set up by the UNFCCC would arguably require more concrete and measurable obligations.

### 2.   A step further: the Kyoto Protocol of 11 December 1997

As in the case of the Vienna Convention on the Protection of the Ozone Layer, it was already clear upon adoption of the UNFCCC that the negotiations would continue with the aim of concluding a Protocol for concrete obligations on emission reduction and limitation. Following the 'Berlin Mandate' in 1995, the Conference of the Parties in Kyoto managed to broker a deal including such 'quantified emission reduction and limitation obligations' by the end of 1997.

At first sight, the outcome in terms of strengthening 'technology transfer disciplines' was meagre. With regard to technology transfer, Article 11 point (c) only generally repeats what is already contained in Article 4(5) of the UNFCCC. However, it also adds clarifications on two issues that have been discussed at length within the relevant bodies set up by the Convention. The first is the insistence by some parties that not all technological knowledge is actually protected by intellectual property rights. Therefore, it was added that the obligation to 'take all practicable steps to promote, facilitate and finance, as appropriate, the transfer of, or access to, environmentally sound technologies' includes 'the formulation of policies and programmes for the effective transfer of environmentally sound technologies that are publicly owned or in the public domain'. The second clarification is linked to the obviously important role that the private sector plays in technology transfer and the corresponding importance of a favourable business climate in the exporting as well as in the importing state, so it was added that such 'practicable steps' include 'the creation of an enabling environment for the private sector'.

Apart from this addition to the existing obligations under Article 4 of the UNFCCC, a closer look reveals that the Kyoto Protocol has certainly taken a large step forward on the issue of technology transfer by inventing the Clean Development Mechanism (CDM), as defined in Article 12.[15] In short, the CDM provides a framework for projects in developing countries achieving reductions in greenhouse gas emission, which generate so-called 'certified emission reduction credits' (CERs) which in turn can be applied to comply with emission reduction obligations in developed countries. The CDM thereby allows 'extraterritorial' emission reduction measures. Depending on the importance of emission reduction obligations in developed countries, this mechanism creates a significant incentive for private investors to finance the use of climate-friendly technologies in developing countries.[16] While I will not go into any more detail on the operation of the CDM in this paper, because other contributions to this volume have taken up the matter, one obvious point should nonetheless be stressed here. While it is undisputed that the 'flexibility mechanisms' under the Kyoto Protocol have great potential for private sector involvement in technology transfer, it is uncertain that developed country parties to the UNFCCC have, by setting up these mechanisms, complied with their obligations to 'take all practicable steps' as required by Article 4(5) of the Convention and Article 11(c) of the Kyoto Protocol.

In conclusion, for those international lawyers who still associate technology transfer in international law with disagreements on 'forced'

---

[15] See J. Werksman, The Clean Development Mechanism: unwrapping the 'Kyoto surprise' (1998) 7 *Review of European Community & International Environmental Law*, 147–58.

[16] *cf.* M. Grubb, C. Vrolijk and D. Brack, *The Kyoto Protocol* (London: Royal Institute of International Affairs, 1999), p. 246.

transfer of deep seabed mining technology and the quest for a new international economic order, it will be interesting to see how technology transfer obligations have developed under the climate change treaties. Most remarkably, there are no provisions that would suggest a dirigistic approach to the transfer of technology, calling into question the validity of intellectual property connected to technology. Rather, the Convention, and indeed the Protocol, foresee public financing of technologies as well as market-orientated mechanisms that give incentives to private business. In this sense, the concepts of a 'new international economic order' are clearly outdated.

## C. Relationship between the UNFCCC and the WTO

What implications do these 'climate-friendly technology transfer disciplines' have for international trade and, more specifically, for the obligations under WTO rules? It seems clear that the fact that the relevant technology transfer provisions are 'tamed' to fit into the structures of market-based economies does not necessarily mean that there can be no conflict with WTO rules either at the level of international law or at the level of implementation of these technology transfer obligations by WTO Members that are parties to the UNFCCC. For instance, given the vagueness and ambiguity of the transfer obligation to take 'all practicable steps' in accordance with Article 4(5) of the Convention, parties enjoy a considerable margin of appreciation in deciding what 'practicable steps' to take in implementing this obligation.

While a number of different WTO rules may be relevant for assessing the WTO compatibility of implementing action, it appears that the Agreement on Trade-Related Intellectual Property Rights (TRIPS) may contain the most relevant legal obligations for WTO Members in the context of technology transfer. A considerable amount — although not all — of the climate technology-related information is protected by patents and will therefore be subject to the standards for the protection of patents laid down in the TRIPS establishing 'a private, free-market system for the transfer of rights to intellectual property'.[17] In general, an assessment of the advantages and disadvantages of patent protection for technologies that are relevant for climate change mitigation would prima facie appear to be similar to any general balancing of the additional

---

[17] M. Matsushita, T. Schoenbaum and P. Mavroidis, *The World Trade Organization* (Oxford University Press, 2006) p. 717.

incentives for technological innovation and development that are created by intellectual property rights, on the one hand and the societal interest of rapid diffusion at low cost of such climate friendly technology, on the other hand. In the above sense, climate change does not, in principle, pose problems and challenges different to those presented in the field of medicines, and implies a similar balancing of the interests involved.

Both the UNFCCC and the TRIPS offer some openness to these considerations and a balanced approach. If the obligation of developed countries under Article 4 of the UNFCCC only to take 'practicable steps', that may vary 'as appropriate', is read in conjunction with Article 3(5) of the Convention which states that 'measures taken to combat climate change, should not constitute a means of arbitrary or unjustifiable discrimination or a disguised restriction on international trade', it is clear that the UNFCCC leaves it to the parties to disregard measures that would conflict with their obligations under WTO rules. Likewise, Article 7 of the TRIPS states that 'the promotion of technological innovation' and 'the transfer and dissemination of technology' are the objectives of the Agreement. Moreover, with regard to least-developed country Members, Article 66(2) contains a self-standing obligation for developed country Members to 'provide incentives to enterprises and institutions in their territories for the purpose of promoting and encouraging technology transfer to least-developed country Members in order to enable them to create a sound and viable technological base'. It does not appear impossible to interpret the two provisions in a mutually supportive way. Moreover, it may be argued that the vagueness of the term 'practicable steps' can be read as rendering any WTO-incompatible action 'not practicable'.

In practice, it seems that the problems of rapid diffusion of climate technology do not centre on these provisions, and so far, there is no evidence of conflict between the obligations stemming from the UNFCCC and the TRIPS. Other WTO rules may, however, also be relevant when assessing the implementation of the technology transfer obligations under the UNFCCC. While it is difficult to draw any abstract conclusions without examining the details of any given 'practicable step' taken by a party in order to comply with the Convention on technology transfer, it is clear that any subsidies granted to support climate-friendly technologies may be scrutinised in the context of the Agreement on Subsidies and Countervailing Measures.

So far, it seems that the transfer of environmentally sound technology has only once been subject to dispute under the Dispute Settlement

Mechanism of the WTO. In the much cited *Shrimp Turtle* case,[18] Malaysia, Pakistan and Thailand asked the Dispute Settlement Body to set up a panel to examine their complaint regarding the prohibition imposed by the United States on the importation of certain shrimp and shrimp products that were not harvested by shrimp trawl vessels using fishing technology comparable in effectiveness to the technology used in the United States. This fishing technology, called 'turtle excluder devices' (TEDs), reduced the risk of sea turtles being caught in the net.

The panel concluded that 'the import ban on shrimp and shrimp products as applied by the United States … is not consistent with Article XI:1 of GATT 1994, and cannot be justified under Article XX of GATT 1994'.[19] When assessing whether or not the ban was justified under the chapeau of Article XX of the GATT 1994, i.e. whether the measure had been applied by the United States in a manner which constituted arbitrary and unjustifiable discrimination between Members of the WTO, the issue of the efforts made by the United States in transferring the required TED technology to specific countries was discussed. The fact that 'differences in the levels of effort made by the United States' could be observed ('Far greater efforts to transfer that technology successfully were made to certain exporting countries — basically the fourteen wider Caribbean/western Atlantic countries cited earlier — than to other exporting countries, including the appellees') eventually led the Appellate Body to conclude that the measure taken by the United States was indeed discriminatory.[20]

In this sense, it can be concluded that the justification of a measure under Article XX of the GATT 1994 may in a given case depend on the non-discriminatory efforts made to transfer the relevant environmentally sound technology to the other Members of the WTO.

Similar considerations could be relevant when laying down standards for the application of climate-friendly technologies and when considering bans for products that have been produced without such technology. In a possible case relating to climate-friendly technology, a future panel might similarly find provisional justification under Article XX(g), but then, in the second step of the 'two-tiered process' of analysing Article

---

[18] *United States — Import Prohibition of Certain Shrimp and Shrimp Products*, panel report, WT/DS58/R, adopted 6 November 1998, as modified by the Appellate Body report, WT/DS58/AB/R.

[19] Panel report, paragraph 8.1.

[20] *cf.* P. Mavroidis, 'Trade and environment after the *Shrimps — Turtles* litigation' (2000) 34 *Journal of World Trade*, 73–88, at 80.

XX of the GATT 1994, be inclined to interpret the chapeau against the background of the non-discriminatory application of the technology transfer obligations set out in the UNFCCC, this obligation constituting a binding rule of international law applicable in the relations between the parties and being relevant to such a case.[21]

## D.   Conclusion

While the need for a rapid transfer of climate-friendly technologies to developing countries is undisputed today, the existing provisions in the relevant international agreements remain vague. So far, there has been no conflict between those provisions and WTO rules since the implementation of these provisions allows for approaches that are fully compatible with WTO rules. The fact that the technology transfer provisions of the UNFCCC and the existing rules under the TRIPS can be interpreted in such a way that they are mutually supportive shows the profound change that the international economic order has gone through following the confrontational 'North–South' discussions in the 1970s and 1980s. Moreover, the relative importance given to private sector investments in climate-friendly technologies highlights the fact that technology transfer can never be a one-way street, where developing countries sit passively at the receiving end and wait for transfer results. Rather, as the Kyoto Protocol points out, the creation of an enabling environment for the private sector is crucial for any successful technology transfer. In this sense, 'good *environmental* governance' must also be expected from developing countries and it is not enough to point out different developmental priorities or even hide behind the slogan of 'common but differentiated responsibilities'. Nonetheless, the main challenge in the past, as well as for the future, is whether or not the developed countries will be ready to commit themselves to effective greenhouse gas mitigation policies, whether by means of emission reduction and limitation targets or other technological solutions. Either way, it will be crucial to have sufficient political will to channel resources into the deployment of climate-friendly technologies in the emerging economies of the developing world. Such resource transfer may either be effected directly through publicly funded programmes, or indirectly by strengthening

---

[21]   *cf. European Communities — Measures Affecting the Approval and Marketing of Biotech Products*, WT/DS291/R, WT/DS292/R, WT/DS293/R, adopted 29 September 2006, p. 328 *et seq.*

commitments to reduction of greenhouse gas emissions in the industrialised countries, thereby giving additional incentives for private sector
investment in the still emerging market for 'certified emission reduction
credits' and the like. Following the approach taken in the Kyoto Protocol,
market-based incentives may be the most effective means for successful
technology transfer.

## Bibliography

Benedick, R., *Ozone Diplomacy* (Harvard University Press, 1998).

Bloch, F., *Technologietransfer zum internationalen Umweltschutz* (Bern: Peter
Lang, 2007).

Bodansky, D., 'The United Nations Framework Convention on Climate Change: a
commentary' (1993) 18 *The Yale Journal of International Law*, 451–558.

Boisson de Chazournes, L., *The Global Environment Facility as a Pioneering
Institution, Lessons Learnt and Looking Ahead*, GEF Working Paper 19
(Washington DC, 2003).

Dolzer, R., 'Konzeption, Finanzierung und Durchführung des globalen
Umweltschutzes', in V. Götz, P. Selmer and R. Wolfrum (eds.), *Liber
amicorum Günther Jaenicke* (Berlin: Springer, 1998), pp. 37–61.

Grubb, M., Vrolijk, C. and Brack, D., *The Kyoto Protocol* (London: Royal Institute
of International Affairs, 1999).

Matsushita, M., Schoenbaum, T. J. and Mavroidis, P. C., *The World Trade
Organization* (Oxford University Press, 2006).

Mavroidis, P. C., 'Trade and environment after the *Shrimps — Turtles* litigation'
(2000) 34 *Journal of World Trade*, 73–88.

Ott, H., 'The new Montreal Protocol: a small step for the protection of the ozone
layer, a big step for international law and relations' (1991) 24 *Verfassung
und Recht in Übersee*, 188–208.

Stern, N., *The Economics of Climate Change* (Cambridge University Press, 2007).

Wälde, T., 'A requiem for the 'new international economic order', in G. Hafner,
G. Loibl, A. Rest, *et al.* (eds.), *Liber Amicorum Professor Seidl-Hohenveldern*
(The Hague: Kluwer Law International, 1998), 771–803.

Werksman, J., The Clean Development Mechanism: unwrapping the 'Kyoto
surprise' (1998) 7 *Review of European Community & International
Environmental Law*, 147–58.

# 15

# TRIMS and the Clean Development Mechanism — potential conflicts

STEFAN RECHSTEINER, CHRISTA PFISTER AND
FABIAN MARTENS

## Introduction

Although investment law and environmental law differ widely in aim
and scope, the likelihood of their overlapping has considerably increased
in recent times. The protection of the environment, particularly in the
field of climate change prevention, has evolved into one of the most
important issues on the agenda of many states and environmental
mechanisms have begun to influence international investment flows in
an unprecedented way. This article focuses on one such mechanism, the
Clean Development Mechanism (CDM), and its possible conflicts with
the WTO Agreement on Trade Related Investment Measures (TRIMS).

This paper also refers to an article on possible conflicts between
international investment law and climate protection policies by
Werksman, Baumert and Dubash.[1-2] The authors of this article pointed
out areas in which conflicts between the CDM and international investment law might occur. Some of their findings will be revisited and tested
against the latest developments in international environmental law.

Following a general introduction of the CDM and the TRIMS as the two
main points of focus of this paper, some general reflections on the relationship between international environmental law and international trade and
investment law will be presented. An analysis of the notion of conflict in
WTO law in particular and in international law in general leads the way to
the identification of possible areas of conflict between the CDM and the
TRIMS. First, some characteristics of the CDM which might be considered

---

[1-2] J. Werksman, K. A. Baumert and N. K. Dubash, *Will International Investment Rules
Obstruct Climate Protection Policies? Climate Notes* (Washington DC: World Resource
Institute, 2001).

to discriminate against certain types of investors will be examined as to their compatibility with the TRIMS. Second, the local content requirements which national regulations might stipulate for CDM projects will be tested against the TRIMS, and third, the special case of unilateral CDM projects will be scrutinised as to its likelihood of leading to violations of the TRIMS.

It will be shown that, due to the increasing popularity of a market-based approach to environment protection, international investment law and international environmental law are likely to overlap and occasionally to conflict. Such conflicts are, however, limited to a few aspects of the CDM mechanism and do not jeopardise its overall compatibility with investment rules according to the TRIMS. As compliance with duties under the Kyoto Protocol does not require states to violate the TRIMS, it will even be seen that careful drafting of host countries' national regulations for CDM projects can reduce the potential for conflict. It will also be suggested that international environmental law and international investment law in general, and the TRIMS and CDM in particular, apart from their potential for conflicts, also offer a certain potential for synergy, as they share some common goals.

## A.    Understanding the Clean Development Mechanism

The United Framework Convention on Climate Change (UNFCCC) is a multilateral international environmental treaty which was opened for signature in Rio de Janeiro in May 1992 and entered into force on 21 March 1994. The UNFCCC aims to stabilise the concentration of greenhouse gases (GHGs) in the atmosphere at safe levels. It does not, however, contain mandatory limits on GHG emissions or enforcement provisions. Rather, it contains provisions for 'protocols' to be decided at the annual Conference of the Parties (COP). The so-called Kyoto Protocol was adopted at COP 3, held in December 1997 in Kyoto, Japan. This Protocol, which has become better known than the UNFCCC itself, introduced mandatory targets for emission reduction and created three mechanisms to support parties in their efforts to achieve them: Joint Implementation, the CDM and Emissions Trading. These three mechanisms have become the pre-eminent example of an attempt to deal with an international environmental problem using a market-based approach.[3] One of these mechanisms, the CDM, will be examined more closely below.

---

[3] M. Wara, *Measuring the Clean Development Mechanism's Performance and Potential*, Program on Energy and Sustainable Development Working Paper #56, Stanford (2006), p. 1.

The CDM, defined in Article 12 of the Kyoto Protocol, is a mechanism which delivers means for development to developing countries in return for lower emissions of GHGs. More precisely, it provides for countries under a commitment to reduce GHG emissions (Annex I countries[4]) to implement project activities that reduce emissions in non-Annex I parties (mostly developing countries), in return for certified emissions reductions (CERs).

Thus, the CDM has a twofold aim: firstly, it helps Annex I countries meet their emission targets using CERs generated in countries where emissions reductions can be achieved at a much lower cost. Second, it advances sustainable development in non-Annex I countries.

After the meeting in Kyoto, the parties needed another four years to finalise most of the operational details for the CDM and to set the stage for nations to ratify the Protocol. The agreement reached at COP 7 in October and November 2001 in Marrakech finally established operational guidelines for the CDM in the Marrakech Accords. The CDM Executive Board was created as a supervising body for CDM projects and a CDM project cycle was introduced. According to the CDM project cycle, a CDM project passes through various stages. One of the stages contains the requirement under the CDM that the Designated National Authority (DNA) of a project's host country must certify that the project meets the standards of sustainability required by the Kyoto Protocol.[5] Article 12 of the Kyoto Protocol creates the notion of sustainable development, but leaves the meaning of this term largely undefined. The implementing directives of later conferences of the parties do not clarify the definition of this important term either.[6] There is thus scope for individual countries to draft regulations and guidelines for ascertaining that a specific project fulfils the sustainability requirement.

Even before the Kyoto Protocol entered into force on 16 February 2005, the registration of CDM projects was taken up. To date, a total of 832 CDM projects have been registered with the CDM Executive Board; more than 2,000 projects are currently in the pipeline. The first CERs were issued in October 2005.[7] India, Brazil, China and Mexico are host

---

[4] Annex I countries: countries contained in Annex I to the UNFCCC (industrialised countries under an obligation to reduce GHG emissions).

[5] UNEP, *Legal Issues Guidebook to the Clean Development Mechanism*, 2nd edition (Roskilde: Baker & McKenzie UNEP, 2004), p. 49.

[6] Wara, *Measuring CDM's Performance*, p. 13; UNEP, *Legal Issues*, p. 33.

[7] *cf.* UNFCCC website, Issuance of CERs, http://cdm.unfccc.int/Issuance/index.html, visited 3 September 2007.

countries to most of the registered projects. The United Kingdom (UK), the Netherlands, Japan and Switzerland have so far been the leading investors.[8]

The CDM has been considered a great success by some,[9] and a (partial) failure by others.[10] In terms of numbers of CERs already issued and to be expected during the next few years, the CDM has undoubtedly grown at an impressive speed. Yet, several commentators have pointed out serious flaws in the mechanism which allow participants to manufacture CERs at little or no cost[11] or have questioned the effect the CDM will have on the environment. Indeed, the subsidy paid through the CDM might prevent countries from reducing emissions through costly regulation. The political incentives for selecting a subsidy paid by an extranational entity over a more restrictive domestic regulation can tempt states to retain a low level of regulatory environmental requirements.[12] Other features of the CDM, such as the high transaction costs and the conversion rules for different kinds of GHG and the counter-productive incentives these rules might lead to, have also been criticised.

In spite of the (justified) criticism concerning flaws in the mechanisms in place, the general concept of using a market-based approach to deal with environmental issues seems to have been widely accepted in the course of the past decade as a viable way of addressing issues that are increasingly perceived as a serious threat to humanity.

## B.   The WTO Agreement on Trade-Related Investment Measures

### 1.   History and structure

The TRIMS came into effect on 1 January 1995 as part of the WTO Uruguay Round negotiations. Negotiations on an agreement regarding the TRIMS had already been started by WTO Members in April 1987. From the outset, it was apparent that two groups of states held opposing views on the matter. Industrialised countries such as the United States (US) argued that, due to their distorting and limiting effect on trade,

---

[8] *cf.* UNFCCC website, CDM Statistics, http://cdm.unfccc.int/Statistics/index.html, visited 3 September 2007.

[9] *cf.* for example: UNFCCC Secretariat, Press Release from 16 February 2007 (Bonn: 2007).

[10] Wara, *Measuring CDM's Performance*, p. 3 *et seq.*, finds that while the CDM has been successful as a political mechanism it has failed as a market and as a subsidy.

[11] *Ibid.*, p. 4.    [12] *Ibid.*, p. 16.

TRIMS ought to be generally ruled out. Developing countries did not support a general ban on the TRIMS, but favoured a limited approach which would only forbid measures having identifiable adverse effects on trade. The current wording of the TRIMS reflects the minimum compromise the parties were able to reach during negotiations. This feature of the TRIMS as a compromise between conflicting interests should always be borne in mind as it is closely connected to the issues discussed below.

The TRIMS consists of nine articles and one annex containing an illustrative list of TRIMS which are inconsistent with WTO rules. The TRIMS confirms the obligation of national treatment provided for in paragraph 4 of Article III of the GATT and the general elimination of quantitative restrictions provided for in paragraph 1 of Article XI of the GATT.

## 2.  Reference to the GATT

As the TRIMS refers to Article III paragraph 4 and Article XI of the GATT, it is necessary to outline these two provisions to show their relevance for the TRIMS.

Article III paragraph 4 of the GATT concerns the principle of national treatment. This principle, in short, obliges countries not to treat foreign products less favourably than products of national origin. A less favourable treatment in the terms of Article III paragraph 4 of the GATT is given if competition is affected negatively by the requirements. The focus of this principle is on the product, not on the investor.[13]

The narrow wording of Article III paragraph 4 of the GATT has been stretched to a certain extent by the GATT panels. For example, ever since the panel ruled in *Canada — Administration of the Foreign Investment Review Act*, it has been clear that even the obligation to buy from local sellers represents a less favourable treatment, because national sellers will typically favour national goods.[14]

Article XI is entitled 'General Elimination of Quantitative Restrictions'. This provision concerns, in particular, restrictions on imports or exports of goods by a company or on access to foreign exchange.

---

[13] Criticised by K. Sidhu, *Die Regelung von Direktinvestitionen in der WTO* (Göttingen: V&R Unipress, 2004), p. 181.

[14] *Ibid.*, p. 141.

### 3.   Definition of the TRIMS

In spite of its brevity, the TRIMS raises a number of questions. Most importantly, the interpretation of its name-giving key element, the investment measure related to goods, is far from clear. The understanding of what constitutes such a measure and what does not defines the scope of the Agreement. For the purposes of this paper, assessing the scope of the TRIMS is a vital pre-requisite for establishing the potential conflicts with the CDM.

In general terms, the TRIMS may be defined as requirements imposed on investors by states that cause a modification of trade flows.[15] The TRIMS itself does not provide for a precise definition of the term. Neither have the panels done this.[16] This is to a certain extent a consequence of the nature of the Agreement as a compromise between the signatory parties rather than a precisely worded consensus. An understanding of the term must therefore be derived from interpretation of the wording (the letter of the law, the preamble and the illustrative list), from the drafting history of the Agreement, from panel decisions and also from the fact that the Agreement itself ought to be seen as a mere compromise. An analysis of these elements leads to the following findings.

#### (a)   'Investment measures'

The definition of the term 'investment measures' has not yet been completely clarified by the panels. Yet, it has been determined that the intention of the state imposing the measure is of no relevance. As the panel *in Indonesia — Autos* stated, 'nothing in the text of the Agreements establishes the requirement that the measure ought to be characterised or explicitly adopted with a view to investment'.[17]

In the same case, the panel had to decide whether the definition of the TRIMS was limited to measures taken specifically with regard to *foreign* investment, as the Indonesian Government argued, or whether measures that are applied equally to foreign and domestic investors could also fall within the definition. The trade-related context of the TRIMS might at first sight imply a limitation to measures imposed on foreign investment. However, the panel rightly stated that the nationality of the ownership of

---

[15]  *Ibid.*, pp. 99–139.
[16]  *Indonesia — Autos, Indonesia — Certain Measures Affecting the Automotive Industry*, WT/DS54/R, WT/DS55/R, WT/DS59/R, report of the panel, adopted 23 July 1998, paragraph 14.80.
[17]  *Indonesia — Autos*, paragraph 14.81.

the enterprise subjected to the particular measure was not a decisive element in determining the applicability of the TRIMS. Deciding otherwise would have allowed governments to implement investment measures safely as long as nationality was no criterion. The wording of the TRIMS confirms this finding, as it does not include a limitation to foreign investment. This is of particular relevance for unilateral CDM projects where domestic investors participate in their home country's CDMs.[18]

### (b) 'Related to trade in goods'

The TRIMS explicitly states in Article 1 that only measures related to the *trade in goods* fall within its scope.[19]

The extent of the required relation to trade has been subject to dispute. Put simply, it is arguable whether any degree of trade relatedness of a measure should suffice or whether it ought to have a trade restrictive and distorting effect on trade. As mentioned above, this question was one of the main causes of disagreement in the negotiation process. In light of the preamble to the TRIMS, where the Punta del Este Declaration is quoted literally, and where it is recognised 'that certain investment measures can cause trade-restrictive and distorting effects', it appears that the parties intended to limit the scope of applicability of the Agreement to measures actually having a restrictive and distorting effect.[20]

### 4. One example of a TRIM: local content requirement

Trade-related investment measures can take many different forms. The main focus of the TRIMS is on trade-balancing requirements, export restrictions and performance requirements. In the context of potential conflicts with the CDM, performance requirements are most likely to be of relevance, in particular in the form of local content requirements. Such requirements, when related to trade in goods, require the investor to assign a certain quota for goods from local producers. Typically, minimum local or national content requirements amount to a less favourable treatment of foreign goods in the sense of Article III paragraph 4 of the GATT.

---

[18] *cf.* D.2(c) below.
[19] The (non-binding) German translation of the Agreement unfortunately fails to make this sufficiently clear when simply referring to '*handelsbezogene Massnahmen*' (*cf.* Swiss SR 0.632.20 Attachment 1A.7, Article 1).
[20] Sidhu, *Direktinvestitionen in der WTO*, p. 129 *et seq.*

The obligation to choose local goods over imported goods would thus be inadmissible under the TRIMS. However, in the CDM context, such an obligation might be considered beneficial with regard to the sustainability requirement. Therefore, local content requirements open up a certain potential for conflict between the CDM and the TRIMS. Before considering this potential conflict in detail,[21] some general reflections on the relationship between international environmental law and international trade law are indicated.

## C.   International environmental law and international trade law

### 1.   Market-based mechanisms in environmental law

International trade law and international environmental law differ in aim and scope. The increasing popularity of a market-based approach to climate change prevention, however, has increased the likelihood of closer contact or even overlap between the two areas.[22] Commentators agree that the market-based approach to environmental issues is here to stay.[23] Therefore, questions regarding the compatibility of market-based environmental mechanisms and established world trade rules have gained importance and are likely to remain relevant in the foreseeable future. As the strengthening of world trade and the protection of the environment are both currently priorities on the agendas of numerous states, the interaction between the two merits special attention. Taking into consideration that most parties to the Kyoto Protocol are also WTO Members, it can be stated that the relationship between the two regimes is indeed a relevant question for many states.[24]

### 2.   The relationship between the UNFCCC and the WTO

Some guidance, but no specific rules, concerning the mutual relationship between the UNFCC and the WTO can be found in the GATT[25] and the

---

[21]  See below D.2(b).

[22]  S. Charnovitz, *Beyond Kyoto — Advancing the International Effort against Climate Change* (Arlington: Pew Center on Global Climate Change 2003), p. 141.

[23]  Wara, *Measuring CDM's Performance*, p. 2.

[24]  For states, such as the US, which are WTO Members but not parties to the Kyoto Protocol, the relationship between the former and the latter might also be of importance, in particular where they are confronted with a state party violating duties under WTO law and seeking to justify such behaviour with obligations under the Kyoto Protocol.

[25]  General Agreement on Tariffs and Trade.

UNFCCC respectively. The UNFCCC declares that measures taken to combat climate change, including unilateral ones, should not constitute a means of arbitrary or unjustifiable discrimination or a disguised restriction on international trade.[26] More specifically, Article 2.3 of the Kyoto Protocol[27] states that the parties shall strive to implement policies and measures in such a way as to minimise adverse effects, including effects on international trade. It can thus be stated that parties to the Kyoto Protocol are under an obligation, although rather vague, to minimise the impact of their implementation of the duties under the Protocol on international trade.

A more general approach is taken in the preamble to the WTO Agreement[28] which recognises that 'relations in the field of trade and economic endeavour should be conducted with a view to raising standards of living … while allowing for the optimal use of the world's resources in accordance with the objective of sustainable development, seeking both to protect and preserve the environment and to enhance the means for doing so'.

As an interim result, it can thus be noted that the GATT and the UNFCCC refer to one another's goals but fail to establish specific rules as to their mutual relationship.

### 3.   Article XX of the GATT as a gateway for environmental concerns

Environmental concerns are, among other issues, reflected in Article XX of the GATT. Under Article XX, measures violating GATT rules can be excused provided that they fit within one of the article's general exceptions and that they are not applied in an arbitrary or unjustifiable manner and are not a disguised restriction on international trade. In the context of measures aimed at the protection of the environment, lit. b) and lit. g) of Article XX of the GATT are of particular interest, as they apply to 'measures necessary to protect human, animal or plant life or health' and 'measures relating to the conservation of exhaustible natural resources if such measures are made effective in conjunction with restrictions on domestic production or consumption', respectively.[29]

---

[26]  Article 3.5 of the UNFCCC.
[27]  The Kyoto Protocol is described in more detail below (cf. A).
[28]  Agreement Establishing the World Trade Organization.
[29]  For more detailed comments on CDM and Article XX of the GATT, see below D.3(b).

Although specific provisions on deference to environmental regimes are absent from the WTO regimes,[30] there is therefore a gateway for environmental concerns in Article XX of the GATT.

When applying this provision, WTO institutions have considered international environmental law to be of relevance for the interpretation of WTO instruments. In the famous *Shrimp — Turtle*[31] case, the Appellate Body turned to international environmental law when interpreting certain terms. Similarly, the panel in the *EC — Biotech*[32] case stressed that it did have the option of taking other treaties into account. It then went on to state, however, that in the present dispute it was not necessary or appropriate to rely on other treaties to interpret the WTO agreements at issue.

## 4.   The Doha Round

The relationship between multilateral environmental agreements and the WTO is one of the subjects discussed within the Doha development Round. The Doha Round was originally scheduled to be concluded within four years after it had begun in Doha in November 2001. The progress of the negotiations has, however, met with considerable difficulties and been stalled several times. Regarding the relationship between multilateral environmental agreements and WTO rules, some parties have suggested an increase in information exchange between countries when implementing trade-related provisions in environmental agreements. Others, in particular the European Union, have called for improved international co-ordination.[33] So far, the Doha Round has contributed little to the clarification of the relationship between trade rules and environmental law.

It is argued here that international environmental law and international trade law are — in spite of their interactions — two different

---

[30]  Charnovitz, *Beyond Kyoto*, p. 154.

[31]  *United States — Import Prohibition of Certain Shrimp and Shrimp Products*, WT/DS 58 RW, adopted 15 June 2001, paragraph 25.

[32]  *European Communities — Measures Affecting the Approval and Marketing of Biotech Products*, WT/DS291, WT/DS292, WT/DS293, panel report circulated on 29 September 2006.

[33]  Bundesministerium für Wirtschaft und Technologie der Bundesrepublik Deutschland, *Stand der Welthandelsrunde, Juli/August 2007*, at www.bmwi.de/BMWi/Redaktion/PDF/ WTO/wto-handelsrunde-stand-juli-august-2007,property=pdf,bereich=bmwi,sprache=de, rwb=true.pdf, visited 3 September 2007.

regimes existing at the same level. In cases where the two regimes clash, each conflict will have to be analysed in its own right.

## D. Potential for conflicts between CDM and the TRIMS

### 1. *The notion of 'conflict'*

For the determination of areas of conflict between CDM and the TRIMS, it is essential to have a clear understanding of what the notion of conflict signifies — and what it does not. The following analysis will summarise the notion of conflict in international law. This outline will then be compared with the findings of WTO panels on conflicts of treaties within the WTO regime.

### (a)   The notion of conflict in public international law

In public international law, conflicts of norms are resolved in accordance with certain principles. The *lex posterior* principle,[34] applicable to conflicting agreements with identical parties, uses chronological criteria when determining which instrument is to be given preference. The *lex specialis* principle[35] gives priority to the most specific provision. Yet, application of these principles is only required in cases where a genuine conflict has been identified. It is argued here that correct interpretation of seemingly conflicting obligations will in many cases lead to the finding that no conflict exists.

Article 31 of the Vienna Convention on the Law of Treaties requires interpretation of norms in good faith, in accordance with their context as well as their object and purpose. Observance of this principle will reduce the number of cases in which a genuine conflict is identified. Article 31 paragraph 3 of the Vienna Convention even states explicitly that 'any relevant rules of international law applicable in the relations between the parties' are to be taken into account.

The number of conflicts in international law is even further reduced by the application of the principle of presumption against conflict. In 1953, Jenks[36] stated: 'A conflict in the strict sense of direct incompatibility arises only when a party to the two treaties cannot simultaneously comply with its obligations under both treaties.' In public international

---

[34] *Lex posterior derogat legi priori* (a later law prevails over an earlier law).

[35] *Lex specialis derogate legi generali* (a more specific law prevails over a more general law).

[36] W. Jenks, 'The conflict of law-making treaties', *British Yearbook of International Law* 30 (1953), 426.

law, this presumption against conflict still acts as the prevailing, though not undisputed,[37] principle for determining whether different legal instruments contain contradictory obligations. According to this presumption, in cases where there are two possible interpretations, of which only one leads to a conflict between two norms, the meaning that allows for harmonisation of the two norms should be given preference.[38]

Such a narrow definition of the notion of conflict is also in line with the main objective of treaty interpretation. When interpreting treaties, the foremost goal is to identify the intention of the parties.[39] Since the parties are signatories to both treaties in question, it must have been their intention to be bound by both. From this perspective, an interpretation which allows a party to comply with the obligations of both treaties must be given preference.

### (b)   WTO panels on conflicts within the WTO regime

The Agreement establishing the World Trade Organization in 1994 contains a general interpretative Note to Annex 1A, dealing with the appropriate procedure for handling a 'conflict' between a provision of the GATT 1994 and a provision of another agreement in Annex 1A. Two questions are essential in this context: (i) when does a 'conflict' exist, and (ii) what are the legal consequences that arise if a conflict exists?

In *EC — Bananas III*,[40] the panel held — with reference to the aforementioned conflict clause of Annex 1A — that a conflict existed when two obligations were mutually exclusive and where a rule in one agreement prohibited what a rule in another agreement explicitly permitted.[41]

Put negatively, this would mean in the view of the panel that:

> a 'conflict' … does not relate to situations where rules contained in one [agreement] provide for different or complementary obligations in addition to those contained in [another]. In such a case, the obligations arising from the former and [the latter] can both be complied with at the same

---

[37]   *cf.* e.g. E. Vranes, 'The definition of "norm conflict" in international law and legal theory', *The European Journal of International Law* 17 (2006), 395 *et seq.*

[38]   J. Pauwelyn, *Conflict of Norms in Public International Law* (Cambridge University Press, 2003), p. 240 *et seq.*

[39]   Similarly G. Marceau, 'Conflicts of norms and conflicts of jurisdictions: the relationship between the WTO Agreement and MEAs and other treaties', *Journal of World Trade* 35 (2001) 1081, 1086.

[40]   *EC — Bananas III, European Commuities — Regime for the Importation, Sale and Distribution of Bananas*, panel report, WT/DS27/R, adopted 25 September 1997, as modified by the Appellate Body, paragraph 7.159.

[41]   *Ibid.*, paragraph 7.160.

time without the need to renounce explicit rights or authorizations. In this latter case, there is no reason to assume that a Member is not capable of, or not required to, meet the obligations of [both agreements].[42]

Therefore, as the panel held in *Indonesia — Autos*, 'no conflict exists if there is no provision contained in [one agreement] that obliges a Member to violate the [other agreement], or vice versa'.[43] Thus, WTO panels have confirmed the presumption against conflicts in international law in their assessment of potential conflicts if only within the WTO regime.

## 2. *Possible conflicts between CDM and the TRIMS*

### (a) Discrimination against foreign investors

The Kyoto Protocol and the other instruments regulating the CDM require states wishing to participate in CDM projects to fulfil certain conditions. First, states must have ratified the Kyoto Protocol and — in the case of the project's host country — must have established a DNA.[44] Additionally, the parties are required to be in compliance with their obligations under the Protocol, as the Marrakech Accords state.

Such prerequisites exclude certain states, such as the United States as the most prominent absentee from the Kyoto Protocol, from participation in CDM projects and might thus — from the investor's perspective — be regarded as discriminatory.

In order to decide whether such discrimination falls within the scope of the TRIMS, it needs to be established whether limiting participation in a CDM project to the parties to the Protocol constitutes a trade-related investment measure. The definition of the TRIMS has been the object of controversial discussion,[45] yet it is clear from the wording of Article 1 of the Agreement that only investment measures related to trade in goods can fall within its scope. The TRIMS aims at the protection not of the investor but of the goods. The exclusion of non-member states of the Protocol from the CDM, therefore, does not in itself constitute a violation of the general ban on the TRIMS as long as trade in goods is not affected.

[42] *Ibid.*, paragraphs 7.159–7.160.  [43] *Indonesia — Autos*, paragraph 14.49.
[44] Report of the Conference of the Parties serving as the meeting of the parties to the Kyoto Protocol on its first session, held at Montreal 28 November–10 December 2005, COP Decision 3/CMP.1, at 29.
[45] *cf.* e.g. Sidhu, *Direktinvestitionen in der WTO*, p. 98.

The limited scope of the TRIMS does not cover the issue of distortion of international investment flows per se. It is only applicable to investment decision-making insofar as a connection with trade in goods exists. Thus, the general exclusion of certain states from investment activity in the CDM context cannot lead to a conflict with the TRIMS, since it does not fall within the narrow scope of this agreement.

(b)    Performance requirements in CDM regulations

The Kyoto Protocol stipulates that CDM projects must assist developing countries in achieving sustainable development. The selection of criteria for sustainability remains a sovereign matter for the host countries. Hence, national authorities can co-ordinate national development policies and CDM projects with the aim of selecting and designing CDM projects in a manner which maximises synergies with local development goals.[46] In addition to social and environmental criteria, it is widely accepted that criteria for economic sustainability can be applied when determining whether a CDM project does indeed assist sustainable development. Examples of such economic criteria are financial returns to local entities, positive impact on balance of payments, or transfer of new technology.[47]

When confronted with such examples of criteria to include in their national regulation regarding the admissibility of CDM projects, states might be tempted to use local content requirements when defining the notion of sustainability. The fact that this term is used rather vaguely in the Kyoto Protocol might even increase the likelihood of a state resorting to easily understandable measures such as the prescription of the use of locally produced goods in CDM projects. The use of local goods in a CDM project can be beneficial from an ecological perspective, as it leads to a reduction of GHG emissions during transport. As far as the development aspect of the CDM is concerned, the infamous 'infant industry argument'[48] could be applied to local content requirements for CDM projects. Since developing countries and their nascent industries cannot compete with their older competitors from developed countries, it might be argued that temporary protection of developing industries from international competition could assist their development. Local content requirements could thus be seen as assisting ecological sustainability as

---

[46]  UNEP, *CDM Information and Guidebook*, p. 16.    [47]  Examples taken from *ibid.*, p. 18.
[48]  Originally developed by F. List, *The National System of Political Economy* (London: 1856).

well as the development of nascent industries in countries not yet industrialised.

From the perspective of the TRIMS, on the other hand, it is evident that such a CDM project rule would constitute a prohibited performance requirement. Restrictions on imports of foreign goods for use in a CDM project would thus constitute a violation of a host country's duties under the TRIMS.

The controversy which characterised the negotiations on the TRIMS reappears in the present context. In the course of negotiations for the TRIMS, developing countries argued in favour of certain TRIMS as they felt such measures could assist them in their development. In the CDM context, the same argument, with the added environmental dimension, resurfaces.

In the case of performance requirements in national CDM regulations, the potential for violations of the TRIMS is striking. Surprisingly, a random sample test of national CDM regulations has not brought to light any examples of local content requirements for CDM projects. An exhaustive analysis might lead to different results.

### (c)   Unilateral CDM Projects

The type of CDM project originally envisaged in the Kyoto Protocol involves more than one party. Typically, an Annex I party or a private entity authorised by such a party participates in the CDM project in the role of investor, whereas a party not listed in Annex I serves as host to the CDM project. It is unclear from Article 12 of the Kyoto Protocol whether the participation of an Annex I party is a mandatory requirement for a CDM project. As it became evident that Annex I countries were hesitant to invest in CDM projects, several developing countries expressed an interest in undertaking such projects independently and selling the CERs thus generated to parties not involved in such projects. The term 'Unilateral CDM Project' was created for this concept.

At their meeting in Marrakech in 2001, the parties agreed that Unilateral CDM Projects should be possible under the Kyoto Protocol but failed to state this clearly in the Marrakech Accords. In February 2005, the CDM Executive Board finally clarified the matter by deciding to allow Unilateral CDM Projects.

Werksman, Baumert and Dubash[49] pointed out that a prohibition of Unilateral CDM Projects would lead to discrimination between

---

[49] Werksman, Baumert, Dubash, *International Investment Rules*, p. 10.

investors. They went on to state that, as such discrimination would be *in favour* of foreign investors, it would not conflict with international investment agreements. As stated above, direct discrimination against investors based on their nationality, provided there is no relation to trade in goods, does not fall within the TRIMS. Therefore, this kind of discrimination, whether against a foreign investor or in favour of this investor, would not infringe the TRIMS.

The recognition of Unilateral CDM Projects enables all parties to the Kyoto Protocol, including non-Annex I countries, to invest in CDM projects. In this respect, all risk of direct discrimination between investors — whether covered by international investment law or not — is eliminated. However, some likelihood of conflict with the TRIMS remains. The absence of a foreign party to the project might tempt DNAs to apply criteria for sustainability which focus completely on local interests. An obligation for investors to buy from domestic sellers (even if they are free to choose the products) might constitute a breach of the TRIMS, for example, because domestic sellers tend to favour domestic products. In such constellations, a violation of international investment law might not be obvious, as no foreign investor is involved.[50] The TRIMS, however, rules out discriminatory treatment of imported and exported *products* generally, even where discriminatory rules are imposed on national and international investors alike.[51] Thus, it is important to point out that even Unilateral CDM Projects, although they might not include any cross-border investment, hold some potential for conflict with the TRIMS.

### 3.  The case of local content requirements in particular

#### (a)  Breach of the TRIMS

Local content requirements in national CDM regulations have been identified as the most likely area of conflict between the CDM and the TRIMS. The following analysis will thus focus on the following situation: A non-Annex I country member of the Kyoto Protocol issues regulations for CDM projects hosted in this country. These regulations contain, in particular, guidelines for the determination of the sustainability

---

[50] The actions of the host country might fall within the definition of government procurement according to the Agreement on Government Procurement. However, most non-Annex I countries (with the exception of China) are not parties to this agreement.

[51] *cf.* D.1(b) above.

requirement. Local content requirements are identified as beneficial with regard to ecological concerns and as suitable to advance the development of said country.

Another country willing to export goods to this country in the context of a CDM project might bring this case to a WTO panel, claiming a violation of the TRIMS. In all probability, the panel would find the country in question to be in breach of the TRIMS.

### (b)  Excused under Article XX of the GATT?

The country found to be in breach could try to argue that the national content requirement contained in its CDM regulations should be excused under Article XX lit. b) or lit. g) of the GATT. According to Article 3 of the TRIMS, all exceptions under the GATT are also applicable under the TRIMS.

Article XX of the GATT requires a three-step test.[52] After establishing that the measure in question falls within the scope of the provision, it needs to be established whether — depending on the specific paragraph — the measure is either 'necessary' or 'relating to' the pursuit of the policy. Third, the measure needs to be applied in conformity with the chapeau.[53] The term chapeau is used to describe the general rule contained in Article XX of the GATT, requiring that measures are not applied in a manner which would constitute a means of arbitrary or unjustifiable discrimination between countries where the same conditions prevail, or a disguised restriction on international trade.

An exhaustive comment on jurisprudence regarding Article XX lit. b) and g) of the GATT is beyond the scope of the present paper. The following analysis is therefore limited to the particular requirements of these provisions which seem to rule out the applicability of the two exceptions to local content requirements for CDM projects.

Article XX lit. b) of the GATT requires that a measure be necessary to protect human, animal or plant life or health. Skipping the first step of the test, the focus shall be on this necessity requirement. It can safely be said that it is unlikely that local content requirements contained in CDM regulations could ever pass the necessity test according to this provision. In the given context, a measure can only be deemed necessary if there is

---

[52]  A. Thiedemann, *WTO und Umwelt* (Münster: LIT Verlag, 2005), p. 13 *et seq.*, p. 192 *et seq.*; T. Cottier and M. Oesch, *International Trade Regulation* (Bern: Stämpfli, 2005), p. 429.

[53]  Cottier and Oesch n. 52 above, p. 429 *et seq.*

no alternative measure consistent with the GATT or less inconsistent with it that could reasonably be expected to achieve the same policy objective.[54] The necessity test was further refined in later decisions,[55] but the underlying rationale remains that as long as an alternative is available, a measure is not necessary under the terms of Article XX lit. b) of the GATT. As the sustainability requirement of Article 12 of the Kyoto Protocol cannot be interpreted as to *require* local content requirements for CDM projects, it can hardly be argued that such measures would constitute the only way of achieving the intended aim. Thus, even if a state succeeded in arguing that the measures in question fell within the scope of Article XX lit. b) of the GATT, their trade-distorting effect could not be excused under this provision.

Article XX lit. g) of the GATT is equally unlikely to justify local content measures for CDM projects, as it only concerns measures related to the conservation of exhaustible natural resources *if such measures are made effective in conjunction with restrictions on domestic production or consumption*. The rather cryptic meaning of this last requirement has been interpreted as referring only to measures brought into effect together with restrictions on domestic production or consumption of natural resources. It was stated that the clause was a requirement of even-handedness in the imposition of restrictions upon domestic and imported products.[56] Considering that local content requirements are by definition only restrictive towards imported goods, their justification under Article XX lit. g) of the GATT can be ruled out. Thus, again, the question of the scope of the provision can remain unanswered, as this second requirement will not be fulfilled.

In conclusion, it appears unlikely that a panel would find local content requirements in national CDM regulations excusable under Article XX lit. b) or lit. g) of the GATT. As the Appellate Body stated in the *Shrimp — Turtle* case, 'WTO Members are free to adopt their own policies aimed at protecting the environment' but only if they 'fulfill

---

[54] *Thailand — Cigarettes, Thailand — Restrictions on Importation of and Internal Taxes on Cigarettes*, panel report, WT/DS10/R, adopted 7 November 1990, BISD 37S/200 (1991).

[55] *US — Gasoline, United States — Standards for Reformulated and Conventional Gasoline*, WT/DS2/R, adopted 20 May 1996, as modified by the Appellate Body report, WT/DS2/AB/R, 29 April 1996; *EC — Asbestos, European Communities — Measures Affecting Asbestos and Asbestos-Containing Products*, WT/DS135/AB/R, 12 March 2001.

[56] *Canada — Herring and Salmon, Canada — Measures Affecting Exports of Unprocesed Herring and Salmon*, report of the panel, adopted 22 March 1988 (L/7268 — 25S/98).

their obligations and respect the rights of other Members under the WTO Agreement'.[57]

### (c)  Conflict between CDM and the TRIMS?

The above findings that local content requirements are reasonably likely to be contained in national CDM regulations and that the TRIMS rules out such requirements might seem to imply the existence of a conflict between the Kyoto Protocol and the TRIMS. However, it is argued in this paper that a narrow definition is to be applied to the notion of conflict in international law. According to this narrow definition, no conflict exists as long as a party to the two treaties can simultaneously comply with its obligations under both treaties.[58]

Neither the Kyoto Protocol nor any of its implementing directives require a state to implement measures that qualify as TRIMS. Rather, parties are obliged to ensure that the CDM projects they host assist sustainable development. Local content requirements are but one measure with the potential to increase sustainability. As there are numerous other measures available, the parties to the Kyoto Protocol are by no means forced to implement the TRIMS in order to achieve compliance with their duties under the CDM of the Kyoto Protocol.

Moreover, the Kyoto Protocol itself states that parties shall strive to implement policies and measures in such a way as to minimise adverse effects, including effects on international trade.[59] Hence, it could even be argued that the Kyoto Protocol requires parties to abstain from implementing measures that would be in breach of trade agreements.

To sum up, it can be stated that the Kyoto Protocol and the TRIMS do not impose conflicting duties on their respective parties. The sustainability requirement of the CDM leads to only a small risk that national regulation could be drafted in a way which is inconsistent with the requirements of the TRIMS.[60]

In the light of these findings, the above statement that there is potential for conflict between the CDM and the TRIMS needs to be put more precisely: there is a risk that *national legislation* drafted in connection with the CDM might conflict with the TRIMS. Consequently, careful

---

[57] *US — Shrimp, United States — Import Prohibition of Certain Shrimp and Shrimp Products,* panel report, WT/DS58/R, adopted 6 November 1998, as modified by the Appellate Body report WT/DS2/AB/R, 12 October 1998, paragraph 186, with reference to *United States — Gasoline* WT/DS2/AB/R, adopted 20 May 1996, paragraph 30.

[58] *cf.* D.1(a) above.    [59] *cf.* A above.    [60] Similarly, Charnovitz, *Beyond Kyoto*, p. 144.

drafting of national regulations, combined with the necessary attention to the obligations of states under the WTO regime, can effectively prevent conflicts.

### E.    Potential synergies between international environmental law and international trade law

Obviously, international environmental law and international trade and investment law strive to achieve different results. One aims at protecting the environment from detrimental human influence, whereas the other is concerned with the global free flow of trade and investment. As Charnovitz points out, there is also a fundamental difference in how these goals can be achieved and whom they benefit, as participation in trade liberalisation is in a country's own interest while the environmental and in particular the climate regime require a high degree of co-operation.[61]

Despite such fundamental differences, however, it must be remembered that both regimes share certain goals, and increasingly use similar means of achieving them. Environmental law and trade law aim to enhance public welfare to promote well-being. Both attempt to accomplish this by increasing economic efficiency. As already mentioned above,[62] environmental law is making increasing use of a market-based approach. This trend, which is expected to continue, further enlarges the common ground shared by the two regimes.

Even in a paper concentrating on potential conflicts between international environmental law and international investment law, it should be noted that, as well as clashing with one another, the two areas also exhibit considerable synergies. Bigger markets spur technological innovation and diffusion, which can reduce the ecological impact of economic growth. As trade promotes higher international incomes, some countries, in particular developing countries, will be better able to afford clean technology.[63] It is, *inter alia*, this effect that the CDM is designed to intensify.

Furthermore, both regimes have in common that they anticipate long-term benefits in return for short-term costs of compliance. Also, both trade law and environmental law are sensitive to the different interests and challenges developing countries are faced with. This common feature is particularly important in the context of the CDM and the TRIMS.

[61]  *Ibid.*, p. 143.    [62]  *cf.* Introduction above.    [63]  Charnovitz, *Beyond Kyoto*, p. 141.

To assist development is one of the main goals of the CDM. Similarly, the TRIMS is based on the belief that the elimination of trade barriers will ultimately improve the situations of developing countries. While the effectiveness of both approaches to development is disputed, it is clear that the underlying mindsets of the two Agreements are comparable.

Finally, a strong common trait of both regimes is that they are met with fierce criticism and have required long and tedious negotiation processes in the past.

## F.   Conclusion

Following a general outline of the pertinent issues and a short analysis of the notion of conflict in international law, one particular source of conflict between the CDM and the TRIMS has been identified in this paper: the inclusion of local content requirements into host country regulations for CDM projects. It was stated that the risk of violation of the TRIMS might be even more serious in the case of unilateral CDM projects, as its applicability is less obvious in such cases.

However, even with regard to local content requirements for CDM projects, no genuine conflict exists between the relevant international agreements. Rather, there is a certain potential for countries to draft national legislation in violation of the TRIMS. Therefore, the main finding of this paper is that careful drafting of national CDM regulations can avoid conflicts with the TRIMS.

To broaden the scope of this paper, the last section looked at the potential for synergy — as opposed to the potential for conflict — between international environmental law and international trade and investment law. This outline of the common traits and potential synergies of environmental and trade law shows that the two regimes in general — just like the CDM and TRIMS in particular — should not be seen primarily as conflicting but rather as able mutually to support partially parallel goals.

# 16

## Balancing investors' interests and global policy objectives in a carbon constrained world: the interface of international economic law with the Clean Development Mechanism

JACOB D. WERKSMAN

As lawyers we are trained to spot issues with our clients' interests in mind. When I teamed up with Baumert and Dubash to assess the relationship between the Kyoto Protocol's Clean Development Mechanism (CDM) and international investment rules,[1] I was working with the Alliance of Small Island States (AOSIS), and my colleagues at the World Resources Institute were keeping an eye out for the interests of the climate system. We were concerned to alert policy-makers that, if they were not careful, putting in place rules that stepped up levels of protection for foreign investors without including environmentally based exceptions to these rules could threaten the effective operation of the CDM.

Our paper was written in the context of wider concerns about the environmental and social impact of international investment agreements (IIAs) in the form of a rapidly growing number of bilateral investment treaties and of bilateral and regional free trade agreements. Capital exporters, particularly the United States (US) and the European Union, were keen on maintaining the momentum and the stability of increasing levels of foreign direct investment (FDI) by using IIAs as a means of strengthening the rights of their investors and providing them with access to compulsory and binding international arbitration.

The Kyoto Protocol was an even more fragile instrument in 2001 than it is now; it had not yet entered into force and the CDM's detailed rules

---

[1] J. Werksman, K. A. Baumert and N. K. Dubash 'Will international investment rules obstruct climate protection policies?' *International Environmental Agreements: Politics, Law and Economics* 3 (2003), 59–86.

had not yet been agreed on. At the same time, foreign direct investors were increasingly triggering the dispute settlement mechanisms attached to IIAs to enforce their rights and, in particular, to challenge the application of environmental regulations. Our paper sought to highlight what we perceived as a growing imbalance between the policy goal of promoting the flow of capital (which restrains government intervention in markets), and the policy goal of directing that capital towards specific environmental and social objectives (which encourages government intervention in markets).

We worried, too, about the imbalance of rights accorded by IIAs to foreign investors vis-à-vis host governments. A number of worrying cases, particularly under the North American Free Trade Agreement, provided examples of investors using that treaty's compulsory arbitration procedures to challenge and successfully overturn environmental measures as being discriminatory or expropriatory. IIAs that expand the definition of investment, to include all forms of real and potential commercial expectations, expand the definition of discrimination and expropriation to include the direct and indirect impacts of regulation that have the potential to shrink significantly the policy space regulators require to manage markets towards important public policy objectives.

Essentially, our goal was to strengthen the resolve of Kyoto negotiators to put in place rules, including facially discriminatory rules where they made sense, and to encourage trade and investment negotiators to create the policy space necessary to make this possible. It seemed appropriate, for example, for CDM rules to exclude the participation of investors and service providers from non-parties to the Protocol. Previous multilateral environmental agreements that have deployed market mechanisms exclude non-parties from, for example, trading in endangered species, ozone-depleting substances and hazardous waste. A CDM host country should be able to deploy performance requirements as a means of promoting the Protocol's climate change and sustainable development objectives even if this means filtering out a foreign investor's commercial expectations.

Our analysis at the time was necessarily speculative, and given that no formal disputes of the nature contemplated have yet arisen, perhaps slightly paranoid. Without detailed rules or examples from CDM projects we had to rely on the text of the Protocol and the limited experience with prototype investment-related mechanisms under the United Nations Framework Convention on Climate Change (UNFCCC). It was thus possible only to speculate about what a CDM project would look like, what measures a host government might put into place to attract these investments, and to anticipate circumstances in which a foreign investor's interests might be affected by these measures.

Essentially, an IIA promotes the flow of FDI between its parties. It does this by limiting the use of performance requirements that host governments put in place as conditions for FDI prior to the establishment of that investment. Classic examples of such measures include conditions requiring a share of domestic ownership, and requirements that manufacturers use a percentage of local content in their products. Once the investment is established, IIAs discourage measures that directly or indirectly discriminate against investors on the basis of their country of origin, either in favour of domestic over foreign investors, or favouring one foreign investor over another. IIAs prohibit host countries from unjustifiably expropriating the assets of a foreign investor, and require these countries to compensate promptly and effectively the investor in any circumstance in which expropriation has taken place. Finally, most IIAs entail the consent of the host country to the binding and compulsory jurisdiction of an arbitral tribunal to resolve claims for breach of the agreement brought by a foreign investor against the host country.

The CDM also seeks to promote FDI, but with the narrower goal of directing capital towards a highly specific set of policy objectives. The CDM is intended to reward investors from countries that have joined the Kyoto Protocol for investing in projects in developing countries that have also joined the Kyoto Protocol when those projects directly result in additional greenhouse gas emissions reductions. Investors whose projects comply with the CDM rules are rewarded with certified emissions reductions (CERs). CERs have a market value because they can be used by a Kyoto Protocol party (that has an emissions reduction commitment) to increase the amount of emissions they are allowed to release during the period of compliance with the Protocol's commitment period. The CDM does not provide for any *sui generis* dispute settlement mechanism for foreign investors feeling hard done by in the context of a CDM transaction.

In 2001, we felt it would be useful for the CDM rules to discriminate against investors from non-parties and from parties that were not in compliance with the CDM rules, but were concerned that these direct forms of discrimination could be interpreted as a violation of the non-discrimination provisions in IIAs. Although not explicit in the Kyoto Protocol, the Marrakesh Accords indeed clarified that a Kyoto Protocol party (and only a Kyoto Protocol party) can authorise the participation of a private entity in a CDM project activity, and that these entities may only transfer and acquire CERs if the authorising party is eligible to do so at that time. This links an investor's ability to benefit from the CDM to the status of its sponsor government as a party, and as a party in compliance with CDM eligibility requirements.

We also noted that the Kyoto Protocol provides that CDM project activities should assist developing countries in achieving sustainable development and should promote real, measurable, and long-term benefits. Such criteria applied by a host country could require a CDM project activity to use locally produced goods or services, build domestic capacity by employing local citizens, or require the transfer of technology to a local firm. Such requirements, to the extent that they affect the import or export of products, could run into conflict with IIAs, including the WTO's Agreement on Trade Related Investment Measures (TRIMS). Similarly, under a high standard IIA, local content requirements even if imposed equally on domestic and foreign investors, would be prohibited. A blanket prohibition on 'performance requirements' could potentially undermine a core objective of the CDM — sustainable development benefits for the host country.

Finally, we noted that the application of any CDM rules by a host country that led to the devaluation of a project could lead to a claim of expropriation. And indeed CDM rules have developed in a way that requires the readjustment of the baseline during the lifetime of the project, effectively reducing its commercial value. These rules reduce the commercial value of the investment but enhance the environmental integrity of the project.

Our paradigm case in 2001, following the US Senate's rejection of what would become the Kyoto Protocol, was a US investor, denied the opportunity to participate in a CDM project using the compulsory investor–state dispute settlement procedure to challenge a host state's rules and to chill the further development of the CDM.

In the companion piece to this chapter, Rechsteiner, Pfister and Martens have selected from these different potential pairings of CDM-related measures and IIA rules, the issue of domestic content requirements and the TRIMS. The analysis is a process of discovery towards just how narrow a set of facts could lead to such a conflict. Because the TRIMS applies only to those investment-related measures that have an impact on the cross-border flow of goods, they would be applicable only to those CDM projects involving such trade. Furthermore, it must be kept in mind that while the TRIMS is subject to the WTO's compulsory dispute settlement mechanism, unlike IIAs, this mechanism can only be triggered by a WTO Member government, and not a private investor. Generally, this means that an apparent legal conflict will not evolve into a formal dispute unless the volume of trade or the political stakes are high enough to move a government to bring a case.

It is possible to imagine a CDM project linked to local content performance requirements, but the authors do not assess here (as we could not, in 2001) the shape of actual CDM projects approved or in the CDM pipeline, whether these projects have a significant trade component and, if so, whether government policies intervened to ensure local content. Nonetheless, the authors arrive at the conceptually sound observation that a domestic content requirement used in the context of a CDM project that could be shown to have an effect on international trade would be actionable.

Along the way, however, the authors make several, tentative observations:

(1) **Unilateral CDM**. The authors rightly observe that the decision by the CDM to certify projects originated within and funded by a developing country host without the direct participation of a foreign investor creates an incentive for host countries to favour domestic investors over foreign investors. However, if a significant pattern of this kind of favouritism towards domestic investors were to arise, it would suggest that the primary rationale behind the CDM — to attract FDI and the North–South transfer of technology — was unwarranted, and that the value of carbon offsets generated unilaterally was higher than the benefit of using them to lure foreign investment and technology.

(2) **Local content restrictions**. As discussed, if a host country were to deploy local content restrictions in the context of a CDM project, these measures would likely be actionable under the TRIMS. But it is unclear whether host countries are in fact deploying them, and if they are, whether they are affecting sufficient volumes in trade to motivate a WTO Member (as opposed to an individual investor) to trigger a dispute.

(3) **The relevance of the Kyoto Protocol to a WTO dispute between parties**. The authors appear to conclude that the Kyoto Protocol could not, legally, have put in place rules that could 'require a breach' of the WTO law. The authors' point is not entirely clear. It is true that the Kyoto Protocol does not require its parties to

depart from their WTO obligations. Indeed, treaty negotiators, in general, seek to avoid clashes between existing obligations and those they are in the process of designing. Environmental treaties are increasingly using language that expresses the parties' desire to avoid such conflicts. But as a matter of treaty law, nothing prevents WTO Members from entering into agreements outside the WTO that in effect require changes in the nature of their WTO obligations. The Convention on International Trade in Endangered Species (CITES), for example, by banning trade in certain products in effect 'required a breach' of the prohibition of the General Agreement on Trade and Tariffs (GATT) on quantitative restrictions. Furthermore, as the WTO Appellate Body recognised in the *Shrimp — Turtle* dispute, WTO law does not operate in isolation from wider developments in international law, and cited international environmental agreements as informing a contemporary interpretation of the GATT's general exceptions. Thus, even though the Protocol does not 'require' a departure from WTO rules a WTO Member could, presumably, invoke the Protocol in the context of a WTO dispute to justify an exception under GATT of the Article XX.

(4) **Parties v. non-parties**. The authors choose not to address the paradigm case of the United States or another non-party as the disappointed CDM investor. They appear to assume that the substantial overlap between UNFCCC parties and WTO Members obviates the need to assess a dispute arising between a WTO Member that is a party to the Kyoto Protocol and one that is not. However, at least until 2012, when the Kyoto Protocol's first commitment period (and, perhaps the Protocol itself) expires, it remains the legal underpinning for the CDM. To bring our exercise in speculation to its full extent we would need to address the relevance of the Protocol to a WTO dispute between a party and a non-party. The WTO panel's discussion in the *EC — Biotech* case on the relevance of the Cartagena Protocol on Biosafety to this dispute between the European Community (EC) (which is a party to that Protocol) and the US, Canada and Argentina (which are not parties) should be brought to bear here. To the surprise of some, the *EC — Biotech* panel suggested that an agreement to which the disputants are not all parties would not be directly relevant to their analysis of a challenged measure.

(5) **The legal character of the Conference of the Parties serving as the meeting of the parties to the Kyoto Protocol (COP/MOP) or CDM Executive Board decisions**. Whether the dispute arose among parties or between parties and non-parties, a WTO panel may also need to address whether the measure at issue drew its legitimacy directly from the text of the Protocol or from subsequent decisions of the Protocol's institutions. The Conference of the Parties, serving as the Meeting of the Parties to the Protocol (COP/MOP) (the Kyoto Protocol's decision-making body), and the CDM Executive Board (responsible for administering the CDM) have taken many detailed decisions affecting the interests of actual and potential CDM investors. The relevance of the legal character of these decisions requires deeper analysis, particularly given recent decisions by local courts questioning whether governments can be considered bound by them.[2]

With a couple of years of CDM behind us, deeper research and analysis of actual state practice and investor behaviour should be possible. According to the UN, 'there are currently more than 840 registered CDM projects in 49 countries, and about another 1800 projects in the project registration pipeline. The CDM is expected to generate more than 2.5 billion CERs by the time the first commitment period of the Kyoto Protocol ends in 2012.'[3] It should now be possible to assess whether there has been a pattern of national implementing legislation or other dimensions of host country policy or practice that might be interpreted as discriminating against or between foreign investors. If we step back from TRIMS, which was the focus of the authors' analysis, to the wider question of the interests of foreign investors de-coupled from the flow of products, can we see patterns of host state discrimination and investor state recrimination emerging?

A detailed response to these questions is beyond the scope of this contribution, but three observations are worth making:

(1) The Kyoto Protocol mechanisms have been operating at the national, regional and global levels for several years, and have excluded the participation of non-parties to the Kyoto Protocol. More specifically, the EU Emissions Trading Scheme, which represents, in financial terms, the largest Kyoto carbon market, precludes

---

[2]  United States Court of Appeals for the District of Columbia Circuit filed August 29, 2006 No. 04-1438 *Natural Resources Defense Council* v. *Petitioner* v. *Environmental Protection Agency*.

[3]  www.unfccc.int

the participation of investors based in non-parties. Perhaps due to the relative ease with which US companies can establish subsidiaries within Europe, no disputes have arisen over these restrictions.[4]

(2) Although CDM investors have not yet triggered an IIA dispute settlement provision, they have found other ways in which to protect what they view as their interests. In a little-observed development, CDM investors frustrated, not by their treatment by host governments, but by their treatment by the CDM Executive Board, have formally complained to the UNFCCC Secretariat. Several 'private legal entities' claimed that they had suffered losses of several million euros and reputational damage as a result of having their projects rejected by the CDM Executive Board for not meeting CDM criteria. They raised concerns about violations of due process and arbitrariness in decision-making reminiscent of domestic law claims against government agencies' violations of administrative procedure. Governments and others sympathetic to their interests have put pressure on the CDM Executive Board to revisit these decisions, and have even gone so far as to suggest that the Board or individual members might be subject to suit if investors' concerns are not addressed. The Board has since reconsidered several of the projects about which complaints were received, and has re-instated some but not others.[5]

(3) The longer-term threat to CDM investors may come not from national governments pursuing protectionist policies, but from local communities resentful of the restrictions that these projects can place on land use and local development priorities. Recently the media has reported a series of citizen 'expropriations' of land set aside in the South by carbon finance to offset pollution of Northern consumers at the expense of local farmers.[6] Should current proposals to scale up the use of carbon markets to finance efforts to reduce deforestation be approved by the UNFCCC or the Kyoto Protocol,

---

[4] D. Goldberg and A. Delfino, 'The impact of the Kyoto Protocol on US business' in M. Gerard (ed.), *Global Climate Change and US Law* (Chicago: American Bar Association, 2007).

[5] Privileges and immunities for individuals serving on constituted bodies under the Kyoto Protocol: implementation of decision 9/CMP.2, FCCC/KP/CMP/2007/2, 12 November 2007, www.unfccc.int. See J. Werkman, 'Balancing public goods with private rights under the climate change regime' in *Carbon and Climate Law Review* Vol 1 No 1 95–104 (Lexxion: 2008)

[6] S. Faris, 'The other side of carbon trading', *Fortune*, 30 August 2007, http://money.cnn.com/2007/08/27/news/international/uganda_carbon_trading.fortune/index.htm

host governments could find themselves caught between the development demands of their citizens and their obligations under IIAs to protect the interests of carbon financiers.

The issues identified above are likely to become increasingly important in relation to a growing range of interests, from international project and portfolio investors, to host and home country governments, as well as to Northern consumers and Southern stakeholders. How these interests will be addressed, and through which legal systems, remains for creative lawyers to discover. But if we are to rely on carbon markets primarily as a means for protecting the planet, rather than primarily as a source of private gain, we must hope that whatever bodies are asked to balance these interests do so with a full appreciation of what is at stake.

# 17

# Procurement policies, Kyoto compliance and the WTO Agreement on Government Procurement: the case of the EU green electricity procurement and the PPMs debate

GARBA I. MALUMFASHI

## 1. Introduction

Public procurement is considered a potent policy tool to address numerous other secondary governmental policies[1] including climate change and energy security concerns. This is more so with the European Union (EU) among other parties to the Kyoto Protocol[2] that have made binding commitments to reduce greenhouse gas (GHG) emissions. This is sought to be achieved through the 'greening' of public procurement by which procuring authorities give preference to products, services or suppliers that are more environment friendly and net energy efficient than others. The climate change benefit of green procurement has been underscored by a study called '*Relief*'[3] conducted between 2001 and 2003 for the European Commission, which shows, for instance, that 'if all public bodies in the EU switched to green electricity,[4]

---

[1] S. Arrowsmith, *Government Procurement in the WTO* (The Hague: Kluwer Law International, 2003) p. 15.

[2] Kyoto Protocol to the United Nations Framework Convention on Climate Change, 10 December 1997, 37 *I.L.M.* 32 (1998) (entered into force 14 February 2005).

[3] The Relief — *Environmental Relief Potential of Urban Action on Avoidance and Detoxification of Waste Streams through Green Public Procurement* — project was co-financed by the European Communities (EC) research programme on Environment and Sustainable Development, called *City of Tomorrow and Cultural Heritage* (see http://cordis.europa.eu/eesd/ka4/brochure.htm). The project 'scientifically' assessed the potential environmental benefits of green public procurement for the EU. Details of the result, available at http://www.iclei-europe.org/index.php?id=relief&type=98, last accessed 12 June 2008.

[4] 'Green electricity' has been defined by Article 2(c) of Directive 2001/77/EC thus: 'Electricity produced from renewable energy sources shall mean electricity produced by plants using only renewable energy sources as well as the proportion of electricity produced from renewable energy sources in hybrid plants also using conventional energy sources …' See infra section 3.2.

they would avoid more than sixty million tonnes of $CO_2$ emissions per year, thus contributing towards 18 per cent of the EU's Kyoto target'.[5] Previously, the EU had aimed to have renewable energy sources providing 21 per cent of electricity by 2010.[6]

Public procurement is regulated by the World Trade Organization (WTO) Agreement on Government Procurement (GPA) 1994. The GPA is a plurilateral agreement binding only the WTO Members that specifically subscribe to it.[7] The EU green procurement policy is informed by the objectives of the EU climate change mitigation and energy security policies.[8] This policy is provided for in the new Public Procurement Directives.[9] It allows for preference to be given to green electricity over electricity produced by the traditional fossil-based sources, even though the two types of electricity are indistinguishable in terms of physical characteristics and performance, but differ in their processes and production methods (PPMs). However, there is still controversy[10] over the extent to which PPMs

---

[5]  See European Commission, *Buying Green!: Handbook on Environmental Public Procurement* (Brussels: European Communities, 2004), p. 5, available at http://ec.europa.eu/internal_market/publicprocurement/docs/keydocs/gpphandbook_en.pdf.

[6]  See EC Communication entitled *The Support of Electricity from Renewable Energy Sources*, Brussels, 7 December 2005 COM(2005)627 final {SEC(2005) 1571}, available at http://ec.europa.eu/energy/res/biomass_action_plan/doc/2005_12_07_comm_biomass_electricity_en.pdf 9, last accessed 13 June 2008. The Communication recognised the benefits of increasing the share of renewables in EU electricity to include: 'Improved security of energy supply' and 'mitigation of GHG emissions by the EU power sector'. This Communication was based on Article 3(4) and recital 7 of Directive 2001/77/EC. See infra n. 49 for the full title of the Directive.

[7]  There are currently thirty-eight parties to the GPA. All but three of these are industrialised nations including the EU and its twenty-seven Member States. See WTO website, www.wto.org/english/tratop_e/gproc_e/memobs_e.htm, last accessed, 21 July 2007. See text of the GPA (also referred to in this paper as 'the Agreement') at www.wto.org/english/docs_e/legal_e/gpr-94_e.pdf, last accessed 11 June 2008.

[8]  European energy policy has three key objectives. These are: (i) the maintenance of security of supply; (ii) the maintenance and improvement of European competitiveness through further development of the internal market as regards energy; and (iii) the contribution to environmentally sustainable development and, in particular, the reduction of emissions of GHGs so as to combat climate change. See, *inter alia*, Decision 280/2004 concerning a mechanism for monitoring Community greenhouse gas emissions and for implementing the Kyoto Protocol (O.J. 2004 L49/1).

[9]  See section 3.

[10]  See L. Assuncao and Z. Zhang, *Domestic Climate Change Policies and the WTO*, United Nations Conference on Trade and Development (UNCTAD) Discussion Paper No. 164, 12–14, (2002); D. Brack, *et al*, *International Trade and Climate Change Policies* (London: The Earthscan/RIIA, 1999), J. Cameron and M. Buck, *International Trade Law and Green Procurement Initiatives*, prepared for International Institute for Sustainable

which are not physically discernible in the final product are relevant in determining the *likeness* of the products.

In order to address the question, the remainder of this paper is structured as follows: the next section discusses the significance of public procurement and the legal bases of green procurement under the GPA and the EU law. This is followed by a discussion under section 3 on EU green electricity procurement and the PPMs debate under the WTO system with a suggestion that green electricity may be covered under the GPA general exceptions as one of the necessary measures taken by the EU to tackle the climate change problem. Section 4 concludes. The sustainable development component of green procurement, a dimension often neglected in the discourse on the subject is beyond the scope of this paper.[11]

## 2. Green public procurement under the WTO GPA: an overview

### 2.1 The GPA and the regulation of public procurement

The object of the GPA (the Agreement) is essentially to enforce the WTO values of 'non-discrimination' and 'transparency' in the conduct of the parties' public procurement policies, with a view 'to achieving greater liberalisation ... [in] the conduct of world trade'.[12] The rights and obligations created under the GPA are due to, and performed by, the parties on a reciprocal basis pursuant to the commitments they made towards each other in their schedules.[13] Article III:1 of the GPA on national treatment (NT) obligation thus provides:

> 1. With respect to all laws, regulations, procedures and practices regarding government procurement covered by this Agreement, each Party shall provide immediately and unconditionally to the products, services and

Development (IISD) Manitoba, 1998. See also van Asselt, *et al.*, 'Greener public purchasing under the WTO and EU rules', *Climate Policy* 6 (2006) 217–29.

[11] This has been discussed in Professor Geert van Calster's comment on this paper in this volume. For a detailed treatment of sustainable procurement, see generally, C. McCrudeen, *Buying Social Justice: Equality, Government Procurement and Legal Change* (Oxford University Press, 2007); C. McCrudden 'Using public procurement to achieve social outcomes', *Natural Resources Forum* 28 (2004) 257–67.

[12] For a detailed overview of the GPA, see S. Arrowsmith, supra n. 1.

[13] On the effect of the reciprocity rule, see M. Trebilcock, and R. Howse, *The Regulation of International Trade*, third edition (London: Routledge, 2005), p. 295; G. van Calster, 'Green procurement and the WTO — shades of grey' RECIEL 11 (3) 2002 (298–305), 298.

suppliers of other Parties offering products or services of the Parties, treatment no less favourable than:

    (a) that accorded to domestic products, services and suppliers; and

    (b) that accorded to products, services and suppliers of any other Party.

Paragraph (2) of this article emphasises that all locally based suppliers should be treated equally, regardless of (i) the degree of their foreign affiliation or ownership, or (ii) the country of production of the good or service in so far as they are all parties to the Agreement. This is otherwise referred to as the most-favoured-nation treatment (MFN) obligation.

These non-discrimination norms draw fundamentally from Articles I and II of the General Agreement on Tariffs and Trade (GATT) and Article II: 1 of the General Agreement on Trade in Services (GATS).[14] By these norms, the GPA parties are required to open up their procurement markets and avail equal opportunity of participation to both domestic and foreign suppliers of goods and services. Similarly, parties should not discriminate among goods, services and supplies of other parties. In order to give effect to these obligations, the Agreement under Articles VII – XVI makes detailed provisions on the need for transparency in the conduct of their procurement practices. These provisions, for instance, require the parties to advertise tender notices in prescribed forms and to allow for adequate time for prospective tenderers to participate in the procurement process, or to qualify to submit tenders. Tender notices should state clearly the technical specifications for the goods and services required.[15]

The GPA under Article XXIII, however, provides for exceptions as derogations from the obligations created under Article III mentioned above. These exceptions are generally similar to the Article XX of the GATT exceptions which are interpreted to include measures taken to protect the environment and other cross-cutting values. These are discussed in section 2.3.

## 2.2   Green procurement and climate change mitigation and the trade effects

In the context of climate change mitigation, green procurement signifies giving preference in government purchasing to those environmentally

---

[14] However, government procurement is excluded from the ambit of the GATT and GATS and is generally regulated by the GPA. See Article III:8(a), Article XVII of the GATT and Article XIII:2 of the GATS: see also G. van Calster's comment, supra n. 11.

[15] See generally sections 2.2 and 3.2 infra.

friendly goods and services that are less carbon intensive and more energy efficient, viewed not only from their physical characteristics and performance of the products but also their PPMs and the impact of their disposal. An example is the preference given to electricity generated from renewable sources over that generated from coal or other similar 'dirty' sources, or preference for biofuels generated through 'sustainable' biomass production methods.[16] For the EU and many other countries included in the Annex I of the United Nations Framework Convention on Climate Change (UNFCCC), the main motivator for a green procurement policy is reduction of GHG emissions pursuant to their climate change mitigation commitments under the Kyoto Protocol. The result of the *Relief* study cited earlier[17] is a good example of the significance of green procurement to the EU climate change and emissions reduction goals.

While the climate change mitigation potential of green public procurement is clear, the PPMs debate, among other issues, as will be seen in section 3 of this paper, means that the compatibility of the said practice with the GPA is still unclear. *Greening* of public procurement may be founded on the GPA provisions regulating the use of technical specifications, namely, Article VI. Technical specifications set 'the minimum quality standard acceptable for performance of the contract'.[18] The GPA stipulates, *inter alia*, that technical specifications inserted in the tender notice should (a) 'be in terms of performance rather than design or descriptive characteristics' of the products or services, and should (b) 'be based on *international standards* where such exist; otherwise, on *national technical regulations*, recognized national standards, or building codes'.[19]

Green procurement, although *origin neutral*, may amount to a de facto discrimination[20] against suppliers from jurisdictions where climate change mitigation is not a major priority, or who see their products as

---

[16] See 'EU makes bold climate and renewables commitment,' (published Friday 9 March 2007, updated Thursday 14 June 2007), available at www.euractiv.com/en/environment/brussels-biofuels-push-met-scepticism/article-160789, last accessed 18 June 2007. If the EU requires government fleets to use a certain percentage of this non-fossil based fuel, then this falls within the purview of government procurement.

[17] See supra nn. 3 and 5.

[18] See *UK Government Timber Procurement Policy*: Timber Procurement Advice Note November 2005 available from the United Kingdom's Central Point of Expertise on Timber Procurement (CPET) website, www.proforest.net/cpet, accessed 12 June 2008.

[19] Article VI:2 of the GPA (emphasis added).

[20] On de facto discrimination, see generally R. E. Hudec, 'GATT/WTO constraints on national regulation: requiem for an "aim and effects" test', available at www.worldtradelaw.net/articles/hudecrequiem.pdf (undated).

exactly the same as the green products in terms of physical characteristics and performance.[21] Indeed, as the Appellate Body (AB) so held that 'the essence of non-discrimination is that like products should be treated equally, irrespective of their origin'.[22] Thus, jurisdictions like the EU where climate change mitigation is a state policy may face challenges that green procurement is discriminatory contrary to Article III of the GPA. In the event of such a challenge, recourse may be had to Article XXIII of the GPA which provides for general exceptions to the general provisions on non-discrimination.

### 2.3    Green procurement under Article XXIII of the GPA exceptions

Article XXIII: 2 provides thus:

> Subject to the requirement that such measures are not applied in a manner which would constitute a means of *arbitrary or unjustifiable discrimination* between countries where the same conditions prevail or *a disguised restriction on international trade*, nothing in this Agreement shall be construed to prevent any Party from imposing or enforcing measures: *necessary to protect public morals, order or safety, human, animal or plant life or health* or intellectual property; or relating to the products or services of handicapped persons, of philanthropic institutions or of prison labour. (emphasis added)

These provisions are similar to those Article XX(b) and (g) of the GATT on general exceptions, and Article XIV of the GATS, Article 2.2 on legitimate objectives of the WTO Agreement on Technical Barriers to Trade (TBT).[23] It should be noted that there is a conspicuous omission, under Article XXIII:2, of the term 'environment' or 'conservation of exhaustible natural resources' in the listing of the issues covered under the exceptions. Nevertheless, greening of procurement policy could be justified generally by reference to the preamble to the WTO Agreement

---

[21]  See infra section 3.2.

[22]  See *EC Bananas III, AB Report EC — Report for the Importation, Sale and Distribution of Bananas, WT/DS27/AB/R* (adopted 25 September, 1997), paragraph 190. See also P. van den Bossche, *The Law and Policy of the World Trade Organization: Text, Cases and Materials*, second edition (Cambridge University Press, 2005), pp. 310–11.

[23]  Under Article 2.2 of the TBT, the *legitimate objectives* for which the exceptions apply include 'national security requirements; the prevention of deceptive practices; protection of human health or safety, animal or plant life or health, or *the environment*' (emphasis added).

which, as held by the AB in the *US — Shrimp* case, expressly states that the objectives of the WTO should be pursued bearing in mind 'the objectives of sustainable development' which seek 'both to protect and preserve the environment'.[24] Indeed by virtue of the numerous AB reports, and in particular the *US — Gasoline*[25] and *US — Shrimp* cases, WTO Members could freely 'adopt their own policies aimed at protecting the environment as long as, in so doing, they fulfil their obligations and respect the rights of other Members under the *WTO Agreement*'.[26]

However, even where justification is established for a green procurement measure, the other major hurdle is how to satisfy the chapeau or introductory part of the exception as cited above. The terms: 'arbitrary or unjustifiable discrimination' and 'arbitrary or unjustifiable discrimination a disguised restriction on international trade' are neither defined in the GPA nor in the GATT or GATS. However, the AB in *US — Shrimp*[27] gives an illustrative interpretation. The AB in that case held, *inter alia*, that the measure for the conservation of sea turtles taken by the United States (US) pursuant to section 609 of its statute[28] constituted 'unjustifiable discrimination' because 'under the terms of the law, the US had an alternative method of attaining its goals through the negotiation of bilateral or multilateral treaties for the conservation of sea turtles ... rather than simply resorting to an import ban'. Further, the US measures amounted to 'arbitrary discrimination' as 'they required countries to obtain certification from the US, but lacked a means of appeal or review of a denied application'.[29] This could mean that the interpretation of these terms is determinable by the circumstances of each case. This is

---

[24] See Appellate Body report: United States — Import Prohibition of Certain Shrimp and Shrimp Products, WTO Doc. WT/DS58/AB/R, 8 October 1998 (see paragraphs 129–30).

[25] *United States — Standards for Reformulated and Conventional Gasoline*, adopted 20 May 1996, WT/DS2/AB/R, paragraph 30.

[26] See WTO, 'We wish to underscore what we have not decided ...' by AB in *US — Shrimp* (paragraphs 185–6) at www.wto.org/english/tratop_e/envir_e/edis08_e.htm, last accessed 5 August 2007.

[27] *US — Shrimp*, supra n. 24 at paragraphs 122–5.

[28] Section 609 of US Public Law 101–102, enacted in 1989, dealing with imports provided, *inter alia*: 'shrimp harvested with technology that may adversely affect certain sea turtles may not be imported into the US — unless the harvesting nation was certified to have a regulatory programme and an incidental take-rate comparable to that of the US, or that the particular fishing environment of the harvesting nation did not pose a threat to sea turtles'. See www.wto.org/english/tratop_e/envir_e/edis08_e.htm

[29] A summary of the relevant section of the AB report is available at the International Law Brief website at www.asil.org/ilib/ilib0107.htm#02, last accessed 5 August 2007, and at www.wto.org/wto/dispute/58abr.doc

what the AB calls a 'case-by-case' approach suggested when interpreting the term 'likeness' which is similarly not defined in the WTO legal texts.[30]

There is, however, lack of judicial guidance on the meaning of the term 'disguised restriction on international trade'.[31] In any event, commentators, including Howse believe that the exceptions in the GPA that relate to, *inter alia*, 'measures *necessary for the protection of human, animal or plant life or health*' (emphasis added) 'would certainly cover environmentally motivated preferences for renewables, given the environmental harms and risks associated with conventional methods of generation'.[32]

The term 'necessary', has also received considerable attention in the GATT/WTO jurisprudence. Given that the wordings in both the GPA and the GATT provisions are similar it is expected that the proof required to show the *necessity* of a measure would also be the same.[33] In the context of the exception relating to the protection of 'human, animal or plant life or health', the AB, in the *EC — Asbestos* case,[34] after extensive reference to previous WTO jurisprudence,[35] came to the conclusion that a measure could be considered 'necessary' in terms of Article XX(b) of the GATT only if there were no alternative measures consistent with the GATT, or less inconsistent with it, which a country could reasonably be expected to employ in order to achieve its health policy objectives.[36] Similarly, in the *Korea — Beef* case, referred to in the *EC — Asbestos* case, the interpretation of the word 'necessary' was considered in the context of Article XX(d) of the GATT dealing with measures aimed at securing compliance with laws and regulations.

The Committee on GPA which administers the GPA is currently revising the GPA, and the new draft GPA is now express in its permission for inclusion of environment-related considerations in public procurement. Under Article X of the new draft, it is provided thus:

---

[30] See, for instance, the AB report in *EC — Asbestos* infra n. 34 at paragraphs 40, 101 and 102.

[31] R. Howse, Post-hearing submission to the International Trade Commission: 'World trade law and renewable energy: the case of non-tariff measures,' Renewable Energy and International Law Project (5 May 2005): 'There is lack of clear judicial guidance so far on the meaning of "disguised restriction on international trade".' (*US — Reformulated Gasoline*).

[32] *Ibid.* [33] R. Howse also supports this assertion. See *ibid.*

[34] Appellate Body report: *European Communities — Measures Affecting Asbestos And Asbestos-Containing Products.* Doc. No. WT/DS135/AB/R (5 April 2000).

[35] See Article XX(b) of the GATT and the corresponding Article XIV(b) of the GATS.

[36] *Ibid.*, paragraphs 170–5.

> For greater certainty, a Party, including its procuring entities, may, in accordance with this Article, prepare, adopt, or apply technical specifications to promote the conservation of natural resources or protect the environment.[37]

This provision, it seems, essentially does not really add any new value in the face of the Article XXIII of the GPA exceptions. Consequently, the EU and other green procurement practitioner countries will still have to prove the chapeau conditionalities when the new GPA comes into force. And in all cases, the defendant maintaining a green procurement measure has the onus to prove that the technical specifications used are 'not ... prepared, adopted or applied with a view to, or with the effect of creating unnecessary obstacle to international trade'.[38] Though not specifically defined by the GPA, the term 'unnecessary obstacle to international trade' has been interpreted as 'any trade obstacle that can be removed without endangering fulfilment of the relevant objective'.[39]

The next section will examine the EU green energy procurement system in the context of both the new EC law and policy which allows for incorporating environmental considerations in public procurement, and the relevant WTO law and policy.

## 3. EU climate policy, green electricity procurement and the PPMs debate

### 3.1 EU law and policy for climate change and green procurement

Pursuant to the ultimate objectives of the UNFCCC,[40] each Annex 1 party[41] to the UNFCCC, including the EU as well as its Member States,

---

[37] See Revised GPA 2007 Article X paragraph 6 at http://docsonline.wto.org/ DDFDocuments/t/PLURI/GPA/W297.docGPA/W/297. For more information on the revised text see WTO, provisional agreement on text of revised Government Procurement Agreement at www.wto.org/english/news_e/news06_e/gproc_8dec06_ e.htm, accessed 13 June 2008.

[38] See J. Early, 'Green Procurement and Trade Policy,' (Background Report for the Commission for Environmental Co-operation (CEC), Montreal: (undated)), p. 7, available at www.cec.org, accessed 22 May 2007.

[39] See G. van Calster, supra n. 11, p. 303, citing E. L. M. Volker, 'The Agreement on Technical Barriers to Trade', in Bourgeois, et al., (eds.), The Uruguay Round Results — A European Lawyer's Perspective (Brussels: European University Press — College of Europe, 1996), p. 281.

[40] Article 2 of the UNFCCC stated the objectives of the Convention to include the 'stabilization of greenhouse gas concentrations in the atmosphere at a level that would prevent dangerous anthropogenic interference with the climate system ...'

[41] The emissions reduction commitments of the UNFCCC Annex 1 parties are listed in Annex B of the KY.

has been enjoined under Article 2 paragraph 1(a)(iv) of the Kyoto Protocol to

> implement and/or further elaborate policies and measures in accordance with its national circumstances, such as: ... (iv) Research on, and promotion, development and increased use of, new and renewable forms of energy.

Hence, the climate change mitigation measures under the Kyoto Protocol are targeted, on the one hand, at the reduction of GHG emissions, and, on the other hand, as embodied in the above provisions, at the development and use of new and renewable sources of energy, and energy efficiency strategies including the provision of alternatives to address the energy security concerns. In the case of the EU, 'action on renewables and energy efficiency, besides tackling climate change, will contribute to security of energy supply and help limit ... dependence on imported energy'.[42] Hence, climate change mitigation policy became, for the EU and most Annex 1 parties an integral part of their energy policy.

The EU as well as its Member States are also signatories to the GPA,[43] and pursuant to Article XXIV:5(a) of the GPA they have the responsibility to ensure consistency of their procurement policies with the GPA provisions. The article states:

> Each government accepting or acceding to this agreement shall ensure ... the conformity of its laws, regulations and administrative procedures and the rules, procedures and practices applied by the entities contained in its lists annexed hereto, with the provisions of this agreement.

GPA parties, accordingly, have modified their procurement systems to bring them in line with the GPA. The sources of the EU public procurement system include the European Community (EC) Treaty,[44] the implementing Regulations, Directives and other communications issuing from the EC institutions, as well as their interpretation by the courts,

---

[42] See also the Commission's Green Paper, *European Strategy for Sustainable, Competitive and Secure Energy* COM (2006)105(final), p. 10.

[43] By Decision 94/800/EC of 22 December 1994 the Council, on behalf of the European Community, approved, *inter alia*, the WTO Agreement on Government Procurement. See P. Trepte, *Public Procurement in the EU: A Practitioner's Guide*, second edition (New York: Oxford University Press, 2007), p. 129.

[44] The EC Treaty refers to The Treaty of Rome 1957 as amended by the Single European Act 1986, the Treaty of Maastricht 1992, officially known as the Treaty of the European Union, the Treaty of Amsterdam 1997 and the Treaty of Nice 2001, published in O. J. C325/124.(12.2002 EN), available at www.europa.eu/eur-lex/pri/en/oj/dat/2002/c_325/c_32520021224en00010184.pdf

especially the European Court of Justice (ECJ). The current state of the EU public procurement law and especially in regard to green procurement could be found in the new Directives on Public Procurement. These are: Council Directive 2004/18/EC (Public Contracts Directive)[45] and Directive 2004/17/EC (Public Works Directive).[46] However, the legal basis for green public procurement in the EU was first established by the *integration rule* provided under Article 6 of the EC Treaty, which says:

> [e]nvironmental requirements must be integrated into the definition *and implementation* of other Community policies in particular with a view to promoting sustainable development. (emphasis added)

Article 6 above imposes a 'legal obligation'[47] upon Member States to incorporate environmental considerations into their public procurement and other policies. This principle was then incorporated into the new Directives which explicitly provided for the inclusion of environmental criteria in public procurement. The Public Contracts Directive in Article 23(3)(a) provides that procurement authorities are to define their technical specifications, *inter alia*, 'by reference to technical specifications as defined in Annex VI' and to certain technical standards. Under Annex VI paragraph 1(a) 'technical specification' (for public supply or services contracts) is defined as:

> [a] specification in a document defining the required characteristics of a product or service, such as quality levels, *environmental performance levels*, design for all requirements, [and] ... *production processes and methods*.[48] (emphasis added)

This provision re-enforced an earlier Directive[49] the purpose of which was 'to promote an increase in the contribution of renewable energy

---

[45] Directive 2004/18/EC of 31 March 2004 on the co-ordination of procedures for the award of public works contracts, public supply contracts and public service contracts, published in O. J. 2004 L134/114.

[46] Directive 2004/17/EC of the European Parliament and of the Council of 31 March 2004 co-ordinating the procurement procedures of entities operating in the water, energy, transport and postal services sectors, published in O. J. 2004 L134/1.

[47] See the Opinion of the Advocate General Jacobs in Case C-379/98 *PreussenElektra AG* v. *Schleswag AG* [2001] ECR I-2099, paragraph 231.

[48] A similar definition is provided by Annex XXI of Directive 2004/17 EC.

[49] Directive 2001/77/EC on the promotion of electricity produced from renewable energy sources in the internal electricity market, published in O.J. 2001 L283/33.

sources to electricity production in the internal market for electricity and to create a basis for a future Community framework'.[50]

Similarly, Directive 2004/17 explicitly states under recital nine that its provisions are 'based on Court of Justice case-law, … on award criteria, which clarifies the possibilities, subject to some stated conditions, for the contracting entities to meet the needs of the public concerned, including *in the environmental and/or social area*' (emphasis added). The 'Court of Justice case-law' referred to by the Directive, is the ECJ decision in the two cases cited earlier, namely:

(a)  Case C-513/99 *Concordia Bus Finland Oy Ab* v. *Helsingin kaupunki and HKL-Bussiliikenne* judgment of the Court of Justice (17 September 2002) *(Finnish Buses)*; and

(b)  Case C-448/01, *Evn AG and Wienstrom Gmbh* v. *Austria/Stadtwerke Klagenfurt AG*, ECJ (4 December 2003) *(Wienstrom)*.[51]

In both cases, the main issue of contention was whether the term '*most economically advantageous*' used as a guiding principle in the assessment and award of public contract under the Directives (in this case Directive 92/50 and Directive 93/36) should include *non-economic* (or 'secondary') objectives of public procurement, and in this case, the environmental and social considerations. The ECJ reasoned that:

> Community legislation on public procurement does not preclude a contract-ing authority from applying, in the context of the assessment of the most economically advantageous tender for a contract for the supply of electricity, a criterion requiring that the electricity supplied be produced from renewable energy sources, provided that that criterion is linked to the subject matter of the contract, does not confer an unrestricted freedom of choice on the authority, is expressly mentioned in the contract documents or the contract notice, and complies with all the fundamental principles of Community law, in particular the principle of non-discrimination.[52]

This in effect is also an affirmation of the earlier EC interpretative communication[53] which sought to clarify the extent to which, pursuant

---

[50]  *Ibid.*, Article 1. The Directive specifically provided for the Member States of the EU to seek to purchase a greater percentage of green electricity from suppliers.

[51]  See G. van Calster's ECJ cases' review, ECJ 4 December 2003, Case C-448/01, *EVN AG and Wienstrom Gmbh* v. *Austria/Stadtwerke Klagenfurt AG* (then not published in ECR) European Case Law Report, October 2003–March 2004 in *RECIEL* 13 (2) 2004 p. 4.

[52]  See Trepte, *supra* n. 43 p. 291.

[53]  The EC *Interpretative Communication of 4 July 2001 on the Community Law Applicable to Public Procurement and the Possibilities for Integrating Environmental Considerations into Public Procurement*, COM(2001)274.

to the earlier EC Directives, environmental considerations could be included in the tendering process. This thus establishes more firmly that the objectives of energy policy and those of environmental protection (climate change mitigation) as well as public procurement can be, and are indeed complementary under the EU system.

### 3.2 The EU green electricity procurement and the PPMs debate

For the EU, the power generation sector is the priority[54] area targeted for its climate policy and GHG emissions reduction efforts. The EU power sector accounts for a major proportion of these emissions: over 50 per cent of EU electricity comes from fossil fuels, mainly coal, which accounts for about 30 per cent of overall electricity generation in the EU.[55] In 2005 $CO_2$ emissions from coal-based electricity generation accounted for 70 per cent of total $CO_2$ emissions due to electricity generation in the EU, and 24 per cent of $CO_2$ emissions from all sectors taken together.[56]

The basis of the EU green electricity procurement is EC Directive 2001/77[57] the purpose of which is 'to promote an increase in the contribution of renewable energy sources to electricity production in the internal market for electricity and to create a basis for a future Community framework'.[58] The Directive explicitly recognises 'the need to promote renewable energy sources *as a priority* measure given that their exploitation contributes *inter alia* to environmental protection, sustainable development, security of supply and to the meeting of Kyoto targets'.[59] The Directive thus required Member States to set

---

[54] See infra n. 59.

[55] See Commission of the European Communities Communication from the Commission to the Council and the European Parliament, *Sustainable Power Generation from Fossil Fuels: Aiming for Near-zero Emissions from Coal After 2020*, (Brussels, 10 January 2007, COM(2006)843final) (summary at http://europa.eu/scadplus/leg/en/lvb/l27068.htm). It states that worldwide, emissions from coal-fired power generation amount to approximately eight billion tonnes of $CO_2$ per year.

[56] *Ibid.*

[57] Directive 2001/77/EC of 27 September 2001 on the promotion of electricity produced from renewable energies sources in the internal electricity market O.J. 2001 L283/33 (Renewables Directive). (The date for the implementation of this Directive was October 2003 and for the new Member States, 1 May 2004.) See also P. Del Rio and M. Gual, 'The promotion of green electricity: Europe's present and future' (2004) 14(4) *European Environment* 219.

[58] Renewables Directive, Article 1.

[59] *Ibid.*, recital 1. Recital 2 also identifies the promotion of electricity from renewable sources as a 'high priority' area.

national indicative targets for the consumption of electricity produced from renewable sources,[60] and to 'take appropriate steps to encourage greater consumption of electricity produced from renewable sources in conformity' with those targets.[61] Article 3(2) of the Directive emphasises that the targets should be consistent with the Community's climate change commitments under the Kyoto Protocol.[62]

This Directive thus requires Member States to tailor their electricity production and consumption in such a way as to favour green electricity over the conventional type which is generated from coal and other fossil-based sources. The issue for trade law is that the two types of electricity are indistinguishable in terms of physical characteristics and performance, and differ only in their processes and production methods (PPMs).

Following the ECJ decisions cited earlier, and the passing of the new Directives, the legality of green procurement is generally less disputable under EU law. What may still be problematic under the GPA is the *green electricity* procurement, in view of the provisions against discrimination under Article III. Thus, in view of the obligation on the GPA members to ensure the compatibility of their procurement systems with the GPA, it is incumbent upon the EU to ensure that the practice of green procurement which discriminates between 'like' products will also be justifiable under the Article XXIII of the GPA exceptions. However, it is necessary first to determine whether green electricity and conventional electricity are 'like' products which would warrant the application of the WTO rule against non-discrimination between them.

### 3.2.1   The 'like products' question

First, the GPA does not use the term 'like products', a term found in the GATT and many other WTO Agreements.[63] Professor Geert van Calster

---

[60] *Ibid.* Article 3 and recital 5.

[61] *Ibid.* Article 1(1). See also J. Zerk, 'Renewables obligation (the requirement that electricity suppliers supply a percentage of their electricity from renewable sources' (2006) *Environmental Information Bulletin* 160, 12–14. See similarly, A. Gunst, 'Impact of European law on the validity and tenure of national support schemes for power generation from renewable energy sources' *JENRL* 23 (2005)2 95–119.

[62] Article 3(2) and recital 6.

[63] For instance, Professor Jackson lists ten GATT provisions: Articles I:1, II:2(a), III:2, III:4, VI:1 (a,b), IX:1, XI:2(c), XIII:1, XVI:4, (J. Jackson, *World Trade and the Law of GATT*, Charlottesville, Va.: The Michie Company, 1969), p. 259, n. 1). Similarly, the 1970 Working Party on Border Tax Adjustments reported that the phrase 'like or similar products' appears sixteen times in the text of the GATT. See BISD, 18th Supp. 97, 101 (1972). See also R. E. Hudec, ' "Like product": the differences in meaning in GATT Articles I and III,' p. 1, in

opines, however, that this term is implicit also in the GPA. This is because the notion of non-discrimination 'requires *like* situations to be treated alike, while … *unlike* situations not be treated alike'.[64] Indeed, he sees the inclusion of the 'likeness' term in the other WTO Agreements as 'superfluous'![65] Consequently, and for the purpose of present analysis, the *likeness* notion is taken as implied in the said provisions of the GPA.[66] It is beyond the scope of this paper to query the wisdom behind the WTO legislation for this omission, even where consistency should be ensured especially as the issue concerns the basic objectives of the multilateral trading rules, namely, national treatment and non-discrimination. Even though the term featured in several provisions of the WTO Agreements it was nowhere defined, hence the difficulty in interpreting it. One could thus think that its omission from the GPA was intended to avoid the controversy and difficulty experienced by various GATT/WTO judicial panels in determining the meaning of the term, especially when interpreting Article III of the GATT on national treatment.

The Report of the 1970 Working Party on Border Tax Adjustment[67] has commonly been cited by the GATT/WTO panels as a guide to the determination of likeness of products. This report first stated that problems arising from the interpretation of the term should be examined on a 'case-by-case basis', to allow for 'a fair assessment in each case of the different elements that constitute a "similar" ['like'] product'. It then suggested some guiding criteria for making this determination, namely '[(i)] the product's end-uses in a given market; [(ii)] consumers' tastes and habits, which change from country to country; [(iii)] the product's properties, nature and quality'.[68] But the panel in *Spain — Unroasted Coffee*[69] did not use the

T. Cottier, and P. Mavroidis (eds.), *Regulatory Barriers and the Principle of Non-Discrimination in World Trade Law* (University of Michigan Press, 2000), pp. 101–23.

[64] See G. van Calster, supra n. 13.    [65] *Ibid.* at p. 301.

[66] Similarly observed is the omission by the GPA of the term 'directly competitive' which might have made the 'like' term unnecessary. See M. Cossy, 'Determining "likeness" under the GATS: squaring the circle?' 4 (Staff Working Paper ERSD-2006-08 WTO, September 2006). On the other hand, Professor Desta believes, and I agree, that the omission of the term 'like' in Article III of the GPA seems to impose an even stricter non-discrimination obligation on the GPA parties, namely that they are required not to discriminate between goods or services regardless of whether they indeed are technically 'like' or not. (Student-Supervisor discussion: 28 May 2008).

[67] See Working Party Report, Border Tax Adjustment, adopted 2 December 1970, BISD 18S/97. The 1970 BTA Working Party reviewed the application of Article III of the GATT.

[68] *Ibid.*, at paragraph 18.

[69] *Spain — Tariff Treatment Of Unroasted Coffee 1981 GATTPD Lexis* 5 (report of the panel adopted on 11 June 1981) *(L/5135 — 28S/102).*

*consumers' tastes and habits* criterion; it introduced 'tariff classification' regimes of other WTO Members as an additional criterion for determining likeness within the meaning of Article I:1 of the GATT.

Similarly, the AB in *EC — Asbestos*, faced with determining whether different asbestos products were 'like' under Article III:4, referred first to a dictionary meaning of the term 'like', which suggested that 'like products' were products that shared a number of characteristics. The AB, emphasising also the 'case-by-case'[70] approach, suggested that three questions of interpretation need to be resolved in order to determine whether products are like, namely:

(a) which characteristics or qualities are important in assessing 'likeness';
(b) to what degree or extent must products share qualities or characteristics in order to be 'like products'; and
(c) from whose perspective should likeness be judged?[71]

In all cases, however, the PPMs used in making the goods or performance of the services in question played a decisive role in determining whether the products are regarded as 'like' or 'unlike'. Hence, the fact that green and conventional electricity are the same in terms of physical design and characteristics as well as performance may or may not necessarily make them the same thing if the PPMs are taken into consideration, and this thus determines what rules are applicable to interpret the two.

### 3.2.2   The PPMs debate

PPMs have equally been a subject of heated debate in the GATT/WTO system. It all depends on the extent to which the processes and methods applied in producing a product are or should be relevant in determining whether one product is like, or substitutable for, the other under consideration. PPMs can be 'product-related', that is they are discernible in the final physical characteristic of the product, or 'non-product-related' not discernible in the final product. The WTO law applies different rules to these two classes of PPMs. The significance of the debate lies in the need to understand when a measure (by which two products or services

---

[70] See *EC — Asbestos* supra n. 30. See also L. Steenkamp, 'Complexities and inadequacies relating to certain provisions of the General Agreement on Trade in Services (GATS)', available at http://wto.tralac.org/pdf/WP_1_04_-_Complexities_and_inadequacies_rela ting_to_certain_provisions_of_the_GATS.doc, accessed 11 August 2007.
[71] See AB in *EC — Asbestos*, paragraph 92, supra n. 30.

are treated differently) can be regarded as discriminatory or protectionist and run into conflict with the non-discrimination rules of the WTO system.[72]

The PPMs issue usually features in procurement tender notices, where technical specifications are outlined for the products or services or suppliers required. Article VI of the GPA says:

> technical specifications laying down the characteristics of the products or services to be procured, such as quality, performance, safety and dimensions, symbols, terminology, packaging, marking and labelling, or the processes and methods for their production and requirements relating to conformity assessment procedures prescribed by procuring entities, *shall not be prepared, adopted or applied with a view to, or with the effect of, creating unnecessary obstacles to international trade.*[73] (emphasis added)

Article VI:2 of the GPA also provides that technical specifications prescribed by procuring entities shall, where appropriate:

(a) be in terms of performance rather than design or descriptive characteristics; and
(b) be based on international standards,[74] where such exist; otherwise, on national technical regulations, recognized national standards,[75] or building codes.

Thus the requirement under paragraph (a) above concerns the physical characteristics as well as the intrinsic value of the product or service procured. Paragraph (b) on the other hand relates to the *source* which forms the basis of the product specifications. The conditions under both (a) and (b) are subject to the overriding requirement that they should not create an 'unnecessary obstacle to international trade'.

As regards the PPMs question, footnote 3 to Article VI of the GPA defines a 'technical regulation' to mean:

---

[72] For detailed analysis on PPMs including country-base measures, see R. Howse and R. Regan, 'The product/process distinction — an illusory basis of disciplining "unilateralism" in trade policy' in *EJIL* 11 (2000) 249–89. See also, for a discourse on like product/service process under GATS: M. Cossy, supra n. 66.

[73] Article VI:1 of the GPA.    [74] Article VI:2(b) of the GPA.

[75] Footnotes 3 and 4 to Article VI of the GPA define 'technical regulations' as 'a document which lays down characteristics of a product or a service or their related processes and production methods, including the applicable administrative provisions, *with which compliance is mandatory*', while a 'standard' is 'a document approved by a recognized body, that provides, for common and repeated use, rules, guidelines or characteristics for products or services or related processes and production methods, *with which compliance is not mandatory*' (emphasis added).

[a] document which lays down characteristics of a product or a service or their *related* processes and production methods, including the applicable administrative provisions, *with which compliance is mandatory*. It may also include or deal exclusively with terminology, symbols, packaging, marking or labelling requirements as they apply to a product, service, *process or production method.* (emphasis added)

This definition refers to *related* processes and production methods (PPMs). The implication of this express mention of *related* PPMs may be seen in its potential to suggest that climate-friendly and energy security-motivated standard-setting for products may not be justified where such measures result in differential treatment being given to otherwise 'like products'[76] as they are not identifiable in the end products.

On the other hand, under the EU law, procurement authorities are permitted to include technical specifications that also define 'the required characteristics of a product or service, such as quality levels, *environmental performance levels*, design for all requirements, [and] ... *production processes and methods'.*[77] PPMs are nowhere defined in the relevant Directives, and there has been no judicial interpretation so far to guide the extent of the application of these provisions. Thus, the EU energy contracting authorities feel empowered to specify electricity produced from renewable energy sources.[78]

---

[76] The notion of 'like products', however, is not express in the GPA. See van Calster, Geert, supra n. 13.

[77] A similar definition is provided by Annex VI, paragraph 1(a) for public works contracts.

[78] See *Buying Green!* supra n. 5. Two practical examples were cited and are reproduced here on how this was achieved in two EU jurisdictions, thus:

> [1] At the beginning of 2002, Sheffield Hallam University in the UK decided to cover 5% of their electricity demand with green electricity and awarded the contract to a green electricity supplier. The purchase of 5% of their electricity [from a green supplier] has enabled the University to lower their carbon emissions by approximately 1.5 to 2% a (sic) year. Further energy efficiency measures will bring this figure to 3%, which is the annual target of the university. More information at: Local Sustainability Case Description, at www3.iclei.org/egpis/egpc-059.html
>
> [2] Nearly all public buildings and street lighting in South-East Brabant in the Netherlands are powered by green electricity. In March 2002, 21 municipalities in the Eindhoven Co-operation Region signed a contract with a supplier to obtain green electricity for 75% of their consumption, representing about 29 million kWh. The municipalities banded together in order to obtain a better price from the utility. As well as the environmental improvement, the negotiated contract offers a cost saving of €620,000 over previous contracts.

It could therefore be observed that insofar as permission for the inclusion of environment-related PPMs at the *production* stage is concerned, both the GPA and the EU law are agreeable. And to that extent, the procurement of green electricity produced from renewable sources is lawful. What is, however, potentially in dispute is the extent to which the PPMs can affect the characteristics of the product at the *consumption* stage so as to warrant a differential treatment between the two types of electricity products. In other words, does this indicate that technical specifications should define or relate to the product at the stage of its *production* rather than at that of its *consumption* (end product and performance) stage?

Traditionally, the WTO system of which the GPA is a part does not allow for a distinction between products to be made on the basis of PPMs (except where these are evident in the end product). This seems to favour the interpretation that product specification should define the product at its *consumption* rather than *production* stage. The pertinent question is whether environment-related PPMs and in particular those related to generation of electricity from renewable sources affect the nature of the product so as to make it different at (i) the production stage, or (ii) consumption stage. As observed earlier and confirmed by EU documents,[79] green electricity is only different from conventional electricity at the production stage (which is irrelevant under the traditional WTO jurisprudence) and absolutely identical at consumption stage.

It is thus clear that the practice which permits preference of green electricity over conventional electricity is contradictory in the sense that the two kinds of electricity are the same at the consumption (end product) stage, even if the processes are different. This is also regardless of the cost element, namely that green electricity, in view of the PPM is more costly to the tax payer.

The principal reason under the WTO for disallowing differential treatment between products based on non-product-related PPMs is that since the goods on their face value and quality are the same and substitutable in terms of their use and performance, then there is no basis for discriminating between them. It may simply be a disguised protectionism. Again, as the PPMs standards vary between countries and processes, it would be impossible, for regulatory purposes, to set a limit of how or which process is acceptable and which is not, and/or from which country or source.

---

[79] e.g. *Buying Green!* supra n. 5.

But in the case of the EU green electricity procurement, the concern simply, as Professor Howse[80] would have it, is the climate protection. Public authorities are the consumers in the case of government procurement. The perception of the public authorities in the EU is that green electricity performs a particular function which conventional electricity does not, namely, helping to reduce GHG emissions. This position is reinforced by the fact that reduction of GHG emissions is a legally binding commitment by the EU under the climate treaties.

### 3.3   Green electricity procurement v. the EU climate policy objectives

#### 3.3.1   Policy preference v. technical legality

Preferential green energy procurement may technically be discriminatory, and also costlier for the tax payer.[81] This is, however, beside the point. The issue in the EU has more to do with policy consideration and preference: green procurement serves the (climate change and energy security) policy objectives of the EU and other Kyoto parties. Thus green electricity procurement would still be acceptable regardless also of the additional initial cost to society at large. Indeed, earlier in *PreussenElektra AG* v. *Schleswag AG*,[82] the ECJ, relying on the integration principle of Article 6 of the EC Treaty, stated:

> [t]he use of renewable energy sources for producing electricity … is useful for protecting the environment in so far as it contributes to the reduction of greenhouse gases which are amongst the main causes of climate change which the European Community and its Member States have pledged to combat.[83]

Of course, the usual conditions imposed by the ECJ judgment in the *Finnish Buses* and *Wienstrom* cases still firmly apply.[84] This position is valid as between the EU Member States. However, this may not hold in

---

[80] See R. Howse, supra n. 72, at pp. 279–80, where he argued that it is a 'misconception' to suggest that all process-based product distinction is, or, is meant to be 'protectionism'.

[81] It is arguable also that from the end-consumer point of view, green electricity procurement also encourages energy efficiency which results in energy saving, hence, cost saving, in the long run.

[82] Case C-379/98 *PreussenElektra AG* v. *Schleswag AG* [2001] ECR I-2099 (*PreussenElektra* case). See also P. Kunzlik, 'Green procurement under the new regime' in *The New EU Public Procurement Directives* (Copenhagen: Djof Publishing, 2005), pp. 130–1; P. Trepte, supra n. 43, at p. 291.

[83] *PreussenElektra* case, paragraph 73.    [84] See supra section 3.1.

relations between the EU and third countries (other members of the GPA). Thus, in the event of a complaint being brought before the WTO Dispute Settlement Body (DSB), the EU has the challenge of placing the measure well under the exceptions.

### 3.3.2 Green electricity procurement and the general exceptions

The general exceptions provided for under Article XXIII of the GPA could be resorted to in order to justify the green electricity procurement policy. Discussion on the said GPA provisions has already appeared in section 2.3 of this paper. This section considers how green electricity may be argued under the exceptions, and draws some analogy from the *EC — Asbestos* case.[85] Thus:

(a) **The peculiarity of the nature of electricity as the subject-matter**   Related to the production/consumption argument for green electricity production and supply, it is difficult to discern the source from which a particular amount of electricity is produced and fed into the grid, or supplied to a particular consumer — unless the whole of it is generated from one source and fed into one grid from which consumers are supplied. Thus, to stick to the traditional rule disallowing differentiation on the basis of PPMs in the case of green electricity is futile. This consideration then may make the procurement of green electricity justifiable under the GPA exceptions.

(b) **Green electricity procurement and the ruling in EC — Asbestos**   The issue in the AB's report in *EC — Asbestos* was France's ban (under Decree No. 96–1133) on imported asbestos (and products containing asbestos). The AB regarded this as a 'technical regulation' and thus covered by the TBT, because, *inter alia*, the products in question were identifiable by reference to their characteristics. The AB, having agreed with the panel that the measure 'protects human life or health' and that 'no reasonably available alternative measure' existed, upheld the panel's finding that the ban was justified as an exception under Article XX(b) of the GATT.[86] The 'necessity' condition was thus satisfied by the particular finding of the unavailability of any alternative applicable measure in the

---

[85]   By extension also, the rules in many other GATT/WTO cases cited, some of which have been cited in section 2.3.

[86]   See AB report in *EC — Asbestos*, supra n. 34.

circumstances. The AB also accepted that measure ultimately satisfied the conditions of the Article XX chapeau.

By analogy, and as informed also by the spirit of the AB report in *US — Shrimp* cited earlier, the author is inclined to opine that preference given for green electricity over conventional electricity in the EU, even if discriminatory and thus contrary to Article III of the GPA, could be justified as being taken ultimately to reduce GHG emissions, hence, environmental protection under Article XXIII of the GPA.

## 4.    Conclusion

Green procurement is a 'necessary' measure in the context of the EU because 'action on renewables and energy efficiency, besides tackling climate change, will contribute to [the EU] security of energy supply and help limit … dependence on imported energy'.[87] It may also be regarded as necessary for the following reasons:

- The huge impact of fossil-based electricity on climate change is a global problem. It is thus an area where actions to reduce GHG emissions should be encouraged.
- The EU's ambitious Kyoto target and the leading role it plays in the fight against climate change requires the adoption of more available domestic measures and strategies to enable it to meet the challenge.
- The high annual EU-wide budget on procurement means that it is a wise idea to pursue other 'secondary objectives', the most prominent of which in the case of EU policy priorities, are climate change mitigation objectives.
- The complex nature of electricity which makes it difficult to determine, at the level of the consumption, which 'part' of the electricity was generated from what sources, thus making the related and non-related PPMs arguments futile.

But whether green procurement could be covered under Article XXIII of the GPA exceptions is a practical issue, and there has not been a pertinent case brought before the WTO DSB. However, because green procurement is increasingly gaining ground, and the current revision of the GPA is giving explicit permission for green procurement, coupled with the fact

---

[87] See also the Commission's Green Paper, *European Strategy for Sustainable, Competitive and Secure Energy* COM (2006)105final, p. 10.

that more members are joining the GPA, there is a clear potential for abuse of the opportunity which could trigger litigation.

The express permission for green procurement under the current review of the GPA is a welcome development. However, it still remains to be seen when the WTO system will reshape the rules, especially those on PPMs, explicitly to allow special considerations (under the exceptions) for climate/energy-related discriminatory procurement measures. With this, the WTO system would then be making a huge contribution to the global climate change mitigation efforts, and establishing synergy out of the fragmented system.

# 18

# Procurement and the World Trade Organization: purchase power or pester power?

GEERT VAN CALSTER[1]

Bringing government procurement within WTO disciplines has obvious benefits. Governments' purchase of goods and services in itself has considerable economic value.[2] Moreover, in their purchase decisions, governments and authorities in general (mis)lead by example. Counting government, regional and local authorities as clients for one's business often amounts to a stamp of approval and helps foster sales to private clients. Government procurement is largely exempt from GATT and GATS disciplines.[3] Interestingly, the original US draft for the Charter on the International Trade Organization (ITO Charter) would have made government procurement subject to most-favoured-nation and national

---

[1] Based on the author's paper delivered at the World Trade Forum 2007 (International Trade on a Warming Globe), World Trade Institute, Bern, Switzerland, September 2007.

[2] For instance, in the European Union, public authorities spend around 16 per cent of Europe's GDP: European Commission, *Buying Green! A Handbook on Environmental Public Procurement* (Brussels: European Communities, 2004). Available at http://ec. europa.eu/environment/gpp/pdf/buying_green_handbook_en.pdf

[3] Article III:8(a) of the GATT: 'The provisions of this Article shall not apply to laws, regulations or requirements governing the procurement by governmental agencies of products purchased for governmental purposes and not with a view to commercial resale or with a view to use in the production of goods for commercial sale.' Note that this language indicates that tax measures leading to prejudice in public procurement are caught by Article III:2 of the GATT and the most-favoured nation principle of Article I of the GATT: see in particular the *Belgian Family Allowances* panel, 1952, G/32 — 1S/59.

Article XVII:2 of the GATT (state trading enterprises): 'The provisions of paragraph 1 of this Article shall not apply to imports of products for immediate or ultimate consumption in governmental use and not otherwise for resale or use in the production of goods* for sale.'

Article XIII:2 of the GATT: 'Articles II, XVI and XVII shall not apply to laws, regulations or requirements governing the procurement by governmental agencies of services purchased for governmental purposes and not with a view to commercial resale or with a view to use in the supply of services for commercial sale.' Article II refers to most-favoured-nation, Article XVI to market access and Article XVII to national treatment.

treatment obligations. The London draft charter, however, deleted the relevant proviso from the text, 'as it appears to the Preparatory Committee that an attempt to reach agreement on such a commitment would lead to exceptions almost as broad as the commitment itself'.[4] Procurement is moreover not the only area where the ITO Charter (at draft or final stage) would have already incorporated the so-called 'Singapore' issues into the multilateral trading system long before the European Union (EU) in particular started its attempts to bring them within the remit of the WTO.[5] With climate change concerns appearing on the horizon of most WTO Members (and firmly entrenched in some, including of course the EU), the scope for and use of so-called 'green' procurement has increased dramatically. This contribution will reflect on this development within the general context of the attempts at recruiting more WTO Members to the WTO Agreement on Government Procurement (GPA).[6]

As environmental awareness diversifies, so too does the matrix of green/environmental issues which authorities may potentially seek to include in their purchasing policies. Procuring printers which have double-sided printing as the default option is one thing (and not legally controversial, if only because of the direct economic savings for the authorities) — insisting on, say, buying GM-free coffee beans from Oxfam fair trade accredited farmers in countries enjoying the benefits of the generalised system of preferences (GSP)+ for having signed up to the Kyoto Protocol, quite another.

In this contribution, I shall not conduct a systematic legal analysis of the ins and outs of the GPA and how that affects green procurement, in particular in the area of climate change.[7] Rather, I shall attempt

---

[4] *London Report*, p. 9, paragraph (d)(iv), as quoted in WTO, *Guide to GATT Law and Practice* (Geneva: WTO and Bernan Press, 1995), vol. 1, p. 190.

[5] Competition policy is another: see the 'restrictive business practices' chapter of the Havana Charter.

[6] Readers will be aware that the GPA is one of two so-called 'plurilateral' agreements that currently exist within the WTO, i.e. agreements which WTO Members are not under an obligation to adhere to (as an exception to the single package rule). The other is the Agreement on Trade in Civil Aircraft.

[7] See Garba Malumfashi's contribution to this forum; see also J. Earley, *Green Procurement in Trade Policy*, Background Report for the Commission for Environmental Co-operation (2003). Available at www.cec.org/files/PDF/ECONOMY/green-procurement-in-trade% 20Policy_en.pdf, last visited 17 September 2007; and see also G. van Calster, 'Green Procurement and the WTO — Shades of Grey', *RECIEL* 11 (2002), 298–305.

to highlight some concerns or challenges which may help in considering the issues.

## 1.  'Green' procurement and the principle of sustainable development

Without wanting to over-complicate the debate, it would seem that the practice of 'green' procurement often unjustifiably focuses on the environmental gains, rather than on the concept of sustainable development[8] as a whole. The origin of the principle is well known, at least in its most visible format, as emanating from the World Commission on Environment and Development, better known by reference to its chair — Dr Gro Harlem Brundtland — as the Brundtland Commission. Its work led to the definition of sustainable development as development 'that meets the needs of the present without compromising the ability of future generations to meet their own needs'.[9] Although not all that evident from the Brundtland report, the sustainable development principle has for some time been seen as a three-tier concept, encompassing ecological, social and economic development. Especially in the 1990s, the principle of sustainable development was often understood in a condensed meaning. Politicians and international negotiators alike (let alone members of the public) effectively equated sustainable development with environmental protection. This led to an explosion in international environmental treaties in the 1990s, and eventually to a re-orientation at the 2002 Johannesburg Summit on Sustainable Development.[10] The Action Plan adopted at the Johannesburg Summit, under pressure from developing countries, firmly took the more or less exclusive focus on environmental protection which had occurred during the 1990s back to the three pillar approach as initially intended.[11]

---

[8] Principle 3 of the Rio Declaration: 'The right to development must be fulfilled so as to equitably meet developmental and environmental needs of present and future generations.' Note that not only Star Trek suffers from split infinitives.

[9] United Nations. 1987. *Report of the World Commission on Environment and Development*. General Assembly Resolution 42/187, 11 December 1987: see www.un. org/documents/ga/res/42/ares42-187.htm. Readers will be aware that the WTO Agreement includes a reference to the principle in its preamble; this has been recalled by a number of WTO dispute settlement reports.

[10] Called ten years after the 1992 Rio de Janeiro Conference, which can rightly be seen as the cradle of a large part of current international environmental agreements.

[11] See Report of the World Summit on Sustainable Development, Johannesburg, South Africa, A/CONF.199/20. Available at http://daccessdds.un.org/doc/UNDOC/GEN/N02/636/93/PDF/N0263693.pdf?OpenElement.

Consequently, a pure focus on 'green' procurement does not do justice to the sustainable development principle which underlies it. Indeed the principle implies a balancing act which inevitably often rules out full environmental return on a given decision: the other two pillars of the principle may not necessarily lead to the same decision. Hence 'development', in the sense of economic development, which lies at the core of current negotiations in the WTO, likewise acts as a flashpoint in 'green' procurement.

The European Commission, in its *Handbook on Green Procurement*[12] — which may be regarded as the global pinnacle of such initiatives — would not entirely seem to appreciate the tension between the three pillars. Indeed the Handbook does not define 'green' procurement, however it firmly clarifies that what it discusses is the environmental performance of the goods and services at issue. Sustainable development is flagged as a contextual part of the debate, without the Commission considering the inherent tensions.

The points made above are not meant as the legal muttering of a regulatory lawyer. The renewed emphasis on the three parts of sustainable development acts as an important driving force in the current development of international environmental law, and may have a knock-on effect on international trade law. Discussions surrounding the Kyoto Protocol to the UNFCCC[13] serve as a good reminder of the impact of the re-orientation. For instance, at a press conference to mark the launch of its June 2007 national climate change programme,[14] the chairman of China's National Development and Reform Commission firmly emphasised China's priority for economic development, in line — so he argued — with the principle of common but differentiated responsibility.[15, 16] China has ratified the Kyoto Protocol — which gives it the

---

[12] n. 2 above.     [13] The United Nations Framework Convention on Climate Change.

[14] http://en.ndrc.gov.cn/newsrelease/P020070604561191006823.pdf, visited 13 September 2007.

[15] Principle 7 Rio Declaration:

> States shall cooperate in a spirit of global partnership to conserve, protect and restore the health and integrity of the Earth's ecosystem. In view of the different contributions to global environmental degradation, States have common but differentiated responsibilities. The developed countries acknowledge the responsibility that they bear in the international pursuit of sustainable development in view of the pressures their societies place on the global environment and of the technologies and financial resources they command.

[16] As reported by the BBC: http://news.bbc.co.uk/2/hi/asia-pacific/6717671.stm, revisited 13 September 2008; and CBC: www.cbc.ca/world/story/2007/06/04/china-climate-070603.html, visited 12 September 2007.

right, for the time being, actually to increase emissions of a number of key greenhouse gases. Hence, say, an indirect climate tax (arguably this would be a customs duty, really[17]) levied by the European Union on the imports of products from China,[18] would face serious hurdles under the WTO regime, not least on the basis of the very principle of sustainable development which would underpin its introduction.

## 2.   Warring acronyms: NPR and PR-PPMs

### 2.1   WTO suspicion of NPR-PPMs: wrong reasoning, but the right outcome

A recurring issue within the debate on regulatory autonomy relates to so-called PR- and NPR-PPMs: product-related and non-product related processes and production methods. PR-PPMs are those PPMs which are directly (physically) linked to the final product: e.g. spray-painting a car with hazardous metals will lead to hazardous metals being present in the car; using hexavalent chrome in a DVD player will lead to that player containing the chrome, etc. NPR-PPMs by contrast are not physically linked to the final product: e.g. the car will not give away the amount of carbon dioxide ($CO_2$) emitted into the atmosphere during its production; the DVD player will not tell you whether a twelve-year-old child or an adult was operating the machinery used in its manufacture.

Other contributions in this volume and indeed a wide range of academic literature discuss the ins and outs of the distinction.[19] Suffice it to point out here that ever since the GATT *Tuna — Dolphin* panel, the GATT and now the WTO have been extremely suspicious of WTO Members employing non-product related distinctions in their regulatory measures. I firmly believe that the reasoning adopted by that panel was flawed[20] and that the panel (and in this it is not alone) misread the

---

[17] See the author's contribution (in Dutch), 'K3: Klimaat, Kyoto, Klaagzang — Over (indirecte) belastingen en de Wereldhandelsorganisatie', in *Liber Amicorum Frans Vanistendael* (Knops Publishing, 2007), 279–84.

[18] In view *arguendo* of the inaction of China vis-à-vis climate change.

[19] See in particular, R. Howse and D. Regan, 'The product/process distinction — an illusory basis for disciplining "unilateralism" in trade policy', *EJIL*11 (2000), 249–89.

[20] It was based on a perceived need for an absolute symmetry between Article III:2 of the GATT (which contains the rules on tax measures within the GATT Agreement) and Article III:4 (which refers to other regulations — now to a large degree superseded by the TBT). See also G. van Calster, *International and EC Trade Law — the Environmental Challenge* (London: Cameron May, 2000), p. 427 ff.

context, aim and implications of the 1970 Working Party Report on Border Tax Adjustment (BTA).[21] Moreover, and with some implications for the current debate, the 1970 Report in fact contained two criteria for considering the likeness of products, which are if not necessarily linked to NPR-PPMs, then at the least open to NPR-PPMs: namely consumers' tastes and habits (consumers may very well distinguish between products on the basis of NPR-PPMs), and the end use in a given market.

Notwithstanding the faulty reasoning of the panel, I have in the meantime warmed to the idea of relocation of NPR-PPMs from Article III/XI to Article XX. In light of the evolving case law of the Appellate Body (AB) on the chapeau of Article XX, with more emphasis on a due process approach than on the specific nitty-gritty legal reasoning of the sub-paragraphs,[22] Article XX would seem better suited than Article III for weeding out abuse. Arguably, NPR-PPMs are more likely to lead to abuse and protectionism than PR-PPMs.

Now that the GATT seems to have moved NPR-PPMs firmly to the exceptions regime of Article XX, the question remains how other WTO Agreements deal with the issue.

## 2.2   NPR-PPMs in the GPA

Article VI of the GPA, which regulates the technical specifications which governments may employ in procurement,[23] itself raises the prospect of processes and production methods representing a potential technical

---

[21] e.g. the Working Party was not meant as the final and definitive GATT/WTO word on Border Tax Adjustment (BTA), rather as a stocktaking of the then current views of the Contracting Parties on BTA.

[22] See, *inter alia*, the author's 'The World Trade Organization panel report on *Brazil Tyres*: advanced waste management theory entering the organisation?', *European Environmental Law Review* 16 (2007), 304–8, and the review of the AB's decision: G. van Calster, '*Faites vos jeux* — regulatory autonomy and the World Trade Organization after *Brazil Tyres*', *Journal of Environmental Law* (2008), 121–36.

[23] '1.  Technical specifications laying down the characteristics of the products or services to be procured, such as quality, performance, safety and dimensions, symbols, terminology, packaging, marking and labelling, or the processes and methods for their production and requirements relating to conformity assessment procedures prescribed by procuring entities, shall not be prepared, adopted or applied with a view to, or with the effect of, creating unnecessary obstacles to international trade.

    2.  Technical specifications prescribed by procuring entities shall, where appropriate:

       (a) be in terms of performance rather than design or descriptive characteristics; and

       (b) be based on international standards, where such exist; otherwise, on national technical regulations, recognized national standards, or building codes.

specification (subject of course to the prohibition on creating unnecessary obstacles to trade). The Agreement includes a specific reference to 'related' PPMs in the footnotes to Article VI.2. Indeed, in footnote 3, 'technical regulation' is defined as 'a document which lays down characteristics of a product or a service or their related processes and production methods, including the applicable administrative provisions, with which compliance is mandatory. It may also include or deal exclusively with terminology, symbols, packaging, marking or labelling requirements as they apply to a product, service, process or production method'. Similar language is included for standards (which are not mandatory).

The qualification 'related' most definitely refers to product-incorporated PPMs, i.e. those PPMs which have a bearing on the physical characteristics of the finished products. There is some uncertainty as to whether the explicit reference to product-related PPMs in Article VI.2 either negates or on the contrary enforces the conclusion that non-product related PPMs are within the limits of Article VI.1 of the GPA. A legalistic analysis (the footnotes are part of Article VI.2 only; Article VI.2 itself recommends recourse to international standards and regulations only where this is 'appropriate') may clash with the presumed internal coherence of the various agreements. Indeed, it would be surprising should Members have introduced such a symbolically and substantially important 'concession' to the international environmental community, without ado and/or fierce preliminary debate. Moreover, the footnotes themselves state that the concept of standard and regulation which they put forward defines these 'for the purpose of this Agreement'.

Whatever the merits of the literal and/or contextual analysis of these provisions (for which there is as yet no authority in WTO dispute settlement), the confusion surrounding this issue underlines the importance of the third element present in Article VI: the prohibition of unnecessary obstacles to trade (Article VI.1 *in fine*). In the author's view, emphasis on this part of the GPA's test would be beneficial. It

3. There shall be no requirement or reference to a particular trademark or trade name, patent, design or type, specific origin, producer or supplier, unless there is no sufficiently precise or intelligible way of describing the procurement requirements and provided that words such as "or equivalent" are included in the tender documentation.

4. Entities shall not seek or accept, in a manner which would have the effect of precluding competition, advice which may be used in the preparation of specifications for a specific procurement from a firm that may have a commercial interest in the procurement.'

would arguably tap into the AB and panels' fairly advanced view on due process requirements and the like.

### 2.3 'Unnecessary obstacles to trade'

The GPA leaves 'unnecessary obstacles to trade' undefined. Some inspiration may be sought from other WTO Agreements (although one must not, of course, simply transfer conclusions from one Agreement to another).

### Compared with the provisions of the TBT

Article 2.2 of the Technical Barriers to Trade Agreement (TBT) provides that technical regulations are not to be regarded as unnecessary obstacles to trade if they are 'not more trade restrictive than necessary' to fulfil a 'legitimate objective'.

The TBT identifies environmental protection in so many words as a possible legitimate objective, with express reference to the 'end use' of a product. What should the necessity test consist of? As in the GPA, no express brief is given in the TBT. Article 2.2 of the TBT does add a specification. Whether the measures are not more trade restrictive than necessary to fulfil the legitimate objective concerned must be assessed 'taking account of the risks non-fulfilment would create'. In the absence of common risk management practice and standards, this does not help in clarifying the assessment. Indeed, who is to judge the severity of the risk?

The crucial issue which is to be resolved is whether the WTO, including the WTO Dispute Settlement Body, should perform a 'proportionality' test, whereby the level of protection would be offset against the trade restrictions which it entails.

The clearest clue to the drafters' intentions in the TBT is given in the preamble, where it states that a Member can take measures to protect national policy objectives 'at the levels it considers appropriate, subject to the requirement that they are not applied in a manner which would constitute a means of arbitrary or unjustifiable discrimination between countries where the same conditions prevail or a disguised restriction on international trade, and are otherwise in accordance with the provisions of this Agreement'. This wording is obviously inspired by the Headnote *Ad* Article XX of the GATT Agreement. It is not in fact repeated in the substantive provisions of the TBT. In the absence, however, of clearer guidance in the Agreement itself, the preamble comes closest to briefing future dispute settlement panels on how to interpret the prohibition of unnecessary obstacles to trade.

The preamble also adds the proviso that Members' measures should be 'otherwise in accordance with the provisions of this Agreement'. The issue is, however, precisely that the TBT does not indicate if and how the WTO institutions themselves are to reconsider the level of (*inter alia*, environmental) protection set by the Members.

In my view, such a test is neither welcome, nor included in the text of the Agreement. Not welcome, as it would take the WTO down the slippery slope of having to draft some sort of a hierarchy of national political choices; not included in the Agreement, because the Agreement does not question the level of the 'legitimate objective'. On the contrary, the TBT specifically adds, with respect to the adherence to existing international standards, that these need not be followed where they would be 'ineffective or inappropriate, for instance, because of an *insufficient level of protection* or fundamental climatic or geographical factors or fundamental technological problems' (emphasis added) (Code of Conduct, point F). This, arguably, amounts to a clear brief for states to determine their own level of desired protection.

Importantly, the TBT does not identify unquestionable scientific evidence as the only justification for standards or regulations. Precautionary action therefore is not a priori excluded. Even though scientific evidence may facilitate proof that no unnecessary obstacle to trade has been put in place, such proof is arguably not dependent upon the production of scientific evidence.

### Compared with the provisions of the SPS

Article 2.2 of the Sanitary and Phytosanitary Measures Agreement (SPS) obliges Members to 'ensure that any sanitary or phytosanitary measure is applied only to the extent necessary to protect human, animal or plant life or health'. Note 3 to Article 5, paragraph 6 adds that 'a measure is not more trade-restrictive than required unless there is another measure, reasonably available taking into account technical and economic feasibility, that achieves the appropriate level of sanitary or phytosanitary protection and is *significantly* less restrictive to trade' (emphasis added). The inclusion of 'significant' arguably gives more breathing space to the WTO Member that has put the measure in place. It is, however, doubtful whether the provisions of either the TBT or GPA can be interpreted through the wording specifically provided for in the SPS.

## The (lack of) provisions in the GPA

Article VI.1 does not offer any indication of the precise meaning of 'unnecessary obstacles to international trade'. There would not seem to be any immediate context which could be called upon to clarify the provision. In particular, while Article XXIII includes language which could be construed to provide clues in this respect, it would seem troublesome to refer to that article's provisions in a similar way to that described above, with respect to the TBT. Indeed, as noted, the preamble to the TBT recalls the non-discrimination test which takes inspiration from Article XX of the GATT. This wording having been included in the Agreement's preamble, one can arguably employ it so as to construe the exact meaning of the Agreement's provisions. This is a lot more cumbersome within the context of Article VI of the GPA. Indeed, Article XXIII offers a general escape clause for any practices with respect to government procurement, which are found to contravene the agreement otherwise.

Given that, as for the similar provision in the GATT, recourse to Article XXIII is only necessary (and possible) to the degree that an infringement of other articles of the Treaty is established, this means by default that some practices infringe upon Article VI, including its necessity test, and yet may pass the necessity test of the Agreement's Article XXIII. This observation may in effect render the test of Article VI of the GPA a rather strict one, offering less leeway than one may deduce at first sight. Again, however, there is no authority in WTO dispute settlement either to back up or to reject this claim.

### 2.4   The experience with NPR-PPMs in the European Community

Above I have argued that the insistence of Article VI of the GPA on the absence of unnecessary obstacles to trade, especially given the uncertainty surrounding the NPR-PPM issue, may well be the one crucial test which a Member has to undergo within the context of its room for manoeuvre in specifications of tenders. Two judgments of the European Court of Justice (ECJ) on the issue of preference for renewable sources of energy are often quoted as textbook examples of how the European Community (EC) balances the preservation of the internal market with modern regulatory requirements such as in the climate change field. These two judgments are *PreussenElektra*[24] and

---

[24] Case C-379/98, *PreussenElektra AG v. Schleswag AG* [2001] ECR I-2099.

*Outokumpu Oy*.[25] I shall briefly review them below, as their precedent value even in the EC itself needs to be handled with caution (especially in the case of *PreussenElektra*).

### *Outokumpu Oy*: strict interpretation of the non-discrimination requirement in EC law

Under Finnish legislation on the taxation of energy, excise duty on electricity is levied in Finland on electrical energy produced there, the amount of the duty depending on the method of production (the highest for electricity produced by nuclear power, lower for electricity produced by water power; for electricity produced by other methods, for example from coal, excise duty is charged on the basis of the amount of input materials used to produce the electricity; finally, for electrical energy produced by some methods, for example in a generator with an output below two megavolt-amperes, no excise duty at all is charged). On imported electricity, the excise duty charged, regardless of the method of production of the electricity, is a set duty, higher than the lowest excise duty chargeable on electricity produced in Finland, but lower than the highest excise duty chargeable on such electricity. The levying of excise duties determined on the basis of the method of production of the energy is founded on environmental grounds in the drafting history of the law.

The ECJ accepted the principle that the rate of an internal tax on electricity may vary according to the manner in which the electricity is produced and the raw materials used for its production, insofar as that differentiation is based on environmental considerations. However, it referred to earlier case law which states that Article 90 (this is the EC's almost identical version of GATT Article III) is infringed where the taxation on the imported product and that on the similar domestic product are calculated in a different manner on the basis of different criteria which lead, if only in certain cases, to higher taxation being imposed on the imported product. Practical difficulties in levying the same kind of tax, in particular because of the specific nature of electricity and the difficulty in determining the method of production of imported electricity, could not justify this breach of the article. The ECJ also seemed to attach particular weight to the fact that the Finnish legislation did not even give the importer the opportunity of demonstrating that the imported electricity had been produced by a particular method in order

---

[25] ECJ judgment of 2 April 1998 in Case C-213/96, *Outokumpu Oy* [1998] ECR I-1777.

to qualify for the rate applicable to electricity of domestic origin produced by the same method.

The ECJ's decision in *Outokumpu Oy* represents a strict interpretation
of the condition of non-discrimination: national legislation can only be
compatible with Article 90 if it excludes higher taxation of imported
products in all instances. This strict approach has subsequently been
confirmed, and represents a firm belief in a de facto interpretation of the
condition of non-discrimination, where the legislator's intent is
irrelevant.

The ECJ's attitude was less absolute in other instances. More specifically with respect to environmental taxation, the Advocate General (AG)
and the Finnish Government had pleaded for leniency in light of the
ecological objectives of the regulations and of technical difficulties relating to the nature of electricity.[26] The ECJ was in no mood for such special
treatment. Practical and technical difficulties were dismissed. The only
way out for the national authorities was to surrender the very system that
had led to inequality. Rather than imposing a tax, calculated as a national
average, Finland should have imposed the lowest tax rate on imported
products. Jacobs AG had suggested an improved version of the Finnish
technique, which would have imposed an average tax which was a better
reflection of the true proportion of Finnish products subject to the
various tax levels. It would have been amended on a regular basis, to
reflect changing consumption patterns.[27]

### *PreussenElektra*: questionable precedent value

The judgment in *PreussenElektra* concerned the German Feeding-in Act
1990 (*Stromeinspeisungsgesetz*), which aims to stimulate the production
of energy from renewable sources. The goal is electricity generated
exclusively from hydroelectric sources, wind energy, solar energy, gas
from waste dumps and sewage treatment plants, or products or residues
and biological waste from agriculture and forestry work.

The Act intervenes both on the demand side of the market and in the
price paid for the electricity concerned. Electricity supply undertakings
which operate a general supply network are obliged to purchase the
electricity produced in their area of supply from renewable sources of
energy and to pay a price for those inputs of electricity in accordance

---

[26] Once produced, it is impossible for the authorities to 'read', from the electricity presented, the production process that was used in manufacturing it.

[27] Opinion of Jacobs AG in Case C-213/96, *Outokumpu Oy*, at 61.

with a number of parameters. Depending on the latter, the minimum price to be paid varies between 65 and 90 per cent of the average sales price per kilowatt hour of electricity supplied to all final customers by electricity supply undertakings.

In a first instance, the Commission regarded the system as being an acceptable form of state aid, *inter alia*, in view of its relatively small impact (given the limited share of the energy concerned in the overall electricity market). However, in view of the increase in this share, the Commission was in the process of reviewing this decision. The state aid aspects of the case are less relevant here — what is of more interest to the international debate on climate change are the ECJ's findings on the free movement articles.

Given that distributors are obliged to purchase electricity produced within the territory in which they are active, there is no doubt that intra-Community trade is affected, at least potentially (ECJ judgment at 71). However, the ECJ found these restrictions to be justified, for two reasons: the aim of the regime (i.e. environmental protection) as well as the specific characteristics of the EC electricity market.

The environmental credentials of the regulations, as identified by the ECJ, were indeed rather impressive: the increased use of renewable sources of energy is a central part of the EC commitment to tackling climate change; this is obviously beneficial for the environment (one of the mandatory requirements of the ECJ's rule of reason) — it also fosters the life and health of humans, animals and plants (one of the exceptions provided for in Article 30 EC). The ECJ also refers to the integration principle of Article 6 of the EC Treaty, so as to emphasise the importance of an 'environmentally conscious' internal market. Finally, the Directive on the Internal Market in Electricity (Directive 96/62, O.J. 1997 L27/20) specifies that the Member States may give priority to the production of electricity from renewable sources of energy.

The recognition of the positive environmental impact of renewable energy is not surprising; neither is the consequential potential priority over the internal market principles. What is, however, more controversial is whether such hindrance of the internal market in the name of environmental protection and/or the life and health of humans, animals and plants is proportionate; in other words, whether there is no disproportionate impact on the internal market. The ECJ did not conduct a proportionality test.

*PreussenElektra* is especially noteworthy in that the ECJ's evaluation of the national measure within the context of Article 30 of the EC Treaty is milder than its similar considerations under Article 90 of the EC Treaty, in particular as compared to *Outokumpu Oy*. To be sure, *PreussenElektra* was arguably only a relevant precedent for as long as no reliable system of certificates of origin existed in the EC. Nevertheless, cases such as *PreussenElektra* would seem to adopt a softer stance on the proportionality test under Articles 28–30, especially within the context of climate change — effectively doing away with proportionality in these cases. That to me would not seem a feature of ECJ case law which the WTO should seek to emulate.

## 3.   The WTO and the positive harmonisation challenge

The WTO's set-up is deficient for dealing with the full spectrum of regulatory challenges. Typically, the end result of the interference of the WTO hence carries weight for the specific dispute at stake, however, strictly speaking does not go beyond the particulars of the specific case. The findings of the panel or the AB may serve as legal precedent to some degree, however, their immediate impact is ad hoc only. Having to seek rulings on an ad hoc basis is the result of the WTO not harmonising positively; it harmonises negatively. If one is to *avoid* tensions over unilateral regulatory regimes rather than 'simply' settling them on an individual basis, some kind of international minimum harmonisation is the only way forward. This holds true for the whole of the regulatory law of WTO Members, including procurement decisions on the basis of sustainability.

The WTO does not have the mandate or the personnel necessary to carry out any positive harmonisation task.[28] The introduction of common minimum standards within the WTO framework is not, however, per se untested. The Agreement on Trade-Related Aspects of Intellectual Property Rights Agreement (TRIPS), for instance, has introduced comprehensive obligations for the protection of private property rights by requiring substantive minimum standards for the availability, scope, use

---

[28] The dispute settlement rulings themselves are aware of the shortcomings of the ad hoc approach. panels and Appellate Body routinely refer to the need and preference for providing multilateral solutions to the regulatory concerns at issue. In more recent dispute settlements they go further, by insisting that where Members have to take recourse to the exceptions regime of the Agreements, they will not be granted the room for manoeuvre which they seek unless they have first actively sought to reach such a multilateral solution. Failure to engage in what the Appellate Body calls 'genuine negotiations', will now inevitably lead to failure of the recourse to this exceptions regime.

and protection of intellectual property rights. Upon signature of the Uruguay Round Agreements, ministers recognised that the TRIPS could serve as an approach that could also be used to harmonise domestic policy in other areas. The WTO Agreement itself, in Article III states that:

> the WTO shall provide the forum for the negotiations among its Members concerning their multilateral trade relations in matters dealt with under the [WTO Agreements]. The WTO may also provide a forum for further negotiations among its Members concerning their multilateral trade relations, and a framework for the implementation of the results of these negotiations, as may be decided by the Ministerial Conference.

Thus, there is arguably a brief for the WTO to step into a wide range of issues with a trade impact, including the co-ordination of environmental harmonisation efforts. However, it is clear that in practice, positive harmonisation as part of the solution to the trade and regulatory debate at the GATT/WTO level will not be done by the WTO itself. Rather the WTO should (and does) take proper account of the developments in other international fora, including the United Nations Environment Programme (UNEP), the International Organization for Standardization (ISO) (not an intergovernmental organisation, but a private one), the Food and Agriculture Organization of the United Nations (FAO), the International Maritime Organization (IMO), and the Organisation for Economic Co-operation and Development (OECD).

The above may be true; it does not, however, serve at the moment to ease the tensions over green or sustainable procurement: indeed examples of international, government-sanctioned standards for what are to be considered environmentally friendly goods or services[29] are, if not few and far between, then at least a minority. As expected, international consensus is more difficult to obtain for PPMs which are *not* integrated in the final product, as opposed to those which are.[30] To give but one, pertinent example: governments worldwide currently have a wide range of measures in place which encourage the production and consumption of so-called 'biofuels'. Yet in the absence of internationally agreed sustainability criteria for these fuels, their piecemeal encouragement at the moment arguably has no proven sustainable impact and indeed may even be counterproductive.[31]

---

[29] With complete 'sustainability' being an even harder challenge.
[30] More detail in n. 7 and section 2 above.
[31] See, e.g. R. Doornbosch and R. Steenblik, *Biofuels: Is the Cure Worse than the Disease?*, OECD Round Table on Sustainable Development (2007), SG/SD/RT(2007)3.

## 4. Private labels and their governance

Adding to the green procurement puzzle are private sustainability labels. The GPA provides that technical specifications in calls for tenders shall, 'where appropriate', be based on international standards, where such exist; otherwise, on national technical regulations, recognised national standards or building codes. It is important to note, first, that this provision obviously does not require technical specifications to be based on international standards only. Neither does it result in any kind of inherent advantage of specifications which are based on international standards (contrary to the situation under the TBT, where alignment with international standards leads to a presumption of legality under the Agreement).

Moreover, the GPA does not prescribe that only standards emanating from international bodies (such as the ISO), or even of national, government-sponsored bodies, are acceptable as a source for technical specifications. The Agreement sets out in a footnote to Article VI.2 a definition of 'standards', which provides that, for the purposes of the GPA, standards may be approved by any 'recognised body' without further ado.[32] This choice of wording in my view can lead to only one conclusion: that the standardisation bodies as meant by the GPA extend beyond the classic group of standing international standardisation bodies (in particular, the ISO) and national standardisation institutions. Whether intended or not, one cannot a priori exclude standardisation efforts by private organisations from being sanctioned for use in tenders covered by the GPA. This raises the stakes for ensuring proper governance of these private organisations, some of which run very successful labels in the sustainability sector.[33]

---

[32] The footnote reads:

> for the purpose of this Agreement, a standard is a document approved by a recognized body, that provides, for common and repeated use, rules, guidelines or characteristics for products or services or related processes and production methods, with which compliance is not mandatory. It may also include or deal exclusively with terminology, symbols, packaging, marking or labelling requirements as they apply to a product, service, process or production method.

[33] Reference can be made to the Forest Stewardship Council (FSC) and, in a wider sustainability context, Oxfam's fair trade label.

## 5.  Conclusion

Regulatory issues, such as 'green' procurement and climate change laws, challenge the WTO in a variety of ways. They also highlight the interdependency of international organisations. Some of the features of sustainable procurement are at odds with more or less long-established trade law principles. The WTO will require creativity and perhaps boldness to accommodate these features. Attention to health, safety and environmental issues in particular is not likely to drop down the agenda.

### Bibliography

Doornbosch, R. and Steenblik, R., *'Biofuels: Is the Cure Worse than the Disease?'*, SG/SD/RT(2007)3, OECD (2007).

Earley, J., *Green Procurement in Trade Policy*, Background Report for the Commission for Environmental Co-operation (2003). Available at www.cec.org/files/PDF/ECONOMY/green-procurement-in-trade%20Policy_en.pdf, last visited 17 September 2007.

European Commission, *Buying Green. A Handbook on Environmental Public Procurement* (Brussels: European Communities, 2004). Available at http://ec.europa.eu/environment/gpp/pdf/buying_green_handbook_en.pdf

Howse, R. and and Regan, D., 'The product/process distinction — an illusory basis for disciplining "unilateralism" in trade policy', *EJIL* 11 (2000), 249–89.

van Calster, G., *International and EC Trade Law — the Environmental Challenge* (London: Cameron May, 2000).

'Green procurement and the WTO — shades of grey', *RECIEL* 11 (2002), 298–05.

'K3: Klimaat, Kyoto, Klaagzang — Over (indirecte) belastingen en de Wereldhandelsorganisatie', in *Liber Amicorum Frans Vanistendael* (Knops Publishing, 2007), pp. 279–84.

'The World Trade Organization panel report on *Brazil Tyres*: advanced waste management theory entering the organisation?', *European Environmental Law Review*, 16 (2007), 304–8.

'*Faites vos jeux* — regulatory autonomy and the World Trade Organization after *Brazil Tyres*', *Journal of Environmental Law* (2008), 121–36.

# PART VI

Institutional challenges and the way forward

# 19

# Institutional challenges to enhance policy co-ordination — how WTO rules could be utilised to meet climate objectives?

MIREILLE COSSY AND GABRIELLE MARCEAU[1]

## I.  Introduction

The debate on the relationship between the United Nations Framework Convention on Climate Change (UNFCCC) and the Kyoto Protocol on the one hand and the World Trade Organization (WTO) on the other hand raises both old and new issues. The old issues are those which have been discussed in the General Agreement on Tariffs and Trade (GATT)/ WTO trade and environment debate for the past fifteen years, in particular the relationship between multilateral environmental agreements (MEAs) and the world trading system and the treatment of process and production methods, among others. The main new elements are the sense of urgency which characterises the climate change debate, as well as the range of different policy measures which may be needed to reach carbon emissions targets; these measures may concern several WTO agreements, including the GATT, the Agreement on Technical Barriers to Trade (TBT), the Agreement on Sanitary and Phytosanitary Measures (SPS), the Agreement on Subsidies and Countervailing Measures (SCM), the General Agreement on Trade in Services (GATS) and the Agreement on Trade-Related Aspects of Intellectual Property Rights (TRIPS). Moreover, the solutions chosen to curb emissions of greenhouse gases (GHGs) may vary from country to country, or groups of countries may get together to implement common regional solutions, thus adding to the diversity of possible scenarios.

Certain measures and policies implemented under climate change treaties will involve interaction with WTO disciplines. They will affect

[1]  We would like to thank Kerry Allbeury and Arancha Gonzalez for their useful inputs. Views and opinions expressed in this article are strictly personal and do not bind the WTO Members or the WTO Secretariat.

competitiveness of the suppliers of goods and services, and it may be tempting for affected parties (economic operators and governments) to resort to trade measures in order to try to 'level the playing field'. As a starting-point, we should assume nevertheless that it is possible for governments to implement their trade and climate change obligations simultaneously and harmoniously. It is a well-accepted principle of international law that states are presumed to undertake their international obligations in good faith so that they can be implemented without conflict. This principle is reflected in Article 3.5 of the UNFCCC:

> The Parties should cooperate to promote a supportive and open international economic system that would lead to sustainable economic growth and development in all Parties, particularly developing country Parties, thus enabling them better to address the problems of climate change. Measures taken to combat climate change, including unilateral ones, should not constitute a means of arbitrary or unjustifiable discrimination or a disguised restriction on international trade.

One should also remember that the WTO has a very specific mandate in the international legal order, which is to promote the liberalisation of international trade (in goods and services) and fight protectionism. At the same time, the WTO framework provides space for governments to pursue and implement non-trade policy objectives and obligations. Importantly, like the Climate Change Convention, the WTO aims at promoting sustainable development.[2]

The primary responsibility for ensuring the coherent development of public international law remains with states. Dialogue among intergovernmental organisations (IGOs) has also an important role to play in building coherence, but it is not sufficient. One of the main challenges in the climate change debate is that it requires extensive collaboration among all actors concerned: states and IGOs, but also non-governmental organisations (NGOs), scientific experts and multinational enterprises,

---

[2] In the first paragraph of the preamble to the WTO Agreement, Members recognise 'that their relations in the field of trade and economic endeavour should be conducted with a view to raising standards of living, ensuring full employment and a large and steadily growing volume of real income and effective demand, and expanding the production of and trade in goods and services, while allowing for the optimal use of the world's resources in accordance with the objective of sustainable development, seeking both to protect and preserve the environment and to enhance the means for doing so in a manner consistent with their respective needs and concerns at different levels of economic development'.

among others, in order to be environmentally effective. As will be briefly discussed below, WTO rules authorise Members, in certain circumstances, to maintain 'unilateral' trade restrictions when such actions comply with the prescriptions of Article XX of the GATT (or Article XIV of the GATS). Yet, such unilateral actions alone will not necessarily be able to address effectively challenges arising from climate change. It will be important to take into account actions by all WTO Members, including actions which may be adopted and implemented by groups of countries (on a regional basis or otherwise). Both the WTO and the UNFCCC will need to ensure the active involvement of developing countries in the discussions, in order to devise appropriate ways to reduce GHG emissions without impairing economic development. It will be essential to gain a full understanding of the environmental alternatives that are most appropriate and efficient among the various measures that are consistent with WTO rules. This task will require very extensive collaboration between scientific experts on climate change, economists and lawyers. In this context, and as stated by Pascal Lamy, '[t]he WTO, far from being hegemonic as it is sometimes portrayed to be, recognizes its limited competence and the specialization of other international organizations'.[3] Indeed the WTO is not the forum where 'standards' are discussed and negotiated, but it does offer a forum where the trade effects of such measures can be discussed, monitored and litigated. Thus the real challenge of the WTO will be to ensure that this non-hegemonic attitude is maintained. This contribution briefly examines various aspects of the WTO institutional framework which are relevant to the climate change debate. It will look at the instruments available in the WTO for conducting policy dialogue with other IGOs and NGOs. It will then discuss the role that standards developed in other IGOs can play in the WTO.

We should also note that most of the questions that arise when examining the institutional aspects of the WTO/UNFCCC relationship are horizontal, in the sense that they extend to other interfaces, such as trade and the environment in general, and trade and human rights, among others. The 'trade and climate change' debate is an extension of the more general 'trade and …' debate.

---

[3] P. Lamy, 'The place of WTO and its law in the international legal order', *European Journal of International Law* 17 (2006), 969.

## II.   Existing basis for co-operation with IGOs and NGOs

### A.   Co-operation between WTO and other IGOs

#### 1.   The various forms of institutional co-operation

The 2006 Report of the Director-General of the WTO on Coherence in Global Policy-making[4] highlights that, through its councils and committees, the WTO maintains extensive institutional relations with numerous other international organisations; there are some 140 international organisations that have observer status in WTO bodies. The WTO also participates as observer in the work of many international organisations. In all, the WTO Secretariat maintains working relations with almost 200 international organisations in activities ranging from statistics, research, standard-setting, and technical assistance to training.

Pursuant to Article V of the Marrakesh Agreement, the General Council must 'make appropriate arrangements for effective cooperation with other intergovernmental organizations that have responsibilities related to those of the WTO'. The General Council regulation allows IGOs to request observer status in WTO committees which is granted subject to a consensus decision by Members. Several IGOs received such status, but in 1999 tensions arose due to the refusal of some Members to grant observer status to the League of Arab Nations. Since then, Members have not been able to reach consensus on any formal request for observership. However, WTO Members and the WTO Secretariat have developed pragmatic alternative solutions for granting ad hoc observership and for collaboration with the secretariats of other IGOs.[5]

The co-operation between UNEP/MEAs and the WTO deserves specific mention. In the 2001 Doha Ministerial Declaration, Ministers welcomed the continued co-operation of the WTO with the United Nations Environment Programme (UNEP) and other intergovernmental environmental organisations and encouraged efforts to promote co-operation between the WTO and relevant international environmental and developmental organisations.[6] The WTO Secretariat has a co-operation

---

[4]  World Trade Organization, *Coherence in Global Economic Policy-Making*, Report (2006) by the Director-General, WT/TF/COH/S/12, 6 March 2007.

[5]  D. Abdel-Motaal, 'The observership of intergovernmental organisations in WTO post-Doha: is there political will to bridge the divide?', *Journal of World Intellectual Property* 5 (2002), 477–89.

[6]  Doha Ministerial Declaration (WT/MIN(01)/DEC/1), adopted on 14 November 2001, paragraph 6.

arrangement with the UNEP extending into such areas as reciprocal representation at meetings, information-sharing, joint research and technical assistance. The WTO Secretariat is an observer of the Governing Council of UNEP and attends annual Council meetings; the UNEP is an observer of various WTO bodies, such as the Committee on Trade and Environment (CTE) and is also invited to attend meetings of the Committee on Trade and Environment in Special Session (CTESS) on an ad hoc meeting-by-meeting basis.

Several MEAs, including the UNFCCC, have observer status in the CTE; together with other MEAs, the UNFCCC is also invited to the CTESS on an ad hoc basis. Ten years ago, the CTE started so-called 'MEA information sessions', which allowed WTO Members to receive first-hand information from MEA secretariats. The UNFCCC Secretariat has participated in seven such exchanges and has submitted several information notes briefing CTE members on developments under the UNFCCC.[7] The WTO Secretariat collaborates with other international organisations on the topic of trade and the environment, including secretariats of MEAs, which allows the conveyance of information on relevant discussions in the CTE and CTESS. Joint activities between the WTO and MEA secretariats, including the UNFCCC, have also developed, such as co-authorship of CTE documents and participation of MEA secretariats in WTO technical co-operation activities on trade and the environment. In some instances, the collaboration goes further. The WTO, the World Health Organization (WHO) and the Codex Alimentarius secretariats work together in the sectors relating to health and SPS measures, and collaborate in bringing attention to the need for policy coherence between trade and health matters at the global and national levels. Indeed, there are WTO provisions which explicitly state that measures complying with standards and norms developed in specified international organisations — such as the Codex — are presumed to be compatible with WTO obligations. Should the WTO envisage a similar approach with the UNFCCC?

When examining the relationships between international organisations, one should distinguish the organisations themselves from their secretariats. The formal relationships between organisations have

---

[7] World Trade Organisation, *Existing Forms of Co-operation and Information Exchange Between UNEP/MEAS and the WTO*, Note by the Secretariat, TN/TE/S/2/Rev.2, 16 January 2007. Papers submitted to the CTE by UNFCCC are found in documents WT/CTE/W/61; – /74: – /123; – /153; – /153; – /174; – /201.

remained rigid; they are essentially limited to granting each other obser-ver status. MEAs with observer status in the WTO do not have an operational role in the negotiations or in dispute settlement, and the same applies to WTO participation in MEAs. This is a direct conse-quence of the fact that, at the WTO and elsewhere, international nego-tiations are carried out, and outcomes defined, by governments. The 'dialogue' between international organisations is not of the same nature as the dialogue between states. This means that policy coherence (whether between trade and climate change, or trade and something else) must be ensured first and foremost at the national level: it is up to each government to ensure that its actions are consistent across the various international institutions of which it is a member. WTO Director-General, Pascal Lamy, has already stressed the responsibility of governments in ensuring synchronisation in global policy-making: '[w]e need to turn the page on the era in which governments would bring conflicting positions to different fora. The right hand of government should not compete with its left hand.'[8] As noted above, there has been increasing collaboration at the level of the secretariats (including tech-nical co-operation, joint notes or studies) and various options have already been explored. However, whether at the WTO or elsewhere, the competences of the secretariats are limited (they do not normally include decision-making) and underlain by their obligation to remain neutral vis-à-vis the membership. Secretariats of international organisations, while they may have somewhat different responsibilities, are not supra-national bodies with independent powers (like the EC Commission, for instance), and this situation is unlikely to change soon. The role they can play in ensuring global policy coherence and mutual support is con-sequently limited.

## 2.   Participation of IGOs in the WTO dispute settlement process

There is no provision dealing specifically with the participation of IGOs in the WTO dispute settlement process. Some WTO provisions impose consultations with another IGO (such as Article XV of the GATT requir-ing consultation with the International Monetary Fund (IMF)). Other provisions, such as those contained in the SPS, require panels to examine, for instance, whether a challenged national measure is consistent with

---

[8] Director-General, Pascal Lamy's address to the UNEP Global Ministerial Environment Forum in Nairobi, 5 February 2007, at www.wto.org/English/news_e/sppl_e/sppl54_e.htm

standards contained in the Codex; in such situations, formal and informal exchanges between the panel and the secretariat concerned take place in order for the WTO panel to be informed of the nature of such standards. More generally, a panel could invoke the right to seek information under Article 13 of the WTO Dispute Settlement Understanding (DSU) to consult an IGO on a technical or other scientific issue; but so far, this provision has been used to consult individual experts, even when IGOs could have been, a priori, adequate interlocutors.[9] Various reasons may deter panels from seeking expertise directly from an IGO, such as the fear of engaging in a cumbersome and time-consuming procedure (especially in cases where the membership of that organisation would have to be consulted) and awareness of the constraints (obligation of neutrality) faced by its secretariat.

Finally, we should recall that the Appellate Body has stated on several occasions that individuals or organisations can submit *amicus curiae* briefs to the Appellate Body or to panels, which have, however, no obligation to consider them.[10] No IGO has taken such an initiative so far. Note that, if accepted, the EC proposal on MEAs tabled in the CTESS (discussed below), would make it compulsory for panels to seek the expertise of relevant MEAs in trade and environment disputes.

## B.    Collaboration with NGOs and other non-state actors

### 1.    The WTO Secretariat and its Director-General

NGOs and other non-state actors can offer very useful expertise and it is thus important to be able to include them in debates. How the WTO should deal with NGOs and more generally how it should improve the transparency of its activities has been an important issue since the entry into force of the WTO. The so-called 'external transparency' of the organisation has been much discussed among its Members, who have traditionally held — and still hold — extreme positions. Even if, arguably, more can still be done, it has to be recognised that considerable efforts have been made over the past ten years to make WTO activities more transparent and to increase interaction with NGOs and other non-governmental actors.

---

[9] For example, in the *EC — Asbestos* case, the panel relied on individual experts and not the WHO. The WHO was consulted informally with respect to providing the names of possible individual experts.

[10] Appellate Body Report on *EC — Sardines*, WT/DS231/ABR paragraphs 156–9.

The basis for establishing relations with non-governmental NGOs is Article V:2 of the WTO Agreement, which stipulates that '[t]he General Council may make appropriate arrangements for consultation and co-operation with non-governmental organizations concerned with matters related to those of the WTO'. The framework for relations with NGOs is further defined in the *Guidelines for Arrangements on Relations with NGOs*, adopted by the General Council in 1996, where Members 'recognize the role NGOs can play to increase the awareness of the public in respect of WTO activities and agree in this regard to improve transparency and develop communication with NGOs'.[11]

According to the Guidelines, the primary vehicles for interaction with NGOs are the WTO Secretariat and its Director-General, who are encouraged to 'play a more active role in its direct contacts with NGOs' through various means, such as 'the organization on an ad hoc basis of symposia on specific WTO-related issues, informal arrangements to receive the information NGOs may wish to make available for consultation by interested delegations and the continuation of past practice of responding to requests for general information and briefings about the WTO'. On this basis, the Secretariat has developed a number of activities with NGOs, including symposia, the annual 'Public Forum', NGOs briefings, circulation of NGO briefing papers on the WTO website, and so-called 'issue specific dialogues with civil society'. Although environmental NGOs have been traditionally very much involved in all these activities, climate change and trade has attracted specific interest only recently: until 2007, no NGO had requested inclusion of this topic on the agenda of the Public Forum and no NGO position paper had been submitted to the WTO Secretariat. However, this is changing: for instance, no less than four sessions were devoted to this theme during the 2007 WTO Public Forum, which was organised by various actors of civil society together with the WTO Secretariat.

The WTO is restrictive when it comes to the participation of NGOs and other non-governmental actors in its bodies. Two main arguments, reflected in the Guidelines, are invoked to keep the doors to its meetings closed. First, the 'special character of the WTO, which is both a legally binding inter-governmental treaty of rights and obligations among its Members and a forum for negotiations', and, second, the view that consultation and co-operation with NGOs must take place primarily at

---

[11] *Guidelines for Arrangements on Relations with Non-Governmental Organizations*, Decision adopted by the General Council on 18 July 1996, WT/L/162.

the national level, 'where lies primary responsibility for taking into account the different elements of public interests which are brought to bear on trade policy-making'.[12] Hence the 'broadly held view' that it is not possible for NGOs to be directly involved in the work of the WTO or its meetings. This position was reaffirmed by many Members on the occasion of a passionate debate in the General Council in relation to the Appellate Body's initiative to issue rules for procedures for *amicus* briefs in the *EC — Asbestos* dispute. NGOs are, however, allowed to attend (without the right to speak) the plenary sessions of ministerial conferences if they demonstrate that their activities are concerned with matters related to those of the WTO.[13] And nothing prevents individual members from including NGO representatives in their national delegation, which some do on a regular basis.

Other organisations, including the UNFCCC, go further than the WTO in this regard by providing a quasi-automatic right for interested non-state actors to be granted observer status. For instance, Article 7.6 of the UNFCCC provides, *inter alia*, that '[a]ny body or agency, whether national or international, governmental or non-governmental, which is qualified in matters covered by the Convention, and which has informed the secretariat of its wish to be represented at a session of the Conference of the Parties as an observer, may be so admitted unless at least one third of the Parties present object'. It would be desirable for the WTO to adopt — or at least come closer to — the more generous practice followed by other international organisations as far as participation by NGOs and other non-state actors is concerned. A number of NGOs would be able to contribute to enhancing the understanding of WTO rules and principles by the public at large and to increasing the legitimacy of the role of the WTO in the international community. However, this issue still meets with strong resistance from many Members, in particular developing countries.

### 2.    Participation of NGOs in the WTO dispute settlement process

The dispute settlement mechanism of the WTO has brought about clarifications on the meaning and the scope of the provisions of the WTO that are related to the environment and, in this context, many

---

[12]  Report of the General Council meeting held on 22 November 2000, WT/GC/M/60.

[13]  The number of NGOs attending WTO ministerial conferences has increased from 108 (235 individuals) in 1996 in Singapore to 801 (2,100 individuals) in 2005 in Hong Kong.

actors — and in particular NGOs — have requested a right to participate in these disputes in order to submit their views.

Under the DSU, only Member governments can initiate a dispute and participate in the proceedings. Nevertheless, NGOs have somehow invited themselves into the process by sending unsolicited *amicus curiae* briefs to panels. The first dispute in which such an initiative was taken was the *US — Shrimp* dispute: some NGOs sent *amicus curiae* briefs to the panel, which decided it could not accept them. On appeal, the Appellate Body reversed the panel decision and found that the 'right to seek information' provided for in Article 13 of the DSU allowed panels to accept unsolicited briefs. Since the *US —Shrimp* dispute, various panels have received such briefs.[14] In *EC — Asbestos*, the Appellate Body adopted special rules of procedure for interested parties to file *amicus curiae* briefs, an initiative which triggered strong reactions among members.[15] The treatment by panels and the Appellate Body of *amicus curiae* briefs is still controversial among WTO Members, as evidenced by proposals made in the DSU review. While some Members, like the European Communities and the United States, are in favour of developing procedural rules for submission of *amicus curiae* briefs,[16] various developing countries have proposed to make it clear that the 'right to seek information' cannot be read as entailing the right for panels to accept unsolicited information.[17]

A related and more recent question in this context concerns the right of NGOs and other interested parties to observe meetings of the panel and Appellate Body. The issue of public hearings was raised in the DSU review where some Members proposed the adoption of measures for making panel and Appellate Body meetings public.[18] Recently, several panels[19] agreed to allow the public to observe meetings, at the request of

---

[14] For further details, see J. Durling and D. Hardin, '*Amicus curiae* participation in WTO dispute settlement: reflections on the past decade', in R. Yerxa and B. Wilson (eds.), *Key Issues in WTO Dispute Settlement — The First Ten Years* (World Trade Organization/ Cambridge University Press, 2005), pp. 221–31.

[15] Report of the General Council meeting held on 22 November 2000, WT/GC/M/60.

[16] Communications by the European Communities (TN/DS/W/1) and by the United States (TN/DS/W/86).

[17] Communications by Cuba, Honduras, India, Malaysia, Pakistan, Sri Lanka, Tanzania and Zimbabwe (TN/DS/W/18); by Kenya (TN/DS/W/42); by India on behalf of Cuba, Dominican Republic, Egypt, Honduras, Jamaica and Malaysia (TN/DS/W/47).

[18] Communications by the European Communities (TN/DS/W/1), Canada (TN/DS/W/41) and the United States (TN/DS/W/86).

[19] The Appellate Body has never held a public hearing so far.

the parties. The event was publicised on the WTO website and those interested were allowed to watch the meeting being broadcast 'live' in a separate room at the WTO. Participation by NGOs in these events was disappointingly low. Incorporating some transparency into the dispute settlement proceedings is desirable as it would contribute to demystifying the processes followed by the panel and Appellate Body and do away with the image of 'faceless bureaucrats'. Publicity of justice is a well-established principle in democracies ('Publicity is the very soul of justice'[20]) and, with the appropriate safeguards in place (for instance to protect confidential business information), allowing the public to watch meetings of the panel and Appellate Body could contribute to reinforcing the legitimacy of the WTO dispute settlement system.

### III.   How does the WTO deal with climate change rules?

#### A.   The WTO and the UNFCCC: two different dispute settlement systems, but ...

The UNFCCC and the Kyoto Protocol impose certain obligations on their signatories and provide for a dispute settlement mechanism to ensure enforcement of such obligations. The WTO imposes different types of obligations, which are enforced through its own dispute settlement system. So, why is the WTO being brought into the climate change debate? Problems may arise in situations involving states that are not parties to the UNFCCC and/or the Kyoto Protocol, or when measures are used which are not clearly mandated in these treaties, such as the use of trade restrictions to realise GHG reduction targets.

Dispute settlement mechanisms in MEAs are different to that of the WTO. A joint note by the UNEP and WTO Secretariats remarks that '[t]he focus of the MEAs is on procedures and mechanisms to assist Parties to remain in compliance and to avoid disputes, not on the use of provisions for the settlement of the disputes'. In contrast to the WTO, MEAs normally do not have a compulsory dispute settlement mechanism and do not issue binding decisions. Moreover, signatories to MEAs rarely resort to these mechanisms.[21]

---

[20]  Wrote Jeremy Bentham (1748–1832).

[21]  World Trade Organization, *Compliance and Dispute Settlement Provisions in the WTO and in Multilateral Environmental Agreements*, Note by the WTO and UNEP Secretariats, WT/CTE/W/191, 6 June 2001.

The compliance mechanisms in the UNFCCC and the Kyoto Protocol have been considered to remain weak.[22] Article 14 of the UNFCCC calls the parties to 'seek a settlement of the dispute through negotiation or any peaceful means of their own choice'. Parties may recognise 'as compulsory *ipso facto*' submission of the dispute to the International Court of Justice (ICJ) or to arbitration in accordance with procedures to be adopted by the Conference of the Parties. If the parties cannot settle their dispute through these means, it can then be submitted, at the request of a party concerned, to a conciliation commission which 'shall render a recommendatory award, which the parties shall consider in good faith' (Article 14.6). Article 14 of the UNFCCC applies *mutatis mutandis* to disputes arising under the Kyoto Protocol (Article 19).[23]

However, the different natures of these dispute settlement mechanisms, and their possible imbalance, should not be a cause for concern in practice as the UNFCCC and the Kyoto Protocol contain different types of obligations from those of the WTO agreements. This means that the competences of WTO and UNFCCC dispute settlement mechanisms should not overlap and have no reason to 'compete'. It also means that there is little scope for governments to do 'forum shopping'. The main question is rather whether, for instance, the mechanisms provided for in the Kyoto Protocol, in particular the flexibilities built therein to reach GHG reduction targets, could be invoked to justify trade restrictions otherwise inconsistent with WTO obligations. Another important question is the weight that would be attached to being a signatory to the UNFCCC or the Kyoto Protocol in assessing compatibility of trade measures with WTO rules, should a non-signatory challenge such measures in the WTO. In other words, the issue at stake is how the WTO

---

[22] According to Birnie and Boyle, the UNFCCC and the Kyoto Protocol 'are strong on reporting, expert inspection and review, and multilateral consultation, but they remain weak on dispute settlement and non-compliance, where further development is awaited'. P. Birnie and A. Boyle, *International Law and the Environment*, second edition (Oxford University Press, 2002), p. 532.

[23] In addition, signatories to the Kyoto Protocol adopted 'Procedures and mechanisms relating to compliance under the Kyoto Protocol' (Decision 24/CP.7, 10 November 2001). This compliance mechanism is detailed and appears to be more stringent than those of other environmental agreements. Under this system, an 'enforcement branch' has the responsibility of determining whether an Annex I party is in compliance with its emission targets. Should it find non-compliance (for instance, when a party has exceeded its emission targets), it can require that party to bring itself into compliance. For that purpose, the enforcement branch can require the party to submit an action plan and suspend the eligibility of that party to make transfers in emissions trading.

dispute settlement system would 'use' non-WTO law in the adjudication of disputes. This is discussed in the following section.[24]

## B.   Non-WTO law in the WTO dispute settlement system

Under the DSU, the jurisdiction of panels and the Appellate Body is limited to claims of violation of WTO agreements. Hence, a WTO Member could not resort to the DSU to seek redress for an alleged breach of an MEA. This does not mean, however, that non-WTO law has no role to play in WTO disputes. The issue is rather how and for what purpose non-WTO law can be used in claims of breach of WTO agreements brought pursuant to the DSU. We believe that generally non-WTO law can be used in two different ways, with two different purposes.

First, non-WTO law can be referred to in the *interpretation* of concepts and terms contained in WTO agreements, with a view to ascertaining their meaning. For instance, more recent environmental treaties have been referred to for the purpose of interpreting in an evolutionary manner GATT provisions which were drafted sixty years ago. The typical example is the *US — Shrimp* dispute in which the Appellate Body decided to resort to 'modern international conventions and declarations' to interpret the concept of 'exhaustible natural resources' found in Article XX(g) of the GATT; it looked at instruments such as the 1982 United Nations Convention on the Law of the Sea (UNCLOS), the Convention on Biological Diversity (CBD) and Agenda 21[25] to conclude that 'exhaustible natural resources' included biological resources, such as sea turtles, and not only finite resources, such as oil and ores (which seemed to have been the intention of the drafters in 1947). Under this scenario, non-WTO law is taken into account if it can be considered to represent a sufficient degree of consensus among WTO Members, but identical membership between the WTO and the environmental treaty concerned is not required.[26] In the context of a climate change-related dispute, this

---

[24]  Another issue which would merit further development is the treatment, under the WTO dispute settlement system, of countermeasures implemented by a WTO Member as a response to another Member for failing to meet international obligations contracted under another treaty (such as the Kyoto Protocol). However, such a discussion is beyond the scope of the present document.

[25]  Appellate Body report in *US — Shrimp*, WT/DS58/ABR, paragraphs 130–1.

[26]  This was presumably the case, in the view of the Appellate Body, for UNCLOS, Agenda 21 and the CBD. In another dispute (*Chile — Price Band*), the Appellate Body refused to agree to a practice developed between some Latin American countries being used for the interpretation of the Agreement on Agriculture.

would mean that, when interpreting Article XX(g) of the GATT, for instance, a panel or the Appellate Body could refer to other treaties, like the UNFCCC or the Montreal Protocol, to determine whether the ozone layer or the atmosphere could be considered 'exhaustible natural resources'.[27]

The second instance in which non-WTO law can be referred to is when assessing whether a specific national measure complies, in casu, with a WTO provision (obligation or exception), or, in other words, when determining the appropriate application of that WTO provision. For instance, in US — Shrimp (Article 21.5 Malaysia), the Appellate Body, when assessing the US measure in light of the chapeau of Article XX of the GATT, considered that the existence of regional fishing arrangements negotiated by the United States demonstrated the good faith of the US in its efforts to protect sea turtles.[28] In this scenario, all relevant treaties can be taken into account, even if they are concluded among a small number of countries, as they are only used as one of the facts that would support an allegation.[29] In this sense, reliance on international or even regional standards may provide a de facto presumption of good faith, as required by Article XX.[30] This brings about another institutional challenge, though: the legitimacy of the WTO to be the one institution assessing whether a trade restriction is effectively 'based on' mechanisms and standards set up in other treaties and IGOs.

However, Pauwelyn and others argue that, in situations where a WTO obligation would conflict with a right granted in another treaty, the WTO panel should first assess which of the two treaties' provisions prevails. Should the panel find that the provision contained in the non-WTO treaty prevails, then the WTO dispute system would need to apply and enforce that treaty.[31] We believe that WTO panels can only

---

[27] In this context, we would like to stress that interpretation of WTO terms is not limited to disputes. What we have just said should be used in 'day-to-day' national policy-making involving trade and environment issues.

[28] Appellate Body report in US — Shrimp (Article 21.5 Malaysia), WT/DS58/ABR/RW, paragraphs 130–4.

[29] For further developments, see G. Marceau, 'Fragmentation in international law: the relationship between WTO law and general international law', in Finnish Yearbook of International Law (Martinus Nijhoff, 2006), vol. 17, p. 31.

[30] G. Marceau, 'A call for coherence in international law', Journal of World Trade 33 (1999), 128.

[31] See, for instance, J. Pauwelyn, Conflict of Norms in Public International Law — How WTO Law Relates to Other Rules of International Law (Cambridge University Press, 2003) and 'How to win a World Trade Organization dispute based on non-World Trade

apply[32] WTO provisions, but in doing so, they will need to look at non-WTO law, often as factual matters, to interpret the relevant applicable WTO provisions; indeed, WTO provisions themselves often induce defending parties to invoke participation in other treaties as evidence of their legitimate policy objective and good faith. Setting aside the debate on 'WTO applicable law', i.e. to what extent and how a treaty not signed between the parties to a WTO dispute could be used in such a dispute,[33] it remains clear that, in the case of a dispute involving national measures allegedly based on the Kyoto Protocol, a WTO panel will examine the Protocol, if only to reject its relevance. We believe that Members cannot disregard their WTO obligations beyond the situations envisaged in WTO exception provisions; in other words, Members can derogate their WTO obligations only in situations defined by the WTO agreements themselves.[34] It is for WTO Members to make the necessary adjustments through new law-making (e.g. amendments or understandings) if they consider that the current WTO legal framework does not allow them to comply simultaneously with other international obligations they have contracted. But it is not up to adjudicating bodies to engage in law-making to fill a legal vacuum.

In our view, Members can find ways to implement the UNFCCC and the Kyoto Protocol harmoniously with the WTO. The Appellate Body has insisted on the need to maintain a balance between trade liberalisation and the right to pursue other policy objectives, as contemplated in exception provisions. This has allowed the preservation of policy and

---

Organization law — questions of jurisdiction and merits', *Journal of World Trade* 37 (2003), 997; L. Bartels, 'Applicable law in WTO dispute settlement proceedings', *Journal of World Trade* 35 (2001), 505; D. Palmeter and P. C. Mavroidis, 'The WTO legal system: sources of law', *American Journal of International Law* 92 (1998), 398.

[32] 'Applicable law' means here the law for which a breach can lead to actual remedies in the WTO. This definition is narrower than the definition given by the International Law Commission (ILC) in its report on the fragmentation of international law (A/CN.4/L.682/Add.1, 13 April 2006), for which 'applicable law' seems to include all legal rules that are necessary to provide an effective answer to legal issues raised in a WTO dispute (including procedural-type obligations, rules of interpretation, etc.).

[33] In addition to the publications referred to in n. 31, see also the Report of the Study Group of the International Law Commission on *Fragmentation of International Law: Difficulties Arising From the Diversification and Expansion of International Law*, A/CN.4/L.682, 13 April 2006, paragraphs 44–5 and 165–71 and bibliographical references therein.

[34] See, for instance, G. Marceau, 'WTO dispute settlement and human rights', *European Journal of International Law* 13 (2002), 753 and 'Conflicts of norms and conflicts of jurisdictions', *Journal of World Trade* 35 (2001), 1081; J. Trachtman, 'The domain of WTO dispute resolution', *Harvard International Law Journal* 40 (1999), 333.

legal space for Members to comply with their rights and obligations under other treaties without undermining WTO objectives. WTO adjudicating bodies have shown that WTO and non-WTO rules can be interpreted and applied in a harmonious manner, thus directly contributing to international legal coherence. The UNFCCC and the Kyoto Protocol, therefore, can find an appropriate place in the adjudication of trade disputes. Measures adopted under the auspices of these two instruments should be found compatible with WTO rules, for instance, if they comply with the provisions of Article XX of the GATT or other relevant WTO agreements (such as the TBT), and assuming that they are taken in good faith and do not pursue protectionist purposes.

### C. The use in the WTO of international standards developed by other organisations

The issue of trade and climate change also presents interesting institutional questions since it may involve situations where a WTO Member decides to adopt a national regulation based on existing international standards developed in another IGO. This begs the question of how the WTO deals with, and considers, norms and international standards negotiated in other fora, and whether the UNFCCC and the Kyoto Protocol can be considered as setting 'international standards'.

Turning to the first question, the WTO does not treat all international standards in the same way: they have a particularly 'high profile' in the TBT and SPS, which deal explicitly with such standards and favour their harmonisation. The definition of 'international standards' contained in Annex A to the SPS appoints the Codex Alimentarius Commission (Codex), International Office of Epizootics (now the World Organisation for Animal Health) (OIE) and International Plant Protection Convention (IPPC) as forums whose standards are given legal weight in WTO disputes. The standards developed by the Codex, OIE and IPPC for human, animal and plant health, respectively, are, under the terms of their own constitutive documents, non-binding. However, Article 3.1 of the SPS provides that 'Members shall base their sanitary or phytosanitary measures on international standards, guidelines or recommendations, where they exist, except as otherwise provided for in this Agreement'. Moreover, Article 3.2 states that SPS measures of WTO Members that are in conformity with international standards, guidelines, or recommendations shall be 'presumed to be consistent with the relevant provisions of this Agreement'. So, while the Codex and other bodies by no means legislate in the normal or full sense, the norms they produce have a certain authority in creating a presumption of WTO compatibility when such international standards are respected. The SPS thus provides important incentives for states to base their national standards upon, or to fit them to, these international standards. Therefore, the WTO encourages Members to negotiate norms in other international fora which they will then implement coherently in the context of the WTO. Members can nevertheless adopt norms higher than the international standards as long as they comply with the SPS, including Article 5 on risk assessments.

The same is true of the TBT. Article 2.4 of the TBT requires Members to use 'relevant international standards' as a basis for their technical regulations, unless the international standards are an inappropriate or ineffective means to achieve legitimate objectives. Article 2.5 of the TBT further stipulates that a technical regulation which is in accordance with relevant international standards 'shall be rebuttably presumed not to create an unnecessary obstacle to international trade'. So, deviations from international standards are discouraged. When interpreting Article 2.4 of the TBT in *EC — Sardines*, the Appellate Body determined that a Codex Alimentarius standard was a 'relevant international standard', despite the fact that it had not been adopted by consensus. The Appellate Body found that in order for a standard to be used 'as a basis for' a technical regulation, it must be 'used as the principal constituent or fundamental principle for the purpose of enacting the technical regulation'. Nevertheless, since Members' measures are presumed to be WTO consistent, it is for the complainant to bear the burden of proving violation of Article 2.4 as a whole.[35]

So, what does this mean for the climate change debate? If a WTO Member adopts a domestic regulation allegedly based on the Kyoto Protocol or the UNFCCC, can this regulation be considered to 'be based on' an international standard within the meaning of Article 2.5 of the TBT, and thus presumed to be TBT/WTO consistent? The answer is not clear, as it depends on how one defines international standards. Many argue that standards should be defined narrowly, which would exclude regulation adopted pursuant to an MEA such as the UNFCCC. Should we argue, nevertheless, that some provisions contained in the Kyoto Protocol or the UNFCCC constitute international standards, then a WTO panel could indeed examine whether a national measure is a

---

[35] Appellate Body report on *EC — Sardines*, paragraphs 243 and 248.

technical regulation within the TBT, and whether that regulation used a Kyoto standard as the 'principal constituent or fundamental principle for the purpose of enacting the technical regulation'. If, on the contrary, provisions of the Kyoto Protocol or the UNFCCC were not considered to qualify as international standards, or if the national measure could not be viewed as a technical regulation within the meaning of the TBT, the only option would be to invoke these provisions to demonstrate justification under an exception provision, such as Article XX of the GATT.

This brings us back to the logic of the argumentation developed by the United States (and approved by the panel and the Appellate Body) in *US — Shrimp (Article 21.5 Malaysia)*. In this dispute, the United States pointed to agreements reached with some WTO Members as examples of logical ways to deal with conservation of turtles. Malaysia opposed any reference to these regional arrangements because it was not a party to any of them. The Appellate Body said that *concluding* an agreement with the country opposing the restriction is *not* necessarily a pre-condition of a WTO consistent import restriction if one has tried in good faith but failed. If a WTO Member can, under the good faith prescriptions of Article XX, maintain an import restriction based on criteria determined unilaterally, there is no reason why the same importing country would be in a worse position if such criteria came from an agreement to which only some of the WTO Members were signatories and the challenging Member was not.

> Clearly, and 'as far as possible', a multilateral approach is strongly preferred. Yet it is one thing to *prefer* a multilateral approach in the application of a measure that is provisionally justified under one of the subparagraphs of Article XX of the GATT 1994; it is another to require the *conclusion* of a multilateral agreement as a condition of avoiding 'arbitrary or unjustifiable discrimination' under the chapeau of Article XX. We see, in this case, no such requirement[36] (emphasis added).

In *US — Shrimp*, the Appellate Body had already stated that 'conditioning access to a Member's domestic market on whether exporting Members comply with, or adopt, a policy or policies unilaterally prescribed by the importing Member may, to some degree, be a common aspect of measures falling within the scope of one or another of the exceptions (a) to (j) of Article XX'.[37]

---

[36] Appellate Body report on *US — Shrimp (Article 21.5 — Malaysia)*, paragraph 124.
[37] Appellate Body report on *US — Shrimp*, paragraph 121.

Consequently, unilateral actions can find justification under Article XX of the GATT and the existence of a multilateral agreement between the parties involved in a dispute is not a pre-condition to benefiting from WTO exception provisions. This jurisprudence is potentially relevant for disputes arising in relation to trade measures taken pursuant to the UNFCCC or the Kyoto Protocol. It means that, whenever relevant, participation in these treaties would be considered as one of the pertinent factual elements to demonstrate that a trade measure otherwise contrary to WTO obligations would nevertheless find justification under an exception provision.

## IV.   WTO and MEAs: the stakes in the negotiations on the Doha Development Agenda

The relationship between the GATT/WTO system and MEAs has been one of the main issues under discussion since 1992, when the topic of trade and environment emerged on the trade agenda. In December 2001, ministers decided to include this topic in the Doha Development Agenda (DDA). As noted by WTO Director-General, Pascal Lamy, '[a]s imperfect as the WTO may be, it continues to offer the only forum worldwide that is exclusively dedicated to discussing the relationship between trade and the environment'.[38]

The mandate agreed at Doha requires Members to negotiate on:

> [t]he relationship between existing WTO rules and specific trade obligations set out in multilateral environmental agreements (MEAs). The negotiations shall be limited in scope to the applicability of such existing WTO rules as among parties to the MEA in question. The negotiations shall not prejudice the WTO rights of any Member that is not a party to the MEA in question.[39]

This mandate, contained in paragraph 31(i) of the Doha Declaration, excludes the most difficult aspect of the relationship between MEAs and WTO rules, i.e. the application of trade measures by MEA signatories to non-MEA signatories. This situation is the only one which had been identified as a potential problem by WTO Members.[40] While the

---

[38] Director-General, Pascal Lamy's address to the UNEP Global Ministerial Environment Forum in Nairobi, 5 February 2007, at www.wto.org/English/news_e/sppl_e/sppl54_e. htm

[39] Doha Ministerial Declaration, adopted on 14 November 2001, WT/MIN(01)/DEC/1.

[40] Report (1996) of the Committee on Trade and Environment, WT/CTE/1, paragraph 8.

UNFCCC and the Kyoto Protocol do not mandate the use of trade measures, whether between signatories or against non-signatories, the Montreal Protocol on Substances that Deplete the Ozone Layer, which is also pertinent in the context of climate change policies, does rely on trade measures.

It is not the purpose of this contribution to undertake a detailed review of the arguments and positions developed by members of the CTESS, nor to discuss the various aspects of the relationships between trade and environment rules.[41] We shall only recall that Members have always held different views on how to tackle this issue and that the negotiations seem to have had difficulties in narrowing the gap. The last report by the chairman of the CTESS indicates that the group has before it two main proposals, which present 'two rather different perspectives with regard to the scope of the mandate in Paragraph 31(i)'.[42]

The proposal by the European Communities (EC) suggests a ministerial decision containing various principles (mutual supportiveness, no subordination, deference and transparency) which would 'govern the relationship between MEAs and WTO rules'. The EC also proposes a right for MEA bodies to be granted observer status in relevant WTO bodies and an obligation for WTO committees and panels to 'call for and defer to' MEA expertise whenever examining issues with environmental content relating to a particular MEA.[43] If accepted, this proposal would raise the profile of international environmental organisations in the WTO. However, it raises various interesting questions, some of which are being discussed in the CTESS. In practice, who will speak on behalf of the 'MEAs'? Assuming this role goes to the secretariats, will they have sufficient independence to give the expertise sought? Would WTO bodies be bound by the opinion given by an MEA? What would be the relationship with Article 13 of the DSU? Why should involvement of

---

[41] This subject has been extensively researched. For reading suggestions, see the selective bibliography contained in WT/CTWE/W/49/Add.1. See also G. Marceau, 'Conflict of Norms and Conflicts of Jurisdiction' (2001), 1081; D. Abdel Motaal, 'Multilateral Environmental Agreements (MEAs) and WTO rules: why the "burden of accommodation" should shift to MEAs', Journal of World Trade 35 (2001), 1215; P. Mavroidis, 'Trade and environment after the Shrimps — Turtle litigation', Journal of World Trade 34 (2000), 73.

[42] Committee on Trade and Environment in Special Session, Report by the Chairman, Ambassador Mario Matus, to the Trade Negotiations Committee, TN/TE/17, 25 July 2007.

[43] Proposal for a Decision of the Ministerial Conference on Trade and Environment, Submission by the European Communities, TN/TB/W/68, 30 June 2006.

IGOs be limited to environment-related issues? What about reciprocity, i.e. WTO being 'called for and deferred to' in trade related issues arising under MEAs?

The second proposal, tabled by Australia and Argentina, is far less ambitious. It suggests that 'a short but substantive report be prepared, highlighting key observations from CTESS discussions and setting out areas of agreement and recommendations'. Examples of possible recommendations are limited to procedural proposals, such as Members 'continuing to share their national experiences relating to negotiating and implementing specific trade obligations set out in MEAs' or reporting 'on their national coordination process'.[44]

Whatever the outcome of this negotiation, one should note that this discussion has been somehow 'overtaken by events' with the developments in WTO case law. Although no dispute involving trade measures taken pursuant to an MEA has taken place so far, several principles found in the Appellate Body jurisprudence, in particular with respect to Article XX of the GATT, would be directly relevant should such a dispute arise (see above).[45] This issue, which raises the more general question of balance in the WTO between the law-making process (i.e. the negotiations, where political considerations can fully enter into play) and the judicial activities (i.e. dispute settlement, where political interference is limited), would be worth a separate discussion.

The second negotiating item contained in paragraph 31 of the Doha Declaration is also directly relevant to the relationships between the WTO and multilateral environmental agreements. It requires Members to negotiate on 'procedures for regular information exchange between MEA Secretariats and the relevant WTO committees, and the criteria for granting observer status'. Over the past ten years or so, collaboration between the WTO and MEA secretariats has developed on an ad hoc basis and has taken several forms. This collaboration is essentially of a technical nature and aims at increasing mutual understanding of the functioning and impact of relevant agreements (see above).

The mandate in paragraph 31(ii) of the Doha Declaration aims at formalising the various forms of collaboration, and appears to be less

---

[44] *Proposal for an Outcome on Trade and Environment Concerning Paragraph 31(i) of the Doha Ministerial Declaration*, Submission from Australia and Argentina, TN/TE/W/72/Rev.1, 7 May 2007.

[45] G. Marceau, 'A call for coherence in international law — praises for the prohibition against "clinical isolation" in WTO dispute settlement', *Journal of World Trade* 33 (1999), 87.

controversial than negotiations under paragraph 31(i). Discussions focus on how to improve information exchange in the CTE, document exchange, future collaboration in the context of technical assistance and capacity-building activities, and criteria for observer status. According to the last chairman's report, these discussions have progressed significantly and 'convergence [has] started to emerge on basic elements for an outcome'.[46] This negotiation may be beneficial if it allows the clarification and even expansion of the activities between the secretariats of the MEAs and the WTO. However, it may also entail the risk of creating a straitjacket which proves unable to adapt quickly to new circumstances.

## V.   Conclusion

Is the WTO equipped to ensure smooth policy co-ordination with climate change instruments and institutions? In our view, the WTO provides an appropriate framework for Members to discuss trade and climate change issues, as part of the more general debate on trade and the environment. In addition, the WTO dispute settlement system has shown that it is able to integrate non-trade values and to make space for non-trade law. Since *US — Shrimp*, we know that WTO Members can implement unilateral measures to deal with environmental concerns. There are, however, several important challenges ahead. The international community may face a proliferation of unilateral or regional standards that may not be the most environmentally effective, even if they can be considered WTO consistent (which is likely to be the case for most of them). In this context, issues of mutual recognition will become difficult and may lead to increased tensions with those Members that are excluded from recognition schemes. Further thought will also have to be given to the interaction of WTO agreements with climate change instruments currently under consideration in some countries, such as carbon tax, cap-and-trade systems, and green certificates. Moreover, the scientific and technical difficulties linked to assessing the real impact of GHG reduction measures on climate change mitigation will complicate assessment of their WTO consistency. Finally, the use of private standards is likely to increase, hence the need to improve the understanding of their interaction with the WTO and to ensure their co-ordination with

---

[46] Committee on Trade and Environment in Special Session, Report by the Chairman, Ambassador Mario Matus, to the Trade Negotiations Committee, TN/TE/17, 25 July 2007.

governmental standards. Another important challenge is the need to involve developing countries, both in the WTO and in the UNFCCC, with due respect for their development needs and priorities. Can the WTO be used to create incentives for developing countries? According to case law (*India — GSP*), market access preferences can be conditioned on development related criteria. The main question here is whether climate change related preferences could be considered (directly) linked to (sustainable) development. Finally, the relationship between trade and climate change cannot be separated from the trade and energy debate, which involves competition and investment issues, and WTO rules are still very much incomplete in these fields.

Ultimately, the main concern of the international community is that environmentally effective measures be adopted. And whether or not such measures are fully WTO consistent is not a prerequisite for efficiency.

The main problem is not institutional because the international institutions will do what their masters tell them to do. The most important question is whether or not there is political commitment by the entire international community to take all necessary measures to fight climate change. The ultimate arbitrators between conflicting values (assuming that trade and environment are conflicting, an assumption that we do not share) are not panels, the Appellate Body or even the WTO, but governments themselves. States are the ultimate arbitrators between opposing or contradictory rights, obligations and values. International institutions, including the WTO, can only play a supportive role in offering fora in which states can devise and implement solutions, as well as strengthen their co-operation and co-ordination.

## Bibliography

### *Publications*

Abdel Motaal, D., 'Multilateral Environmental Agreements (MEAs) and WTO rules: why the "burden of accommodation" should shift to MEAs', *Journal of World Trade* 35 (2001), 1215–33.

 'The observership of intergovernmental organizations in WTO post-Doha: is there political will to bridge the divide?', *Journal of World Intellectual Property* 5 (2002), 477–89.

Bartels, L., 'Applicable law in WTO dispute settlement proceedings', *Journal of World Trade* 35 (2001), 499–19.

Birnie, P. and Boyle, A., *International Law and the Environment* (Oxford University Press, 2002).

Durling, J. and Hardin, D., 'Amicus curiae participation in WTO dispute settlement: reflections on the past decade', in Yerxa, R. and Wilson, B. (eds.), *Key Issues in WTO Dispute Settlement — The First Ten Years* (World Trade Organization/ Cambridge University Press, 2005).

Lamy, P., 'The place of WTO and its law in the international legal order', *European Journal of International Law* 17 (2006), 969–84.

Marceau, G., 'A call for coherence in international law — praises for the prohibition against "clinical isolation" in WTO dispute settlement', *Journal of World Trade* 33 (1999), 87–152.

'Conflict of norms and conflicts of jurisdiction — the relationship between the WTO Agreement and MEAs and other treaties', *Journal of World Trade* 35 (2001), 1081–131.

'WTO dispute settlement and human rights', *European Journal of International Law* 13 (2002), 753–814.

'Fragmentation in international law: the relationship between WTO law and general international law — a few comments from a WTO perspective or the search to understand non-WTO dispute', in *Finnish Yearbook of International Law* (Leiden: Martinus Nijhoff, 2006), vol. 17, p. 31.

Mavroidis, P., 'Trade and environment after the *Shrimps — Turtle* litigation', *Journal of World Trade* 34 (2000), 73–88.

Palmeter, D. and Mavroidis, P. C., 'The WTO legal system: sources of law', *American Journal of International Law* 92 (1998), 398–413.

Pauwelyn, J., *Conflict of Norms in Public International Law — How WTO Law Related to Other Rules of International Law* (Cambridge University Press, 2003).

'How to win a World Trade Organization dispute based on non-World Trade Organization law — questions of jurisdiction and merits', *Journal of World Trade*, 37 (2003), 997–1030.

Trachtman, J., 'The domain of WTO Dispute Resolution', *Harvard International Law Journal* 40 (1999), 333–77.

### WTO case law

*EC — Sardines, European Communities — Trade Description of Sardines*, Appellate Body report, WT/DS231/ABR, adopted 12 January 2000, DSR 2002:VIII, paragraphs 156–9.

*US — Shrimp, United States — Import Prohibition of Certain Shrimp and Shrimp Products*, Appellate Body report, WT/DS58/AB/R, DSR 1998:VII.

*US — Shrimp (Article 21.5 — Malaysia), United States — Import Prohibition of Certain Shrimp and Shrimp Products — Recourse to Article 21.5 of the DSU by Malaysia*, Appellate Body report, WT/DS58/AB/RW, adopted 21 November 2001, DSR 2001:XIII, paragraphs 130–4.

# 20

# Environmental goods and services: the Environmental Area Initiative approach and climate change

THOMAS COTTIER AND DONAH BARACOL-PINHÃO[1]

## I. Introduction

An inquiry into the potential contribution of international trade regulation and the law of the World Trade Organization (WTO) to climate change mitigation[2] inevitably focuses attention on the basket of negotiations on environmental goods and services (EGS), mandated by paragraph 31(iii) of the Doha Ministerial Declaration (DMD).[3] This effort stems from established insights that trade liberalisation and environmental protection are potential 'win-win' constellations. The same philosophy applies to policies which seek to promote investment and trade in technologies for combating emissions of greenhouse gases (GHGs). It equally applies to the promotion of renewable and alternative energy sources. Relevant goods and services may be identified and brought to the negotiating table and could result in appropriate sectoral initiatives with a view to lowering trade barriers in these

---

[1] The paper draws upon a research report prepared by the authors for the Secretariat of the United Nations Conference on Trade and Development (UNCTAD) in 2007.

[2] Climate change mitigation addresses the future reduction of greenhouse gases and essentially carbon dioxide ($CO_2$) emissions into the atmosphere. Climate change adaptation addresses policies dealing with the consequences of and disruptions caused by climate change. The paper is limited to addressing the former and does not take into account the latter.

[3] Paragraph 31. With a view to enhancing the mutual supportiveness of trade and environment, we agree to negotiations, without prejudging their outcome, on:

> (iii) The reduction or, as appropriate, elimination of tariff and non-tariff barriers to environmental goods and services.

Available at www.wto.org/english/thewto_e/minist_e/min01_e/mindecl_e.htm

fields in terms of tariff protection, discrimination in services, technical barriers to trade, intellectual property protection and technology transfer.

The EGS negotiations so far, however, have witnessed major difficulties in bringing about such results. Several reasons lie behind the stalemate in the negotiations up to the close of 2007. The definition of environmental goods and its demarcation from regular non-agricultural market access negotiations (NAMA) pose consensus problems. The proposed listings of potential goods are considered to be too broadly defined and over-inclusive, arguably leading to NAMA negotiations in disguise. Moreover, since most of these goods and advanced technologies are concentrated in developed countries, an appropriate balance of interests is difficult to achieve, even taking into account so called environmentally preferable products (EPPs) from developing countries.

With the intention of addressing these imbalances, India proposed an approach seeking to facilitate nationally defined environmental programmes and projects. Others suggested an integrated approach, combining both recourse to listings and defined project areas and multilateral environmental agreements (MEAs). Yet, all these proposals focused mainly on goods. The area of services, as well as of technical barriers to trade — both equally mentioned in paragraph 31(iii) of the DMD — were largely left aside, except for the issue of services classification.[4] The same is true for intellectual property and related problems of technology transfer and licensing.

The pressing need to address climate change mitigation multilaterally offers the potential for a focused and more balanced approach to the negotiations. A proposed avenue discussed in a United Nations Conference on Trade and Development (UNCTAD) study by the authors, may be particularly useful in the present context. An Environmental Area Initiative (EAI) approach could be launched, comprehensively addressing services, goods, technical barriers to trade and intellectual property issues in an a priori defined field of reducing GHGs. Once political decisions have been taken to focus on this and perhaps additional areas, operational requirements will focus on appropriate operational structures of the negotiations being sought.

This paper explores the potential of the EAI approach in a post-Doha agenda of the WTO to address climate change goals by applying it to the promotion of renewable energy. It also explores the potential of linking the liberalisation of environmental services and related goods and

---

[4] See the contribution in this volume by Olga Nartova, 'Assessment of GATS' impact on climate change mitigation'.

appropriate rules on technical barriers to trade and intellectual property with the Kyoto Protocol mechanisms, in particular within the context of the Clean Development Mechanism (CDM),[5] in order to bring about enhanced investment in, and transfer of, technology to developing countries. The possibility of emissions trading[6] and other innovative forms of investment brings an entirely new dimension to the table which calls for further exploration.

## II.   Main EGS proposals on the table

The current EGS negotiations may be characterised by the following main proposals:

(1)   Negotiating and defining a *list of industrial products* with a view to lowering or eliminating tariffs thereof. The products amount to relevant technology input in fields such as sewage, clean water, climate change, noise abatement, and renewable energy. This approach, mainly based upon lists prepared by the Organisation for Economic Co-operation and Development (OECD) and the Asia-Pacific Economic Co-operation (APEC), is essentially supported by industrial countries. (e.g. Submission by the United States, TN/TE/W/52 T, TN/MA/W/18/Add.7, 4 July 2005; Submission by the European Communities, TN/TE/W/56, 5 July 2005).[7]

(2)   Negotiating and defining a *list of environmentally preferable products* (EPPs) with a view to lowering or eliminating tariffs thereof. These are products which, because of their nature or method of production, are beneficial to sustainable development and ecology. Such products include non-timber forest products such as jute and coir, eco-labelled products, organic agricultural products, and biofuels such as ethanol and biodiesel. This approach, based upon a list prepared by

---

[5] Article 12 of the Kyoto Protocol, which defines the CDM, provides for Annex I parties to implement projects that reduce emissions in non-Annex I parties, or absorb carbon through forestation or reforestation activities, in return for certified emission reductions, and assist the host parties in achieving sustainable development and contributing to the ultimate objective of the UN Framework Convention on Climate Change. Available at http://unfccc.int/kyoto_protocol/mechanisms/items/2998.php

[6] Article 17 of the Kyoto Protocol, which sets out emissions trading, provides for Annex I parties to acquire units ('assigned amount units' a unit of which is equal to one metric tonne of emission in $CO_2$-equivalent terms) from other Annex I parties. Available at http://unfccc.int/kyoto_protocol/mechanisms/items/2998.php

[7] These and the following proposals can be found at www.wto.org (visited September 2007).

the UNCTAD, was submitted by a number of developing countries.[8] It is equally endorsed in proposals submitted by industrialised countries (e.g. Submission by Switzerland, TN/TE/W/57, 6 July 2005).

(3) The *Environmental Project Approach* (EPA) covers goods and services and envisages extending market access facilitation during the implementation of specific projects, essentially defined by national governments through a Designated National Authority (DNA), within parameters to be negotiated within the WTO Committee on Trade and Environment Special Session (CTESS). If approved, the goods and services included in the project would qualify for specified concessions for the duration of the project. The main proponent of this approach is India (*cf.* Submission by India, TN/TE/W/54, 4 July 2005).

(4) The *integrated approach* proposed originally by Argentina combines elements of both list and EPA approaches. Categories of environmental projects to be identified by the CTESS will include a list of goods applicable to national projects that would be eligible for preferential access during the project period.[9] Uruguay suggested defining environmental activities of concern to members in order to provide an appropriate framework.[10] In a subsequent joint proposal by Argentina and India, explicit and indicative reference was made to specific fields and linked to the activities of public and private entities in these fields. Eligibility for concessions on tariffs and all other relevant trade areas will be conditioned on whether or not entities are included in a WTO-notified list. The list may be subject to amendment through periodic negotiations.[11]

## III.   Assessment of current proposals

The four models all have their advantages and disadvantages.

(1) Listing technological products based on APEC and OECD lists allows the reduction of tariffs and the creation of legal security through binding commitments. The approach is fully in line with

[8]  See S. Singh, 'Environmental goods negotiations: issues and options for ensuring win-win outcomes', International Institute for Sustainable Development (2005), 3–5. Available at www.iisd.org/pdf/2005/trade_environmental_goods.pdf
[9]  Submission by Argentina, TN/TE/W/62, 14 October 2005.
[10]  Submission by Uruguay, JOB (06)/44.
[11]  Submission by Argentina and India, JOB (07)/77, 6 June 2007.

traditional WTO policies and instruments of tariff reductions. While products chosen are relevant for environmental technology, they also apply to other areas of technology (dual use), and thus cannot be separated from regular NAMA negotiations. Since environmental technology is often advanced technology, the listing will naturally favour the interests of industrialised countries. The emphasis on technology can partly be balanced by including EPPs in the overall list. Importantly, listing fails to comply with the mandate of the Doha Development Agenda (DDA) to include non-tariff barriers (NTBs) and services.

(2) Listing EPPs equally allows for the reduction of tariffs and the creation of legal security through binding commitments. The approach is also fully in line with traditional WTO policies and instruments of tariff reductions. The UNCTAD list of inherently environmentally friendly products mainly benefits developing countries. Yet, the benefits are likely to be unevenly spread; some members are likely to benefit more than others. The list also is limited to commodities and fails to consider the problem of NTBs. Similarly, the potential of services liberalisation in solving these problems remains to be explored.

(3) The EPA offers coherence and focus, and leaves the eclectic enumeration of numerous randomly defined items behind. It puts the achievement of progress in defined areas first, followed by a process of implementation for the goods and services involved. Tariff and non-tariff negotiations, as well as access to services, are placed within a framework and environmental agenda. The proposal, supported mainly by India, however, focuses on unilateralism, subject to guidelines and co-ordination within the WTO. It is essentially up to individual members to define projects, and subsequently to facilitate market access for relevant products and services limited to the project defined, in terms of subject-matter coverage. Such facilitation is also limited in time and expires upon the completion of the project. Tariff reductions thus remain of a temporary nature and do not lend themselves to binding. The same is true for relevant services. The approach therefore does not respond to the expectations of enduring reductions in tariff and NTBs, and of permanent service commitments.

(4) The model is not truly compatible with the precepts of WTO law, and the two avenues are difficult to reconcile legally. First, it creates difficult transitional issues, such as how to treat components

requiring maintenance, and the expansion of a project. Second, the approach focuses on government-defined projects. It potentially creates differential treatment between products used for the project, and those used outside the project — the problem of dual use. The distinction faces difficulties under a like-product analysis. It may deter investment outside projects defined. Alternatively, concessions may be extended to all like products, irrespective of their use. In this case, commitments would inherently need to be of a lasting nature, given their effects outside the project properly speaking. Finally, it should be noted that the EPA lacks a true multilateral dimension. Projects are neither defined nor implemented multilaterally, lacking a basis for working out meaningful package deals in the field. There is nothing to prevent a government from operating the EPA at any time within the range of bound tariffs and service commitments as well as other rules, and to reduce market access restrictions in support of its programmes on a most-favoured-nation (MFN) basis.

(5) The more recent joint submission of Argentina and India merges the concepts of listing and environmental areas, and introduces the idea of sequencing the definition of goals and targets and actors. The approach is no longer based upon specific projects, but on the basis of listing private and public entities undertaking environmental activities and services in pre-defined fields. For the first time, it has been suggested that targets should be defined in advance at the multilateral level. It establishes the idea of sequencing. First, it is a matter of defining environmental goals and sectors, and second, of implementation of these goals by the entities listed in the WTO benefiting from specified concessions.

(6) This idea is interesting as it relies upon the *ex ante* definition of specific targets and areas. It was first expressed in the submissions which link such requirements to rights and obligations under MEAs. At the same time, the approach raises a number of complex legal issues. It relies upon privileging the importation of specific goods and services for specific purposes and specific operators and thus entails the potential for discrimination inconsistent with WTO obligations. The analysis of WTO law shows a number of uncertainties and tends to deny justifications for the approach.[12] Members, however, may overcome these difficulties by agreement. Irrespective of

---

[12] For a detailed legal analysis of the project approach, see T. Cottier and D. Baracol-Pinhão, 'The WTO negotiations on environmental goods and services: a potential

existing WTO law, WTO Members are free to negotiate a framework which accommodates the needs of the EPA/integrated approach. This is essentially a matter of political will and consensus. Such an agreement would form part of the WTO system. It is placed on a par with other agreements and will prevail as *lex specialis* over more general provisions.

## IV.  The Environmental Area Initiative (EAI) as an alternative approach

### A.   The philosophy

In light of the limitations of the main proposals, it is submitted that members should agree to work on the basis of a multilateral EAI approach. By organising negotiations on the basis of specific target areas and goals, the EAI can provide a key to manage the complexity. The negotiations do not pertain to specific environmental projects in countries, but address an overall regulatory goal, and apply to all relevant products, including dual use, on the basis of MFN. Finally, they lead to binding and lasting commitments in the WTO. Under the EAI, negotiations would cover tariffs, making use of listings, non-tariff measures and services and technical co-operation, as well as linkages to other regulatory areas, including intellectual property rights (IPRs) to the extent that they are relevant for the chosen field.

While the bulk of WTO rules seek to create equal conditions for products, irrespective of purpose and use in a particular sector, sector initiatives are not alien to the WTO tradition. We recall MFN-based sector initiatives in the Uruguay Round in the field of medical equipment, as well as a special agreement on subsidies in the aircraft industry. In the field of intellectual property, the problem of access to essential drugs was addressed by special rules on compulsory licensing for pharmaceutical products in the Trade Related Aspects of Intellectual Property Rights Agreement (TRIPS). WTO law therefore is capable of making special efforts in identified areas and of contributing to the solution of specific problems.[13]

---

contribution to the millennium development goals', in *Trade and Environment Report 2007*, UNCTAD (forthcoming, 2009).

[13] For these examples see T. Cottier and M. Oesch, *International Trade Regulation: Law and Policy in the WTO, the European Union and Switzerland*, (London: Cameron May and Bern: Staempfli Publishers, 2005), pp. 594–5, 933–4.

In the field of environmental goods and services, such a focus could draw from areas identified by other international fora. EAIs could, for example, relate to the following fields:

- targeted reduction of GHGs
- access to, and supply of, clean water; treatment of waste water and disposal of sewage (sanitation)
- solid waste management (not limited to hazardous waste, including disposal of information technology equipment)
- promotion of renewable energies and fuel efficiency (possibly limited to transportation)
- promotion of extensively produced agricultural goods (organic foodstuffs).

Adopting such goals and targets partly draw from commitments to the United Nations (UN) Millennium Development Goals (MDGs)[14] and obligations under existing MEAs. Negotiating trade commitments within the framework of such goals shows that there can be mutual supportiveness between trade and development objectives.

The EAI approach requires the preparatory step of first addressing the problems of definitions and classification that have underlined the failure of the negotiations so far. Environmental areas and regulatory goals will then be identified in a political process of agenda setting and prioritising. In order to establish a linkage between environmental services and goods that has been absent from the proposals on the table, commitments will be undertaken sequentially with services providing a starting-point. This angle is important as it promises to achieve a more balanced approach than placing negotiations on goods at the top of the agenda. Defining environmental goods for liberalisation will thus be mainly linked to their use as a component for the delivery of a service, except in the case of EPPs. The EAI approach makes a special case for EPPs in favour of the developing countries as an offsetting mechanism for the huge technological advantage and export dominance of developed countries in the global environmental goods and services market. This is also a direct response to repeated calls by developing countries for explicit rules on the inclusion of EPPs in any listing that would eventually result. Modalities will then be agreed which provide flexibility for members to undertake commitments according to nationally defined priorities. Finally, drafting a framework agreement will secure coherence and

---

[14] www.un.org/millenniumgoals/ (visited January 2008).

co-operation among different relevant fields in the WTO and across pertinent negotiating groups towards the pre-determined goals.

It will be necessary to explore further linkages to technical barriers to trade and intellectual property rights (IPRs) in target areas. Market access will be strongly defined by product standards which may need harmonisation. This can be done under appropriate provisions of the framework agreement, either by incorporating relevant standards or referring to adopted international bodies in WTO Members' schedules of commitments. The same holds true for IPRs. Market access will be influenced by conditions for technology transfer and thus the intellectual property regime. The issue of subsidies is pertinent to many environmental areas and thus needs to be addressed. Likewise, the implications of government procurement need to be studied. Finally, questions of financial support arise and the linkages to the CDM and to emissions trading need examination.

The steps outlined take into account synergies between the provision of environmental goods and services, and ensure more coherence in the negotiating process, so that discussions do not occur in a seemingly fragmented manner. More important, the approach facilitates the achievement of the *entire* mandate of paragraph 31(iii) of the DMD.

## B.   Operational requirements in preparing for EAI

### 1.   Preparatory work: updating the GATS W/120 classification

The Harmonized System (HS) of tariff classification underlying WTO tariff commitments is sufficient for the purposes of environmental goods. However, shortcomings exist in relation to the classification of services. In particular, the current W/120 list suffers from a 'dual use' problem where some types of environmental services overlap with services classified within other services sectors.[15] It also lacks organisation in terms of services for specific aspects of the environment (water, soil, air, and noise). The classification, moreover, no longer reflects the evolving structure of the industry resulting from expansion and change of focus from 'end-of-pipe' technologies to prevention and cleaner processes and products and the increasingly integrated nature of some service sectors.[16]

---

[15] Such as construction, engineering, consulting, and technical analysis services.

[16] Organisation for Economic Development and Co-operation (OECD), *Environmental Goods and Services: The Benefits of Further Global Trade Liberalisation* (Paris: OECD, 2001), pp. 15–20.

The negotiating proposals calling for a revised classification with new categorisations aim to address such limitations.[17]

Two important considerations should be noted in the updating process: first, the mutual exclusivity of each service sector needs to be maintained (as required for the W/120 list). Second, an adequate mechanism has to be found to address integrated environmental services that may require a cross-sectoral approach. Establishing a 'core' and a 'cluster' list may provide a good starting-point.[18]

### 2. Identifying environmental areas and regulatory goals

The UN MDG targets or specific goals of MEAs can and should be used as a starting-point in identifying environmental areas and regulatory goals. They provide a high level of legitimacy to the goal and process and link the efforts within the WTO with the agenda agreed upon in the UN. The identification of specific target areas should take place in high level and non-technical negotiations. The CTESS would eventually need to secure horizontal co-ordination between the different fields involved.

Goals have to be *time-bound*, e.g. a ten-year target for the elimination of trade barriers relevant to the identified environmental area. This, however, does not preclude any member from pursuing unilateral liberalisation ahead of this goal-setting exercise and of the time-frame ultimately agreed upon.[19] By setting definite time-frames for the achievement of specific goals, the WTO will help drive timely and meaningful responses to urgent environmental problems and development challenges.

In order to address the interests of developing countries properly and fairly, any combination of environmental areas identified needs to include an area which directly promotes the trade of EPPs, especially organic and natural products.[20]

---

[17] Proposals from the United States (S/CSS/W/25), the European Communities (S/CSC/W/25), Switzerland (S/CSS/W/76), Australia (S/CSS/W/112), and Colombia (S/CSS/W/121).

[18] The idea of a core list and undertaking commitments in related services is mentioned in the EC proposal and supported by Australia and Switzerland (see above), as well as Canada (S/SS/W/51) and the United States (S/CSS/W/25).

[19] Needless to say, since current commitments in environmental services remain in force, partial fulfilment of goals in some environmental areas is already taking place and should be counted against future commitments.

[20] This is not to say that developing countries are not efficient exporters of other types of environmental goods, as trends show that they have developed export capacity in manufactured goods and are increasingly trading with other developing countries.

### 3.   Establishing criteria for the inclusion of relevant services and goods[21]

Once Members have agreed upon and defined a certain environmental target area, all pertinent environmental services under the updated W/120 classification that are significant to the achievement of the goals for that area have to be identified. The identification of goods to be liberalised then follows, provided that one or other of these conditions is met: (a) the good is *essential* to the delivery of the said services, or (b) it is a good or cluster of goods that is common to more than one type of environmental service.[22] To determine what can be considered 'essential', specific criteria have to be developed by the Members. Any good complying with either of the two conditions makes it to the list, whether or not it has dual use. The only exception is the mandatory additional identification of EPPs for inclusion in the list, which will not be conditioned on the provision of an environmental service.

Defining essential services and goods for this purpose entails issues of demarcation in the negotiating process, requiring an analysis of like products. The application of stringent criteria based upon WTO jurisprudence on goods may render such demarcations difficult as goods are essentially defined on the basis of physical characteristics and end uses, for the purpose of assessing competitive relationships.[23] This may limit the possibility for product differentiation as Article XX(d) and Article XX(g) of the General Agreement on Tariffs and Trade (GATT) 1994 merely allow exemptions if the exemptions are necessary to implement GATT-consistent domestic market regulations and for the protection of non-renewable resources. For example, it would be difficult to distinguish between fuel efficient and less fuel efficient motor cars on this basis.

In the field of services, the doctrine of like products is far from settled. Article XVII: 3 of the General Agreement on Trade in Services (GATS) essentially relies upon the concept of modification of competition between different products and service providers. The combined approach to services and goods in the context of EGS may suggest reviewing in the final analysis the potential of the aims and effects test

---

[21] A comprehensive discussion of practical considerations in liberalising environmental goods is provided by R. Steenblik, 'Liberalising Trade in "Environmental Goods": Some Practical Considerations', OECD Trade and Environment Working Paper 2005–5 (2005). Available at www.oecd.org/dataoecd/25/8/35978987.pdf

[22] Examples of goods commonly used in several types of services are certain chemicals, catalysts, ion exchangers, laboratory refractory equipment.

[23] Cottier and Oesch, *International Trade Regulation*, pp. 389–418.

which applies to Article III:2 of the GATT second sentence and is also suggested to be suitable in the context of the GATS.[24] To the extent that a service and product differentiation does not have the effect of protecting domestic producers, Members are entitled, under this doctrine, to operate product differentiation for regulatory purposes, including taxation. The same philosophy could also apply as a guideline for defining essential products in the context of implementing a specific environmental goal. It is pertinent, for example, in deciding whether to include certain engineering services, but not others. It is likewise applicable to the decision on whether to include products used for specific purposes, while excluding other products which on the basis of standard criteria may be considered like, but are mainly used in a different context.

Anticipating newer and more environmentally efficient products coming on to the market on a more or less regular basis, as a result of continuous innovation in the industry, the list of goods has to be open-ended and subject to periodic review and updating. This addresses the concern about the list becoming obsolete and irrelevant for tariff purposes.

### 4. Agreeing on modalities for undertaking commitments within a specified environmental area

Many environmental problems can be linked to particular market or policy failures to internalise environmental costs. Against such a background, liberalising trade in EGS will have a minimal effect unless the operation is undertaken or embedded within programmes that specifically target the particular market or policy failure. The EAI approach takes this into account by providing the necessary flexibility for Members to choose the mix or package of services and goods that corresponds to their national environmental priorities. Since liberalisation of services strongly depends upon individual capacities to regulate and monitor markets, Members are expected to take their level of regulatory development into account when scheduling commitments, for example in the field of competition policy. The structure of schedules of commitments in services and in goods offers the necessary flexibility to accommodate the individual needs of countries in a process of progressive liberalisation.

---

[24] M. Cossy, 'Determining "Likeness" under GATS: Squaring the Circle?', WTO, Staff Working Paper ERSD 2006–08 (2006). Available at www.wto.org/english/res_e/reser_e/ersd200608_e.pdf

It is crucial that the approach to environmental services commitments be undertaken as a package. In effect, any Member who chooses to grant market access in a 'core' service has also to make basic commitments in the related service ('cluster') that is classified elsewhere in the W/120 sectoral list. This addresses the often heterogeneous nature of the providers where entities making up the sector cut across 'vertical' sectoral lines of the list involving 'vertical' functional specialists of 'horizontal' service providers.[25] The schedule of any commitment in environment related services not classified under 'core', however, has to state the restriction that this applies only to services rendered in relation to a cross-referenced 'core' environmental service.[26]

The next step will be committing to reduce or eliminate tariffs and NTBs for a number of goods within the identified and agreed list of eligible goods. Recalling the flexibility provided in the modalities for agriculture during the Uruguay Round wherein countries were free to choose which tariff lines to reduce, we suggest similar options in the case of environmental goods: (i) a minimum number of goods from the set of eligible goods will be subject to a mandatory reduction of tariffs; (ii) an overall average tariff cut with minimum cuts at the tariff line level at levels differentiated for developed and developing countries; (iii) or a combination of both, that is, a minimum number of goods and a minimum tariff cut. The mix of goods will vary between Members, where resulting commitments could consist of either a larger number of goods with shallow cuts, or a smaller set of goods with deeper cuts or zero tariffs. The question of how to deal with the remaining tariffs for eligible goods, with a view to their elimination in the long run, will presumably be the subject of subsequent rounds of negotiations. These options provide Members with sufficient flexibility to prioritise liberalisation objectives depending on national policies and goals. National programmes will essentially drive the choice of the mix which is demand driven.

---

[25] OECD, *Environmental Goods and Services: The Benefits of Further Global Trade Liberalisation* (Paris: OECD, 2001) provides some examples such as (1) engineering, consulting, and project management services being provided across functional segments by environmental divisions of big engineering firms, which enter into contract and partnership arrangements with smaller firms, (2) pollution remediation and prevention activities involving the integrated provision of equipment, technology and services, with project managers and engineers calling in the required medium specialist (in water, air, soil, habitat) on a contract basis.

[26] An alternative proposal regarding 'dual use' has been mentioned by the OECD (2001) which specifically incorporates environmental end-use services under the environmental services sectoral classification, with a clear description of the specific environmental aspect of the service, for example, design and architecture services for the construction of waste management facilities.

In terms of EPPs, separate modalities will operate and should ensure mandatory commitments on a minimum number of such products. These commitments will not be counted against the minimum or average reductions in the general modalities. As a matter of special and differential treatment, it could be contemplated that developing countries may opt not to undertake commitments on EPPs, although this does not preclude any unilateral liberalisation on their part at any time. Placing EPPs on this separate but parallel liberalisation track is aimed at restoring an overall balance of interests between the developed and developing countries that would otherwise not be readily achieved within the general tariff reduction framework.

EAI allows both for uniform, multilateral tariff reductions across the board, or for bilaterally negotiated reductions, commensurate with the principles of GATT tariff negotiations and GATS services' liberalisation. The commitments may vary from area to area and cannot be generally determined except for the fact that liberalisation takes place on the basis of broadly reciprocal commitments and is subject to the principle of MFN.

## 5.   Drafting an EGS framework agreement

In order to develop an appropriate mechanism of implementation, and consolidation of the approach, we suggest that an agreement on environmental goods and services be drafted. Provisions have to set out the modalities for the reduction of tariff and non-tariff barriers in environmental goods and services, and for the scheduling of commitments. Where appropriate, they have to establish or clarify existing linkages with other WTO agreements or with efforts undertaken by other negotiating groups in overlapping areas.

By introducing modalities requiring mandatory, but differentiated, commitments across both 'core' and 'cluster' services, barriers to trade in environmental services are dealt with in a coherent way by addressing, at the same time, current market access restrictions in interrelated service sectors which impact on environmental services, such as construction, engineering, and consulting services. Licensing, qualification, and work experience requirements also serve as barriers[27] that need to be addressed, and appropriate provisions will have to be introduced.

---

[27] R. Hamwey, U. Hoffmann, A. Vikhlyaev, and R. Vossenaar, *Liberalisation of International Trade in Environmental Goods and Services*, UNCTAD (2003), 8. Available at http://r0.unctad.org/trade_env/test1/meetings/bangkok4/EGS.pdf

In order to respond to the mandate of paragraph 31(iii) of the DMD on NTBs, relevant provisions will need to be introduced. Subsidies, technical standards and issues of eco-labelling are the major NTBs commonly identified. They are often not addressed with sufficient clarity in other agreements, and supplementary or newly designed special provisions may be elaborated, as necessary. The agreement would need to address the relationship to MEAs, seeking to prevent potential conflicts. Otherwise, the flexibility in MEAs, for example of the Kyoto Protocol for countries to choose domestic policies to meet their emission targets, may conflict with specific WTO obligations by unfairly favouring domestic producers over foreign ones. Such policies include carbon or energy taxes, subsidies, energy efficiency standards, eco-labels, and government procurement policy.[28]

The subsidy issue is particularly relevant for the promotion of renewable energy sources.[29] With the temporary expiry, however, of Article 8 of the Agreement on Subsidies and Countervailing Measures (ASCM), which permitted certain non-actionable subsidies, Members' subsidy programmes, including those for renewables, are open to challenge. The proposed agreement could aim to resolve this dilemma through an exception clause or the identification of non-actionable 'green' subsidies, basically returning to the philosophy of Article 8 of the ASCM.[30] The issue of subsidies is also relevant for many environmental areas which are fundamentally linked with development goals. The promotion of renewable energy sources, with the concurrent aim of reducing GHGs, could provide viable off-grid sources for rural electrification. Similarly, with regard to clean water and access to drinking water, cross-subsidisation to ensure universal coverage may be necessary. Further flexibilities for developing countries may be introduced where the purpose of subsidies is to support basic social services, such as those mentioned above. Regarding subsidies for biofuels, the proposed agreement has to refer to the domestic support provisions of the WTO Agreement on

---

[28] L. Assunção and Z. X. Zhang, 'Domestic Climate Change Policies and the WTO', Discussion Paper No. 164, UNCTAD (2002), 2–3. Available at www.unctad.org/en/docs/osgdp164_en.pdf

[29] R. Howse, Post-Hearing Submission to the International Trade Commission: *World Trade Law and Renewable Energy: The Case of Non-Tariff Measures*, Renewable Energy and International Law Project (2005).

[30] The revisiting of Article 8 of the ASCM and a reinstatement of a similar clause has been raised by several authors. See Assunção and Zhang, *Domestic Climate Change Policies*, 2–3.

Agriculture. Where necessary, it has to adopt special rules to promote their trade in a sustainable manner, taking into account the possible adverse effects on food prices in developing countries where crop sources may compete for exports for fuel purposes.

Standards and certification requirements are of paramount importance in the present context. They are of particular interest to developing countries, as they especially affect EPPs. Niche products seeking new markets may be hindered by a lack of appropriate standards, or in the case of 'novel' food products, may be subject to stringent import requirements.[31] Certification can be a useful tool to promote sustainable practices but can pose enormous challenges in enforcement and control. In order to avoid the result of a mere segmentation of the market, certification has to be undertaken multilaterally. A uniform certification process also avoids higher costs and increased bureaucracy for potential suppliers.[32] In order to avoid measures becoming disguised restrictions to trade, the agreement may oblige Members to establish uniform certification, particularly in EPPs and biofuels, and to establish linkages with relevant rules in the WTO Agreement on Technical Barriers to Trade (TBT) and the WTO Agreement on the Application of Sanitary and Phytosanitary Measures (SPS). In areas deemed insufficiently covered within these agreements, such as certification based on non-product related production and process methods (PPMs), discussions and any agreement reached in the Committee on Trade and Environment on labelling for environmental purposes are to be reflected through appropriate wording in the proposed agreement.[33]

Additional NTBs that are used widely need to be addressed and removed. They include the following broad types of measures: para-tariff measures (such as customs surcharges), price control measures (administrative pricing), finance measures (e.g. advance payment requirements and transfer delays), automatic licences and prior surveillance, quantity control measures (non-automatic licensing), monopolistic measures (single channel for imports), and technical measures (pre-shipment inspection and special customs formalities).[34] Most of

---

[31] Hamwey *et al.* (see above n. 27).    [32] Doornbosch and Steenblik, p. 8.

[33] UNCTAD, *Legal and Policy Issues in the Market Access Implications of Labelling for Environmental Purposes* (2003) gives a good background on labelling issues for environmental purposes as considered under the TBT.

[34] Based on a typology done by UNCTAD. See L. Fontagné, F. von Kirchbach and M. Mimouni, *A First Assessment of Environment-Related Trade Barriers*, Working Paper 2001–10, CEPII Research Center (2001). Available at www.intracen.org/mas/pdfs/pubs/etb_english.pdf

these measures relate to trade facilitation, hence, reference to discussions within the Negotiating Group on Trade Facilitation is necessary.

Provisions also have to address the overlaps with other WTO agreements, e.g. clarifying the relationship between publicly owned and operated monopolies or exclusive service suppliers and public procurement. The relevant provisions are those in Article VIII of the GATS, and in the Agreement on Government Procurement. Links with the GATS Annex on Financial Services also need to be clarified, especially in relation to the issue of trade in emission certificates and similar schemes to fulfil Kyoto Protocol obligations, to the extent that members agree to resolve definitional issues of whether they are deemed to be financial instruments.

Specific provisions on technology transfer to assist developing countries in improving domestic capacity, as well as technical assistance to help in strengthening their regulatory capacity, have to be included. Technology transfer is crucial especially in the context of combating climate change. The agreement could provide a technology transfer obligation for developed countries to be written into some kind of a scheduling commitment. Members could agree on establishing a specific funding mechanism for this purpose, which will also be used to improve the regulatory framework of developing countries to enable them to prepare for and to maximise the opportunities to be gained from the new technologies, e.g. in the area of protection of intellectual property. Technology transfer has to be an explicit commitment above and beyond existing and rather weak obligations in the context of the implementation of mechanisms such as the CDM under the Kyoto Protocol.[35]

Finally, there should be a mandate for a regular review of classification issues in services, and until no longer applicable, in goods (as eventually tariffs will be eliminated and thus obviate the need for a review), keeping the list of goods open-ended to allow for the inclusion of innovations and new products as necessary. Provisions to cover transparency and notification procedures, as well as integrating the field into WTO dispute settlement, form equally necessary parts of the framework agreement.

## V.   Linking EGS and climate change mitigation

### A.   EGS and the Kyoto Protocol

The challenge of climate change mitigation is of an unprecedented scale, requiring enhanced commitments and global co-operation of states. It

---

[35]  cf. Felix Bloch, in this volume.

calls for the creation of innovative solutions both technologically and institutionally. We submit that the EAI approach can potentially support the objective of stabilising disastrous climatic developments. It is suitable to address specific policies of reducing GHGs. We propose to start by linking the approach to the Kyoto Protocol, in particular its application within the context of the CDM. It must be reiterated, however, that the EAI approach is not limited to these fields and can equally apply to similar initiatives outside the Kyoto Protocol mechanisms.

### B.    Potential environmental areas

The sectors and activities covered by the Kyoto Protocol and eligible for the CDM are potential and eligible environmental areas of services and goods in the context of the EGS negotiations. The sectors include, among others, renewable energy technologies, energy efficiency improvements, in particular in construction, fuel switching (e.g. coal to natural gas or coal to sustainable biomass), reduction of emissions from industrial processes, in the transport sector, and in the agricultural sector.[36]

Under the current Kyoto Protocol, members are entitled to define unilaterally their priorities and seek CDM projects within the given structure of service regulations, tariff and NTBs relating to corresponding products. Developing countries therefore should have an interest in making available advantageous conditions for trade in order to attract investments under the CDM. Attractive terms and conditions for investments can be created unilaterally. However, they could also be created and reinforced on the basis of multilateral trade negotiations. This is where the EAI approach enters the stage and offers new opportunities: in accordance with the approach described above, WTO Members will decide on the selection and the prioritisation of the above-mentioned project areas for inclusion in the WTO negotiations. Relevant environmental and energy-related services will then be grouped according to the sectors and industries selected. Table 3 lists possible areas. For developing countries, liberalisation commitments for an agreed set of services and goods signal their national priority areas for development to prospective investors (from Annex I countries).

Specific environmental services and goods relevant to a proposed CDM project that are among a host (developing) country's WTO

---

[36] United Nations Environment Programme (UNEP), *Baseline Methodologies for Clean Development Projects: A Guidebook* (Roskilde: UNEP, 2005), pp. 12–13. Available at www.cd4cdm.org/Publications/UNEP_CDM%20Baseline%20Meth%20Guidebook.pdf

Table 3 *Examples of key mitigation technologies and practices by sector*

| Sector | Relevant technologies and practices |
| --- | --- |
| Energy supply | Improved supply and distribution efficiency; fuel switching from coal to gas; nuclear power; renewable heat and power (hydropower, solar, wind, geothermal and bio energy); combined heat and power |
| Transport | More fuel efficient vehicles; hybrid vehicles; cleaner diesel vehicles; biofuels; modal shifts from road transport to rail and public transport systems; land use and transport planning |
| Buildings | Efficient lighting and daylighting; more efficient electrical appliances and heating and cooling devices; improved cook stoves, improved insulation; passive and active solar design for heating and cooling; alternative refrigeration fluids, recovery and recycling of refluorinated gases |
| Industry | More efficient end-use electrical equipment; heat and power recovery; material recycling and substitution; control of non-$CO_2$ gas emissions; and a wide array of process-specific technologies |

*Source*: Adapted from IPCC Fourth Assessment Report Summary for Policymakers, 2007.[37]

commitments will be subject to agreed reductions of domestic preferences (services) and tariff reduction or elimination (goods). Services related to the implementation of the CDM and financial services rendered in emissions trading are likely to be considered under the GATS.[38] All of the CDM project development services may be covered by the GATS, but it is important to define specifically which are 'core' and which are 'cluster' services under the EAI initiative.

In identifying the goods essential to the delivery of the environmental services, members may be guided by the categorisation of relevant technologies and practices by the Intergovernmental Panel on Climate Change (IPCC).[39]

---

[37] *Ibid.*

[38] For reference and an analysis of the interface between CDM and GATS rules, see G. Wiser, 'Frontiers in trade: the clean development mechanism and the general agreement on trade in services', *Int. J. Global Environmental Issues* 2 (2002), 288–309.

[39] Available at www.ipcc.ch/SPM040507.pdf

## C. The example of renewable energy

We take renewable energy as an example of the identified environmental area. First, and following the EAI approach, WTO Members identify which environmental and energy-related services would be pertinent to this area. Members may opt to implement immediately and simultaneously the entire range of activities and sectors under the Kyoto Protocol relating to renewable energy, covering electricity generation, transport, and industrial processes. Alternatively, a sectoral limit may be agreed on by the Members as an initial target, say, in relation to electricity generation. Second, whatever the scope of sectors to be covered, relevant services and goods are defined accordingly.[40] Third, goods following the EAI criteria are identified, from which Members formulate and negotiate their commitments following the proposed modalities, guided by individual national priorities and programmes in the area of energy. In terms of services, where renewable energy obligations for electricity are being imposed on grid operators and retailers, they constitute GATS commitments under energy services and have to be specified in their schedules accordingly.

An important issue for coherence in the area of renewable energy, is the overlap with certain areas of negotiation in the GATS on energy services, in particular how commitments are to be scheduled. Energy services are not classified under the current W/120 list; instead, three specific energy-related activities are listed explicitly as separate subsectors: transportation of fuel under transport services, services relating to upstream activities for oil and gas under other business services, and services incidental to energy distribution also under other business services. Under the Doha Round request offer process for energy services, references made to the concepts of 'technological neutrality' and 'neutrality of energy source' could have implications for the flexibility to undertake market opening commitments affecting renewable energy. These need to be considered. It may help if Members decide whether to treat this as a sectoral or as a horizontal issue.[41]

---

[40] See the contribution in this volume by Olga Nartova, 'Assessment of GATS' impact on climate change mitigation'.

[41] S. Zarilli *Managing Request-Offer Negotiations Under the GATS: The Case of Energy Services* TD/TC/WP(2003)24/FINAL, OECD (2003). Available at www.olis.oecd.org/ olis/2003doc.nsf/LinkTo/td-tc-wp(2003)24-final

A discussion of renewable energy inevitably leads to the issue of renewable energy certificates (RECs). Whether they are to be classified as goods or services within the general framework of emission trading, is currently a matter for debate.[42] Where they apply to energy being generated by renewable sources and sold in the same jurisdiction, international trade is limited to certificates, and not the energy. It should therefore be considered as a trade in services and addressed and regulated as for financial services.[43] Members may have to adopt a definition and specify the conditions under which they are to be considered a good or a service, and which WTO Agreement they are governed by.

Subsidies for fossil fuels and nuclear energy are considered as the most significant barriers to renewable energy.[44] Such subsidies significantly lower final energy prices putting renewable energy at a competitive disadvantage. They usually take the form of direct budgetary transfers, tax incentives, research and development spending, liability insurance, leases, land rights of way, waste disposal, and guarantees to mitigate project financing or fuel price risks.[45] While many of these subsidies can be 'actionable' within the meaning of the WTO ASCM, it is a politically difficult issue and Members seek to avoid a legal challenge of their own support programmes in dispute settlement under the Dispute Settlement Understanding (DSU). It is submitted that the proposed return to non-actionable subsidies under the EAI approach could present a more practical alternative. Howse[46] suggests the establishment of a non-actionable 'green box' for renewable energy subsidies. He also suggests the adoption of a cap-and-reduction scheme for environmentally unfriendly subsidies in the energy sector.

---

[42] Including discussions in the WTO Committee on Trade and Environment on, generally, emission credits. Brokerage, consulting and insurance services associated with emissions trading, however, could be considered commercial services under GATS (T. Brewer, *International Trade, the WTO and International Climate Arrangements*, paper presented at the International Forum for Environmental Issues, Tokyo (2003), 9). Wiser (*Frontiers in Trade*, 2002) also supports this argument. Delimatsis and Mavromati (in this volume), however, argue more specifically that in the absence of an entry listing energy-related services separately, the trading of RECs and the services involved therein fall under the Financial Services Annex to the GATS.

[43] Howse, *Renewable Energy* (2005), 18–19.

[44] See, for example, Howse (*ibid.*) and F. Beck and E. Martinot, 'Renewable energy policies and barriers' in C. Cleveland (ed.), *Encyclopedia of Energy* (San Diego: Academic Press/ Elsevier Science, 2004).

[45] *Ibid.* See n. 39 p. 4.      [46] Howse, *Renewable Energy* (2005), 29.

Apart from the obvious and direct benefits to the environment of renewable energy sources, the liberalisation of associated services and goods can support the export capacities of many developing countries as well as contributing to their rural and social development. This is the case for biofuels.

Resources and capacity for biofuel production are distributed fairly widely across developing countries and require less sophisticated technologies than for the production of other renewables.[47] Developing countries thus have a huge export potential in biofuels. The issue, however, is how well they are able to balance their export interests, by supplying the anticipated global demand, against their own environmental sustainability. This leads to the question of regulation, which likewise can be addressed through specific provisions in the proposed EGS framework agreement. The labelling of sustainable biofuel products offers a viable approach to bring about such a balance.

Currently, European Union tariffs on biodiesel are around 6.5 per cent, but tariffs on ethanol range between 40 and 100 per cent, depending on the price.[48] The differential rates essentially depend on whether the biofuel is regarded as an agricultural product, and therefore is subject to higher rates under the current WTO Agreement on Agriculture, or as an industrial product, with relatively low tariffs. Under the current regime, there is a structural bias against some important biofuel products of developing countries. We submit that the matter can be dealt with within the EAI approach, and negotiations can be co-ordinated with negotiations on agriculture.

Relative to conventional energy, renewable energy can provide a cheaper alternative source of power and electricity in the rural areas of developing countries. The installation of solar photovoltaic systems (which are stand-alone systems) for supplying off-grid power to remote and low income households and communities is an example. Lowering tariffs for such products, which are still at 15 per cent or higher in developing countries,[49] will not only address connectivity in remote

---

[47] www.greencarcongress.com, cited by R. Steenblik, *Liberalisation of Trade in Renewable-energy Products and Associated Goods: Biodiesel, Solar Thermal and Geothermal Energy*, OECD Trade and Environment Working Paper 2006–01 (2006), 8.

[48] Swedish National Board of Trade, *Trade Aspects of Biofuels* (2007). Available at www.kommers.se/upload/Analysarkiv/In%20English/Trade%20Aspects%20of%20Biofuels.pdf

[49] R. Steenblik, *Liberalisation of Trade in Renewable-energy Products and Associated Goods: Charcoal, Solar Photovoltaic Cells, and Wind Pumps and Turbines'*, OECD Trade and Environment Working Paper, 2005–07 (2005), 5.

areas through cheaper and more sustainable means, but could increase export opportunities for the new regional players.[50]

In terms of NTBs, SPS measures mainly affect feedstocks due to their biological origin. Because there is no way of determining the product's end use at the border, strict regulations on residues are applied equally to crops destined for animal or human consumption and to vegetative biomass feedstocks. Increasingly important to trade in biofuels are sustainability standards and regulations currently being contemplated.[51] In this regard, the adoption of varying standards, which render compliance burdensome for prospective suppliers, needs to be avoided. Coordination and harmonisation towards internationally agreed standards is thus imperative and, more important, is in keeping with the mandate of paragraph 31(iii) of the DMD to reduce or eliminate NTBs.

## VI.   Conclusions

This paper submits that the EAI offers a viable approach to linking trade negotiations and climate change mitigation policies, building upon the win-win philosophy entailed in many facets of the trade and development agenda. The approach offers a method which reduces complexity by proceeding in certain steps, from political decisions in identifying relevant areas, to technical implementation in the fields of both services and goods. The integrated approach, also entailing other NTBs, including technical barriers to trade, food standards, subsidies and intellectual property require close co-ordination with other regulatory areas of WTO law. We submit that such co-ordination, as well as that with the pertinent MEAs, in particular the Kyoto Protocol, should be undertaken within an EGS framework agreement. Vice-versa, the framework requirements of the WTO should also be taken into account in future negotiations on the Kyoto Protocol, hopefully taking effect at the end of the first commitment period in 2012.[52] Efforts to negotiate the instruments in a mutually coherent manner are imperative. Much work

---

[50] There is a growing number of companies based in developing countries that have emerged in recent years, such as for photovoltaic based-systems and as affiliates for large wind turbine manufacturers. In their own regions, Brazil, China, India and South Africa are becoming centres for sales of renewable energy technologies See Steenblik (2005).

[51] R. Doornbosch and R. Steenblik, *Biofuels: Is the Cure Worse than the Disease?*, SG/SD/RT (2007)3, OECD (2007), 31–32, 39. Available at www.foeeurope.org/publications/2007/OECD_Biofuels_Cure_Worse_Than_Disease_Sept07.pdf

[52] Article 3 of the Kyoto Protocol indicates 2008–2012 as the first commitment period. Available at http://unfccc.int/resource/docs/convkp/kpeng.html

needs to be done. The present paper merely flags the main pertinent issues which, in one way or another, need to be addressed when framing appropriate rules in the WTO in support of climate change mitigation. The issue of the extent to which modalities should be defined multilaterally, concessions need to be negotiated, and Members need to be able to define unilaterally their levels of commitments, requires further discussion and research.

## Bibliography

Assunção, L. and Zhang, Z. X., *Domestic Climate Change Policies and the WTO* Discussion Paper No. 164, UNCTAD (2002). Available at www.unctad.org/en/docs/osgdp164_en.pdf

Beck, F. and Martinot, E. , 'Renewable energy policies and barriers', in C. Cleveland (ed.), *Encyclopedia of Energy* (San Diego: Academic Press/Elsevier Science, 2004)

Brewer, T. *International Trade, the WTO and International Climate Arrangements* paper presented at the International Forum for Environmental Issues, Tokyo (2003).

Cossy, M., *Determining 'Likeness' under GATS: Squaring the Circle?*, WTO, Staff Working Paper ERSD 2006–08 (2006).

Cottier, T. and Baracol-Pinhão, D. (in press) 'The WTO negotiations on environmental goods and services: a potential contribution to the millennium development goals' in *Trade and Environment Report 2007*, UNCTAD (forthcoming, 2008).

Cottier, T. and Oesch. M., *International Trade Regulation: Law and Policy in the WTO, the European Union and Switzerland* (London: Cameron May and Bern: Staempfli Publishers, 2005).

Delimatsis, P. and Mavromati See n. 42, D., 'GATS, financial services, and trade in renewable energy certificates (RECs) — just another market-based solution to cope with the tragedy of the commons?', in this volume.

Doornbosch, R. and Steenblik, R., *Biofuels: Is the Cure Worse than the Disease?* SG/SD/RT(2007)3, OECD (2007). Available at www.foeeurope.org/ publications/2007/OECD_Biofuels_Cure_Worse_Than_Disease_Sept07.pdf

Fontagné, L., von Kirchback, F. and Mimouni, M. (2001) *A First assessment of Environment-related Trade Barriers*, Working Paper 2001–10, CEPII Research Center (2001). Available at www.intracen.org/mas/pdfs/pubs/etb_english.pdf

Hamwey, R., *Environmental Goods: Where do the Dynamic Opportunities for Developing Countries Lie?*, Cen2eco Working Paper (2005). Available at http://129.3.20.41/eps/it/papers/0512/0512015.pdf

Hamwey, R., Hoffmann, U., Vikhlyaev, A. and Vossenaar, R., *Liberalisation of International Trade in Environmental Goods and Services*, UNCTAD (2003). Available at http://r0.unctad.org/trade_env/test1/meetings/bangkok4/EGS.pdf

Howse, R., Post-Hearing Submission to the International Trade Commission: *World Trade Law and Renewable Energy: The Case of Non-Tariff Measures*, Renewable Energy and International Law Project (2005).

International Panel for Climate Change, *IPCC Fourth Assessment Report Summary for Policymakers* (2007). Available at www.ipcc.ch/SPM040507.pdf

OECD, *Environmental Goods and Services: the Benefits of Further Global Trade Liberalisation* (Paris: OECD, 2001).

Steenblik, R., *Liberalisation of Trade in Renewable-energy Products and Associated Goods: Charcoal, Solar Photovoltaic Cells, and Wind Pumps and Turbines* COM/ENV/TR(2005)23/FINAL, OECD Trade and Environment Working Paper 2005–07 (2005).

    *Liberalising Trade in 'Environmental Goods': Some Practical Considerations*, OECD Trade and Environment Working Paper 2005–5 (2005). Available at www.oecd.org/dataoecd/25/8/35978987.pdf

    *Liberalisation of Trade in Renewable-energy Products and Associated Goods: Biodiesel, Solar Thermal and Geothermal Energy*, COM/ENV/TR(2005)78/FINAL, OECD Trade and Environment Working Paper 2006–01 (2006).

Steenblik, R., Drouet, D. and Stubbs, G., *Synergies between Trade in Environmental Services and Trade in Environmental Goods*, OECD Trade and Environment Working Paper 2005–01 (2005). Available at www.oecd.org/dataoecd/21/48/35161237.pdf

Singh, S., 'Environmental goods negotiations: issues and options for ensuring win-win outcomes', International Institute for Sustainable Development (2005). Available at www.iisd.org/pdf/2005/trade_environmental_goods.pdf

Swedish National Board of Trade, *Trade Aspects of Biofuels* (2007). Available at www.kommers.se/upload/Analysarkiv/In%20English/Trade%20Aspects%20of%20Biofuels.pdf

UNCTAD, *Legal and Policy Issues in the Market Access Implications of Labelling for Environmental Purposes* (2003). Available at www.unctad.org/trade_env/test1/meetings/bangkok4/ecolabelling briefing paper.pdf

    *Managing Request-Offer Negotiations Under the GATS: The Case of Energy Services* (2003). Available at www.unctad.org/en/docs/ditctncd20035_en.pdf

UNEP, *Baseline Methodologies for Clean Development Mechanism Projects: A Guidebook* (Roskilde: UNEP, 2005). Available at www.cd4cdm.org/Publications/UNEP_CDM%20Baseline%20Meth%20Guidebook.pdf

Wiser, G., 'Frontiers in trade: the clean development mechanism and the general agreement on trade in services', *Int. J. Global Environmental Issues* 2 (2002), 288–309.

World Trade Organization, various submissions by members. Available at www.wto.org/english/docs_e/docs_e.htm

Zarrilli, S., *Managing Request-Offer Negotiations under the GATS: the Case of Energy Services* TD/TC/WP(2003)24/FINAL, OECD (2003). Available at www.olis.oecd.org/olis/2003doc.nsf/LinkTo/td-tc-wp(2003)24-final

# INDEX